Dr Maurice M. Mizrahi

Commentaries on the Weekly Torah Portion and the Jewish Holy Days

Volume 2

Dr Maurice M. Mizrahi

Commentaries on the Weekly Torah Portion and the Jewish Holy Days

Volume 2

הַיּוֹם בּוֹ נוֹלַדְתָּ הוּא הַיּוֹם בּוֹ הֶחְלִיט הקב"ה שֶׁהָעוֹלָם אֵינוֹ יָכוֹל לְהִתְקַיֵּים בַּלְעָדֶיךָ.

The day that you were born is the day God decided the world could not be preserved without you.

Rav Nachman of Breslov

Copyright © 2021 by Maurice M. Mizrahi.

All rights reserved.

To the memory of my mother,

Victoria Hallak Mizrahi,

who gave me life, Jewishness, and unconditional love.

The Author

Dr Maurice M. Mizrahi was born and raised in Egypt, which he was forced to leave in 1967, at age eighteen, after the Six-Day War. He earned a PhD in theoretical physics from the University of Texas at Austin and worked in the U.S. Defense Department for 34 years, specializing in science and technology matters, arms control, strategic stability, and defenses against weapons of mass destruction. He has always been fascinated by the interactions between his two main loves, Science and Judaism. He created and led a monthly discussion group on the subject, which met for six years, has been Scholar in Residence on the subject, and has been teaching Judaism to teenagers and adults since 1984. From 1988 to 1991, he and his oldest son Michael have produced, exhibited, and marketed many Judaica computer programs.

In 2006 he received the Distinguished Civilian Service Award, the highest award available to U.S. civil servants. He lives in Burke, Virginia, and is married to pianist/psychologist Joan Berman Mizrahi. They have three adult children: Michael, Trina, and Jonathan; and five grandchildren. He frequently leads services and discussion sessions and gives Judaica talks and Torah commentaries at his synagogue and at the local Jewish Community Center.

Foreword

This book is my second collection of presentations on each of the 54 Torah portions, the 8 main Jewish holidays, and my background. Like the first set, these essays are intended to be consistent with mainline Jewish tradition, while still heavily influenced by my personal background (a Jewish refugee from Egypt) and my scientific and rational outlook (a doctorate in theoretical physics and a career as a defense analyst). Direct quotations from the Tanach, the Talmud, the Midrash, the classical commentators and other traditional Jewish sources abound and form the basis of my presentations.

This book is written for people who are serious about studying Judaism from both a spiritual and a rational point of view, in the tradition of Maimonides.

I made videos of some of these presentations on my YouTube channel:
https://www.youtube.com/user/mizrahim11/videos

Maurice M. Mizrahi
Burke, Virginia
21 February 2021 / 9 Adar 5781

Table of Contents

Bereshit (Genesis)

Is this, too, for the Good? (Bereshit)
What does Judaism Expect from Gentiles? (Noach)
Why did God Choose Abraham? (Lech Lecha)
Why the Binding of Isaac? (Vayera)
The Cave of Machpelah (Chayye Sarah)
Antisemitism (Toldot)
Is Love all you Need? (Vayetze)
Jacob's Mysterious Assailant (Vayishlach)
The Jewish View of Dreams (Vayeshev)
The Evil Eye (Miketz)
I am Joseph. Is my Father Still Alive? (Vayigash)
Why Didn't Jacob Go Back to Israel? (Vayechi)

Shemot (Exodus)

The Righteous Women of the Exodus (Shemot)
Did the Exodus Really Happen? (Vaera)
Promptness in Performing Commandments (Bo)
The Slave Mentality (Beshallach)
Honor your Father and your Mother (Yitro)
Do not Mix Milk and Meat (Mishpatim)
Where is God? (Terumah)
Of Jews and Olives (Tetzaveh)
The Quest for Knowledge in Judaism (Ki Tisa)
The Shabbat Goy (Vayakhel)
Should you Care What Others Think? (Pekudei)

Vayikra (Leviticus)

Do Bad Thoughts Break Commandments? (Vayikra)
Thanksgiving (Tzav)
When Does Speculation Become Evil Gossip? (Shemini)
Is Gossip Good? (Tazria)
In Praise of Praise (Metzora)
Imagine! (Acharei Mot)
Love Your Neighbor as Yourself (Kedoshim)
Why is Blasphemy Such a Major Infraction? (Emor)
The Meaning of Freedom (Behar)
Why did God Create Predators? (Bechukkotai)

Bamidbar (Numbers)

Counting Jews (Bamidbar)
Queen Berenice - Heroine or Traitor? (Naso)
Democracy and Judaism (Behaalotecha)
Fear of Success (Shlach Lecha)
What did Korach do Wrong? (Korach)
What did Moses do Wrong? (Chukat)
Was the Prophet Balaam Good or Bad? (Balak)
The Fate of Moses' Children (Pinchas)
Are Jews Responsible for One Another? (Matot)
The Wandering Jews (Massei)

Devarim (Deuteronomy)

Esau, Edom, Rome and the Jews (Devarim)
The Mission of Judaism (Va'etchanan)
Why Did Moses Break the Tablets? (Ekev)
Why Eat Only Kosher Foods? (Re'eh)
Violence and Judaism (Shoftim)

The Rebellious Son (Ki Tetze)
Is Life a Zero-Sum Game? (Ki Tavo)
The Jewish View of the Afterlife (Nitzavim)
When it's Time to Die (Vayelech)
The Resurrection of the Dead (Haazinu)
The (Reluctant) Death of Moses (V'Zot HaBracha)

Chagim (Holidays)

When Can Repentance Be Considered Complete? (Yamim Noraim)
You Shall Rejoice! (Sukkot)
Hanukkah and Purim: Similar yet Different (Hanukkah)
Does Antisemitism Preserve Judaism? (Purim)
Why an Egg on the Seder Plate? (Pessah)
The Secrets of Jewish Survival (Yom Haatsmaut)
The Law of the Land is the Law (Shavuot)
What is the Proper Response to Being Wronged? (Tish'a b'Av)

Personal

The (Jewish) Lessons of (My) Life

Table of Contents Pages and Links

Is this, too, for the Good? 32
What Does Judaism Expect from Gentiles? 38
Why did God Choose Abraham? 43
Why the Binding of Isaac? 50
The Cave of Machpelah 55
Antisemitism 60
Is Love All You Need? 66
Jacob's Mysterious Assailant 72
The Jewish View of Dreams 80
The Evil Eye 86
I Am Joseph -- Is My Father Still Alive? 93
Why Didn't Jacob Go Back to Israel? 98
The Righteous Women of the Exodus 105
Did the Exodus Really Happen? 111
Promptness in Performing Commandments 115
The Slave Mentality 121
Honor Your Father and Your Mother 125
Do not Mix Milk and Meat 136
Where is God? 141
Of Jews and Olives 147
The Quest for Knowledge in Judaism 150
The Shabbat Goy 156
Should you Care What Others Think? 159
Do Bad Thoughts Break Commandments? 164
Thanksgiving 168
When Does Speculation Become Evil Gossip? 173
Is Gossip Good? 179
In Praise of Praise 183

Imagine!	189
Love Your Neighbor as Yourself	194
Why is Blasphemy Such a Major Infraction?	201
The Meaning of Freedom	204
Why Did God Create Predators?	207
Counting Jews	214
Queen Berenice: Heroine or Traitor?	219
Democracy and Judaism	222
Fear of Success	230
What did Korach do Wrong?	234
What Did Moses Do Wrong?	238
Was the Prophet Balaam Good or Bad?	243
The Fate of Moses' Children	250
Are Jews Responsible for One Another?	257
The Wandering Jews	263
Esau, Edom, Rome and the Jews	270
The Mission of Judaism	274
Why Did Moses Break the Tablets?	281
Why Eat Only Kosher Foods?	289
Violence and Judaism	295
The Rebellious Son	302
Is Life a Zero-Sum Game?	309
The Jewish View of the Afterlife	314
When it's Time to Die	320
The Resurrection of the Dead	327
The (Reluctant) Death of Moses	333
When Can Repentance Be Considered Complete?	342
You Shall Rejoice!	348
Hanukkah and Purim: Similar yet Different	352
Does Antisemitism Preserve Judaism?	358
Why an Egg on the Seder Plate?	365

The Secrets of Jewish Survival	369
The Law of the Land is the Law	376
What is the Proper Response to Being Wronged?	385
The (Jewish) Lessons of (My) Life	395

Brief Summaries

Bereshit (Genesis)

Bereshit: Is this, too, for the Good?

In this week's Torah portion, *Bereshit*, the story of Creation is told, concluding with, "And God saw every thing that He had made, and, behold, it was very good." [Genesis 1:31] But is the world really "very good"? We look around us and see a lot of evil, wars, accidents, natural disasters, etc. Yet some say, like first-century rabbi Nahum ish Gamzu, "*Gam zu le-tovah* -- This, too, is for the good." They believe that everything that happens ultimately leads to good. Let us examine this attitude.

Noach: What does Judaism Expect from Gentiles?

In this week's Torah portion, *Noach*, God makes a covenant with Noah: God will never again flood the earth, but people must observe certain commandments. These are the seven Noahide Laws: To establish courts of justice, and refrain from blasphemy, idolatry, adultery, murder, stealing, and eating the flesh of live animals. But can Gentiles observe the rest of the 613 commandments, applicable only to Jews? In general, the answer is yes, but there are some exceptions.

Lech Lecha: Why did God Choose Abraham?

In this week's Torah portion, *Lech Lecha*, God promises Abraham a bright future if he moves to a new place. [Genesis 12:1-5] But why does God take an interest in Abraham in particular? We are not told. Contrast with Noah, before him, introduced as "righteous" and "perfect"; or Moses, after him, introduced as a man showing leadership, compassion, and courage. Let us explore possible reasons why Abraham was singled out.

Vayera: Why the Binding of Isaac?

This week's Torah portion, *Vayera*, relates the story of Abraham coming close to sacrificing his son Isaac on God's command, as a test of faith, until God stops him right before he does it. [Genesis 22] What can we learn from this episode? Did Abraham pass the test? What questions and issues does it suggest? What lessons can be derived from it?

Chayye Sarah: The Cave of Machpelah

In this week's Torah portion, *Chayye Sarah*, Abraham purchases the Cave of Machpelah as a burial site for his wife Sarah, in a typical Middle-Eastern negotiating session with Ephron the Hittite. The Zohar says that the site is the entrance to the Garden of Eden. When Israel retook the area in 1967, it gave control to Muslim authorities, who sharply limit Jewish visits.

Toldot: Antisemitism

In this week's Torah portion, *Toldot*, the patriarch Isaac becomes wealthy and successful. So his neighbors envy him, fill his water-wells with earth, and finally expel him from their midst. This is the beginning of antisemitism, cause and effect. It will continue for as long as Jews are successful.

Vayetze: Is Love all you Need?

In this week's Torah portion, *Vayetze*, we read about how Jacob fell in love with Rachel at first sight. Love is often mentioned in the Torah: Romantic love, spousal love, parental love, love of God for Israel and vice-versa, etc. We are commanded to love our neighbor. We are even commanded to love strangers! But is love all you need? Isn't justice needed also? How does one differ from the other and how do find the right balance between the two?

Vayishlach: Jacob's Mysterious Assailant

In this week's portion, *Vayishlach*, Jacob is attacked by a mysterious entity and he wrestles with it for an entire night. Who was that entity? A man? An angel? God? He describes himself as "beings both divine and human". Why the plural since there was only one entity? The entity asks Jacob: "What is your name?" Did he not know all along whom he was fighting? What was his mission? When the entity sees that he cannot defeat Jacob, he wrenches Jacob's hip. How can this be considered cause and effect? Why does the entity have to leave at dawn? Why does Jacob want to be blessed by it after fighting it and getting injured? In response to Jacob's request for a blessing, the entity changes Jacob's name. Is that a blessing and why? Why did Jacob ask for the entity's name and why would he not reveal it? How does Jacob know it was a "divine being"? Why is Jacob's wound so important that it led to a dietary restriction for Jews? Let us discuss possible answers.

Vayeshev: The Jewish View of Dreams

In this week's Torah portion, *Vayeshev*, Joseph dreams and interprets dreams. [Genesis 37:5-10] All cultures have a special niche for dreams, and Judaism is no exception. But are all dreams significant? Do they all bear a message? Is God involved in all of them? Let's examine what our Sages say about them.

Miketz: The Evil Eye

In this week's Torah portion, *Miketz*, Jacob charges his sons with a mission to buy grain in Egypt, adding: "Why do you keep looking at one another?" [Genesis 42:1] What does this strange phrase mean? The Talmud and the Midrash say it means: "Do not stand together in one place, lest the evil eye prevail over you." In other words, do not show off your blessings to those who don't enjoy the same. The evil eye (עַיִן הָרַע -- *ayin hara*) is an entrenched belief in Judaism. Let us explore it together.

Vayigash: I am Joseph. Is my Father Still Alive?

In this week's Torah portion, *Vayigash*, Joseph is visited by ten of his brothers, who sold him into slavery in Egypt. He toys with them, but finally reveals his identity, saying: "I am Joseph. Is my father still alive?" It is a strange question, because he had just asked it and gotten an answer. How should we interpret his question? Let us explore what our Sages said on the matter, especially Naḥmanides.

Vayechi: Why Didn't Jacob Go Back to Israel?

Jacob and his entire family of seventy move from the Holy Land to Egypt because of a famine. They are invited by Joseph, now viceroy of Egypt. Joseph tells them: "It is now two years that there has been famine in the land, and there are still five years to come in which there shall be no yield from tilling." [Genesis 45:6] This week's portion, *Vayechi*, opens with: "Jacob lived 17 years in the land of Egypt." [Genesis 47:28] So Jacob lived in Egypt for 12 years after the famine, and his clan stayed in Egypt after he died. Why did they? They hadn't been enslaved yet. Why didn't Jacob and his family go back to Israel, where God wanted them to live? Let's explore possible reasons.

Shemot (Exodus)

Shemot: The Righteous Women of the Exodus

This week's Torah portion, *Shemot*, abounds with righteous women working behind the scenes to foil the evil plans of men. Let's examine their contributions one by one and ask: Are women more righteous than men?

Vaera: Did the Exodus Really Happen?

In this week's Torah portion, *Vaera*, we read about the first seven plagues that befall the Egyptians for refusing to let the Israelite slaves go. The groundwork for the Exodus has begun. For Jews, it is such a central event that we are commanded to remember it every day, commemorate it every year in a major holiday, and even act as if we were personally part of it. But did the Exodus really happen? Most secular scholars say no, that it's purely a matter of faith. But while we do not have direct, archeological proof, we do have hints, indirect evidence, and are discovering more of them. Let's explore this matter.

Bo: Promptness in Performing Commandments

In this week's Torah portion, *Bo*, we are told to "watch over the matzot" in preparation for Passover. [Exodus 12:17] Going beyond the obvious meaning, some commentators learn from this injunction that we must be prompt in performing commandments. Let us explore the "timing" component of the commandments.

Beshallach: The Slave Mentality

In this week's Torah portion, *Beshallach*, the Israelites show they are still suffering from the "slave mentality" -- complaining a lot and talking about returning to Egypt. This is why God arranged for a 40-year trek through the desert: so the generation of the Exodus could die out and be replaced in the Promised Land by a new generation not burdened with the memory of slavery. Let us explore the phenomenon of the "slave mentality".

Yitro: Honor your Father and your Mother

This week's Torah portion, *Yitro*, tells us: Honor your father and your mother. Why should you? What if your parents have not been good to you? Who must honor parents? How important is that commandment? What's my reward if I honor parents? What does it actually mean to "honor" and "revere" your parents? How far must that honoring extend? Who are good examples of honoring parents? Let us answer these questions in light of the Jewish tradition.

Mishpatim: Do not Mix Milk and Meat

In this week's Torah portion, *Mishpatim*, we are commanded not to cook a kid in its mother's milk. [Exodus 23:19] This was interpreted to mean that milk products and meat products, in Hebrew *bassar be-chalav*, must never be together. Let's explore this Jewish law in some detail and try to fathom the reasons for it.

Terumah: Where is God?

In this week's Torah portion, *Terumah*, God tells the Israelites "Make Me a sanctuary and I will dwell in their midst." [Exodus 25:1-2, 8] What does this mean? Does God really need a place to stay? Aren't we taught that God is ubiquitous, that He is everywhere? So where is God, really?

Tetzaveh: Of Jews and Olives

This week's Torah portion, *Tetzaveh*, tells us that only olive oil must be used for kindling the menorah in the Tabernacle. [Exodus 27:20] Why only olive oil? The Sources give us nine reasons why the Jewish people can be compared to olives. Let us explore them one by one.

Ki Tisa: The Quest for Knowledge in Judaism

In this week's portion, *Ki Tisa*, Moses wants answers to ultimate questions, but God only tells him: "I will make all my goodness pass before you... but You may not see my face... You shall see my back; but my face shall not be seen." [Exodus 33:13-23] So God will drop hints, but not give straight answers. Why not? We Jews have always sought knowledge in all its forms. How can knowledge be bad? Let's examine this question.

Vayakhel: The Shabbat Goy

In this week's Torah portion, *Vayakhel*, we are told that no work must be done on Shabbat. However, a tradition developed in Eastern Europe to hire a Gentile to work for Jews on Shabbat, particularly to keep the heat going in cold weather. He is known as the "Shabbat goy". In reality, Jewish law allows this practice only to save lives or avoid a large financial loss, not for comfort. Let us examine the details of when it is permitted and when not.

Pekudei: Should you Care What Others Think?

This week's Torah portion is *Pekudei*, meaning "Accountings". Moses provides a detailed balance sheet to prove that he responsibly directed the use of every single item entrusted to him to build the Tabernacle. He wants everything to be transparent, above-board and in the open, so as to be beyond suspicion. He was applying the Jewish principle of מַרְאִית עַיִן -- *Marit Ayin*, literally: "Appearance to the eye". It means that some permitted behavior is prohibited because it may appear to casual observers to be prohibited behavior. This would cause them to assume it is permitted, or, if they know it isn't, cause them to think ill of the one doing it. Let us explore this principle.

Vayikra (Leviticus)

Vayikra: Do Bad Thoughts Break Commandments?

In this week's Torah portion, *Vayikra*, we learn about the "burnt offering". The Midrash says that it was not brought for sins, but for bad thoughts. [Tanḥuma Tzav 13:13] How can that be, since Judaism is a religion of deed, not one of thought or belief? We are judged by what we do, not by what we think. The Talmud explains that bad thoughts alone are not punished, but if followed by bad action they are. [Kiddushin 40a] So it is better to avoid them to the extent possible, and we apologize for them on Yom Kippur when we say: "*Al chet shechatanu lefanecha b'harhor ha-lev* -- For the sin that we have committed before You by sinful thoughts."

Tzav: Thanksgiving

In this week's Torah portion, *Tzav*, we learn about the Thanksgiving Offering. How is it special and different from the other offerings? Who must make it? How often must Jews give thanks? Does God really need praise and thanks? Should American Jews celebrate Thanksgiving? Let's answer these questions in light of our tradition.

Shemini: When Does Speculation Become Evil Gossip?

In this week's Torah portion, *Shemini*, we learn about the tragic and mysterious death of two of Aaron's sons, Nadav and Avihu, for offering "strange fire". What is this "strange fire" and why is it such a major infraction? We are not told. This left the field open for a lot of disturbing speculation that seems to "dump" on the brothers. When does such speculation become *lashon hara*, or "evil gossip", and when does it serve a useful purpose?

Tazria: Is Gossip Good?

The Torah portion for this week, *Tazria*, deals with skin diseases, but commentators say they really refer to spiritual impurity, in the form of *lashon hara*, that is, gossip. The Jewish tradition unequivocally characterizes gossip as bad. But psychological studies conducted in the past few years have concluded that gossip can sometimes be beneficial. So who is right? Should we engage in it?

Metzora: In Praise of Praise

In this week's Torah portion, *Metzora*, we read about the rituals for cleansing people who are afflicted with a skin disease. Miriam was punished with it for badmouthing her brother Moses. [Numbers 12:1–15] Because of this, the Sages understood the disease to be caused by *lashon hara*, "the evil tongue" or malicious speech. Some commentators have argued that if speaking ill of others is forbidden, then speaking well of them should be required. The opposite of *lashon hara* should be *lashon hatov* -- the "good tongue". Let us explore this matter: To what extent should we go out of our way to praise others?

Acharei Mot: Imagine!

This week's Torah portion, *Acharei Mot*, contains 79 commandments, or 13% of the total, more than any other single portion. If you follow them diligently, you are guaranteed a place in the World to Come, heaven. If not, you will spend up to a year in Gehennom, and if you are not cleansed, your soul and your name will be erased forever. Using John Lennon's song as a springboard, let's "imagine" a world where none of this applies: No heaven, above us only sky, and no religion too; no countries, one united world; no possessions, all the people sharing all the world; a brotherhood of man, all the people living life in peace. Is this nirvana? Let's analyze it. The answer may surprise you. Be careful what you wish for: You might get it.

Kedoshim: Love Your Neighbor as Yourself

This week's Torah portion, *Kedoshim*, includes the most quoted line in the Bible: "And you shall love your neighbor as yourself." [Leviticus 19:18] What does it really mean? Who is my neighbor? Who is not? Should I love my enemy? If I hate myself, should I hate my neighbor also? What is love? How can you be commanded to love? Is it even possible to truly love another as you love yourself? Can we realistically ask a mother to love all children as much as she loves her own children? Let us try to give Jewish answers to these questions.

Emor : Why is Blasphemy Such a Major Infraction?

In this week's Torah portion, *Emor*, we are commanded not to "blaspheme the name of the Lord". [Leviticus 24:10-16] It is also the third of the Ten Commandments and one of the seven Noahide laws, binding on all humankind. Why is "No blasphemy" so major a commandment? What about freedom of speech? Let's examine this question.

Behar: The Meaning of Freedom

This week's Torah portion, *Behar*, contains the famous words: "And you shall proclaim liberty throughout the land, unto all the inhabitants thereof." [Leviticus 25:10] But what, exactly, is freedom, when we are surrounded on all sides by laws, commandments, rules, regulations, conventions, customs and practices, and have to conform to society's expectations? There is an answer in the Jewish tradition.

Bechukkotai: Why did God Create Predators?

In this week's Torah portion, *Bechukkotai*, God promises that if we follow His commandments, He will cause many good things to happen to us, including removing wild beasts from the land, so they no longer pose a threat. [Leviticus 26:6] But why did God create those beasts, who must kill and inflict pain just to survive? Let us speculate on possible reasons in light of the Jewish tradition.

Bamidbar (Numbers)

Bamidbar: Counting Jews

The first portion in the Book of Numbers, *Bamidbar*, begins with a census of the Israelites, the third in the space of a year. Why all these censuses? Let's explore possible reasons and understand why Jewish tradition prohibits counting Jews overtly.

Naso : Queen Berenice - Heroine or Traitor?

This week's Torah portion, *Naso*, tells us about people who took Nazirite vows, to set themselves apart "for the sake of the Lord", and thereby achieve a higher level of holiness. [Numbers 6:2] Let us examine the case of one such Nazirite, first-century Queen Berenice of Judea, sister of King Herod Agrippa

II, with whom she shared power. Hers is a complicated story. Was she a heroine or a traitor?

Behaalotecha: Democracy and Judaism

In this week's Torah portion, *Behaalotecha*, Moses appoints 70 elders to help him judge and govern Israel. [Numbers 11:16-17] The Sanhedrin is born: A body of 71 Sages ruling on Torah matters, making decisions by majority vote, in an early example of democracy. To what extent is democracy as practiced in the West today consistent with Judaism? Let us explore the matter, with some examples.

Shlach Lecha: Fear of Success

In this week's Torah portion, *Shlach Lecha*, Moses sends twelve spies to scout the land of Israel. Ten of them bring back an alarming report and say that the enemies cannot be defeated, which demoralizes the Israelites. What did they do wrong? Some commentators argue that the spies were not afraid that the campaign to settle the Holy Land will fail, but that it will succeed. Why? Read on.

Korach: What did Korach do Wrong?

This week's Torah portion, *Korach*, tells us about Korach -- the rebel, the bad guy, the one who dared to challenge the authority of Moses. But what did Korach actually do wrong? Can we condemn him when he appears to be striking a blow for democracy? Let's explore the matter together.

Chukat: What did Moses do Wrong?

In this week's Torah portion, *Chukat*, the people complain of thirst. So God tells Moses to speak to a rock so it yields its water. Moses strikes the rock instead and water comes out. God punishes him by not allowing him to go into the Promised Land. It seems a bit out of proportion. The mystery deepens when we remember that forty years earlier, God had indeed told Moses to strike a rock to bring water. [Exodus 17:6] Let us explore this strange event.

Balak: Was the Prophet Balaam Good or Bad?

In this week's Torah portion, *Balak*, we learn that Balak, the king of Moab, enlists Balaam, a non-Jewish prophet, to curse Israel. Yet Balaam ends up blessing Israel, against his will. Who was this Gentile prophet, and was he good or bad?

Pinchas: The Fate of Moses' Children

In this week's Torah portion, *Pinchas*, God orders Moses to pass the mantle of leadership to Joshua. Why not to Moses' two sons? Indeed, what happened to them? They seem to disappear from the narrative. From the few clues we have in the Bible, let's reconstruct their troubled story.

Matot: Are Jews Responsible for One Another?

In this week's Torah portion, *Matot*, the Israelites are at the gates of the Promised Land. But some prefer to live just outside it. Is it mandatory for Jews to live in Israel? More generally, what is our responsibility towards other Jews? The Talmud says: "All Jews are responsible for one another." What exactly does it mean? Let us explore some possible answers.

Massei: The Wandering Jews

This week's Torah portion, *Massei*, recounts all 42 places where the Israelites encamped in their 40-year saga from Egypt to Israel. An average of about one move a year. Little did they know that what they were experiencing was merely a harbinger of things to come! We have been "the wandering Jews" for most of our history, forced to roam the earth in the elusive search of a home.

Let us recounts the history of our wandering and its impact on ourselves and on the world.

Devarim (Deuteronomy)

Devarim: Esau, Edom, Rome and the Jews

In this week's Torah portion, *Devarim*, the Israelites must pass through the land of the Edomites, the descendants of Esau, Jacob's "evil twin". The Edomites refuse passage, so God tells the Israelites to bypass them. [Deuteronomy 2:2-5] Why is God being so protective of the Edomites? Isn't Esau a "bad guy"? Moreover, our tradition tells us that the Romans descend from the Edomites. The Romans oppressed the Jews, destroyed their Temple, and exiled them from their land. Why did God protect them and allow them to do this? What's special about Esau that requires such divine indulgence?

Va'etchanan: The Mission of Judaism

This week's Torah portion, *Va'etchanan*, features the Ten Commandments, a good starting point to reflect on the meaning and mission of Judaism in the world. That mission is not clearly spelled out in the Torah. Some say it is to spread Jewish values and teachings. Others say that it is to excel for the benefit of mankind. Still others say that it is to perform *Tikkun 'Olam*, the "repair of the world", that is, to make the world a better place. Which is right? Or do they all apply, in proper balance? Let's discuss the matter.

Ekev: Why Did Moses Break the Tablets?

In this week's portion, *Ekev*, Moses recounts to the Israelites how he broke the first set of tablets of the Law once he saw that they had engaged in idolatry by building and worshiping a golden calf. Why did he do that? What purpose did it accomplish? Wasn't it an affront to God, since the tablets were holy? Didn't it shatter the authority of the very commandments that told the Israelites not to worship idols? Was it just a spontaneous reaction, a public display of anger, a temper tantrum? Did Moses just forget himself? Why didn't he just return them to God, or at least get God's approval before smashing them? Yet he was not admonished! Let us explore this incident in some detail.

Re'eh: Why Eat Only Kosher Foods?

This week's portion, *Re'eh*, summarizes the Jewish dietary laws. Let us review what foods are deemed kosher and speculate on possible reasons why we are not allowed to eat the other foods.

Shoftim: Violence and Judaism

This week's Torah portion, *Shoftim*, contains the so-called law of retaliation: "An eye for an eye, a tooth for a tooth." [Deuteronomy 19:21] In reality, the rabbis have always interpreted this law to mean monetary compensation, not physical violence. In fact, Jews are traditionally against using violence to settle disputes. Let us review in some detail Jewish teachings about the use of violence -- retaliation, death penalty, corporal punishment, and war.

Ki Tetze: The Rebellious Son

In this week's Torah portion, *Ki Tetze*, we are told that a "stubborn and rebellious son" who does not listen to his parents, who is "a glutton and a drunkard", should be executed! [Deuteronomy 21:18-21] This does not sound right. These are not capital sins! In fact, there are no commandments against them. Even if he stole to buy food and drink, it is not a capital offense. Also, he must be given the opportunity to repent. Moreover, if he is an adult, his parents do not have authority over him. If he is a minor, he not responsible for any commandments! Our Sages concluded: This never happened and never will. Let us study their arguments and their speculations on why this passage is in the Torah.

Ki Tavo: Is Life a Zero-Sum Game?

In this week's Torah portion, *Ki Tavo*, we read about offering God the first fruit of the harvest. People have a deep feeling that life is a zero-sum game: If they want to get something, they must give something in return. In ancient days, they went as far as sacrificing their own children to angry gods. Where does this belief come from? Where is it today? Where is it going?

Nitzavim: The Jewish View of the Afterlife

In this week's Torah portion, *Nitzavim*, God says, "I have set before you life and death. Choose life!" [Deuteronomy 30:19] Because of that exhortation, the Jewish emphasis has always been on the "here and now". There is never any encouragement to die because what comes after death is better than this life. But our tradition gives a fascinating picture of life, death, and the afterlife. Let us explore it together.

Vayelech: When it's Time to Die

This week's Torah portion, *Vayelech*, is the end of the road for Moses, physically and spiritually. It is the endpoint of the journey to the Promised Land (and God did not allow him to go into it); he is going to die on that very day; and he must pass the mantle of leadership to Joshua, as instructed by God. It begins with "And Moses went". Where did he go? He says "I can no longer go out and come in." Go out where and come in where? Did he feel incapable of continuing? God tells him he must die, but he resists and argues. Let us explore our Sages' views of these events and try to answer our central question: When is it time to die?

Haazinu: The Resurrection of the Dead

In this week's Torah portion, *Haazinu*, God says: "I kill and I give life. I have wounded and I will heal." [Deuteronomy 32:39] The Talmud sees there an implication of life after death. Indeed, the resurrection of the dead is one of Maimonides'

13 principles of faith. Let us examine in detail what it means and what evidence the Sages presented.

V'Zot HaBracha: The (Reluctant) Death of Moses

In the last Torah portion of the year, *V'zot Ha-Bracha*, we hear about the death of Moses. "And Moses was 120 years old when he died. His eye was not dim, nor had his natural force abated." [Deuteronomy 34:7] The Midrash on Deuteronomy gives a detailed account of the death of Moses. It reads like a thriller, which is unusual for ancient commentary. Let us discover it together.

Chagim (Holidays)

Yamim Noraim: When Can Repentance Be Considered Complete?

On the High Holy Days, we must repent for bad behavior. But when can repentance be considered complete? Is it when you realize what you did was wrong, feel bad about it, and resolve not to do it again? Is it when you also make restitution whenever possible? Is it when you also ask and receive forgiveness? Is it when you also make the matter public? Let us explore how the Jewish tradition answers these questions.

Sukkot: You Shall Rejoice!

The Torah tells us, relative to the Jewish holiday of Sukkot: "*Vesamachta bechagecha* -- And you shall rejoice in your feast." How can you be commanded to rejoice? How can you command an emotion? Our Sages gave us six ways.

Hanukkah: Hanukkah and Purim: Similar yet Different

The holidays of Hanukkah and Purim have many fascinating similarities and differences. Let us explore them in some detail.

Purim: Does Antisemitism Preserve Judaism?

In discussing the story of Purim, the Talmud [Megillah 14a] says that when Haman tried to kill all the Jews, he was more effective in preserving Judaism than all the prophets who tried to steer the Jews to the right path! This message, that antisemitism can preserve Judaism, has been echoed by many commentators over the ages, and history supports it. Let us examine the evidence and ponder what it implies.

Pessaḥ: Why an Egg on the Seder Plate?

Why do we place an egg on the seder plate? That egg is never mentioned in the Haggadah, and is never eaten! No one knows. It is not mentioned in ancient sources. The first reference to it dates from the 12th century. Since then, a lot of commentators have speculated on its significance. Let us hear what they said.

Yom Ha-Atzmaut: The Secrets of Jewish Survival

Yom Ha-Atzmaut is Israel's Independence Day. It is a modern-day miracle, born phoenix-like from the ashes of the Holocaust. The Jewish people have suffered many tragedies over history, each of which, by itself, could have led to the disappearance of Judaism. But none did. Why? What made the Jews survive as a distinct people, when so many other civilizations have disappeared?

Shavuot: The Law of the Land is the Law

When the Diaspora began and Jews were forced to live in foreign lands, the rabbis laid down a basic principle: *Dina de-Malkhuta Dina*, meaning "The Law of the Land is the Law". Jews committed themselves to being good citizens and always following local laws, as long as the freedom to teach, worship and conduct religious rituals is granted. How does this principle square with

Jewish law? To what extent does it apply? What are its limits? Let us explore answers to these questions.

Tish'a b'Av: What is the Proper Response to Being Wronged?

History is full of catastrophic events that befell us Jews on Tish'a B'Av. What should our attitude be towards the perpetrators of all these atrocities, and more generally towards anyone who has wronged us? Retaliate in kind? Hate them, but take no action yet? Forgive them? Love them? Ignore them? Let's examine these five possible reactions one by one in light of the Jewish tradition.

Personal

The (Jewish) Lessons of (My) Life

When I turned seventy I asked myself: What have I learned? What have I contributed? Did I do what I was supposed to do? What did I do right and what did I do wrong? Here are the top twelve lessons I learned and their connection to Judaism.

Bereshit
Gen. 1:1-6:8

B"H

Is this, too, for the Good?

This week's Torah portion, *Bereshit*, meaning "In the beginning", is the first one in the Torah, and begins a new reading cycle. In it, the Story of Creation is told, concluding with:

וַיַּרְא אֱלֹהִים אֶת־כָּל־אֲשֶׁר עָשָׂה וְהִנֵּה־טוֹב מְאֹד
Vayyar Elokim et kol asher 'asa v'hinne: tov me'od
And God saw all that He had made, and, behold, it was very good. [Genesis 1:31]

But is the world really "very good"? We look around us and see wars, death and devastation; hatred and murders; unspeakable evil and atrocities carried out in the name of some ideology; natural disasters, such as floods, famine, earthquakes, or tornadoes; accidents galore; senseless deaths, and the like. How can any of this be good?

Well, some people believe there is a purpose behind it all; that good things always emerge from bad things, and justifies them; that all suffering is for some greater good, whether it's for the individual, the community, the country, the earth, or the universe. Note that all these are not all the same. The greater good of a community as a whole might require that some individuals suffer more than others. Others believe it all averages out in the afterlife, in what Judaism calls *olam haba*, the "World to Come". Let us take a close view at these attitudes.

There are two sets of justifications for this position: Religious and scientific. From the religious angle, we are told that everything God does is good. In our Torah portion, as we saw, God declares the world "very good". The psalmist says:

טוֹב־יְהוָה לַכֹּל וְרַחֲמָיו עַל־כָּל־מַעֲשָׂיו:
Tov HaShem lakol, verachamav 'al kol maasav
The Lord is good to all and His mercy is over all His works. [Psalms 145:9]

Jews recite that line at least three times a day. So we must have faith that it's all to the good.

From the scientific angle (I am a physicist), we note that nature is always optimizing. One example is the principle of least time: Between two points, light takes the path it can cross in the least time. This is why objects at the bottom of a pool seem closer to the surface than they are: Refracted light follows a broken line. Likewise, soap bubbles form so as to minimize surface area. An oddly-shaped metal loop dipped in a soapy solution will be spanned by an odd-looking surface. Of all possible surfaces joining the metal parts, this one has the smallest area.

There is also the principle of least action. When an object is subjected to various forces and follows an odd path as a result, that path is the one that minimizes a function called the "action". My doctoral dissertation was based on the principle of least action. It is a very powerful insight into the workings of nature.

Also, evolution is nature optimizing life. Nature gradually makes changes in the make-up of living things in order to maximize their chances for survival in their environment.

So, the thinking goes, why not assume nature optimizes absolutely everything, including matters where human beings are involved? This is where the word "optimism" comes from. It is the belief that everything that happens is somehow for the best. The German philosopher Leibnitz preached that "Everything is for the best in the best of all possible worlds." He was satirized by Voltaire in his novel *Candide or Optimism*.

But one wonders: What function, exactly, is God optimizing? That is totally unknown.

An objection can be quickly made: Why can't we always *see* the good? Some say: Because of our limited understanding. A primitive man in a dentist's chair or a surgeon's table only knows that he is being hurt. He does not see it's for his own good. In the Torah, Moses could not see the good either:
> Moses returned to God and said: "My God, why have You done evil to this people? Why have You sent me? For since I came to Pharaoh to speak in Your name, [Pharaoh] has done worse to this nation; and You have not saved Your people!"
> [Exodus 5:22-23]

First-century rabbi Nachum ish Gamzu was severely afflicted, yet he was always optimistic. No matter what happened to him or around him, he would say: "*Gam zu l'tovah* -- This, too, is for the good". He always saw a silver lining. The Talmud recounts his story:
> It is related of Nachum of Gamzu that he was blind in both his eyes, his two hands and legs were amputated, his whole body was covered with boils, and he was lying in a dilapidated house on a bed whose feet were standing in bowls of water to prevent the ants from crawling on to him…
> Why was he called Nachum of Gamzu? Because whatever befell him he would declare, "*Gam zu l'tovah* -- This, too, is for the good." [Taanit 21a]

Rabbi Akiva was a student of his, and followed in his footsteps. He used to say:
> כָּל דְּעָבֵיד רַחֲמָנָא לְטָב עָבֵיד -- *Kol da'avad rachmanah litav aved.*
> Everything God does is for the good.

The Talmud illustrates this notion with a story from Rabbi Akiva's life:

> It was taught in the name of Rabbi Akiva: A man should always accustom himself to say "Whatever the All-Merciful does is for the good".
>
> [As an example, consider] the following incident. Rabbi Akiva was once traveling along the road. He came to a certain town and looked for a place to stay but was turned away everywhere. He said "Whatever the All-Merciful does is for the good".
>
> He went and spent the night in an open field. He had with him a rooster [to wake him up in the morning], an ass [to carry his luggage], and a lamp [to study Torah at

night]. A gust of wind came and blew out the lamp. A weasel came and ate the rooster. A lion came and ate the ass. He said "Whatever the All-Merciful does is for the good".

That same night some bandits came and carried off the inhabitants of the town. He said: Did I not say to you, "Whatever the All-Merciful does is all for the good?" [The light from the lamp or the sounds from the rooster or the ass would have revealed my location to the bandits and I would have suffered the fate of the town's inhabitants.] [Berakhot 60b]

Note that the rabbis said everything is for the "good", not for the "best". The difference is important. The "best" could simply mean the "least bad" of several bad alternatives, but still bad. But no, they meant "positively good", not "least bad".

Can one always find a silver lining, no matter what tragedies occur around us? Long after the event, one can sometimes say "yes", especially when there is plenty of uncertainty. For example:

-The destruction of Temple led to a Judaism centered on synagogue, prayer, study, and spiritual matters.

-The Diaspora helped us learn new skills from the host countries, and prevented the destruction of all the Jews. When some countries were hostile, others were friendly.

-The various expulsions, from Spain and elsewhere, led us to seed our knowledge and bring new skills to the world at large.

-The Holocaust led to the world allowing the creation of the State of Israel.

-The State of Israel may be under perpetual siege and surrounded by implacable enemies, but this keeps the country together, increases the determination to keep the state Jewish, and minimizes intermarriage with Arabs. This avoids an explosion in the number of children with mixed parentage, uncertain identity, little or no Jewish commitment, or even practicing antisemitism, and who might annul the Law of Return. It also relegates internal feuding between secular and religious factions to the background. Note that the Talmud ascribes the fall of the second Temple to just such internal feuding – to *sin'at chinam*, or senseless hatred, as it puts it.

On the personal level, I can say that without the expulsion from Spain, my parents would not have met and I would never have existed. If I had not been forced out of Egypt, I would never have met my wife, had my children and grandchildren, and led as satisfying a life.

Some will object and say, "Even so, it's not worth it." I am not arguing that it is, just that some might consider it so. It is, of course, a subjective matter.

Now, is saying that everything that happens is for the good lead to a fatalistic attitude? That is, does it lead, not only to acceptance of bad events, but also to not doing much to counter them before they occur, or to react to them only after they happen? Not necessarily, but for some people yes, and that is dangerous.

Some rabbis argue that when bad things happen to us, it means we did something wrong. But the Torah tells us that is not always the case. Take slavery in Egypt, for example. God tells Abraham in the Book of Genesis:

יָדֹעַ תֵּדַע כִּי־גֵר ׀ יִהְיֶה זַרְעֲךָ בְּאֶרֶץ לֹא לָהֶם וַעֲבָדוּם וְעִנּוּ אֹתָם אַרְבַּע מֵאוֹת שָׁנָה

Know for certain that your offspring will be strangers in a strange land, and will be enslaved and afflicted for four hundred years. [Genesis 15:13]

It does not state a reason, and none is obvious. So evidently God thought slavery was necessary and led to some good. But how, and why for so long? There are many possible answers, which I described in another d'var Torah. In brief, slavery was necessary for our protection: Jacob's clan in Israel was an easy target for neighbors, but in Egypt, a superpower protected us, albeit to exploit us. Slavery also allowed us build up our numbers in safety. It allowed us to build up our identity and community spirit: We were all in the same boat and followed the same customs. Slavery minimized contact with the outside world, which reduced the practice of idolatry and eliminated the possibility of intermarriage. Slavery created a scenario that allowed God to show the Jews and the whole world that He was in charge, as He did when He freed us. Both the gratitude that we felt upon liberation and the slave mentality we had acquired made it easier for us to accept the Torah, as God wanted us to do.

But why couldn't God have made slavery less brutal and more tolerable? Because then few Israelites would have wanted to leave. Even as it is, the Midrash tells us that 80% of the Israelites refused to go and died in the plague of darkness [Tanḥuma, Beshallach 1:4]. And the rest may have left, but they grumbled incessantly about going back.

So, in conclusion, yes, it is always possible to find some good things emerging from bad things. In the absence of a definitive answer, looking for the good is not a bad attitude to have, if it does not lead to resignation and passive acceptance.

Shabbat shalom.

# Noach
Gen. 6:9-11:32

B"H

What Does Judaism Expect from Gentiles?

In this week's Torah portion, *Noach*, Noah and his family survive the Flood in the Ark full of animals. After the Flood, God makes a covenant with Noah, a covenant binding on all mankind: God will never again flood the earth, but people must observe certain commandments:
> I establish My covenant with you, and with your seed after you ... for perpetual generations… You shall not eat flesh with its life-blood [in it]. Whoever sheds man's blood, his blood shall be shed by man; for God made Man in His image… I have set My bow in the cloud, and it shall be the token of a covenant between Me and the earth. [Genesis 9:4-13]

The Talmud derives seven laws that are applicable to all mankind. They are called the Noahide Laws. We read in Tractate Sanhedrin:
> Our Rabbis taught: Seven precepts were the sons of Noah commanded: To establish courts of justice; and refrain from blasphemy, idolatry, adultery, murder, stealing, and eating the flesh of live animals. [Sanhedrin 56a-b]

The Talmud then explains how these laws are derived. Curiously, the Sages derived them from a single line in Genesis:
> And the Lord God commanded the man saying, "Of every tree of the garden you may freely eat". [Gen. 2:16]

Here is how:

-"Establish courts of justice" is derived from "And the Lord God commanded", because "command" relates to justice and judgment.

-"No blasphemy" is derived from the words "The Lord", which are used in connection with blasphemy in Leviticus:

38

> And he who blasphemes the name of the Lord, he shall surely be put to death. [Lev. 24:16]

-"No idolatry" is derived from the word "God", because the word "God" is used in that context in Exodus:
> You shall have no other gods before Me. [Ex. 20:3]

-"No murder" is derived from "the man", because the word "man" is used in that context in Genesis:
> Whoever sheds man's blood, by man shall his blood be shed. [Gen. 9:6]

-"No adultery" is derived from the word "saying", because it used in that context in Jeremiah:
> [The word of the Lord came to me] saying: "If a man divorces his wife, and she leaves him, and marries another man …" [Jer. 3:1]

-"No stealing" is derived from "Of every tree of the garden you may freely eat". Since it was necessary to authorize Adam to eat of the trees of the garden, it follows that without such authorization it was forbidden, since the trees did not belong to him.

-"No eating flesh from live animals" is derived from "You may freely eat", because it implies "You may eat only what is ready for eating", which is not the case while the animal is alive.

A commentator marveled that a verse giving permission to enjoy was interpreted as a series of prohibitions. This is a common theme in the Talmud: Freedom to enjoy is limited by ethical considerations, and only attains its value when so limited. The Mishnah says:
> No man is free but he who labors in the Torah. [Avot 6:2]

The question now arises: Jews have 613 commandments in the Torah, but Gentiles have only seven. Should Gentiles keep some of the other laws, such as eating only kosher food, observing Shabbat, honoring parents, affixing a mezuzah, refraining from certain mixtures, etc.? It's up to them. There is no merit or demerit if they do. There are, however, two notable exceptions.

First, there are restrictions on Gentiles studying the Torah. The Talmud says
[Sanhedrin 59a]:
> Rabbi Yohanan said: A Gentile who studies the Torah deserves death [*chayyav mita* in Aramaic].

It must be noted that the phrase "deserves death" just expresses disapproval, and is not to be taken literally. Certainly, no human action is called for. The phrase is common in the Talmud. Another example is:
> He who transgresses the words of the Sages deserves death. [Berakhot 6b]

Now, what is the Talmud's reasoning for forbidding Gentiles from studying Torah? It is written in Deuteronomy:
> תּוֹרָה צִוָּה־לָנוּ מֹשֶׁה מוֹרָשָׁה קְהִלַּת יַעֲקֹב׃
> *Torah tzivah lanu Moshe, morasha kehillat Yaakov*
> Moses commanded us the Torah, the inheritance of the congregation of Jacob.
> [Deut. 33:4]

The implication is understood to be: It is the *Jews'* inheritance, not the Gentiles'.

In that case, the Talmud continues, why is this prohibition not included in the Noahide laws? It *is*, the Sages argued: If you take someone's inheritance, you steal it, and one Noahide law is not to steal.

But objections were raised. Rabbi Meir went so far as to say: A Gentile who studies the Torah is like a High Priest. We learn that from the verse [in Leviticus]:
> וּשְׁמַרְתֶּם אֶת־חֻקֹּתַי וְאֶת־מִשְׁפָּטַי אֲשֶׁר יַעֲשֶׂה אֹתָם הָאָדָם וָחַי בָּהֶם
> Keep my statutes and my judgments, for the man who obeys them will live by them.
> [Lev. 18:5]

It does not say "Priest, Levite, or Israelite", but *adam* -- "man". So we learn that even a Gentile who studies [and observes] the Torah is like a High Priest! But another rabbi countered that Gentiles should study only the parts of the Torah that pertain to their own seven Noahide laws, not the rest. [Sanhedrin 59a, Bava Kamma 38a]

Why this restriction? One can only speculate. Studying Torah yields knowledge that can be used against Jews, especially if it can be easily (or intentionally) misinterpreted. For a long time the Talmud was not translated for that reason. Also, we don't want others to take our rituals and twist their meaning, as Messianics sometimes do.

Second, there are restrictions on Gentiles keeping Shabbat in full. The argument is that Shabbat is a sign between God and Jews only. In Exodus, we read the *Veshamru* prayer, recited at every Shabbat:

וְשָׁמְרוּ בְנֵי־יִשְׂרָאֵל אֶת־הַשַּׁבָּת לַעֲשׂוֹת אֶת־הַשַּׁבָּת לְדֹרֹתָם בְּרִית עוֹלָם:

בֵּינִי וּבֵין בְּנֵי יִשְׂרָאֵל אוֹת הִוא לְעֹלָם כִּי־שֵׁשֶׁת יָמִים עָשָׂה יְהוָה אֶת־הַשָּׁמַיִם וְאֶת־הָאָרֶץ וּבַיּוֹם הַשְּׁבִיעִי שָׁבַת וַיִּנָּפַשׁ:

The Children of Israel shall observe Shabbat, to make Shabbat an eternal covenant for generations. It is a sign between Me and the Children of Israel forever... [Exodus 31:16-17]

The Talmud adds:

Resh Lakish also said: A Gentile who keeps a day of rest deserves death... Ravina said: Even if he rested on a Monday. [Sanhedrin 58b-59a]

The Talmud asks again: If so, why is this prohibition not included in the seven Noahide laws? The Sages replied that the Noahide laws include only negative injunctions, and "Don't observe Shabbat" means "Do work", which is a positive commandment. If so, then why is the positive commandment to establish social laws included in the Noahide laws? The Sages replied: It is both positive and negative. Positive in the sense of: "Dispense justice" and negative in the sense of: "Refrain from injustice".

For this reason, candidates for conversion to Judaism are instructed to violate some rules of Shabbat privately as they practice observance. An example might be simply to turn a light on.

One possible concern was that Early Christians observed Shabbat in full (and some current Messianic Jews also do it), and the rabbis did not want faithful Jews to be confused with them.

The Rambam summed it up by saying:
> The principle is that one may not make innovations in religion or create new commandments. [Gentiles] may become true converts [to Judaism] by accepting all the commandments or they must observe their own (seven Noahide) laws only, and not add or detract from them. [Mishneh Torah, Kings and Wars 10:9]

In other words, Judaism is a package deal: No picking some parts of it and rejecting the rest.

Now, Gentiles are by no means disparaged in Judaism. A well-known principle is:

חסידי אומות העולם יש להם חלק לעוה"ב

> The righteous of all nations have a share in the World to Come. [Tosefta Sanhedrin 13, based on Sanhedrin 105a]

The Mishnah says:

אַל תְּהִי בָז לְכָל אָדָם, וְאַל תְּהִי מַפְלִיג לְכָל דָּבָר, שֶׁאֵין לְךָ אָדָם שֶׁאֵין לוֹ שָׁעָה וְאֵין לְךָ דָבָר שֶׁאֵין לוֹ מָקוֹם

> Do not despise any man, and do not discriminate against any thing, for there is no man that does not have his hour, and there is no thing that does not have its place. [Avot 4:3]

In the Midrash, we read:
> I call heaven and earth as witnesses: Any individual, whether Gentile or Jew, man or woman, servant or maid, can bring the Divine Presence upon himself in accordance with his deeds. [Tanna Devei Eliyahu Rabbah 9]

Consequently, Judaism also holds that no proselytizing among Gentiles is necessary. Judaism is not an "upgrade".

So, let us summarize. Jews must observe the 613 commandments in the Torah. Gentiles must observe the seven Noahide laws. Gentiles may study Torah or observe Shabbat only partially. For all other commandments, it is up to them whether to observe them or not.

Shabbat shalom.

Lech Lecha
Gen. 12:1-17:27

B"H

Why did God Choose Abraham?

This week's Torah portion, *Lech Lecha*, is all about Abraham. God promises him a bright future if he moves to a new place. He goes there, but faces a famine; goes to Egypt; separates from his nephew Lot; participates in the War of the Four against the Five and wins; enters into the "Covenant between the Parts" with God; and has a son, Ishmael, by his maid Hagar since his wife, Sarah, is childless. God promises him a son by Sarah, changes his name from Abram to Abraham, and orders him to circumcize himself and his household.

OK. But why does God take an interest in Abraham in particular? We are not told. Contrast with Noah, before him, and Moses after him.
-Noah is introduced as "righteous" and "perfect":

וְנֹחַ מָצָא חֵן בְּעֵינֵי יְהוָה אֵלֶּה תּוֹלְדֹת נֹחַ נֹחַ אִישׁ צַדִּיק תָּמִים הָיָה בְּדֹרֹתָיו אֶת־הָאֱלֹהִים הִתְהַלֶּךְ־נֹחַ:

And Noah found grace in the eyes of the Lord... Noah was a righteous man and perfect in his generations, and Noah walked with God. [Gen. 6:8-9]

-Moses is introduced by actions that show leadership, compassion, and courage:
    -He kills an Egyptian taskmaster who is beating a Jew. [Ex. 2:11]
    -He intervenes in a fight between two Jews, telling one, "Why do you strike your fellow?" [Ex. 2:13]
    -He defends the daughters of Yitro from the shepherds who drove them away from the well. [Ex. 2:17]

Only *then*, God talks to him at the burning bush and gives him his mission. [Ex. 3]

We understand *why* those two were picked. But Abraham is introduced only as follows:

> Terach fathered Abram, Nachor, and Haran; and Haran fathered Lot...
> And Abram and Nachor took wives. The name of Abram's wife was Sarai... But Sarai was barren; she had no child.
> And Terach took Abram his son, and Lot [his grandson] the son of Haran...and Sarai his daughter-in-law... and they went... from [their homeland] Ur Kasdim [Ur of the Chaldeans] to...the land of Canaan. And they came to Haran, and lived there... And Terach died in Haran. [Gen. 11:27-32]

This passage is really about Abraham's father Terach, not about Abraham himself. Why did they want to move to Canaan? We are not told. Then, suddenly, without transition or justification:

> And the Lord said to Abram, "Get out from your country, and from your family, and from your father's house, to a land that I will show you.
> And I will make of you a great nation, and I will bless you, and make your name great; and you shall be a blessing.
> And I will bless those who bless you, and curse those who curse you..."
> So Abram departed, as the Lord had spoken to him; and Lot went with him; and Abram was seventy-five years old when he departed from Haran.
> And Abram took Sarai his wife, and Lot his brother's son, and all their possessions that they had gathered, and the souls that they had made in Haran; and they went forth to go to the land of Canaan; and to the land of Canaan they came. [Gen. 12:1-5]

And, a little later, God tells him:

> All the land that you see, I give to you and to your seed forever...
> Your seed shall be as the dust of the earth. [Gen. 13:15-6]

Why? God doesn't say. Abraham doesn't ask. There is no obvious reason. Why him? Unknown. The Ramban, in 13th-century Spain, poses the question as follows:

> This section of the Torah has not adequately explained the issue.
> Why should God tell Abraham, "Leave your land and I will extend to you the greatest good that has ever been", without first indicating to us that Abraham was a servant of God or a perfectly righteous individual?
> Or, the text should state a reason for God's injunction to Abraham to leave his land, namely that he will achieve closeness to God in the new location. The convention of the Torah is to state, "Walk before Me, listen to My voice, and I will reward you."... This is the pattern throughout the Torah. [For example, the Torah says:]
>> -If you will follow My statutes..., then I will provide the rains in their due season. [Lev. 26:3]

-If you will surely listen to My voice..., then [I] will raise you above all other nations of the earth. [Deut. 28:1]

But to promise Abraham such reward solely on account of his leaving his land makes no sense.

Let's examine some possible reasons why Abraham was chosen.

First possibility: Abraham was chosen by default. Perhaps God approached others, such as Abraham's father or brothers, but they were unwilling to comply. Note that the Midrash also suggests that Israel was "chosen" by default. It says that God offered the Torah to various nations, and they all turned Him down, except Israel. [Sifri to Deut. 33:2] We only hear about Abraham because he was the only one willing to accept an invisible God. So, was Abraham the best by default, although not particularly worthy?

Second possibility: Abraham was chosen because he was intelligent. This is the answer given in the Midrash. Abraham proceeded logically to deduce the existence of God and the futility of idolatry, on his own, without revelation:

> -Rabbi Chiyya said: Terach was a manufacturer of idols. He once went away somewhere and left [his son] Abraham to sell them in his place. A man came and wished to buy one.
> Abraham asked him, "How old are you?"
> "Fifty years", was the reply.
> [Abraham] exclaimed, "Woe to [you]! You are fifty years old and would worship a day-old object!"
> [The man] became ashamed and left.
>
> -On another occasion a woman came with a plateful of flour and asked him, "Take this and offer it to [the idols]." So he took a stick, broke [the idols], and put the stick in the hand of the largest [idol].
> When his father returned, he asked, "What have you done to [the idols]?"
> [Abraham] rejoined, "...A woman came with... fine meal and asked me to offer it to [the idols]. One [idol] claimed, "I must eat first," while another claimed, "*I* must eat first." So the largest [idol] arose, took the stick, and broke [the other idols]."
> -The father cried out, "Why do you make fun of me? Do [these idols] have any knowledge?"

[Abraham] retorted: "Your ears should listen to what your mouth is saying."

-Thereupon [the father] seized [the son] and delivered him to [King] Nimrod.
[Nimrod] proposed, "Let us worship the fire!"
[Abraham] replied, "Let us rather worship water, which extinguishes the fire."
"Then let us worship water!"
"Let us rather worship the clouds which bear the water."
"Then let us worship the clouds!"
"Let us rather worship the winds which disperse the clouds."
"Then let us worship the wind!"
"Let us rather worship human beings, who withstand the wind."
[Nimrod] exclaimed, "You are just bandying words. We will worship only the fire. Behold, I will cast you into [the fire], and let your God, whom you adore, come and save you from it... [But] when Abram descended into the fiery furnace, he was saved...
[Gen. R. 38:13]

So Abraham derived the truth on his own. The Talmud goes even further:
> Rav said: Our father Abraham kept the whole Torah. [Yoma 28b]

So Abraham observed the Torah before it was revealed because he figured it out. The basis for this is actually the Torah itself: God tells Abraham's son Isaac that he will receive blessings...

> עֵקֶב אֲשֶׁר־שָׁמַע אַבְרָהָם בְּקֹלִי וַיִּשְׁמֹר מִשְׁמַרְתִּי מִצְוֺתַי חֻקּוֹתַי וְתוֹרֹתָי
>
> ...because Abraham obeyed my voice, and kept my charge, my commandments, My laws, and My Torah. [Gen. 26:5]

But why doesn't the Torah tell us his merit, as it did with Noah and Moses? The Ramban argues that the Torah did not want to dwell on the terrible things Abraham witnessed in Ur. This would publicize idolatry. But this is not convincing because later the Torah lists what practices are forbidden. It also does speak of wickedness in the time of Noah:

> And God saw that the wickedness of man was great in the earth, and that every imagination of the thoughts of his heart was only evil continually. [Gen. 6:5]

The Maharal, in 6th-century Prague, notes that Noah and Moses had only one-time missions: "Noah, build the ark and save each species", and "Moses, free the Jews, teach them Torah, and lead them to Israel." But Abraham's mission was for eternity. God said to him, "I will make you a great nation". God was choosing the progenitor of a nation, not just *one* individual for *one* task.

Third possibility: Abraham was chosen because he was obedient.
He did what God asked him without questioning. He had faith God was right. That's what God wanted at the time, for that mission. God was not looking for a righteous man (like Noah) or a compassionate man (like Moses), but an *obedient* one, one who would say, like the Israelites at Mount Sinai:

> נַעֲשֶׂה וְנִשְׁמָע -- *Naaseh venish'ma*
> We will do first, and understand later. [Ex. 24:7]

The Torah could not say at first that Abraham was selected because he was "obedient", because he had done nothing yet to prove that. But he soon proved it. The strange commandment, "Leave everything and go", was followed without question. Later, the order, "Sacrifice your son Isaac", was followed without question. (However, Abraham did argue against the destruction of Sodom, but there was nothing there that God asked him to do, and righteousness *was* important to him).

In the Torah, God says of Abraham:

> יְדַעְתִּיו לְמַעַן אֲשֶׁר יְצַוֶּה אֶת־בָּנָיו וְאֶת־בֵּיתוֹ אַחֲרָיו וְשָׁמְרוּ דֶּרֶךְ יְהוָה לַעֲשׂוֹת צְדָקָה וּמִשְׁפָּט
> I know him: He will command his children and his household after him, and they shall keep the way of the Lord, to do righteousness and justice... [Gen. 18:19]

However, the Mishna does say that God tested Abraham to make sure he was the right one:

> With ten tests Abraham, our father, was tested; and he passed them all, in order to show how great his love was. [Avot 5:3]

The Rambam's list of these ten tests is:

>   1. God orders him to leave his homeland for Canaan. [Gen. 12:1]
>   2. When he gets there, he faces a famine. [Gen. 12:10]
>   3. The Egyptians capture his wife, Sarah, and bring her to Pharaoh. [Gen. 12:15]
>   4. He must fight in the battle of the Four against the Five. [Gen. 14:14]
>   5. He has a child with Hagar after not being able to have children with Sarah. [Gen. 16:3]
>   6. God orders him to circumcise himself in his old age. [Gen. 17:24]
>   7. The king of Gerar captures Sarah, to take her for himself. [Gen. 20:2]
>   8. God orders him to send Hagar away after their son Ishmael was born. [Gen. 21:12]
>   9. He becomes estranged from his son Ishmael. [Gen. 21:12]

10. God orders him to sacrifice his son Isaac. [Gen. 22:2]

Some lists include the fact that God tells him that his descendants will be enslaved in a strange land. [Gen. 15:13] Other lists exist, which include Midrash stories, outside Torah, such as that Abraham was thrown into a fiery furnace by King Nimrod.

Fourth possibility: Abraham was chosen because he could get things done. He got to work right away spreading the message, without even being commanded. The Midrash says:
> Abraham made converts, for it is written, "And Abraham took Sarai his wife... and all the souls that they had made in Haran." [Gen. 12:5]
> Rabbi Eleazar observed in the name of Rabbi Yosei ben Zimra: If all the nations assembled to create one insect, they could not give it life, yet you say, "And all the souls that they had made in Haran!"
> It refers to the converts.
> Then let [the Torah] say, "That they had converted". Why "That they had made?" That is to teach you that if one brings a convert near [God], it is as though he had created him.
> Now why does it not say "That *he* had made" instead of "That *they* had made"? Rabbi Hunia said: Abraham converted the men and Sarah converted the women. [Gen. R. 84:4]

The *Avot* prayer in the Amidah begins by calling God "God of our fathers, God of Abraham, God of Isaac, God of Jacob", but ends with calling God *Magen Avraham* -- "Shield of Abraham". Why not "Shield of the Patriarchs"? Because Abraham was different from the others. He was the first. He was the enabler. He taught his children but no one taught him. [Rambam, Hilkhot Avodat Kokhavim 1:3] He grew up among pagans, but his children did not. He is called *bechir ha-avot* -- "the best of the patriarchs". [Midrash Sekhel Tov on Gen. 33]

So we conclude that God chose Abraham because he was intelligent, obedient, and knew how to get things done. He had reached knowledge of God on his own, without revelation, did as told, and did it well. That was the combination God needed at that time.

Shabbat shalom.

Vayera
Gen. 18:1-22:24

B"H

Why the Binding of Isaac?

This week's Torah portion, *Vayera*, relates the story of when Abraham came close to sacrificing his son Isaac, on God's command, as a test of faith. The Torah says, in Genesis:

> And it came to pass... that
> God tested Abraham, and said to him, Abraham!
> And he said: Behold, here I am!
> And he said: Take now your son, your only son, Isaac, the one you love, and go to the land of Moriah; and offer him there for a burnt offering upon one of the mountains which I will tell you. [Genesis 22:1-2]

Abraham proceeds as told, but at the last minute, God stops him right before Isaac is about to be killed. This is a strange and disturbing story. It is called the *Akedah*, or "The Binding of Isaac". It raises many questions. There is no reference to it anywhere else in the Tanach, the Bible. Why, if it's such a defining moment in Judaism? There are no lessons tied specifically to the Akedah. It's just there. What are we supposed to make of it?

First, we are told that God tested Abraham.
So, we ask: Did Abraham pass the test?
The traditional answer is, of course, yes. The Torah says:

> And [God] said, "Do not lay your hand upon the lad, nor do anything to him; for now I know that you fear God, seeing that you did not withhold your son, your only son, from me." [Gen. 22:12]

So, since Abraham was willing to sacrifice what he loved most, as a sign of submission to God's will no matter what, as a sign of faith, he must have passed the test. But there are clues in our tradition that suggest that in some respects Abraham failed the test.

-First, he did not ask questions or protest. Previously, in the Torah, we hear Abraham arguing strenuously with God that Sodom should not be destroyed. He extracts a promise from God that Sodom will not be destroyed if ten righteous people are found there. So Abraham has a record of arguing with God, but here he did not argue. One may say he never argued only when God told him to *do* something, which was not the case for Sodom.

-Second, right after this story, the Midrash tells us that Isaac's mother, Sarah, died of grief when she heard a false report that Abraham had sacrificed Isaac. [Genesis Rabbah 58:5]

-Third, the Talmud records a tradition that the patriarchs followed Jewish law, *halacha*, even before the Torah was given to all, because the Torah says:
> Abraham obeyed my voice, and kept my charge, my commandments, my statutes, and my laws. [Genesis 26:5]

Well, one of the most loathsome practices outlawed by *halacha* is child sacrifice. So Abraham wasn't *supposed* to obey, because God's instruction was against *halacha*. To counter this argument, the Talmud asserts the right of a prophet to suspend a law [Sanhedrin 89b-90a]. So, they argue, even murder would have been permissible to Abraham, as an established prophet, if it was really God's will.

-Fourth, God never speaks to Abraham again after the *Akedah*. Rabbi Shlomo Riskin explains that this was because God was unhappy with Abraham for being eager to obey the command to slaughter Isaac. (God can't very well tell Abraham he failed the test, since Abraham was obeying God in the first place, but He can think it!)

In a parallel teaching, the Hassidic masters say that the *Akedah* was punishment for Abraham's mistreatment of his elder son Ishmael, whom he expelled from his household. Since Abraham failed to show compassion for his first son, God punished him by ostensibly failing to show compassion for Abraham's second son.

There are other views. My personal one is that Abraham was stalling, and never intended to kill his son. At the last second, he would have stopped his own hand if God hadn't done it. So Abraham was, in a sense, also testing God. He and God were engaged in a game of chicken, as it were. What evidence do we have for that? Well, we read about Abraham's actions, but we don't know his thoughts. He takes his time, he cuts the wood slowly, he loads his animals slowly, he plods slowly toward the mountains... He hopes that God will intercede! He never means to kill Isaac. That's why he tells his servants, "The boy and I...will worship and return to you."

Another view is that God never intended to let Abraham actually sacrifice Isaac. The Book of Jeremiah says:
> And they have built... high places... to burn their sons and their daughters in the fire, which I [God] did not command them; nor did it enter My mind that they should do this. [Jeremiah 7:31]

Rashi interprets this verse as God saying, "Don't think for a moment that I, God, ever had any intention of actually having Abraham kill his son. This never even occurred to Me!"

Abraham Ibn Ezra, from 12th-century Spain, records an opinion that Isaac was killed by Abraham then resurrected. Why? Because the Torah says:
> So Abraham returned to his young men, and they rose up and went together to Beersheba. [Gen. 22:19]

So Abraham returned together with the young men who accompanied him, but nothing is said of Isaac. However, Ibn Ezra himself rejects that view.

Many insightful observations have been put forth on the *Akedah*. Here are some of them.

-First, the *Akedah* refers to Jewish martyrdom. The Jewish people must be ready at all times to give up life itself *l'kiddush Ha-Shem,* for the sanctification of God's name.

-Second, if you place yourself or your children in harm's way for a higher cause (for example, by going to war, going on a risky mission, or just living in antisemitic societies), are you not doing essentially what Abraham did?
The Talmud tells the story of a woman who had seven sons. All seven were tortured to death rather than bow to an idol as commanded:
> She said to [her last son, before he was killed]: My son, go and say to your father Abraham, "You did bind one [of your sons] to the altar, but I have bound [all seven of my my sons to] seven altars [and they, unlike your son, did not survive!]." [Gittin 57b]

Was this different from the Akedah? To this one may answer: Yes, because we see a purpose. Did Abraham see a purpose?

-Third, does God really test us all the time? The Book of Job elaborates on that. Is our evil inclination, our *yetzer hara*, a perpetual "test"?

-Fourth, was Abraham "just following orders"? Is that always correct?

-Fifth, how did Abraham know it was really God making this demand? How would anyone ever know?

-Sixth, why is such a premium placed on faith, without proof, when we were given a mind that asks for proof?

-Seventh, Maimonides, in his Guide of the Perplexed, says:
> "God tested Abraham" does not mean that God put Abraham through a test, but that God made the example of Abraham serve as a test case of the extreme limits of the love and fear of God. [Rambam, Guide of the Perplexed 3.24]

-Eighth, the *shofar*, or ram's horn, is to remind us of the ram that was substituted for Isaac. This is why the story of the *Akedah* is always read on Rosh Hashanah.

-Finally, the Sages tell us that Isaac was really a grown man, strong enough to prevent the elderly Abraham from tying him up if he had wanted to resist.

Why didn't he resist? Note that the story isn't called "The Testing of Abraham", but "The Binding of Isaac", so we must focus on Isaac's acceptance of his fate.

Perhaps that is the lesson of the *Akedah*: Acceptance of bad things, after doing all we can to avoid them, in spite of not understanding the reasons, with faith that in some mysterious fashion it's all for the best, and moving on with our lives to build a better tomorrow.

Shabbat shalom.

Chayye Sarah
Gen. 23:1-25:18

B"H

The Cave of Machpelah

This week's Torah portion is *Chayye Sarah*, "The Life of Sarah". It is the only portion bearing a woman's name. Sarah has just died at 127, of grief, when she saw her husband Abraham come back from the mountain without their son, Isaac, and concluded Isaac must have died. She is the only biblical woman whose age is mentioned.

Abraham must now bury Sarah. He had been a wanderer in the land for 62 years. The Torah says:

> Abraham...spoke to the Hittites, saying, "I am a stranger and a sojourner with you. Give me burial property... so that I may bury my dead..."
>
> And the Hittites answered, "Listen to us, my lord. You are a prince of God among us. Bury your dead in the best of our graves. None of us will withhold his grave from you..."
>
> And Abraham stood up and bowed to the Hittites, saying... "If it is your will that I bury my dead... intercede for me with Ephron ben Tzohar, that he may give me the Cave of Machpelah, which belongs to him... Let him give it to me... as burial property for full price."...
>
> Ephron the Hittite answered Abraham: ... "No, my lord, listen to me. I am *giving* you the field, and the cave that is in it. I am *giving* it to you. Before the eyes of the sons of my people, I am *giving* it to you. Bury your dead."
>
> And Abraham bowed down before the people of the land, saying, "But, if only *you* would listen to me. I am giving you the *money* for the field. Take it from me, and I will bury my dead there."
>
> And Ephron replied, "My lord, listen to me; a piece of land worth four hundred shekels of silver, what is that between you and me? Bury your dead."
>
> And Abraham listened to Ephron, and [gave] Ephron... four hundred shekels of silver. [Genesis 23:3-16]

Welcome to the Middle East! If you understand this story, you understand the Middle East. This was a typical scene in a typical Middle-Eastern bazaar. Consider:

-Everybody is very polite and outwardly friendly and hospitable.

-Everybody flatters everybody else in public. Abraham is called נְשִׂיא אֱלֹהִים *N'si Elokim* -- "A prince of God" – and אֲדֹנִי *Adoni* -- "My Lord".

-There are loud and exaggerated expressions of friendship, such as "What is this matter between me and you?", meaning: Between two great friends such as the two of us, shall we even *talk* about money? Your happiness and satisfaction are the only things that count! Never mind the fact that we just met and belong to different ethnic groups.

-"Listen to me" שְׁמָעֵנִי (*Shma'eni*) means "Don't listen to me". People don't speak their true minds. Ephron never intended to give away his property. In fact he exacted a very high price for it. Ephron said, "I give it to you! Take it!" He said that *three* times! If you believe that, you'll believe anything.

-Always let the shopkeepers quote a price first.

-People love to gather and watch others argue and negotiate. It's a free show! And negotiations are frequently disguised. Yes, they negotiated! Listen:
> -Abraham clearly says at the outset he wants to buy just the cave. But Ephron responds, "I am *giving* you the field, and the cave that is in it." Translation: Sorry, you have to buy the field also: Package deal or no deal.
> -Ephron says, "Bury your dead." Translation: I know you need it fast, I know Jewish tradition says you must bury the dead quickly, and so you are in a poor bargaining position.
> -Ephron says, "Let's not haggle over something worth only 400 shekels of silver." Ephron talks as if the price is low, but it is really exorbitant. He takes advantage of Abraham's grief.

How do we know the price is exorbitant?
> -Because later, King David pays only one-eighth of that, fifty shekels, to buy a site on which to build the Temple. [2 Samuel 24:24-25].
> -And the prophet Jeremiah pays only 17 shekels of silver for an entire field. [Jer. 32:9]
> -And King Omri pays only 6,000 shekels for the entire territory of Samaria. [1 Kings 16:24]

Normally, at this point, serious negotiations would begin and the land would be sold for a fraction of the asking price. And we know Abraham can drive a hard bargain: We've seen him haggle with God Himself over Sodom and Gomorrah. But Abraham immediately agrees to the price without haggling, and pays. Maybe he is overcome by grief and is in no mood for bargaining. Maybe he feels it's an insult to Sarah's memory to haggle over the price of her grave. Maybe he feels he can well afford it, and doesn't bargain for sport. Maybe he feels it is beneath him to argue with such scoundrels as Ephron.

Or maybe he knows the true value of the cave! Consider this. Ephron, no doubt, was laughing all the way to the bank after the deal. But if he had taken a peek in the Zohar, the Book of Jewish mysticism (an anachronistic peek, to be sure!), he would have found out *why* Abraham had his heart set on this particular cave. Listen to the Zohar (if you are over forty!):
> Rabbi Yehudah said: "Abraham recognized the cave of Machpelah by a certain mark, and he had long set his mind and heart on it, for he had once entered that cave and seen Adam and Eve buried there. He knew that they were Adam and Eve because he saw the form of a man, and, while he was gazing, a door opened into the Garden of Eden, and he perceived the same form standing near it. Now, whoever looks at the form of Adam cannot escape death, for when a man is about to pass out of the world he catches sight of Adam and at that moment he dies. Abraham, however, did look at him, and saw his form and yet survived. He saw, moreover, a shining light that illumined the cave, and a lamp burning. Abraham then coveted that cave for his burial place, and his mind and heart were set upon it."
> ...
> Rabbi Shim'on said: "When Abraham brought Sarah in there for burial, Adam and Eve arose and refused to receive her. They said: "Is not our shame already great enough before the Holy One in the other world on account of our sin, which brought death into the world, that you should come to shame us further with your good deeds?" Abraham answered: "I am already destined to make atonement for you

before the Almighty, so that you may not be shamed before Him anymore." After taking upon himself this obligation, Abraham buried Sarah his wife. Adam then returned to his place, but not Eve, until Abraham came and placed her beside Adam, who received her for his sake." [Zohar 1:128a]

So Abraham wanted that cave because it was the entrance to the Garden of Eden. He wanted to buy Heaven!

The most important part of this episode is that possession of the Promised Land began with a legal purchase, in front of many witnesses. It was a purchase that was clearly eternal, because the dead are not going anywhere. This is why Torah dwells on it at length. So it was with the Zionist movement much later. The Jews bought the land they settled, parcel by parcel. They felt the land may be ours by divine right, but we must still compensate, even generously, those who live there.

Another teaching from this episode is that when Jews move to a new place, their first concern is to buy a plot of land for a cemetery.

Tradition holds that four couples are buried at Machpelah, now known as the Tomb of the Patriarchs: Adam and Eve, Abraham and Sarah, Isaac and Rebecca, Jacob and Leah. It is called *Machpelah*, meaning "doubled" [Genesis Rabbah 58:8], because it has two levels. It is the second-holiest Jewish site after Temple Mount.

What is the history of the Cave of Machpelah, in Hebrew מְעָרַת הַמַּכְפֵּלָה *Ma'arat Ha-Machpelah*? The building on the site was originally a synagogue, built 2,000 years ago. Then Byzantine and Crusader conquerors turned it into a church. Then Muslim conquerors turned it into a mosque. They did not allow Jews to enter it. Jews were allowed only up to the 7th step on the outside staircase.

When Israel retook the area in 1967, it gave control of the site to Muslim authorities. Muslims have unlimited access, but Jews do not. There are three rooms: Ohel Avraham, Ohel Yitzhak, and Ohel Ya'akov. Jews can freely access Ohel Avraham and Ohel Yaacob, but have no access to Ohel Yitzhak, the largest one, except for ten days a year. Over 300,000 people visit every year.

The actual cave was uncovered several years ago, under the building, and revealed artifacts from 3,000 years ago, the Early Israelite Period. This strong link to Jewish history is why many Israelis insist on retaining that area. They call the city around it, as the Torah does, Kiryat Arba -- the city of the four, because four couples are buried there [Sotah 13a]. It is a Jewish town where some 8,000 Jews live today. It is near Hebron, where close to 1,000 Jews live, surrounded by a sea of hostile Arabs.

The irony is that, if Jews own any part of the Land of Israel, surely they own Machpelah, whose Jewish acquisition is fully detailed in Scripture. There is no theology there! Likewise, the Bible records the Jewish acquisition of both Joseph's Tomb and Temple Mount. [Genesis Rabbah 79:7] Let us work to ensure that a final peace treaty between the Arabs and Israel does not relinquish Jewish rights to these three areas.

Shabbat shalom.

Toldot
Gen. 25:19-28:9

B"H

Antisemitism

The Midrash recounts the following story:

> A Jew passed in front of Hadrian [the Roman Emperor] and greeted him.
> The king asked, "Who are you?" He answered, "I am a Jew."
> He exclaimed, "Does a Jew dare to pass in front of Hadrian and greet him!" He ordered, "Take him and cut off his head.""
> Another Jew passed, and seeing what had happened to the first man, did not greet him.
> The king asked, "Who are you?" He answered, "A Jew."
> He exclaimed, "Does a Jew dare to pass in front of Hadrian without giving greeting!" He ordered, "Take him and cut off his head.""
> His senators said to him, "We cannot understand your actions. The one who greeted you was killed and the one who did not greet you was killed!"
> He replied to them, "I do not need your advice about killing the people I hate."
> [Lamentations Rabbah 3:20]

Why do so many people hate us Jews? Why do so many people hate us Americans?

Legions of scholars and pseudo-scholars have written mountains of books on the subject, providing us with 1,001 reasons why we ourselves are to blame for antisemitism. We are told we Jews are hated because we are greedy, domineering, scheming, deceitful, unscrupulous, clannish, arrogant, because we don't accept Jesus, because we killed Jesus, because we don't accept Muhammad, because we care for no one but ourselves, because our claim to divine chosenness infuriates others, because we are a convenient small and vulnerable scapegoat during hard times, because we incite fear by being too different, because we refuse to assimilate, because our loyalties are divided, because too many of us are on the left (or the right) of the political spectrum, because we support the State of Israel – "an illegal, bloodthirsty, and genocidal colonialist power". We are told we don't interact enough with others and explain ourselves, and ignorance leads people to believe the most outrageous accusations against us, such as the blood libel or plots to take over the world. We are told most people believe there is no smoke without fire, and that if so many people hated the Jews for so long, there must be good reasons for it, and they might as well join in, etc., etc., ad nauseam.

There are two strong reasons to believe that these alleged reasons are, by and large, pretexts. First, antisemitism predated most of them. Second, other groups, perceived to be just as "guilty" as the Jews on many of these counts, were not hated, or at least not as consistently or to the same extent. Did you ever hear of anybody hating the Amish?

The real cause of anti-Semitism is staring at us right in the face in this week's Torah portion, *Toldot*. It is near the very beginning of the Torah, in the story of the patriarch Isaac, the first person born Jewish. Let me quote directly:

> Then Isaac sowed in that land, and reaped in the same year a hundredfold; and the Lord blessed him.
> And the man became rich, and gained more and more, until he became very wealthy.
> He had possessions of flocks, and possessions of herds, and large numbers of servants. And the Philistines envied him.
> And the Philistines stopped up all the wells which his father's servants had dug, in the days of Abraham his father, and filled them with earth.
> And Abimelech [king of the Philistines] said to Isaac, "Go away from us, because you are much mightier than we are."
> And Isaac departed from there, and encamped in the valley of Gerar, and dwelt there. [Genesis 26:12-17]

So, to summarize, Isaac lives peacefully among his neighbors, then, through hard and honest work, becomes fabulously wealthy and powerful. So his neighbors hate him, then harm him by depriving him of water – the very source of life – and finally expel him.

There you have it, the *only* reason for antisemitism, right at the beginning of the Torah, in the story of the very first person born Jewish: Jealousy. The envy of those who are perceived as more successful, more prosperous, more intelligent, who have more of the qualities or achievements perceived as desirable. Antisemites never acknowledge this reason because it makes *them* look bad, and Jews don't publicize it for fear of exacerbating antisemitism. That's why you don't hear much about it.

This reason is not the same as the so-called "disparity of wealth among the nations", that is often bandied about. The division of the world into the haves and the have-nots is a myth. The Earth is rich in natural resources almost everywhere. The real division in the world is between the well-managed and the mismanaged. There are plenty of countries that enjoy prosperity and achievement in spite of being poor in natural resources. Israel comes to mind. And there are even more countries that are basically rich, yet whose people live in squalor, poverty and ignorance, because of corruption, oppression and mismanagement on the part of their leaders.

Jealousy is deeply rooted in human nature. As the old Jewish saying goes, "We anger God with our vices and men with our virtues". So important is the need to control this feeling that the Torah found it necessary to include, right up there in the Ten Commandments, "You will not covet."

Jews and Americans are prime victims of this phenomenon.

Jews are perceived as successful -- not always individually, to be sure, but certainly as a group:
-Material wealth is the most visible aspect of this success, but it is not the only one.
-Jews also possess intellectual wealth: Only one person in 500 is Jewish in the world, yet one Nobel Prize in 3 or 4 goes to a Jew. So Jews are

getting Nobel prizes at a rate 150 times higher than you might expect given their small numbers.
-Jews exhibit military prowess -- tiny Israel victorious against large and mighty Arab armies.
-Jews exhibit economic prowess -- Israel's meteoric rise in the world of modernity and technology.
-Jews enjoy disproportional representation in the professions (physicians, lawyers, accountants, teachers, researchers, etc.), disproportional representation among holders of college degrees, disproportional representation wherever revolutionary ideas are brewing, and the influence that comes with all these achievements.
-And the biblical teaching that the Jews are "God's chosen people" only exacerbates this feeling of jealousy.

Rising anti-Americanism in the world drinks from the same source. A nation cannot be the world's only superpower, the world's richest nation, the world's most technologically advanced nation, a fairly generous and sharing nation, a nation where freedom and democracy reign supreme, a nation that, while not perfect, contains within its institutions the seeds for continual improvement and renewal, without inciting envy and enmity. Those who believe that the United States (or Israel, for that matter) will be more loved and respected throughout the world if only it would change this or that policy are dangerously deluded.

Unfortunately, jealousy is the most intractable of all grievances, because no amount of goodwill and generosity can alter it. As the saying goes, "No good deed goes unpunished". Any initiative, any form of interaction, however well-intentioned, can, and will, be viewed as patronizing and condescending. It may even exacerbate it. People are proud and resent what they perceive as pity, handouts, or charity. This is all the more true if their own country or ethnic group was dominant in the past: It's tough to be a has-been. This goes a long way towards explaining the attitudes and actions of some European countries or the Islamic world.

So what can be done to prevent matters from reaching the boiling point?

Act humble? Not only would this be contrary to human nature, but others would see through it. There is much wisdom in Golda Meir's tongue-in-cheek comment, "Don't be so humble. You are not that great." Certainly, being careful to eliminate the appearance of arrogance or cockiness would help, but only at the margin, because the root cause would still be there.

Reduce achievement? "Dumb yourself down"? This is so contrary to human nature that it is not worth discussing as a serious option. Even its weaker companion, "Letting others take the credit for your achievements", is totally unrealistic.

Retreat into isolationism? Actively promote complete separation between the successful and the less successful? In today's interconnected world, this is practically impossible. Economies must always expand into new markets. Ethical concerns do not allow us to deny, say, new drugs, even to potential adversaries. Interaction also prevents dangerous misunderstandings. Finally, progress in all fields requires as much collaboration as possible.

Proselytize and conquer? Tell others: "Join us and you'll get the benefits for which you resent us so much?" For the Jews, it would mean trying to convert others to Judaism. For the United States, it would mean conquering and annexing other countries. Although such methods *have* met with partial success in history, they go against the basic principles of both groups, which include letting people make their own choices freely. And, some say, the sudden and massive infusion of outsiders in any group is certain to change the character and values of the group.

There is only one possible conclusion. The successful must learn to live with the inevitable consequences of their success. This means, first and foremost, protecting themselves, being strong, and never letting their guard down, because they are likely to be continually attacked. They must also strive to keep their ethical principles and ideals, and not allow themselves to go down to the level of those who resent them. This includes continuing to share what they have to offer with the world. Fortunately, such a course of action is possible in the case of the Jews (thanks to Israel) and in the case the United States (thanks to its size and power).

This, too, is a form of peace. Peace is, at its root, the absence of war. One certainly hopes that it would also include friendship, love, respect, tolerance, cooperation, collaboration, civil interaction, cultural exchanges, trade relations -- but these are not essential to avoid the death and destruction that accompanies war. As the saying goes, "A cold peace is better than a hot war."

Unless ways to alter basic human nature are discovered, this is the best we can do.

In conclusion, all I can do is repeat what Joshua told the Israelites in the Book of Joshua:
> חֲזַק וֶאֱמָץ *Ḥazzak ve'ematz* – Be strong and of good courage. Do not be afraid and do not be dismayed, for the Lord your God is with you wherever you go. [Joshua 1:9]

Shabbat shalom.

Vayetze
Gen. 28:10-32:3

B"H

Is Love All You Need?

In this week's Torah portion, *Vayetze*, we read about love at first sight:
>-Now Laban had two daughters: ... Leah ... and Rachel. Leah had weak eyes. Rachel was shapely and beautiful. Jacob loved Rachel, so he [told Laban], "I will serve you seven years for your younger daughter Rachel." [Gen. 29:16-18]
>-And Jacob served seven years for Rachel. And they seemed to him only a few days, because of the love he had for her. [Genesis 29:20]

Jacob is tricked into marrying Leah and serving another seven years for Rachel. Married to both, he does not hide his feelings:
>וַיָּבֹא גַּם אֶל־רָחֵל וַיֶּאֱהַב גַּם־אֶת־רָחֵל מִלֵּאָה   And Jacob also slept with Rachel. [But] Jacob also loved Rachel more than Leah. [Gen. 29:30]

But at least he did "love" Leah. Yet immediately afterwards it says:
>The Lord saw that Leah was hated [שְׂנוּאָה] and he opened her womb. But Rachel was barren. [Gen. 29:31]

The phrase is repeated. Leah says:
>שְׂנוּאָה אָנֹכִי – *Snu-ah anochi* -- I was hated. [Gen. 29:33]

Leah was "loved" but "hated". How can that be? Neglected? A love-hate relationship? Jacob wishes she would just go away. She was in the way.

Love, the most irrational of feelings. As the 17th-century French writer Pascal said:
>*Le cœur a ses raisons que la raison ne connaît point.*
>The heart has its reasons that reason does not know. [Pascal, *Pensées* 277]

Love (*ahavah* in Hebrew -- אַהֲבָה) is mentioned very often in the Torah.

First there is romantic love, as in Jacob's love for Rachel, mentioned above, or Shechem's love for Dinah:
> [Shechem] was strongly drawn to Dinah, daughter of Jacob, and in **love** with the maiden, and he spoke to her tenderly. [Genesis 34:3]

Then there is spousal love, as in Isaac's love for Rebecca:
> Isaac **loved** [Rebecca], and thus found comfort after his mother's death. [Genesis 22:2]

Then there is parental love, as evidenced by the three patriarchs:

> -And [God] said [to Abraham]: Take, I pray you, your son, your only one, the one you **love**, Isaac, and go to the land of Moriah. [Genesis 22:2]

> -Now Isaac **loved** Esau, because he did eat of his venison; and Rebecca **loved** Jacob. [Genesis 25:28]

> And Israel [that is, Jacob] **loved** Joseph more than all his sons, for he was the son of his old age. [Genesis 37:3]

There is also love of God for Israel. In the Torah, the Israelites are told:

> -The Lord did not set his **love** upon you, nor choose you, because you were more in number than any people; for you were the fewest of all peoples… [Deut 7: 6-7; 14:2] …The Lord your God does not give you this good land to possess because of your righteousness, for you are a stiff-necked people. [Deut 9:6]

> -[If you sin and repent,] then the Lord your God will restore your fortunes and take you back in **love**. [Deuteronomy 30:3]

During religious services, we recognize God's love:
> -In the morning, we say *Ahava Rabbah* (אַהֲבָה רַבָּה): You [God] have **loved** us with abundant **love**, and You have bestowed great compassion on us.
> -In the evening, we say *Ahavat Olam* (אַהֲבַת עוֹלָם): With everlasting **love** You have **loved** the House of Israel your people.
> -And we conclude with the blessing: בָּרוּךְ אַתָּה יְהֹוָה הַבּוֹחֵר בְּעַמּוֹ יִשְׂרָאֵל בְּאַהֲבָה -- Blessed are You O Lord, Who has chosen his people Israel in **love**.

The *Song of Songs* likens the love between God and Israel to romantic love. In the Torah, God is often described as "jealous", as a lover would be. Note that this is a first among religions: Other so-called "deities" were always angry and needed to be "pacified".

Then there is the love of Israel for God, which is actually a commandment. In the Shema, we chant this line from the Torah:

וְאָהַבְתָּ אֵת יְהוָה אֱלֹהֶיךָ בְּכָל־לְבָבְךָ וּבְכָל־נַפְשְׁךָ וּבְכָל־מְאֹדֶךָ:-
You shall **love** the Lord your God with all your heart, with all your soul and with all your might. [Deuteronomy 6:5]

Finally, there is love of a neighbor, even a stranger, also a commandment). The Torah enjoins us:

וְאָהַבְתָּ לְרֵעֲךָ כָּמוֹךָ- -- You shall **love** your neighbor as yourself. [Leviticus 19:18]

-You shall **love** the stranger as yourself, for you were once strangers in the Land of Egypt. [Leviticus 19:34]

So now is a good time to ask our main question: Is love all you need? Of course not. You need justice too. In fact, "loving" and "fearing" God are two recurring themes in the Torah.

Love unites, as in Jacob and Rachel. But love also divides, as in the case of Jacob and Leah; or the case of Rachel and Leah, two sisters married to the same man.

Love unites, as when Abraham, Isaac and Jacob each had a preferred son. But love also divides, because the other sons were jealous. This is unfair!

Love is particular and selective. Justice is universal.

Love can vary in intensity. Justice does not. The Talmud says about the diminishing love between couples:

When love was strong, we could have made our bed on the blade of a sword. Now that our love has grown weak, a 60-cubit [90-foot] bed is not large enough for us.
[Sanhedrin 7a]

Love calls for no punishment. Justice does. Thus, love allows the proliferation of wrongdoing. Justice does not.

Indeed, the Torah says:
צֶדֶק צֶדֶק תִּרְדֹּף לְמַעַן תִּחְיֶה -- *Tzedek, tzedek tirdof lemaan tichyeh*
Justice, justice shall you pursue that you may live. (Deut. 16:20)
We simply can't live without justice. The world cannot endure with love alone.

In the Torah, we are told that the physical world was created with God's attribute of justice:
בְּרֵאשִׁית בָּרָא אֱלֹהִים -- *Bereshit bara Elokim...*
In the beginning, Elokim created... [Gen. 1:1]
The name *Elokim* for God is associated with God's attribute of justice, that is: Laws, order, cold equations.

A few lines later in the Torah, God's other main name, יְהוָה HaShem [the Tetragrammaton] is introduced, representing the attribute of mercy.

The Midrash quotes God as saying:
If I create the world with the attribute of mercy, sin will be plentiful; and if I create it with the attribute of justice, how can the world [continue to] exist? Therefore I will create it with both the attributes of mercy and justice, and thus may it endure. [Gen. R. 12:15]

On Yom Kippur, we sing:
אָבִינוּ מַלְכֵּנוּ - עֲשֵׂה עִמָּנוּ צְדָקָה וָחֶסֶד
Avinu malkenu 'aseh 'imanu tzedakah va-chesed
Our Father, our King, deal with us with justice and with mercy.

How *do* you temper justice with mercy? How much of each do you allow? How do you rule in a court of law? Extenuating circumstances may encourage a judge to reduce a sentence, but by how much?

The problem is that justice is defined in great detail, but mercy is not. Since mercy is poorly defined, it cannot be a direct commandment. One must use compassion and judgment to apply mercy, but there is no guidance on "how much is enough". The Mishnah says this clearly:
> The practice of loving-kindness [*gemilut ḥasadim*] is one of the things for which no definite quantity is prescribed. [Peah 1:1]

There are *some* answers in our tradition. The prophet Micah said: [Micah 6:8]
הִגִּיד לְךָ אָדָם מַה־טּוֹב וּמָה־יְהֹוָה דּוֹרֵשׁ מִמְּךָ כִּי אִם־עֲשׂוֹת מִשְׁפָּט וְאַהֲבַת חֶסֶד וְהַצְנֵעַ לֶכֶת עִם־אֱלֹהֶיךָ:
It has been told you, O man, what is good and what the Lord requires of you:
>   -Only to act justly *['asot mishpat]*,
>   -to love mercy *[ahavat chesed]*
>   -and to walk humbly with your God *[v'hatznea' lechet 'im elokecha]*.

Note that the word *lechet*, to walk, comes from the same root as *halacha*, or Jewish law. Some say the verse means: Justice, mercy, and *halacha*, in that order. In truth, *halacha* does include justice and mercy, but only in its ethical commandments, not in its ritual commandments.

Along those lines, the Talmud says: [Sukkah 49b]
> "To do justly" means [to act using] justice [which includes charity].
> "To love mercy" refers to acts of loving-kindness …
> [But] loving-kindness is greater than charity, for it is said [in the Book of Hosea]:
>> Sow to yourselves according to your charity, but reap according to your mercy. [Hosea 10:12]
>
> Mercy means loving-kindness. If a man sows, it is not certain that he will eat [the harvest], but when a man reaps, he will certainly eat… *So the reward of charity depends entirely on the extent of the loving-kindness in it…*

> Our Rabbis taught: Loving-kindness is greater than charity in three respects:
>   -Charity can be done only with one's money, but loving-kindness can be done both with one's person and one's money.
>   -Charity can be given only to the poor, but loving-kindness can be given both to the rich and the poor.
>   -Charity can be given only to the living, but loving-kindness can be given both to the living and to the dead.

In conclusion, we certainly need both love and justice in our lives. Only one of them is not enough. However, we have much leeway in deciding how much of each to apply in any given situation. We must rely on our instincts, with little guidance.

Shabbat shalom.

Vayishlach
Gen. 32:4-36:43

B"H

Jacob's Mysterious Assailant

In this week's portion, *Vayishlach*, Jacob is on his way back to the Holy Land to reconnect with his brother Esau. He had been fleeing from him for twenty years because he was afraid Esau would kill him for stealing their father Isaac's blessing from him.

Suddenly, a mysterious entity attacks him and he wrestles with it for an entire night:

> וַיִּוָּתֵר יַעֲקֹב לְבַדּוֹ וַיֵּאָבֵק אִישׁ עִמּוֹ עַד עֲלוֹת הַשָּׁחַר:
> Jacob was left alone. And a man wrestled with him until the break of dawn.
> When [the man] saw that he had not prevailed against [Jacob], he wrenched Jacob's hip at its socket, so that the socket of his hip was strained as he wrestled with him.
> Then [the man] said, "Let me go, for dawn is breaking."
> But [Jacob] answered, "I will not let you go, unless you bless me."
> The [man] said, "What is your name?"
> [Jacob] replied, "Jacob."
> The [man] said, "Your name shall no longer be Jacob, but Israel, for you have striven with beings both divine and human (וְעִם־אֲנָשִׁים כִּי־שָׂרִיתָ עִם־אֱלֹהִים), and have prevailed."
> Jacob asked, "Please tell me your name."
> But the [man] said, "You must not ask my name!"
> וַיְבָרֶךְ אֹתוֹ שָׁם: -- And he blessed him there.
> So Jacob named the place Peniel [פְּנִיאֵל meaning "face of God"), because, he thought, "I have seen a divine being (אֱלֹהִים) face to face, yet my life has been preserved."
> The sun shone for him as he passed Penuel, limping on his hip.

That is why the children of Israel to this day do not eat the thigh muscle that is on the socket of the hip, since Jacob's hip socket was wrenched at the thigh muscle. [Genesis 32:25-33]

Indeed, Jews may not eat the sciatic nerve attached to the hip socket. [Hullin 7, Shulḥan Arukh Yoreh Deah 65:5–14] This mitzvah is called *gid hanasheh* (הַגִּיד הַנָּשֶׁה) or displaced tendon.

This passage raises a host of questions:

-Who was that entity? A man? An angel? God?
-He describes himself as "beings both divine and human". Why the plural since there was only one entity?
-The entity asks Jacob: "What is your name?" Did he not know all along whom he was fighting?
-What was his mission?
-When the entity sees that he cannot defeat Jacob, he wrenches Jacob's hip. How can this be considered cause and effect?
-Why does the entity have to leave at dawn?
-Why does Jacob want to be blessed by it after fighting it and getting injured?
-In response to Jacob's request for a blessing, the entity changes Jacob's name. Is that a blessing and why?
-Why did Jacob ask for the entity's name and why would he not reveal it?
-How does Jacob know it was a "divine being"?
-Why is Jacob's wound so important that it led to a dietary restriction for Jews?

Let us explore some possible answers.

First, who was the entity? There are three main answers.

Maimonides, from 12th-century Egypt, believed that the incident was a dream, "a prophetic vision". [Rambam, Guide for the Perplexed 2:42:2] Abravanel, from 15th-century Spain, strongly disagrees, asking: Why would Jacob limp after a dream?

Another view is that there was no entity. It all happened in Jacob's head. Jacob was alone. Indeed, the Torah itself says: "Jacob was left alone and a man wrestled with him". But if he was "alone", who was he "wrestling" with? It must have been with himself. He was engaged in an inner struggle, in profound introspection, repenting for past misdeeds. In the mystical view, the fight represents the struggle between the good inclination and the evil inclination. The Zohar tells us that the latter, the dark side, is most powerful at night, and the incident happened at night. [Zohar 1:170b]

A third view is that the entity was an angel. Indeed, this is how the prophet Hosea describes him: A *malakh* – an angel. [Hosea 12:4] The Midrash specifies that he was Esau's guardian angel, Samael. [Genesis Rabbah 77:3, Yalkut Shimoni 1:110, Zohar Bereshit 170a]

Note that in Jewish tradition everyone, good or evil, has a guardian angel sent by God to look after his interests. Everyone is entitled to a lawyer!

What is the significance of the wound Jacob received? The Zohar says that the entity struck Jacob's thigh, the place where sexual desire originates, and only *there* was he able to wound him because it is the most vulnerable place. [Zohar 1:170b] Therefore, we do not eat the sciatic nerve to remind us that sexual desire is one place where the urge is so strong that even the greatest are powerless against it.

However, Chizkuni sees the prohibition as punishment to "the children of Israel" for not being with their father in his time of peril. He writes:
> [Jacob was left alone.] It is right and proper to punish the Israelites [by not allowing them] to eat that particular sinew as they should not have allowed their founding father to be exposed to hostile forces at night. Jacob's sons were physically strong, and they should have been at hand to assist their father if the need arose to do so. Seeing that they failed to do this, the blame for the injury sustained by their father was theirs. From now on they would have learned their lesson and would practice the commandment to accompany their father, or for that matter, any older and wiser person, especially at night.

Why did Jacob ask the entity for his blessing? Rashi, from 11th-century France, believed Jacob wanted the angel to bless him to confirm that the blessing Isaac gave him was valid. Rabbenu Baḥya, from 14th-century Spain, writes:
> [Why did Jacob say:] "I will not let you go unless you first bless me."? He wanted Esau's angel to acknowledge that the blessing he had received from Isaac was acknowledged by Esau as being rightfully his…
>
> [By saying] "Your name will no longer be Jacob but Israel" the angel meant that from now on people will no longer say that you obtained the blessings by subterfuge, but they will admit that you are their rightful recipient… This was confirmed when the prophet Micah said:
>
> תִּתֵּן אֱמֶת לְיַעֲקֹב -- You have given truth to Jacob. [Micah 7:20]

Why did the entity ask Jacob his name? Didn't he know whom he was attacking? Tur HaAroch, from 13th-century Spain, says:
> The angel wanted to know Jacob's exact name because the healer must know the person's exact name if his efforts are to be crowned with success.

And why did Jacob ask the entity for *his* name? Sforno, from 16th-century Italy, says:
> [Jacob asking for the angel's name means: Your name] would describe your essence, your function, and how you would go about performing same. This would enable me to understand why you attacked me in the first place. I would then be able to do penitence for my sin, something I cannot do as long as I do not know what precisely my sin consists of.

In Jewish tradition, the name speaks volumes about a person.

Why did the entity refuse to give his name? The Midrash says the reason is that an angel's name can change. It has the entity reply:
> We have no fixed names. Our names change, depending on what we are commanded to carry out. [Genesis Rabbah 78:4]

But the Ramban interprets "You must not ask my name!" as meaning: "There is no benefit in you knowing my name because only God can answer your prayers."

Rabbenu Baḥya sees it as a sign of modesty, saying:

> He does not want a human being to go around saying: "This or that angel has performed such and such a miracle." He is a servant, a mere extension of his Master in Heaven.

Another reason is that the entity wanted to avoid embarrassment at having "lost" the fight. The loser would not want his name known.

Now let us turn to the most important question: What was the entity's mission? There are five main views.

First, he came to prevent Jacob from escaping from Esau. This is the Rashbam's view, from 12th-century France. He believes Jacob is attempting to flee from Esau. But since God wants the brothers to meet, He sends an angel to make sure Jacob does not escape. The angel dislocates his hip joint, thereby laming him and preventing any possibility of escape. The lesson is: You may not run away from your troubles.

Second, he came to find fault with Jacob. This is Rabbenu Bahya's view:
> The angel came to find a sin Jacob was guilty of to use it as a weapon to overpower him. He did not succeed. The only sin he could find was that Jacob had married two sisters during their lifetime, something the Torah later forbade. The writing: "He inflicted an injury on Jacob's hip joint" is a euphemism for his sexual organs and the seat of sexual desire. The punishment was administered near that organ so that Jacob limped for a while.

Third, he came to strengthen Jacob. This is Radak's view, from 13th-century France:
> God sent this angel to Jacob to strengthen his courage so he will not fear Esau. If Jacob could prevail over an angel, surely he had no reason to be afraid of an encounter with someone like Esau! The fact that the struggle lasted until daybreak was an allusion to Jacob that after a period of night, meaning problems and adversity, there would come a period of light, meaning peace and prosperity coupled with security.

Fourth, he came to issue a warning against antisemites. The Ramban, from 13th-century Catalonia, writes that the fight represents the never-ending battle between Jews and antisemites:

> The whole matter represents an allusion to our future history, that there would come a time when the descendants of Esau would overcome Jacob almost to the point of total destruction. This happened during the days of the Sages of the Mishnah... There were other generations who did... worse things to us. But we endured all and it passed us by. [Also in Lekach Tov]

The antisemites may wound us, as the entity wounded Jacob's hip, but they will not destroy us. After that incident, the Torah says:

וַיָּבֹא יַעֲקֹב שָׁלֵם עִיר שְׁכֶם

Jacob arrived whole (*shalem*) in the city of Shechem. [Gen. 33:18]

The battle will end "at the break of dawn", which is the time of the final Redemption.

The Ramban generally taught that "the deeds of the patriarchs are a sign to their descendants."

The Torah says that the battle was with "beings both divine and human". The humans are the antisemites. The Divine is God, from Whom we seek answers He withholds from us: Why is there evil? Why is there suffering? The lesson is that God likes thinkers, questioners, iconoclasts, whence our collective name, Yisrael – "he who struggles with God". The change of name implies that our mission is to struggle with people and with God until we prevail.

Tur HaAroch concurs, saying:
> This injury too was intended to serve as a warning to the Jewish people in the future that a descendant of Esau would arise, the Roman Empire, who would threaten to totally annihilate the people.

Rashi interprets the text literally. He notes that the Torah uses the *past* tense: "You have striven [past tense, not future] with beings both divine and human and have prevailed". He concludes that the divine is God and the human beings are Esau and Laban.

Fifth, He came to provoke a turning point in Jacob's life. "What is your name?" means: Are you still Jacob, the serial deceiver, the "one who steals by grabbing onto other people's heels", as your name, Yaakov, indicates? Or have you matured enough to become Israel, the righteous man "who struggles with God" for lofty spiritual purposes?

Later in the Torah, God confirms what the entity told Jacob:
> God said to him, "You, whose name is Jacob, You shall be no longer be called Jacob, but Israel shall be your name." Thus He named him Israel. [Gen. 35:10]

Rashi, commenting on this verse, says:
> [The verse means you shall no longer be Jacob,] a man who comes as a lurker and a trickster, but you shall be Israel (ישראל), which means Prince and Chief [meaning: one who wields authority].

Note that the Jews are called "the children of Israel" *right* after the incident with the entity.

The Midrash adds that this also teaches us that the righteous are superior to the angels: Jacob seized the mighty angel and vanquished him. [Midrash Tanḥuma]

Note also that this was not the only time a mysterious entity came a night to assault a biblical figure. The Torah reports another instance involving Moses, who did not circumcize his son on time:
> At a night encampment on the way, the Lord encountered [Moses] and sought to kill him. So Zipporah [his wife] took a flint and cut off her son's foreskin, and touched his legs with it, saying, "You are truly a bridegroom of blood to me!" And when He left [Moses] alone, she added, "A bridegroom of blood because of the circumcision." [Ex. 4:24-26]

What can we conclude? The incident can be interpreted many ways, but the facts in the narrative imply that this was the moment when Jacob, who has a history as a deceiver, becomes transformed into Jacob the righteous patriarch and builder of Israel, of the Jewish people.

Shabbat shalom.

Vayeshev
Gen. 37:1-40:23

B"H

The Jewish View of Dreams

In this week's Torah portion, *Vayeshev*, Joseph dreams and interprets dreams:
    And Joseph had a dream and told his brothers...,
    "We were binding sheaves ... and behold, my sheaf arose and... stood upright,
    and... your sheaves encircled [it] and prostrated themselves to my sheaf."
    So his brothers said to him, "Will you reign over us? Will you govern us?" And they
    continued further to hate him on account of his dreams and on account of his words.
    And [later] he... said, "Behold, I have had another dream: ...The sun, the moon, and
    eleven stars were prostrating themselves to me." And he told [this] to his father and
    to his brothers. His father rebuked him and said to him, "What is this dream...? Will
    we come, I, your mother, and your brothers to prostrate ourselves to you to the
    ground?" [Gen. 37:5-10]

Later, when Joseph is in jail, he correctly interprets the dreams of other inmates, and news of his ability spreads fast. Pharaoh summons him and he correctly interprets Pharaoh's dreams. He is then put in charge of all of Egypt to manage the consequences of his interpretations. [Gen. 40:5ff]

Dreams. The Torah is full of them. Sometimes it says specifically that they convey a message directly from God:
    -But God came to Abimelech in a dream by night. [Gen. 20:3]
    -And [Jacob] dreamed, and behold, [there was] a ladder on the ground and its top
    reached to heaven; and behold, angels of God were going up and down on it; and
    behold, the Lord was standing over him. [Gen. 28:12-13]
    -And God appeared to Laban the Aramean in a dream by night. [Gen. 31:24]
    -The Lord appeared to [King] Solomon in a dream by night. [1Kings 3:5]

A man dreamed that Gideon, a Judge of Israel, would defeat the Midianites, and so he did. [Judges 7:13] The prophet Daniel successfully interpreted the dreams of the wicked king Nebuchadnezzar. [Daniel 2:1ff]

All cultures have a special niche for dreams, and Judaism is no exception. I searched the Tanach, Talmud, Midrash and Zohar (electronically!); and found close to a thousand references to dreams. People were scared by them. There was even a custom of fasting to prevent bad dreams [Shabbat 11a]. But are all dreams significant? Do they all bear a message? Is God involved in all of them? Let's examine what our Sages say about them.

First of all, the Talmud notes that dreams are never completely fulfilled:
> Rabbi Berekiah said: While part of a dream *may* be fulfilled, the whole of it is *never* fulfilled. How do we know this?
> From Joseph, as it [says in Genesis]: "The sun and the moon [and eleven stars bowed down to me], [meaning his father, mother, and brothers] [Gen.37:9]. But, at that time, his mother was dead, [so she could not possibly bow to him]. [Berakhot 55a-b]

The Talmud also considers dreams to be a weaker form of prophecy:
> A dream is one-sixtieth of prophecy. [Berakhot 57b]

This implies that there is something to them, but usually not much:
> Rabbi Yoḥanan said in the name of Rabbi Shim'on bar Yoḥai: Just as wheat cannot be without straw, so there cannot be a dream without some nonsense. [Berakhot 55a]

The Midrash amplifies this idea:
> Rabbi Ḥanina bar Yitzhaq said: There are three incomplete phenomena:
> -The incomplete form of death is sleep;
> -The incomplete form of prophecy is dreaming;
> -The incomplete form of the World to Come is Shabbat. [Gen. R. 17:5]

Some even believed that a dream is no more than a crazy, disorganized, mixed-up assemblage of one's thoughts during the day:
> Rabbi Shmuel bar Naḥmani said in the name of Rabbi Yonatan: A man is shown in a dream only what is suggested by his own thoughts during the day. [Berakhot 55b]

Freud said the same thing many centuries later: Dreams reflect nothing but the self.

One of these skeptics was 2nd-century Rabbi Meir, who said:
> Dreams neither help nor harm. [Hor. 13b]

Another was Abbahu, 3rd-century rabbi:
> Dreams have no influence whatsoever. [Gen. R. 68:12]

In Jewish law, all information obtained in a dream is disregarded.

A dream must not be the cause of profound changes. The Talmud says:
> If a non-Jew wants to embrace Judaism because he has been advised to do so in a dream, he is not accepted. [Yevamot 24b]

But the dream itself is not enough. One wants to know: What does it mean? Some interpretation is always needed:
> -Rabbi Chisda... said: A dream that is not interpreted is like a letter that is not read. [Berakhot 55a-b]
> -Bar Kappara taught: No dream is without its interpretation. [Gen. R. 68:12]

But the most far-reaching assessment of dreams by the Sages is their teaching that:
> All dreams follow their interpretation. [Berakhot 55b]

This means that what is suggested in the interpretation is what will actually happen. Call it auto-suggestion, psychological influence, or mind over matter, but it implies that the dreamer is so profoundly shaken by the alleged meaning of his dream that somehow he makes it happen:
> Rabbi Bana'ah [said]: There were 24 interpreters of dreams in Jerusalem. I had a dream once and went around to all of them, and they all gave different interpretations, and all were fulfilled. This confirms that... "All dreams follow [their interpretation]"... [for the Torah says in Genesis]... :
>> And it came to pass *as [Joseph] interpreted [the dreams] to us*, and so it was. [Gen. 41:13]
>
> [Berakhot 55b]

The decisive influence of the interpreter can have disastrous consequences, as this story from the Midrash shows:
> A certain woman went to Rabbi Eliezer and said to him: "I saw in a dream that the loft of the upper story of my house was split open."
> "You will conceive a son," he told her. And so it happened.
> [Years later] she had the same dream, told it to Rabbi Eliezer, and he gave her the same interpretation. And so it happened.
> She dreamed this a third time and went to him but did not find him, so she told his students... They told her, "You will bury your husband," and this did happen.
> [They informed] Rabbi Eliezer... and he upbraided them, saying: "You have killed the man!" [Gen. R. 89:8]

The Talmud has a similar, chilling story:
> [The Chaldean] Bar Hedya was an interpreter of dreams. He used to give a favorable interpretation to those who paid him and an unfavorable interpretation to those who did not pay him.
> Abaye and Rava each had a dream. Abaye gave him a zuz, but Rava did not give him anything. [So, to Abaye he gave many good interpretations and to Rava many bad ones]...
> One day Rava [learned the teaching:] "All dreams follow [their interpretations]". He [understood that the interpreter was *making* these bad things happen to him and] exclaimed: You wretch! It all depended on you and you gave me all this pain! ... May it be God's will that [you] be delivered up to the Government, and that they have no mercy on [you]!
> Bar Hedya said to himself: What am I to do? A curse uttered by a Sage, even when undeserved, comes to pass. How much more so this [one], which was deserved! He [went] into exile, for a Master has said: "Exile procures atonement for iniquity". He... fled to the Romans [but refused to interpret dreams for them unless they paid him. They refused, bad things happened to them, so they executed him.] [Berakhot 56a]

The Zohar, the book of Jewish mysticism, confirms this view:
> A dream contains both falsehood and truth. The word has power over it. Therefore, it is advisable that every dream be interpreted in a good sense. [Zohar, Berakhot 1:183a]

The Zohar bases this on the Torah itself, from this week's portion:
> [The Torah says that Joseph] said to [his brothers]:

> "Hear, I beg you, this dream I had... We were binding sheaves in the field, and my sheaf arose, and stood upright, and your sheaves... bowed to my sheaf". And his brothers said to him, "Will you reign over us? Will you govern us?" [Gen. 37:6-8] We see here how [Joseph's brothers, not Joseph himself, interpreted the dream negatively. If they had interpreted it positively, it would have been fulfilled accordingly.] But they said to him: "Will you reign over us? Will you govern us?" And with these words they sealed their own doom. [Zohar, Berakhot 1:183b]

The Talmud even recommends a ceremony called *hatavat chalom*, the improvement of a dream:

> Rabbi Huna ben Ammi said in the name of Rabbi Pedath who had it from Rabbi Yohanan: If one has a dream which makes him sad he should go and have three people give it a good twist ... They should say to him, [Your dream is] good... May the All-Merciful turn it to good ... May it be decreed from heaven that it should be good and will become good. [Berakhot 55b; Artscroll weekday siddur, pp 549-552]

So the Sages took pains to provide good interpretations to the dreams of the people. Even when the people dreamt that they committed terrible capital crimes, the Sages found ways to make it sound good, witness this very surprising Talmudic passage:

> -If one dreams that he has intercourse with his mother, he can expect understanding, since it says [in the Book of Proverbs], "You will call understanding 'mother'." [Prov. 2:3]
> -If one dreams he has intercourse with a woman who is engaged, he can expect knowledge of Torah, since it says [in Deuteronomy]:
> > *Torah tziva lanu Moshe, morashah kehillat Yaakov* -- Moses commanded us [the Torah], an inheritance of the congregation of Jacob. [Deut. 33:4]
>
> *Morashah*, meaning inheritance, can also be read *Me'orasah*, meaning engaged.
> -If one dreams he has intercourse with his sister, he can expect wisdom, since it says [in Proverbs], "Say to wisdom: you are my sister." [Prov. 7:4]
> -If one dreams he has intercourse with a married woman [he does not know], he can be confident that he is destined for the World to Come. [Berakhot 57a]

There is not even a hint of a rebuke, because none of this actually happened, none of this was planned, and people are not responsible for their dreams!

So, opinions vary, and the final answer on dreams is still in the future.

Let me conclude with a prayer found in the Talmud. It is to be recited during the *Birkat Kohanim*, the priestly blessing. Many communities still recite it today. It is sufficiently broad to accommodate a wide range of positions:

> Sovereign of the Universe, I am Yours and my dreams are Yours. I had a dream and I do not know what it is. Whether I have dreamt about myself, or my friends have dreamt about me, or I have dreamt about others, if they are good dreams, confirm and reinforce them like the dreams of Joseph. And if they require a remedy, heal them, as the waters of Marah were healed by Moses our teacher, and as Miriam was healed of her leprosy, and [King] Hezekiah of his sickness, and the waters of Jericho by [the prophet] Elisha. As You turned the curse of the wicked Balaam into a blessing, so turn all my dreams into something good for me. [Berakhot 55b]

And let us say: Amen.

Shabbat shalom.

Miketz
Gen. 41:1-44:17

B"H

The Evil Eye

In this week's Torah portion, *Miketz*, we learn that there was an intense famine in the Land. Jacob gathered his sons and charged them with the mission to go buy grain in Egypt, not knowing that his son Joseph was in charge of Egypt and had just rescued Egypt from a famine. We read:

וַיַּרְא יַעֲקֹב כִּי יֶשׁ־שֶׁבֶר בְּמִצְרָיִם וַיֹּאמֶר יַעֲקֹב לְבָנָיו לָמָּה תִּתְרָאוּ:
When Jacob saw that there was grain being sold in Egypt, he said to his sons, "Why do you keep looking at one another?" [Gen. 42:1]

What does this strange phrase mean? There are many interpretations.

Rashi and the Ramban say it means: "What are you waiting for? Why aren't you out already looking for food?" But then, what's the reason for informing us of that?

Sforno says it means: "Why are you looking at one another as if each one of you expects another of you to go buy the food? Remember that our Sages said: 'Too many cooks spoil the broth.'" In other words, when more than one person is in charge, nobody is. There is indeed a teaching there.

Perhaps it means that their condition was so dire that they felt numb and froze in place?

The Midrash says it means:
> Since you are strong and handsome, do not stand together in one place, lest the evil eye prevail over you. [Midrash Tanḥuma, Miketz 8:1]

In other words, I don't want to lose all of you at once.

Along the same lines, the Talmud tells us it means:
> Do not show yourselves, when you are satiated, before [the house of] Esau or [the house of] Ishmael, so that they not be jealous of you [considering they suffer from hunger. This teaches that one should not show he is full when others are hungry.] [Taanit 10b]

In other words, do not show off your blessings to those who don't enjoy the same. This explanation became the dominant one (although it is not obvious from the text, which assumes Jacob's clan was also suffering).

The Shulḥan Arukh codified it into law:
> If you go from a place where they are not fasting to a place where they are fasting, you should fast with them. If you forgot and eat and drink, you should not let yourself be seen. [Rambam, Mishneh Torah, Fasts 1:15; Shulḥan Arukh, Orach Ḥayyim 574:3]

The Zohar goes so far as to say that even God is displeased when you flaunt your blessings. By provoking the envy of your neighbors, you also provoke Heavenly judgment. [Quoted in Shenei Luchot HaBrit, Torah Shebiktav, Vayeshev, Miketz, Vayigash, Derekh Ḥayyim, Miketz 5]

This teaches that we must be sensitive and not flaunt what we have, if only for the sake of others who don't have what we have. Even though they should not be jealous, the pain they suffer when they see us is real.

The rabbis of the Talmud maintained that the Evil Eye was involved in many biblical events. For example:

-Sarah cast an evil eye on Hagar while Hagar was pregnant, causing her to miscarry before becoming pregnant with Ishmael. [Genesis Rabbah 45:5]

-The first set of tablets of the Law was given to the Jews openly, so the Evil Eye prevailed over them and they were smashed. But the second set of tablets was given in secret, after God said to Moses:

> No one else shall come up with you, and no one else shall be seen anywhere on the mountain. [Ex. 34:3]

As a result, they were not destroyed. [Midrash Tanḥuma Ki Tisa 31]

Rabbenu Baḥya says:
> The power of the evil eye is so great that it can even interfere with miracles!

-Leah "became subject to the power of the evil eye" because the Torah says she thanked God for having allowed her to bear a fourth son, and immediately after that it says "she stopped giving birth." [Genesis 29:35]
[Rabbenu Baḥya on Gen. 30:38]

-The Book of Numbers says:
> And Balaam lifted up his eyes and saw Israel. [Num. 24:2]

Rashi says it means he cast his evil eye on Israel, since God would not allow him to curse them as he wished.

-Joshua advised those enjoying good fortune to live in a forest to avoid the evil eye:
> Joshua said to them: "If you are a great people, you should go up to the forest." [Joshua 17:14–15]

The Talmud explains that it means:
> Go and hide in the forest, so that the evil eye will not have dominion over you, since you are such a large number of people. [Sotah 36b]

-King Saul was jealous of the future King David and gave him an evil eye:
> From that day on Saul kept a jealous eye on David. [1 Samuel 18:9]
> And it came to pass that David was successful in all his ways, and the Lord was with him. [1 Samuel 18:14]

-Hananiah, Mishael, and Azariah were thrown in a fiery furnace by the King of Babylon after they refused to bow before an idol. But God saved them, so the King, impressed, promoted them to high office. [Daniel 3] The Talmud says they later died as a result of the evil eye:
> Where did these Sages go [after their miraculous deliverance? They are not mentioned anymore.] Rav said: They died as the result of the evil eye [cast by people who were jealous of their deliverance.] [Sanhedrin 93a]

The evil eye (עַיִן הָרַע -- *ayin hara'*) is an entrenched belief in Judaism. It is said to be an evil force generated by our evil inclination. The Talmud asserts flatly:
> Damage caused by looking is also damage. [Bava Batra 2b]

This implies that you can harm by mere thought. Coveting is damaging even if no action results from it.

The Talmud also says: Don't advertise your good fortune, because this will cause envy, which will cause harm to fall on you. The Sage Rav was said to enter cemeteries and determine that 99% of the people buried there died prematurely because an evil eye was cast on them. [Bava Metzia 107b, Pesaḥim 50b]

-However, other rabbis in the Talmud said this does not apply to Jews. [Berakhot 20a, 55b] For example, when a woman tried to cast a spell on Rabbi Ḥanina, he said:
> Try as you will, you will not succeed, for [the Torah says [Deut. 4:35]] "There is none beside God." [Hullin 76b]

In another story, Rabbi Yoḥanan boasted about his beauty:
> The Rabbis said to him: Do you not fear an evil eye? He replied, I am of the seed of Joseph, against whom an evil eye is powerless. [Bava Metzia 84a]

Is there a way to ward off the evil eye? The Talmud describes a ceremonial to do just that:
> One who enters a city and fears the evil eye should hold the thumb of his right hand in his left hand and the thumb of his left hand in his right hand and recite the following: "I, so-and-so, son of so-and-so, come from the descendants of Joseph, over whom the evil eye has no dominion." [Berakhot 55b]

Some Jews, when mentioning their good fortune, will add: *b'li ayin hara*, meaning "without an evil eye", or *kenahora*, meaning "Let there be no evil eye" (Yiddish corruption of *ken ayin hara*). The response used to be to spit three times; now it is to say "ptoo, ptoo, ptoo" as standards of decency change.

To ward off the evil eye, some Jews wear a blue pearl, or a *khamsa* (Hand of Fatma), or tie red strings around their wrists. In Israel, some women perform, for a fee, a ceremony called "Evil Eye Remover".

Some Talmudic rabbis believed that having daughters wards off the evil eye:
> Rabbi Hisda said: [If a] daughter [is born] first, it is a good sign for the children. [Why?] Some say it's because she rears her brothers. Others say it's because the evil eye has no influence over her [because a girl is not the subject of envy]. ...To me, however, daughters are dearer than sons. [Bava Batra 141a]

Maimonides, who hated every form of superstition with a passion, nevertheless made allowances to set people's minds at ease:
> A person bitten by a scorpion or serpent may whisper a charm over the wound even on Shabbat, in order to settle his mind and to strengthen his heart. The thing is of no avail whatsoever, but, since he is in danger, he is permitted to do it, so he won't feel troubled. [Rambam, On Idolatry 2:11-12]

The Mishnah even tells us that we must be careful not to cast the evil eye ourselves:
> -Rabbi Yehoshua says: The evil eye, the evil inclination, and hatred of the creations remove a person from the world. [Avot 2:11]
> -An evil eye, a haughty spirit, and a proud soul, are the marks of the disciples of Balaam the Wicked. [Avot 5:19]

Even the Sages are not immune to casting the evil eye, witness this story in the Talmud:
> Every thirty days, Rabbi Zeira would ignite an oven, climb in and sit inside it [to test his holiness], and the fire would not affect him [on account of his great Torah erudition]. One day, the Sages gave him the evil eye and his legs became singed in the fire. [Bava Metzia 85a]

(Some have said that the story really means that you must examine yourself critically and regularly, and make corrections when necessary.)

Even family members can cast the evil eye:
> A father and his son should not have the same name for fear of the evil eye, even if they profess not to mind. [Kitzur Shulḥan Arukh 23:13]

You can be a victim of the evil eye even if you just *appear* blessed:
> One who sells canes or jars will never see blessing from them. Why? Because their size is large, so the evil eye dominates them. [Pesaḥim 50b, Derekh Eretz Rabbah 11:8, Kallah Rabbati 10:16]

This means that people believe he sells more than he actually does.

It may be nearly impossible to hide your blessings:
> A certain woman came before Rabbi Yoḥanan and told him that every time she came out of the mikvah, she would see blood before she had intercourse with her husband [so they couldn't proceed].
> He said: Maybe the gossip and evil eye of the women in your city has reached you. [They are jealous of the love between you and your husband.] Go and immerse in the river and have intercourse with your husband on the bank of the river [so that other women will not see you coming out of the mikvah.] [Niddah 66a]

The Talmud even places restrictions on people on the assumption that they are *certain* to cast the evil eye:
> It is prohibited for a person to stand in someone else's field and look at his crop while the grain is standing, because he casts an evil eye upon it and thereby causes him damage. [Bava Batra 2b]

To counterbalance the evil eye, there is the "good eye" (טוֹב עַיִן – *tov ayin*). It belongs to one who is satisfied with what he has and does not covet what others have. The Mishna says:
> Whoever possesses these three things is of the disciples of Abraham our Father: ... a good eye, a humble spirit and a moderate appetite. [Avot 5:19]

Should you seek people who have a "good eye"? Examples may be your parents or grandparents, who will rejoice at your good fortune and not envy you for it. They may reinforce your blessings and perhaps invite more of the same. I could not find such encouragement in the Sources -- only exhortations to avoid the evil eye.

The belief in the evil eye is that you can harm by mere thought. Coveting is damaging even if no action results from it. How so? Can mere thoughts harm? Is mind over matter possible?

Controlled experiments in the laboratory have not verified any claims of obvious, direct "mind over matter" effects.

But this does not mean these effects are not real. There is the well-documented "placebo effect". The development of new drugs against diseases requires three groups of patients. One is given nothing, a second is given the real experimental drug, and the third is given a placebo. The last two groups don't know who got what. Frequently, people given a placebo get better on average than people who are given nothing. To be accepted, the new drug has to show that it performs significantly better than a placebo.

A lot of people will go well beyond the "evil eye" and translate their envy and jealousy into direct physical harm to others. Antisemitism is a prime example. Should Jews be extra-modest about their achievements on the grounds that they fuel antisemitism? This is not clear, since it would still be known they deserve the credit. Should they hide them or give credit to others? This would be unrealistic. The only solution is: We should be prepared to endure and fight the consequences of our good fortune.

Belief in superstition is widespread and not backed by hard science. However, this does not mean there is absolutely nothing to it. As the wag said, "I don't believe in superstitious nonsense. However, I am given to understand it works whether or not you believe in it."

Shabbat shalom.

Vayigash
Gen. 44:18-47:27

B"H

I Am Joseph -- Is My Father Still Alive?

In this week's Torah portion, *Vayigash*, Joseph, viceroy of Egypt, is visited by ten of his brothers, who sold him into slavery in Egypt. They "bow low to him" and wish to buy food, as the famine is ravaging the Land. Joseph knows who they are, but they do not recognize him. He toys with them: "You are spies. Go back and bring me your brother Benjamin, whom you left behind. I am keeping Simeon as hostage." They do so and come back with Benjamin.

Joseph greets them and says: "How is your aged father of whom you spoke? Is he still in good health?" They reply: "It is well with your servant our father; he is still in good health."

Joseph then accuses Benjamin of stealing a special goblet and threatens to enslave him as punishment. Judah defends Benjamin and offers to take his place. [Gen. 42:1-45:2]

At that point, Joseph finally reveals his identity to his brothers, saying:

> אֲנִי יוֹסֵף הַעוֹד אָבִי חָי? -- "I am Joseph. Is my father still alive?"
> And his brothers could not answer him, for they were startled by his presence. [Gen. 45:3]

This is a strange question for Joseph to ask, right after he reveals himself, especially since he had just asked that very question. One would think he would start by explaining to his startled brothers how he got to where he is.

How should we interpret Joseph's question? Many commentators have provided possible answers.

Sforno believes Joseph was pretentiously incredulous: How could my father have survived so many years of worry over my fate after what you did to me?

Tur HaAroch argues that Joseph's question was just to start a conversation, to make his brothers feel at ease, and to make personal contact with them. Also, to reinforce his identity: He did not say "your father", as he had so far, but "my father".

Joseph is overwhelmed with emotion and thinks of his father first. Judah offers himself as a substitute slave for Benjamin in an impassioned speech that mentions Jacob "our father" fourteen times. Then, the Torah says:
> Joseph could no longer control himself before all his attendants, and he cried out, "Have everyone withdraw from me!"... His sobs were so loud that the Egyptians could hear, and so the news reached Pharaoh's palace. [Gen. 45:1-2]

Bet HaLevi hears Joseph as saying: "You hypocrites! You tell me you are concerned my father will die if Benjamin does not return. But when you disposed of me, why were you not concerned he might have died when *I* did not return? Isn't my father still alive, even though he knows Benjamin is with you and may never return to him?"

Torah Temimah says that Joseph knew his brothers had a habit of lying, as when they lied to Jacob about his death, so he asked again: "Is my father *really* alive?"

Kli Yakar says it depends on whose point of view: Joseph's or his brothers'. From Joseph's point of view, he thought his brothers first told him Jacob was alive hoping he would take pity on an old man and not cause his death over the possible loss of Benjamin. So he asked again: "Tell me *as your brother*: Is my father really still alive?" From the brothers' point of view, Joseph was reminding them of their sin. He said: "my father", meaning: "He is my father and not your father because you did not take pity on his suffering, as if he were not your father." So they were terrified and unable to speak.

This explanation builds on the Midrash:
> They were "startled by his presence" because they were embarrassed. [Midrash Tanḥuma, Vayigash 5]

When Joseph realized this, he spoke again: "I am Joseph, your brother" (אֲנִי יוֹסֵף אֲחִיכֶם), not just "I am Joseph".

Our second question is: Why didn't Joseph notify his father Jacob that he was still alive? If he loved his father so much, why did he let him mourn for him for 22 years instead of notifying him he was alive and viceroy of Egypt?

The Midrash says it was God's plan:
> [The brothers] decided: "Let us make a vow to excommunicate any one of us who tells our father, Jacob, that Joseph is alive." Judah said: "Reuben is not here, and a vow of excommunication cannot be executed unless ten witnesses are present." So what did they do? They included the Holy One, blessed be He, in their pact of excommunication [and God agreed]. [Midrash Tanchuma, Vayeshev 2:5]

So God agreed that Jacob must not be told, because it suited His plan.

Another Midrash tells us that Jacob's father Isaac knew prophetically that Joseph was alive, but said nothing. The Torah says:
> And all of Jacob's sons and all his daughters rose up to comfort him [for the loss of Joseph]. But he refused to be comforted and said: "No, I will go down to the grave mourning for my son." And his father wept for him. [Gen. 37:35]

This does not refer to Jacob weeping for Joseph, but Isaac weeping because of Jacob's deep pain... And why did Isaac not reveal to Jacob that Joseph was alive? Because Isaac thought: If the Holy One, blessed be He, has not revealed it to him, who am I to reveal it to him? [Genesis Rabbah 84:21]

The Lubavitcher Rebbe [Likutei Sichot 10 p 129ff] adds that Joseph followed the same logic. If God didn't want Jacob to know Joseph was alive, he was not going to inform Jacob either.

Some say Joseph was determined to forget the past and move on.

Iturei Torah, from 20th-century Israel argues that Joseph was afraid God would punish his brothers for selling him. He wanted them to repent. Since they sold him into slavery out in Egypt out of jealousy, he resolved to test whether they still had feelings of jealousy. So he gave his brothers gifts, but gave Benjamin even bigger gifts. He framed Benjamin as a thief and said he would enslave him to see the brothers' reaction. Would they tacitly applaud the move because they envied him as his father's favorite and the other son of his beloved Rachel? No! They argued passionately in favor of Benjamin, and Judah even offered himself as a slave in place of Benjamin. Then Joseph knew they had repented. He could then reveal himself and tell his brothers to let Jacob know that he was still alive.

Rabbi Jonathan Sacks, citing others, says that Joseph was not sure Jacob would welcome finding out he was alive. He wondered: Does *my* father still love me? He was afraid his father stopped caring about him even before they parted. Why? Because Jacob was known to hold grudges.

He held grudges against his three eldest sons: Shimon and Levi (for killing the people of Shechem) and Reuben (for allegedly sleeping with his concubine Bilhah), even severely criticizing them on his deathbed. That is how the fourth son, Judah, became the key figure. Now, Jacob was also mad at Joseph for his dream and rebuked him, as recorded in the Torah:
> What is this dream of yours? Are we to come, I and your mother and your brothers, and bow low to you to the ground? So his brothers were jealous of him *and his father kept the matter in mind*. [Gen. 37:10-11]

So Jacob could very well have written off Joseph. Before the brothers acted against Joseph, the Torah says:
> Israel said to Joseph, "Your brothers are pasturing at Shechem… Go and see how they are and how the flocks are faring, and bring word back to me." [Gen. 37:12–14]

Jacob knew the brothers were jealous of Joseph, yet he sent Joseph *alone* to meet them *far* from home? Jacob knew the power of sibling jealousy from his own brother Esau planning to kill him. Did he not suspect that might happen to Joseph? Joseph later wondered why his father sent him on this mission.

The point when Joseph could no longer control himself and revealed his identity to his brothers was when Judah, in his impassioned defense of Benjamin, said:
> Your servant my father said to us, "As you know, my wife [Rachel] bore me two sons. But one [Joseph] is gone from me, and I said: Alas, he was torn by a beast, and I have not seen him since. If you take this one [Benjamin] from me, too, and he meets with disaster, you will send my white head down to Sheol in sorrow." [Gen. 44:27–31]

That's when Joseph finally knew that his father grieved for him and still loved him! His question "Is my father still alive?" meant he wanted further reassurance that he would soon be reunited with him.

The Ramban (Naḥmanides) [on Genesis 42:9] notes that the Torah says:
> Recalling the dreams that he had dreamed about them, Joseph said to [his brothers]: "You are spies." [Genesis 42:9]

How does it follow? Joseph believed his dreams were prophetic and will be fulfilled in order. In his first dream, his eleven brothers bowed down to him. In the second, his father was included too. If he had told Jacob he was alive, Jacob and his clan would have come to see him and the second dream would have come true before the first. He therefore waited until after all eleven of his brothers, including Benjamin, had come to him.

That last interpretation, the Ramban's, is the one I prefer: It neatly explains the entire chain of events, including why Joseph wanted Benjamin there.

Shabbat shalom.

Vayechi
Gen. 47:28-50:26

B"H

Why Didn't Jacob Go Back to Israel?

In last week's portion, Jacob and his entire family of seventy moved to Egypt because of the famine. They were invited by Joseph, now viceroy of Egypt. Joseph tells them:
> It is now two years that there has been famine in the land, and there are still five years to come in which there shall be no yield from tilling. [Gen. 45:6]

This week's portion, *Vayechi*, opens with:
> וַיְחִי יַעֲקֹב בְּאֶרֶץ מִצְרַיִם שְׁבַע עֶשְׂרֵה שָׁנָה
> Jacob lived seventeen years in the land of Egypt. [Gen. 47:28]

So Jacob lived in Egypt for twelve years after the famine, and his clan stayed in Egypt after he died. Why did they? Why didn't Jacob and his family go back to Israel, where, presumably, God wanted them to live?

Seven reasons have been advanced.

First, because they were waiting for God to take them out. Jacob at first hesitated about going to Egypt. The Midrash says he was thinking:
> Can I forsake the land of my fathers, the land of my birth, the land of the sojournings of my fathers, the land where the Shekhinah of the Holy One, blessed be He, is in its midst, and go to an unclean land where there is no fear of Heaven?
> [Pirkei DeRabbi Eliezer 39:1]

But God not only reassured him, but said that *He* will bring him back:
> God called to Israel in a vision by night: "Jacob! Jacob!"
> He answered, "Here I am."

> And He said, "I am God, the God of your father. Do not fear going down to Egypt, because there I will make you into a great nation. I Myself will go down with you to Egypt, and I Myself will also bring you back; and Joseph's hand shall close your eyes." [Gen. 46:2-4]

However, the last comment seems to apply to Jacob's remains, not to him and his clan while living. [Sotah Y 1:10]

Also, why could they not become "a great nation" in their own homeland? Because remaining in Egypt was necessary to enjoy the safety needed to become "a great nation". Also, to appreciate something, in this case freedom, you have to lose it then reacquire it.

Second, because God commanded them to do stay in Egypt. Abravanel argues that Jacob stayed in Egypt after the famine because God commanded him to do so. But the text says God only *allowed* him to go, at most *encouraged* him, but did not *command* him.

Third, because the Egyptians would not let them return. Joseph was too precious to them. And Jacob wants a united Israel. Even to go bury his father in Israel, Joseph has to get Pharaoh's permission, as the Torah says:
> Joseph spoke to Pharaoh's court, saying: Do me this favor and intercede on my behalf with Pharaoh. My father made me swear, saying, "I am about to die. Be sure to bury me in the grave which I made ready for myself in the land of Canaan." Now, therefore, let me go up and bury my father; then I shall return. And Pharaoh said, "Go up and bury your father, as he made you promise on oath." [Gen. 50:4-6]

Pharaoh then sends a large delegation with Joseph, probably to ensure he would return:
> Joseph went up to bury his father; and with him went up all the officials of Pharaoh, the senior members of his court, and all of Egypt's dignitaries. [Gen. 50:7]

However, the children have to stay back in Egypt (perhaps as hostages?):
> Their children, their flocks, and their herds were left in the region of Goshen. [Gen. 50:8]

Fourth, because they could no longer travel as a group. When the Jews could have left, they had grown so numerous that they could not travel as a group. Even the original family of 70 had to wait for Joseph to help. Joseph gave his brothers wagons and supplies and instructed them not to even bring their belongings:
> [Joseph told his brothers:] "Take from the land of Egypt wagons for your children and your wives, and bring your father here. And never mind your belongings, for the best of all the land of Egypt shall be yours." The sons of Israel did so. Joseph gave them wagons as Pharaoh had commanded, and he supplied them with provisions for the journey. [Gen. 45:19-21]

But could they not go back in individual families? No, because Jacob wanted the Israelites to remain united.

Fifth, because Jacob thought the time for slavery had come. Jacob was no doubt aware that God had told his grandfather Abraham:
> Know for certain that your offspring will be strangers in a strange land, and will be enslaved and afflicted for four hundred years. But know with equal certainty that I will judge the nation that enslaved them, and that afterwards they will leave with great substance. [Genesis 15:13-14]

He also knew God did not say it was punishment for anything. So he concluded slavery was necessary to God's plan, and he might as well get it over with. What reasons might have come to his mind?

> **1-Protection.** In the Land of Israel, Jacob's clan was an easy target for its neighbors. In Egypt, a superpower protected the Jews, albeit to exploit them.
>
> **2-Building large numbers in safety.** If 210 years equal ten generations, and if numbers double with each generation, assuming four children per couple, the original number would be multiplied a thousandfold: 2^{10} is 1024.
>
> **3-Building up identity and community spirit.** All Jews were in the same boat and followed the same customs. The Midrash says that the Jews deserved redemption from Egypt because they kept their distinct names, dress, food and language. [Lev. R. 32:5 for names and language; Minor Pesikta, Devarim on Ki Tavo 41a for clothing and food]
>
> **4-Minimizing contact with the outside world.** Such contact might have led to idolatry and other practices later forbidden by the Torah.

5-Eliminating the possibility of intermarriage. Egyptians wouldn't want to marry slaves, and Israelite women raped by Egyptians would raise their children as Israelites.

6-Creating a scenario that allowed God to show the Jews and the whole world that He was in charge, with miracles and wonders that make a big impression.

7-Creating feelings of gratitude that would make it easier for the Jews to accept the Torah.

8-Creating a slave mentality that would make it easier for the Jews to accept the Torah. Indeed, after being a slave for so many generations, the first instinctive response when given a command is to say "Yes, sir!" However, once they accepted the Torah, the slave mentality became a burden, so God waited until the generation of the Exodus died out in the desert before letting them into the Promised Land.

Sixth, because of the danger of intermarriage. Sforno argues that "I am the God of your father" means "I am the God who told your father not to go to Egypt [Gen. 26:2], yet I am telling *you* to go." God was telling him: If you remain here your offspring will intermarry with the Canaanites. This will not happen in Egypt because the populace will not even eat with the Hebrews. Indeed, the Torah says:
> The Egyptians could not dine with the Hebrews, since that would be abhorrent to them. [Gen. 43:32]

And seventh, because they were too comfortable in Egypt. They felt comfortable until it was too late. The same happened to the Jews of Europe, of Babylonia, of the Diaspora in general. Even 4/5 of the Jews of Egypt refused to follow Moses in the Exodus, even though they were enslaved; and 4/5 of the Jews remained in Babylonia when permission was given to go back to Israel. They were born there, were used to the place and to their condition, and wanted to stay. Changes are hard.

Herzl's most difficult battles were with all the Jews who were too assimilated to embrace his dream of a revived homeland in Eretz Yisrael. He wrote:
> Even the Jew-haters have more respect for the Zionists than do other Jews. [Die Welt, 4 March 1898]

About Jacob's death and burial, the Torah says:
> And when the time approached for Israel to die, he summoned his son Joseph and said to him, "Do me this favor ... please do not bury me in Egypt. When I lie down with my fathers, carry me out of Egypt and bury me in their burial-place." He replied, "I will do as you have spoken." [Gen. 47:29-30]

Why did Jacob want to be buried in Israel?

Let us begin with the prophecy of Ezekiel:
> Thus said the Lord God: "I am going to open your graves and lift you out of the graves, O My people, and bring you to the land of Israel... I will put My breath into you and you shall live again, and I will set you upon your own soil." [Ez. 37:12-14]

The Sources add that the dead in Israel will be first to be resurrected and enjoy the Messianic Age. The others have to roll or tunnel underground to Israel.

The Midrash says:
> Our Sages said... that there were two reasons why the patriarchs longed to be buried in the land of Israel: The dead in the land of Israel would be the first to be resurrected in the Messianic Age, and they would be the first to enjoy the years brought by the Messiah. [Tanḥuma Vayechi 3:4]

The Zohar says:
> We have learned that all the dead in the land of Israel will be resurrected first, because the Holy One, blessed be He, will arouse them and revive them... This is because the spirit of life dwells only in the Holy Land of Israel... The bodies of those outside [the Land] will be created, but they will be resurrected as a body with no spirit. Thereafter, they will roll under the soil until they reach the land of Israel, where they will receive a soul. [Zohar 1:131a]

The Talmud says:

> The righteous outside of Eretz Yisrael will be resurrected and roll [until they reach Eretz Yisrael]… Rabbi Abba Salla Rava strongly objects to this: Rolling entails suffering for the righteous. Abaye said: Tunnels are prepared for them in the ground. Karna said…: Our Patriarch Jacob knew that he was completely righteous, and that the dead outside of Eretz Yisrael are resurrected [anyway], so why did he trouble his sons [to bury him in Eretz Yisrael]? Because he thought he may not be worthy of the tunnels [however righteous he may be]. [Ketubot 111a]

This explains why a lot of Jews want to be buried in Israel, even if they don't live there. Not all Sages of the Talmud were sympathetic with that practice:

> Rabbi bar Kiri and Rabbi Elazar were strolling in Istrina, and they saw coffins arriving in the Land of Israel from the Diaspora. Rabbi bar Kiri said to Rabbi Elazar, "What are they achieving? I apply to them the verse [from the Book of Jeremiah]:
>> You made My inheritance desolate [in your lives], and you came and defiled My land [in your deaths]. [Jeremiah 2:7]"
>
> Rabbi Elazar replied, "When they arrive in the Land of Israel, a clod of earth is placed in the coffin, as it is written:
>> וְכִפֶּר אַדְמָתוֹ עַמּוֹ -- His land will atone for His people. [Deut. 32:43]"
>
> [Kilayim Y 9:3, Ketubot Y 12:3]

Rabbi Elazar's view is the halacha: The Land atones for the people. In fact, a common substitute is to put some earth from Israel in the coffin of a Jew buried outside Israel.

Let us conclude with this. A rabbi in the Talmud made this extraordinary claim: Jacob did not die:

> Rabbi Yitzḥak said to Rav Naḥman that Rabbi Yoḥanan said as follows: Our patriarch Jacob did not die.
>
> Rav Naḥman asked him in surprise: And was it for nothing that the eulogizers eulogized him and the embalmers embalmed him and the buriers buried him?
>
> Rabbi Yitzḥak replied to Rav Naḥman: I am interpreting this verse [in Jeremiah]:
>> Therefore do not fear, Jacob My servant, says the Lord, neither be dismayed, Israel, for I will save you from afar, and your seed from the land of their captivity. [Jeremiah 30:10]
>
> This verse juxtaposes Jacob to his seed: Just as his seed is alive, so too, Jacob himself is alive. [Taanit 5b]

Jacob was Israel. We, the Jews, are Israel. Israel did not die and will not die.

Shabbat shalom.

Shemot
Ex. 1:1-6:1
B"H

The Righteous Women of the Exodus

In this week's Torah portion, *Shemot*, the Book of Exodus begins. This book abounds with righteous women working behind the scenes to foil the evil plans of men. Both the Talmud and the Midrash say:
> רב עוירא דרש בשכר נשים צדקניות שהיו באותו הדור נגאלו ישראל ממצרים
> Rabbi Avira expounded: The Israelites were delivered from Egypt as a reward for the righteous women who lived in that generation. [Sotah 11b; Ex. R. 1:12]

Who are these women? They are the midwives Shifrah and Puah; Moses' mother Yocheved; Moses' sister Miriam; Pharaoh's daughter Bitya; Jethro's seven daughters; Moses' wife Tzipporah; Aaron's wife Elisheva; and all Israelite women as a group. Let's examine their contributions one by one.

First, the Israelite women as a whole. They give birth to a lot of babies. The Torah says:
> And the children of Israel were fruitful, and proliferated, and multiplied, and grew very, very strong. [Ex. 1:7]

The Midrash quantifies this statement:
> [This means the women] would give birth to six [children]: Fruitful, one; proliferated, two; multiplied, three; grew strong, four; very, very; five and six. [Midrash Tanḥuma; Rashi]

The Midrash tells us how Pharaoh planned to reduce the Jewish birth rate:
> Pharaoh [made the Israelites build bricks without straw] and commanded that they should not be allowed to sleep in their homes… He reasoned: If they are not allowed to sleep in their homes [with their wives], they will not be able to give birth to children. [Exodus R. 1:12]

But the Talmud tells us how the women devised a strategy to thwart Pharaoh's plan:

When [the Israelite women] went to draw water, the Holy One, blessed be He, arranged that small fishes should enter their pitchers, which they drew up half full of water and half full of fishes. They then set two pots on the fire, one for hot water and the other for the fish, which they carried to their husbands in the field. They washed [their husbands], anointed them, fed them, and gave them to drink. After eating and drinking, the women took bronze mirrors and looked at them with their husbands. The wives said "I'm prettier than you," and the husbands replied, "I'm more beautiful than you." In this manner they aroused themselves to desire, had intercourse and were "fruitful and multiplied"... After the women had conceived they returned to their homes, and when the time of childbirth arrived, they went and were delivered in the field beneath the apple-tree... The Holy One, blessed be He, sent down someone from the high heavens who washed and straightened the limbs [of the babies] as a midwife would... When the Egyptians noticed [the babies], they went to kill them, but a miracle occurred so that [the babies and their mothers] were swallowed in the ground and [the Egyptians] brought oxen and ploughed over them... After they had departed, [the Israelite women with their babies] broke through [the earth] and came forth like the grass of the field... and when [the babies] had grown up, they came in flocks to their homes... At the time the Holy One, blessed be He, revealed Himself by the Sea of Reeds, they recognized Him first, as it is said [in the Torah]:

זֶה אֵלִי וְאַנְוֵהוּ -- This is my God and I will praise Him. [Ex. 15:2]
[Sotah 11b; Midrash Tanḥuma, Pekudei 9]

The Midrash adds in connection with that incident:

When God told Moses to make the Tabernacle, the whole people stood up and offered whatever they had -- silver, gold, copper, etc. Everyone eagerly offered their treasures. The women... brought [their]... mirrors... Moses... was furious... What do I need mirrors for? Then God said to Moses, "Moses, these you despise! These mirrors raised up all these babies in Egypt! Take them, and make of them a copper basin with a copper stand for the priests to sanctify themselves." And it is said [in the Torah]:

And he made the basin of bronze, and its pedestal of bronze, from the mirrors of the women. [Ex. 38:8]
[Midrash Tanḥuma, Pekudei 9]

Second, **Shifrah and Puah**, the Egyptian midwives, are ordered by Pharaoh to kill all male Jewish babies. They don't, saying:

The Hebrew women are not like the Egyptian women. They are lively, and deliver before we midwives arrive!

> Therefore God dealt well with the midwives, and the [Jewish] people multiplied, and became very mighty. And it came to pass, because the midwives feared God, that He made them houses [that is, a distinguished descendance]. [Ex. 1:19-21]

They knew what was morally right and had the courage to act on it.

So, having failed with the midwives, Pharaoh resorts to Plan B:
> And Pharaoh charged all his people, saying: Every son who is born you shall throw into the river, and every daughter you shall let live. [Ex. 1:22]

The Talmud tells us that Moses' father, Amram, reacts by saying "Then we will all divorce our wives and stop having children altogether!"

But his daughter **Miriam,** Moses' sister, successfully argues with him and makes him reverse his decision:
> Amram, Moses' father, said that it was useless for the Israelites to beget children. So he stopped having intercourse with his wife Yocheved, and even divorced her, even though she was already three months pregnant. Then, all the Israelites arose and divorced their wives. Then his daughter Miriam said to him: "Your decree is more severe than Pharaoh's decree: Pharaoh's decree affects only the male children, but your decree affects males and females alike. [Pharaoh's decree affects only this world, but yours also affects the World to Come, because babies born and killed will enjoy the afterlife, but unborn babies will not.] Besides, since Pharaoh is wicked, there is some doubt whether his decree will be fulfilled, but you are righteous and your decree will definitely be fulfilled." So he took his wife back and was followed by all the Israelites, who also took their wives back. [Ex. R. 1:13; Sotah 12a]

Then, **Yocheved,** Moses' mother, gives birth to Moses, and three months later puts him in a basket on the river, hoping someone finds him and saves him from Pharaoh's decree.

Bitya, Pharaoh's daughter, saves the baby, defying her father's wishes. The Midrash tells us that her maidens object, and God strikes them dead:
> They said to her: "Your Highness, it is the general rule that when a king makes a decree, his own family will obey that decree even if everyone else transgresses it. But you are flagrantly disobeying your father's command." Whereupon [the angel] Gabriel came and smote all of them [but one] to the ground. [Ex. R. 1:23]

Miriam, Moses' sister, watches the scene and offers to get a Hebrew wet nurse for Baby Moses, who turns out to be his own mother Yocheved!

Now, Pharaoh must have found out what his daughter did. Why did he allow her to raise a Hebrew child in his own house? The Midrash answers: Against all expectations, Pharaoh liked Moses!
> Pharaoh also used to kiss and hug [Moses]. [Ex. R. 1:26]

Maybe he expected him to grow up hating his own people, adding insult to injury.

Later, Moses rescues **Jethro's seven daughters** at the well. They introduce him to Jethro, who helps him:
> And the priest of Midian [Jethro] had seven daughters. They came and drew water, and filled the troughs to water their father's flock. And the shepherds came and drove them away. But Moses stood up and helped them, and watered their flock. And when they came to... their father, he said, "How is it that you have come so soon today?"
> And they said, "An Egyptian delivered us from the hand of the shepherds, and also drew enough water for us, and watered the flock."
> And he said to his daughters, "And where is he? Why is it that you have left the man? Call him, that he may eat bread."
> And Moses was content to dwell with the man, and [Jethro] gave him his daughter Tzipporah [in marriage]. [Ex. 2:16-21]

A son is born to **Tzipporah** and Moses. Tzipporah saves Moses' life when he fails to circumcize their son on time:
> The Lord met [Moses] and sought to kill him. Then [Moses' wife] Tzipporah took a sharp stone, and cut off the foreskin of her [newborn] son... So [God] let [Moses] go. [Ex. 4:24-26]

Aaron's wife **Elisheva** suffers and bears high highs and low lows on the same day. The Midrash tells us:
> Elisheva did not enjoy happiness in the world. True, she experienced five joys in one day: Her brother-in-law [Moses] was [like] a king, her brother [Nachshon] was a prince, her husband [Aaron] was High Priest, her two sons [Nadav and Avihu] were Deputy High Priests, and her grandson Pinchas [was Deputy High] Priest to lead in

> battle... But her sons entered to offer incense and were burnt [to death], and her joy was changed to mourning. [Lev. R. 19:2, Song of Songs R. 3:13, Eccl. R. 2:3, Zev. 102a]

Women never "get over" the loss of a child.

All of this is in our weekly portion, *Shemot*. Beyond *Shemot*, women distinguished themselves in three ways in the Torah:

-First, they were not a party to the sin of the spies. The Torah says:
> The Lord spoke to Moses and to Eleazar the son of Aaron the priest, saying, "Take a census of the entire congregation, from twenty years old and upward... who are able to go to war in Israel..." In this [census] no man survived from the original census of Moses and Aaron, for the Lord had said of them, "They shall surely die in the wilderness." And there was not a single man them left. [Num 26:64-5]

The census mentions men only. Why were the women not counted? Because they were not subject to the decree against the spies, as they loved the Holy Land. The Torah makes it clear that only the men complained:
> Why has the Lord brought us to this land, to fall by the sword, that *our wives* and our children should be a prey? And they said to one another: Let us appoint a leader to return [us] to Egypt. [Num. 14:3-4]

-Second, the women were not a party to the sin of the Golden Calf. The Midrash says:
> In that generation, women would repair what men tore down. When Aaron said, "Take off your golden earrings [to make the Golden Calf]," the women refused and protested. [Ex 32:2-3]. They did not participate in making the Golden Calf. [Midrash Tanḥuma, Pinḥas 7]

-Third, the women were particularly cheerful in celebrating the Exodus. The Torah says:
> Miriam the prophetess, the sister of Aaron, took a tambourine in her hand, and all the women went out after her with tambourines, dancing. And Miriam answered them, "Sing to the Lord, for he has triumphed gloriously..." [Ex. 15:20-21]

Now, let us conclude with a few questions and observations about women.

First, note that all four matriarchs came from families with dubious ethical standards, yet were not corrupted by them. Of the three patriarchs, only Abraham did.

Collective judgments on women in the Talmud are a mixed bag.
-On the positive side, it mentions their superior compassion [Megillah 14b], their charity [Taanit 23b], their faithfulness [Eruvin 21b], their piety [Sotah 11b], their understanding [Niddah 45b], and their primary role in educating their children and keeping their husbands from transgressing the Torah [Yevamot 63a].
-On the negative side, it mentions their idle curiosity [Taharot 7:9], their excessive talk [Berakhot 48b], their belief in superstitions [Sanhedrin 67a], and their weak will [Shabbat 33b].

So, are women as a whole truly more righteous than men, or are the rabbis simply building them up to defend themselves against charges of misogyny in a patriarchal society? I believe the former. At the risk of being accused of reverse sexism, I venture to say that if the world were run by women, it would be a better place. At least, women are not prone to violence.

Rabbi Isaac Luria, known as the Arizal, a top Jewish mystic of 16th-century Israel, summed it up when he said:
> The future redemption will follow the pattern of the Exodus, and so will also come as a result of the merit of the righteous women of that generation.

Shabbat shalom.

Vaera
Ex. 6:2-9:35

B"H

Did the Exodus Really Happen?

In this week's Torah portion, *Vaera*, we read about the first seven plagues that befall the Egyptians for refusing to let the Israelite slaves go: Blood, frogs, lice, insects, pestilence, boils, and hail. The groundwork for the Exodus has begun. The time is about 1500 BCE.

For Jews, it is such a central event that we are commanded to remember it every day, commemorate it every year in a major holiday, and even act as if we were personally part of it.

But did the Exodus really happen? Most secular scholars say no. There is no archaeological evidence for it. How could 2-3 million people leave Egypt and travel 40 years in the desert without a trace? So it's purely a matter of faith.

But absence of evidence is not evidence of absence. Besides, we do have hints, indirect evidence:

First, we know that Ancient Egypt had plenty of Semitic people who came because of famine. The tomb of the high priest Khnumhotep II, 20th century BCE, shows Semitic traders bringing offerings. A papyrus talks about a rich Egyptian who had 77 slaves, of which 48 were of Semitic origin. A scroll from the time of Ramses II, 13th century BCE, describes slaves from Canaan and Syria making bricks.

Second, we know that the Hyksos, who ruled Egypt for a century, came from Canaan. Pharaoh Ahmose I booted them out in 1530 BCE. The 3rd-century

BCE Egyptian historian Manetho says that after their expulsion, they wandered in the desert and established Jerusalem. The 1st-century CE Jewish historian Josephus says the Hyksos were the Israelites. However, the Hyksos were expelled as rulers, not slaves. But perhaps they were enslaved first?

Third, we have the Ipuwer Papyrus (Ipou-Our), dated about 1500 BCE, which says:
> Plague is throughout the land... Blood is everywhere. The river is blood... The hearts of all animals weep. Cattle moan... The land is without light... The children of princes are dashed against the walls... He who places his brother in the ground is everywhere... It is groaning throughout the land, mingled with lamentations... The fire has mounted up on high... The necks of female slaves are fastened with gold and lapis lazuli, silver and malachite, carnelian and bronze.

All these statements are strongly suggestive of the biblical plagues on Egypt and their aftermath.

Fourth, we discovered Aper-El's tomb, from 1350 BCE, saying that he was an advisor to Akhenaton, the monotheistic Pharaoh. The ending "El" may indicate a Hebrew origin. Perhaps he steered the Pharaoh towards monotheism?

Fifth, we discovered the Stele of Merneptah, from 1207 BCE, which says: "Israel is laid waste and his seed is no more." (Wishful thinking!) It is the only mention of "Israel" in ancient Egyptian records.

Sixth, the Exodus was said to have been witnessed by millions of people. If the story was made up, it would mean an awful lot of people had to agree to lie to their descendants. Unlikely!

Time may produce more evidence. It took until 1993 for extra-biblical evidence for the existence of King David to be found. The Tel Dan Stele, from the 9th-century BCE, found in northern Israel, mentions in Aramaic a "king of Israel" and a "house of David".

Much later, Manetho, from the 3rd-century BCE, speaks of an Egyptian priest who embraced monotheism and led his followers out of Egypt. He was encouraged by his monotheistic Pharaoh Akhenaton, because Egypt was not ready for him. His name was Osarseph, but he changed it to Moses, meaning "child of". Indeed, Ramses was Ra-Moses, son of the god Ra; Thutmose was Thoth-Moses, son of the god Thoth; etc. He may have removed the prefix to his name that indicated what god he was a son of, since he did not believe in them.

In Thomas Mann's novel *Joseph and His Brothers*, Osarseph is Joseph. Likewise, Sigmund Freud, in his *Moses and Monotheism*, theorizes that Moses was Egyptian, not Hebrew.

Next, we must note that removing traces of embarrassing stories is common. Ancient Egypt in particular has a long history of removing evidence of inconvenient facts. Pharaoh Thutmose III, from the 15th century BCE, worked to erase the memory of his predecessor, Queen Hatshepsut. He removed her cartouches, statues, monuments. Even her name was removed from the official records. Pharaoh Seti I, from the 14th century BCE, did the same with the memory of Akhenaton, because of his failed experiment with monotheism.

This trend continues even today. Modern Egypt hides the predominant role of the Jews in building the country, as well as their harassment, dispossession and expulsion. (I am one of these Jews.) Modern Muslims try to erase evidence of the Jewish past on Temple Mount. Turkey refuses to acknowledge it carried out the genocide of the Armenians. Antisemites the world over promote the fiction that the Holocaust is a myth.

The Jews have an opposite view. They expose all flaws, warts and inconvenient facts. Why would they invent a story about having been slaves? Most people prefer to connect their origins to royalty or nobility.

Many thinkers accept the Exodus, but explain the miracles as natural phenomena. Take, for example, Immanuel Velikovsky. He was a Russian-born American psychiatrist, Jewish and Zionist. In middle age, he became interested in whether biblical events, such as the Exodus from Egypt, were due to natural phenomena rather than divine intervention. He wondered whether the unusual motions of planets, comets, stars, etc., caused these biblical events.

He concluded that Venus was a comet ejected from Jupiter. It had several close encounters with the Earth, and one of them caused the sun to stand still, as reported in the Book of Joshua. [Joshua 10:12-13] In another encounter, its tail sprayed a red pigment on the Nile, causing the plague of blood, and insects that caused the plagues of lice, boils and locusts.

His theories were very well-received by the general public. He wrote such huge best-sellers as *Worlds in Collision*, in 1950; *Ages in Chaos, in* 1952; *Earth in Upheaval, in* 1955; etc. All of them were savaged by all mainline scientists.

Whether the Exodus really happened is, at present, a matter of faith. Parables were frequent in olden days, and not always identified as such. All that mattered was the morals, the teachings they inspired. And we should not, as some have tried to do, excise ritual and biblical history and keep only ethical teachings, either. Ritual commandments preserve Judaism and ethical commandments make Judaism worth preserving. Both are needed.

Shabbat shalom.

Bo
Ex. 10:1-13:16

B"H

Promptness in Performing Commandments

In this week's Torah portion, *Bo*, we read this injunction about Passover:
> וּשְׁמַרְתֶּם אֶת-הַמַּצּוֹת
> And you shall watch over the matzot. [Ex. 12:17]

What does it mean? Well, there are four levels of understanding of the Torah: The *pshat*, or plain meaning of text, the *remez*, or meaning that is only hinted at, the *drash*, or scholarly interpretation, and the *sod*, or the deep, mystical interpretation.

Let us examine two related levels of understanding of this verse.

First, the *pshat*. The verse says that we must watch the dough of the matzah carefully and finish baking it quickly so it does not rise. Time is of the essence.

To be specific, in the process of making *shmurah* matzah (that is, "watched" matzah), the bakers, who must be observant Jews, must combine flour with water and turn it into matzah in just 18 minutes. So they roll the dough into flat circles, make tiny holes in it, and put it into an oven at 1,300 degrees for 20 seconds. After it cools, they inspect it and box it. Then, they repeat the process. However, between baking cycles, every surface that the dough has touched must be scoured or replaced. If any dough from the previous cycle remains, it contaminates the dough of the next cycle. Then, they must wash their hands and cover all work surfaces with fresh paper.

Why emphasize the haste? The Torah says:

> The [Israelites] baked unleavened cakes of the dough which they brought forth out of Egypt... because they were thrust out of Egypt and could not tarry, and had not prepared any provisions for themselves. [Ex. 12:39]

And later, in Deuteronomy:
> For seven days you should eat matzot... because you left Egypt in haste. [Deut. 16:3]

So we must eat matzah on Pessah to remind us of the haste with which we had to leave Egypt. But why is it so important to remember that the Exodus from Egypt happened swiftly and suddenly? In fact, there are only two positive commandments regarding Pessah. One is precisely to eat matzah. The other is telling the story.

The Maharal, from 16th-century Prague, wrote a great deal about this verse. In his view, the lesson of the haste is that God Himself took us out of Egypt (and not human or natural forces). God makes things happen very fast. We emphasize this in the Haggadah, in which God is quoted as saying:
> I will pass through the land of Egypt on that night – I, and not an angel.
> And I will slay all the firstborn in the land of Egypt – I and not a seraph.
> And I will execute judgment upon all the gods of Egypt– I and not a messenger.
> I, God – it is I and no other. [Pessah Haggadah]

By remembering the *swiftness* of the exodus, we remember that *God* made it happen, and that's why the matzah is central. The other symbols are not as important.

My own view about the special character of matzah is this. First, let me list the other symbols of Pessah:
- The *maror*, which reminds us of the bitterness of slavery;
- The *haroset*, which reminds us of the mortar the slaves used;
- The shankbone, or Pessah, which reminds us that God "passed over" the houses of the Israelites and did not kill the firstborn in it, because the blood of the paschal lamb was smeared on the doorposts;
- The wine, which reminds us that we were freed, since it is a royal drink;
- The leaning on the left, which also reminds us that we were freed, because that's what free people did back then;
- Etc.

Now, note that, while some Pessah symbols reflect life b*efore* the Exodus (such as the *maror*, the *haroset*, or the shankbone) and some reflect life *after* the Exodus (such as the wine, or reclining), only the matzah refers to life *during* the Exodus.

Now, let us look for a deeper meaning for our quote:
>And you shall watch over the matzot. [Ex. 12:17]

The Midrash says:
>Rabbi Yoshiyah says: Do not read אֶת-הַמַּצּוֹת, [watch over] the matzot, but אֶת-הַמִּצְוֹת, [watch over] the commandments. [The letters are the same, but the vowels are different.] Just as we may not allow the matzot to become leavened, so we may not allow the commandments to become leavened [by waiting too long to perform them]. If [a commandment] comes your way, perform it immediately. [Mechilta d'Rabbi Yishmael 12:17]

Thus, the deeper lesson is that we must be prompt in performing *all* commandments. The Maharal notes that if the Torah only wanted to talk about matzah, it would have stated "Watch for ḥametz", that is, make sure the matzah is not contaminated. Since the Torah said "Watch over the matzot", there must be a deeper meaning. So a teaching is needed: Mitzvot must be performed with alacrity, promptly and with cheerful readiness.

There is a tie to the *pshat* above: We must emulate God. Just as He was "prompt" with the Exodus, let us be "prompt" in performing mitzvot.

There is a basis in the Torah for this attitude. On two occasions, Abraham was swift to obey God's commandments:

-First, in the matter of circumcision:
>And... the Lord... said to [Abraham]... Every male... among you shall be circumcised.... and it shall be a sign of the covenant between me and you... And Abraham took Ishmael his son, and... every male [in his] house, and circumcised the flesh of their foreskin *in the same day*, as God had said to him. And Abraham was ninety-nine years old, when he was circumcised in the flesh of his foreskin. [Gen. 17]

-Second, in the matter of the binding of his son Isaac:

> And Abraham rose up early in the morning [to take his son Isaac to be sacrificed].
> [Gen. 22:3]

The Talmud reinforces this notion:

> -The zealous are early in the performance of commandments. [Pesachim 4a]
>
> -One should always run for a matter of halakha, even on Shabbat. [Berakhot 6b]
>
> -If [a candidate for conversion is] accepted, he is quickly circumcised. [Why "quickly"? Because] the performance of a commandment must not in any way be delayed. [Yevamot 47b]
>
> -The school of Rabbi Yishmael taught that any place where the word "Command" is stated, its only purpose is to denote exhortation [to speed], for that time and for all time. "Exhortation", because it is written: "And command Joshua, and encourage him and strengthen him" [Deut. 3:28], and "for all time" because it is written: "From the day that the Lord commanded and onward throughout your generations." [Num. 15:23] [Kiddushin 29a]

The Talmud also relates in vivid imagery the story of Gamzu, in which a man died because Gamzu was too slow in helping him:

> Nahum of Gamzu was blind in both his eyes, his two hands and legs were amputated, and his whole body was covered with boils. He was lying in a dilapidated house on a bed whose feet were standing in bowls of water, to prevent the ants from crawling on to him...
> His disciples said to him, "Master, since you are wholly righteous, why has all this happened to you?"
> He replied: "I have brought it all upon myself. Once I was journeying on the road and was making for the house of my father-in-law. I had with me three asses, one laden with food, one with drink, and one with all kinds of dainties. A poor man met me and stopped me on the road and said to me, "Master, give me something to eat." I replied to him, "Wait until I have unloaded something from the ass." I had hardly managed to unload something from the ass when the man died [from hunger]. I then went and laid myself on him and exclaimed, "May my eyes which had no pity upon your eyes become blind, may my hands which had no pity upon your hands be cut off, may my legs which had no pity upon your legs be amputated!" My mind was not at rest until I added: "May my whole body be covered with boils"." [Taanit 21a]

The Mishnah concludes by tapping its foot:
> Rabbi Tarfon said: The day is short and the work is much, and the workers are lazy, and the reward is great, and the Master of the house is pressing...
> לֹא עָלֶיךָ הַמְּלָאכָה לִגְמֹר, וְלֹא אַתָּה בֶן חוֹרִין לִבָּטֵל מִמֶּנָּה
> It is not your responsibility to finish the work, but neither are you free to desist from it. [Avot 2:15-16]

So we must perform mitzvot promptly. Death is a deadline that enjoins us not to delay. Another point emphasized by commentators is that we must not perform mitzvot quickly just to "get them out of the way", but because we are eager to perform them.

The Radbaz, from 16th-century Spain, Egypt and Israel, even said: It is better to perform commandments quickly than to delay them so we can perform them better later. Thus, in his view, the best can be the enemy of the good. Some disagree.

Let's be specific: How much time do we have? Not all mitzvot are equally time-sensitive. Some are very time-sensitive, such as matzah-making, Shabbat and holiday observance, Shema, tefillin, and circumcision. Most Jews understand and respect this time-sensitivity. Others are not time-sensitive at all, such as all negative commandments. So the teaching that concerns us here, performing commandments with alacrity, refers primarily to positive commandments that are not time-bound, such as studying Torah, giving charity, performing good deeds, making peace between people, loving one's neighbor, pursuing justice, honoring parents and teachers, procreating, repenting for misdeeds, making restitution, etc. We must be particularly careful to perform *these* mitzvot promptly. The Mishnah says:
> -Hillel said: Do not say "When I have time I will study" because you may never have the time. [Avot 2:5]
> -Shammai said: Make your study of Torah a practice fixed [in time]. [Avot 1:15]
> -Rabbi Eliezer said: Repent one day before your death. [Avot 2:10]

The Mishnah also states that women are exempted from positive time-bound commandments:

> Men are liable and women are exempt from all positive commandments [that must be performed at specific times]. But all positive commandments not limited to time are binding upon both men and women. And all negative precepts, whether or not limited to time, are binding on both men and women. [Kiddushin 29a]

The reason for that exemption is that women are expected to bear children, raise them, and run their household. Nevertheless, there is no universal agreement on the full list of the commandments from which women are exempt. Among those listed in the Talmud are residing in the sukkah, raising the *lulav*, listening to the *shofar*, wearing *tzitzit* or *tefillin*, counting the *Omer* and saying the *Shema*.

Some time-bound mitzvot have specific times attached to them. For example, after you say *Hamotzi* over bread, you have one halachic unit of time to eat the bread. What is a halachic "unit of time"? It's called *Kdei Achilat Pras* פרס אכילת, the time required to eat half a loaf of bread. It has been estimated to range from 3 to 9 minutes. Chabad rules that it is 4 minutes.

In conclusion, the Maharal's overarching view is that a mitzvah is the vehicle that takes us from the physical to the metaphysical. Performing mitzvot *promptly* expresses our desire to go beyond the physical and break through to the metaphysical, and in so doing establish a relationship with God, who transcends time.

Shabbat shalom.

Beshallach
Ex. 13:17-17:16

B"H

The Slave Mentality

This week's Torah portion, *Beshallach*, begins with:
> וַיְהִ֗י בְּשַׁלַּ֣ח פַּרְעֹה֮ אֶת־הָעָם֒ וְלֹא־נָחָ֣ם אֱלֹהִ֗ים דֶּ֚רֶךְ אֶ֣רֶץ פְּלִשְׁתִּ֔ים כִּ֥י קָר֖וֹב ה֑וּא כִּ֣י ׀ אָמַ֣ר אֱלֹהִ֗ים פֶּֽן־יִנָּחֵ֥ם הָעָ֛ם בִּרְאֹתָ֥ם מִלְחָמָ֖ה וְשָׁ֥בוּ מִצְרָֽיְמָה׃
>
> And it came to pass, when Pharaoh let the people go, that God did not lead them [by] way of the land of the Philistines, even though it was the closest route, because God said, "The people may have a change of heart when they see war, and return to Egypt". [Ex. 13:17-18]

Let me begin with two points.

First, it says: *Vayehi* וַיְהִ֗י – And it came to pass. The Talmud tells us that this phrase always implies that a bad thing is about to happen:
> We received this tradition from the Men of the Great Assembly: Anywhere [the Torah] says *Vayehi*, [and it came to pass], it [indicates] nothing but [impending] grief, [as if the word were a contraction of the words *vai* and *hi*, meaning woe and mourning]. [Megillah 10b]

Why is it used here to introduce a sentence saying that the Israelites were freed from Egypt? Isn't this a happy occasion?

Second, it says: *Beshallach Par'o et haam* בְּשַׁלַּ֣ח פַּרְעֹה֮ אֶת־הָעָם֒ – When Pharaoh let the people go. Why does Pharaoh get the credit? Why doesn't it say: When God (or Moses) freed the people? Also, the phrase is translated variously as "When Pharaoh let the people go", "dismissed the people", "released the people", "discharged the people", "accompanied the people", or "escorted the people".

All these questions are answered by the same observation: Pharaoh "accompanying" us means we were still carrying our negative experience in Egypt along with us. We were still carrying Pharaoh, as it were. We left

Egypt physically, but not emotionally. Egypt was still with us. We were not really free. We were afflicted with the **slave mentality**.

This is why *Vayehi*, implies "a bad thing follows" here also. This is why Pharaoh is mentioned and not Moses. This is why God says "I'd better send them on a longer route, to get them used to the idea of having left Egypt permanently."

Why were the Israelites enslaved in the first place? It was not divine punishment. God tells Abraham in the Book of Genesis:
> Know for certain that your offspring will be strangers in a strange land, and will be enslaved and afflicted for four hundred years. [Genesis 15:13-14]

It does not state a reason, and none is obvious. So evidently God thought slavery was necessary for His plan and led to some good. But how? There are many possible answers:
- First, slavery was necessary for our protection. Jacob's clan in Israel was an easy target for strong marauding neighbors, but in Egypt, a superpower protected them, albeit to exploit them.
- Second, slavery also allowed us build up our numbers in safety, to build up our identity and community spirit. We were all in the same boat and followed the same customs.
- Third, slavery minimized contact with the outside world, which reduced the practice of idolatry and eliminated the possibility of intermarriage. Egyptians wouldn't marry slaves and the children of rape would be raised by their mothers as Jews, away from their fathers.
- Fourth, slavery created a scenario that allowed God to show the Jews and the whole world that He was in charge, as He did when He freed us.
- Fifth, the gratitude that we felt upon liberation and the slave mentality we had acquired made it easier for us to accept the Torah, as God wanted us to do.

So slavery served God's plan, up to the time of the giving of the Torah. But why couldn't God have made slavery less brutal and more tolerable? Because then few Israelites would have wanted to leave. Even as it is, the

Midrash tells us that 80% of the Israelites refused to go and died in the plague of darkness [Tanḥuma, Beshallach 1]. The remaining 20% may have left, but they grumbled incessantly about going back, and some even staged an open revolt.

Fear of change is normal and universal. People prefer the devil-they-know, in this case slavery, to the devil-they-don't-know, in this case the uncertainty of the desert and a radically new way of life. Change is always hard, especially for older people, and leaders tend to be older. Yes, life in Egypt was supremely painful, but Egypt was also home; it was also familiar. In Egypt, they worked hard as slaves for people who beat them and despised them, but they had life, food, shelter, clothing, protection, regularity, predictability. They did not want to face problems they never had before.

We see that God decides not to take the Israelites through the land of the Philistines, because, the Torah says, they might get "scared by war and return to Egypt" [Ex. 13:17-18]. Rather, He takes them by the Sea of Reeds, a circuitous route. Nevertheless, this is exactly what happens anyway! The Israelites do face the Egyptian army at the Sea of Reeds and do ask to return to Egypt! [Ex. 14:11-12]. And they also have to face Amalek in battle. So why bother to avoid the shortcut through the land of the Philistines in the first place? Also, why should the Israelites fear war? After all, they have 600,000 men and they are armed. And they know they will have to fight their way into the Promised Land anyway. And why did they complain after the splitting of the Sea? Didn't God just perform a whole bunch of miracles for them?

All these questions have the same answer: Their slave mentality, which God is trying to break. The Israelites feared war in part because, in their mind, it is inconceivable for slaves to rise up against their masters. Rabbi Menachem Leibtag says that the whole point of our parasha, *Beshallach*, is to liberate the Israelites from the slave mentality.

Fast forward to modern times. I was born and raised in that same Egypt, and lived there until I was eighteen. I saw the Jewish community shrink around me from 100,000 to 1,000, and I was one of the last Jews to be forced out, in late 1967. In retrospect, it was all to the good: The Jews from Egypt did better *outside* of Egypt than they could ever have done *in* Egypt, even under the best of conditions. But the uprooting was still excruciatingly painful to the heads of families, who continued, to their dying day, to wax nostalgic about their life in Egypt. They may have been harassed, persecuted, dispossessed, and finally forced out, but they glossed over all that and frequently said, "Well, at least they didn't kill us!" As if not being quite as bad as the Nazis was a virtue that exonerated the Egyptians!

All this is typical in the slave mentality. That's why God engineered the forty-year trek through the desert. He wanted all those who were adult at the time of the Exodus to die out, so that a new generation, one that has not known slavery and truly wanted to live in freedom with no misgivings, would take over and start the new country in the Promised Land, with no regrets about life in Egypt, with **no slave mentality.**

Shabbat shalom.

Yitro
Ex. 18:1-20:23

B"H

Honor Your Father and Your Mother

In this week's Torah portion, Yitro, in the Book of Exodus, we hear the Ten Commandments, and in particular the fifth:

> כַּבֵּד אֶת־אָבִיךָ וְאֶת־אִמֶּךָ לְמַעַן יַאֲרִכוּן יָמֶיךָ עַל הָאֲדָמָה אֲשֶׁר־יְהוָה אֱלֹהֶיךָ נֹתֵן לָךְ
> Kabed et avicha ve-et immecha…
> Honor your father and your mother, so that your days may be long in the land the Lord your God gives you. [Exodus 20:12]

This commandment, called *Kibbud Av V'Em,* is repeated three times in the Torah. The second version, in Leviticus, is:

> אִישׁ אִמּוֹ וְאָבִיו תִּירָאוּ -- *Ish immo v'aviv tira-u.*

It is usually translated as:

> Every man shall revere his mother and his father. [Leviticus 19:3]

Note that the preferred translation is "revere" or "be in awe of", not "fear". The third version, in Deuteronomy, is:

> Honor your father and your mother, as the Lord your God has commanded you, so that your days may be prolonged, and that it may go well with you, in the land the Lord your God gives you. [Deut. 5:16]

Note that when it comes to honoring, the father is mentioned first, but when it comes to revering, the mother is mentioned first. Why? The Mishnah explains:

> You might think... the honor due to the father exceeds the honor due to the mother, [but] the Torah stated [later], "Every man shall revere his mother and his father" to teach that both are equal. [K'ritot 6:9 - 28a; Genesis R. 1:15]

The Talmud is a bit more specific:

> It was taught that Rabbi [Yehudah HaNasi] said:

> ...A son honors his mother more than his father, because she sways him with her words. Therefore, the Holy One, blessed be He, placed the honor of the father before that of the mother...
> A son reveres his father more than his mother, because he teaches him Torah. Therefore, the Holy One, blessed be He, mentioned the reverence of the mother before that of the father. [Kiddushin 30b-31a]

The Torah also says that one must not hit [Ex. 21:15], curse [Ex. 21:17], or dishonor [Deut. 27:16] one's parents. Maimonides believed these injunctions are so important that he chose to count them as three separate commandments. [Sefer Hamitzvot 2:218,219,195; Hilkhot Mamrim 5ff]

Let us now proceed to analyze this commandment, so we can better understand it. Several questions come to mind:
- Why honor parents, especially if they haven't been good to you?
- Who must honor parents?
- How important is that commandment?
- What's my reward if I honor parents?
- What does it mean to "honor" and "revere" your parents?
- How far must that honoring extend?
- Who are good examples of honoring parents?

First, why honor parents? Two reasons: Gratitude and self-interest.
The Sefer HaChinuch, from 13th-century Spain, covers gratitude:
> One should appreciate the fact that his parents are the source of his very existence in this world, and it is therefore appropriate for him to act as respectfully and beneficially as he can. Besides having brought him into the world, they also expended tremendous effort in raising him as a child. [Sefer HaChinuch 33]

And Saadia Gaon, from 10th-century Egypt, covers self-interest:
If you take care of your parents, your children will take care of you in your old age, and you will live longer!

Why is the commandment necessary? After all, the Torah does not command us to do what we would do naturally. But is it natural to want to honor parents? Contemporary American Rabbi Yissachar Frand thinks not:

> Honoring parents…goes against human nature. It requires us to acknowledge all they've done for us and show gratitude. It requires us to admit that we needed them, that we could not have done it ourselves. This is a difficult thing for the human ego. The ego would have us view ourselves as independent, self-sufficient and invincible. We can bring ourselves to thank strangers who do small things for us now and then, because this does not really affect our egotistical self-image. But when it comes to our parents, if we admit they did anything, we also have to admit they did everything for us. Our egos do not allow us to say, "I owe you everything." This, then, is [as the Talmud puts it] the "most difficult of the difficult" mitzvot. [Rabbi Yissachar Frand on Ki Tetze]

Also, many children (perhaps most) grow up to rebel against their parents, which does not set the stage for honoring them.

What if my parents have not been good to me? Answer: You must honor your parents even if they have not taken good care of their children, because the Torah says:

> Honor your father and your mother, as the Lord your God has commanded you. [Deut. 5:16]

It implies this may be a *chok,* that is, a commandment whose rationale escapes us. Rabbi Meir Simcha of Dvinsk, from 19th-century Eastern Europe, writes:

> Even if your father and mother abandoned you and did not raise you, you should still honor them "as the Lord your God has commanded you." [Meir Simcha of Dvinsk, 19th-century Eastern Europe, Meshech Chochma on Deut. 5:16]

Why? For several reasons. They transmitted the Tradition to us. Even if not, they transmitted the knowledge that we are Jewish, thereby giving us the impetus to discover the Tradition on our own, knowing that we belong. And even if not that, they gave us life: That alone is sufficient reason.

Who must honor parents? Obviously, everybody. But the question is not trivial:

> -What if the children are adopted? Then, they are exempt. The Talmud says:
>> Rabbi Aha ben Yaakov raised his daughter's son, Rabbi Yaakov. When he grew up, [the grandfather] said to him: "Give me some water to drink". He replied: "I am not your son." [Sotah 49a]
>
> -Also, converts are exempt: Prior family ties are not recognized.

-Non-Jews are also exempt: Honoring parents is not one of the seven Noahide laws, which are binding on all mankind. So, if the biological parents are not Jewish, they do not have to be honored.

Nevertheless, there is still a moral obligation. The Talmud says:
> If anyone brings up an orphan boy or girl in his house, Scripture accounts it as if he had begotten him. [Megillah 13a]

The Midrash adds:
> He who brings up children is called the father, not he who gives birth. [Ex. R. 46:5]

Contemporary Rav Moshe Feinstein says:
> A convert must not curse his non-Jewish father or hit him, or disgrace him... but should treat his parents with... honor. [Rav Moshe Feinstein, Igrot Moshe YD 2:130]

The Maharal says that non-Jews should honor their parents more than most Jews, because two non-Jews are paragons of honoring parents, as we shall discuss later.

Are adopted children obligated to search for their biological parents so they can honor them? I do not know the answer.

How important is that commandment? The Mishnah goes so far as to say that the Torah compares the honor and reverence due to father and mother to the honor and reverence due to God Himself. [Peah Y 1:1, 6b] A contemporary rabbi adds:
> Even if one were to honor father and mother as he would a king and queen, he would still not fulfill his obligation, since the Torah compares their honor to the honor due to God Himself. Therefore, one should imagine how he would feel if God were to show up at his doorstep. With what trepidation would he receive Him! One should honor parents with that same attitude. [Shmuel Houminer, 20th-century Jerusalem, Eved Hamelech]

Note that the first five of the Ten Commandments address obligations to God, whereas the second five address duties towards individuals. Why is honoring parents among the first five? Because by honoring parents we also honor God.

That commandment is one of only two commandments for which long life is promised. The other is to shoo away the mother bird before taking her eggs or

her young (שילוח הקן -- *Shiluach HaKen*). [Deut. 22:6] The Mishnah also elevates this commandment:
> The following are the things for which a man enjoys the fruits in this world while the principal remains for him in the World to Come: Honoring father and mother, practicing charity, and making peace between a man and his friend; but the study of Torah is equal to them all. [Peah 1:1, Shabbat 127a]

Now, let us tackle the all-important practical question. What does it actually mean, to "honor" and "revere" your parents?

First and most importantly, it does not mean "Obey your parents". This is especially true if they tell you to go against the Torah. The Midrash explains:
> It might be supposed that even if his father tells him: "Slaughter or cook for me on Shabbat", he must obey. The Torah therefore explicitly states [in the same verse]: Every man shall revere his mother and his father, and keep my Sabbaths. I am the Lord your God. [Leviticus 19:3].
> This implies [that...] if [any] mortal rages against you to make you transgress the commandments of the Torah, do not be cowed by his anger into following his counsel. [Numbers R. 14:6]

The Talmud confirms:
> -One might have assumed that honoring father and mother supersedes Shabbat [but the rest of the verse shows that it is not so.] [Yevamot 5b]
> -[Also,] Torah study is greater than the mitzvah of honoring parents. [Megillah 16b]

In the same vein, the Zohar says:
> Rabbi Yosei said: Reverence of mother and father is put next to keeping Shabbat [because] it is all one: He who reveres one keeps the other. [Zohar, Vayikra 3:81b]

Maimonides summarizes:
> A child must not listen to a parent asking him to transgress a commandment of the Torah or of the rabbis. [Rambam, Hilchot Mamrim 6:12]

Later rabbis even added: Even if the parents' request does not contradict the Torah, you don't have to obey:

19th-century Russian rabbi Eisenstadt said:
> If someone wants to pray in a synagogue where [the congregation] prays with more devotion, and his mother protests, he does not have to listen to his mother. [Rabbi Eisenstadt, Pitchei Teshuva, Yoreh Deah 240:22]

The Rema, commenting on the Shulḥan Arukh, said:

If the father protests against the son marrying a specific woman that he wishes [to marry], the son does not have to listen to his father. [Rema on Shulḥan Arukh Yoreh Deah 240:25]

To which Chaim Hezekiah Medini, 19th-century Jerusalem rabbi, adds:
But if she is not Jewish, or not moral, or not religious, he must listen to his father. [Chaim Hezekiah Medini, 19th-century Jerusalem rabbi, Sdei Chemed, Ma'arechet Caf 147]

Contemporary rabbi Moshe Lieber comments:
Many rabbis say that the mitzvah to dwell in Israel overrides the obligation to honor parents. Some disagree. [Rabbi Moshe Lieber, The Fifth Commandment, p 131]

Rabbi Shlomo Zalman Braun comments:
If a parent asks a son to shave his beard, he need not listen. If a parent tells a child not to speak to a certain person, the child need not obey. [Shulḥan Arukh, Yoreh Deah 240:16]. [Rabbi Shlomo Zalman Braun, She'arim Metzuyyanim Bahalakhah 143]

What is the difference between "honor" and "revere" your parents? The Talmud answers:
"Honor" means you must give them food, drink, clothing; and help them in and out. "Revere" means you must neither stand nor sit in their place, nor contradict them, nor tip the scales against them. [Kiddushin 31b]

Rashi explains:
If the father is in dispute with another scholar, the son must not side with his opponent... He must not even say: I agree with my father. This holds only in the father's presence, otherwise he may state his view freely. Even then, he should avoid mentioning his father's name when refuting his view, if possible.

Also, no financial loss need be incurred in helping parents. The Talmud explains:
At whose expense [must the parents be helped]?
Rav Yehudah said: The son's.
Rabbi Naḥman ben Oshaia said: The father's.
The Rabbis [ruled:] At the father's expense.
An objection is raised: It is said: "Honor your father and your mother", and it is also said: "Honor the Lord with your substance." [Proverbs 3:9] Just as the latter means at personal cost, so does the former. But if you say: At the father's [expense], how does it affect [the son]? [What personal loss is there?] Loss of time. [Kiddushin 32a]

The law, summarized in the Shulḥan Arukh, is:

The son provides food and drink from the resources of the father and mother. That is, he is not required to pay for serving his parents. However, he is obligated to honor his parents through his physical presence even if by doing so he will miss work...But if the son himself does not have [enough food for one day], he is not obligated to miss work and end up a beggar. [Shulḥan Arukh, Yoreh Deah 240:5]

A joke illustrates the requirement to visit parents:
> A man goes to his rabbi and says, "Rabbi, my parents insist that I go visit them. But they live on the other coast, and I have a very demanding job that keeps me busy six days a week, and I have little time for a social life. Besides, I call them regularly, and send them things. So tell me, rabbi: Do I *have* to fly out to see my parents?"
> The rabbi replies: "No. You can walk."

Rabbenu Yonah, from 13th-century Catalonia, adds that you must gratify your parents:
> The main way to honor parents is to gratify them, through words or deeds. [Rabbenu Yonah, Iggeret Ha-Teshuvah 3:70]

You must also be sincere in honoring parents. Sefer Charedim says:
> Honoring father and mother applies to feelings and emotions as well as actions. If one displays honor for parents only in superficial speech and deed, without heartfelt concern, he shows that in reality he considers them lowly and honors them only "because God says so." Rather, he must see them as truly great and honorable people. This is the main aspect of honoring parents. Once one has developed this attitude, it will be easy to honor them sincerely in both speech and action. [Sefer Charedim 1:35]

You must also look for your parents' qualities and achievements. Rav Chaim Shmuelevitz says:
> True fulfillment of honoring parents is only possible if you feel real respect and admiration toward them. You must therefore find areas or character traits in which they excel. If you do not cultivate a deep feeling of esteem for them, even if you go through all external motions of acting respectfully, you have not fulfilled the Torah's goal at all. [Rav Chaim Shmuelevitz, Sichot Mussar, p 158]

The Shulḥan Arukh says that you must not call your parents by their first names. [Shulḥan Arukh, Yoreh Deah 240:2]

You must remember that the word *Kavod* is dignity, not just honor. Just feeding and clothing parents is not honor, but only charity.

You must also remember your parents after they die. This includes saying Kaddish, following mourning rites, remembering their teachings and merits, and mentioning them often for the good.

Now, how far must the honoring of one's parents extend? There is no easy answer. In fact, the Mishnah says that it is the most difficult mitzvah:
> Rabbi Ba bar Kahana said: The Torah put the most minor of minor commandments on the same level as the most major of major commandments. The easiest is sending away the mother bird, and the most difficult is honoring father and mother. And with regard to each, it is written [in the Torah]: "So that you may live long." [Peah Y 1:1, 7a]

The Talmud adds that this "bracketing" implies that all mitzvot get at least this reward:
> A man may not take the mother bird along with the young... If in respect of so light a precept... the Torah said, "that it may be well with you", and "that you may prolong your days", how much more [must the reward be] for observing the more difficult precepts of the Torah! [Ḥullin 142a]

In the Midrash, Rabbi Shim'on bar Yoḥai concludes clearly:
> The most difficult of all mitzvot is "Honor your father and your mother". [Tanḥuma, Ekev 2]

In fact, it is practically impossible to fully perform the mitzvah of honoring parents. The Talmud says:
> Rabbi Yoḥanan said: *Ashrei mi she-lo raah chama-an* -- Happy is he who has not seen [his parents]. Rabbi Yoḥanan's father died when his mother conceived him, and his mother died when he was born; and likewise for Abaye. [Kiddushin 31b]

Rashi explains:
> Only one who never saw his parents can be considered not to have violated the commandment of honoring parents, [the most difficult one].

For this reason, no blessing is said before honoring parents. Rabbi Chaim Hezekiah Medini, from 19th-century Jerusalem, writes:
> No blessing is recited for fulfilling this mitzvah, because you never know if you have fulfilled it properly. [And saying a blessing in vain is prohibited.] [Sdei Chemed v6, Berakhot 1:16]

The Mishnah adds that you can never do enough for your parents:
> Rabbi Tarfon's mother… took a walk [and her shoes tore].
> He went and placed his two hands under her feet, and she walked on them until she reached her bed.
> One time, [Rabbi Tarfon] became ill, and the Sages came to visit him. His mother said to them, "Pray for my son, for he treats me with exceptional honor." They said to her, "What does he do for you?", and she relayed this incident to them.
> They said to her, "Even if he were to do that thousands upon thousands [of times], he still would not have achieved half of the honor the Torah requires." [Peah Y 3b]

It is important that you honor your parents personally. The Talmud says:
> Rabbi Avahu said, "My son Avimi is an example of one who has fulfilled the mitzvah of honoring [one's parents]." Avimi had five children who were ordained [as rabbis] while his father was still alive. Yet, when Rabbi Avahu came [to visit] and called out at the door, Avimi himself hurried and went to open it for him saying, "Yes, yes!" [I am coming to open the door] until he reached there. One day [Rabbi Avahu] said, "Bring me a drink of water." He [Avimi] brought him [water and found him] sleeping. He stood over him [and waited] until he awoke. [Kiddushin 31b]

The Mishnah says that you must honor your parents willingly and cheerfully.
> One can feed his father birds of delicacy and be punished; one can make his father grind with a millstone and be rewarded.
> -How can one feed his father birds of delicacy and be punished?
> Once there was a son who always fed his father birds of delicacy. The father asked his son how he could afford to do so. The son answered him, "Old man! What do you care? Chew and eat! Even dogs eat quietly."
> -How can one make his father grind with a millstone and be rewarded?
> A man who worked at a mill had an elderly father. One day the king drafted the father for forced labor. The man told his father: "Father, you work here on the millstone and I will go in your place, so that if I incur ridicule and lashes, better me than you." [Peah Y 1:1]

However, the Shulḥan Arukh has a word of admonition for parents. Parents should just teach children the importance of the commandment, but may not demand the honor due them:
> It is forbidden to burden your children by being particular about them honoring you. [This is so that] you will not pose a stumbling block before them, rather you should forego [your honor] and close your eyes to their actions... [Shulḥan Arukh, Yoreh Deah 240:19]

The Talmud says that parents may be rebuked, but very gently:
> Rabbi Eliezer was asked: "How far does the honor of parents [extend]"?
> If your father is transgressing a precept of the Torah, you must not say to him, "Father, you are transgressing a precept of the Torah", but... "Father, such and such a verse is written in the Torah." [Kiddushin 32a]

Does the commandment to honor parents take precedence over other commandments? The Talmud answers: Not always:
> Eleazar ben Mathia said: If my father orders me, "Give me a drink of water", while I have a commandment to perform, I disregard my father's honor and perform the commandment... [But] Issi ben Yehudah maintained: If the commandment can be performed by others, it should be performed by others, while he should bestir himself for his father's honor.
> Rabbi Mattena said: The law agrees with Issi ben Yehudah. [Kiddushin 32a]

Who are good examples of honoring parents, in our tradition? Believe it or not, it turns out the best examples are... an idolatrous Gentile and a "bad guy"!

The Mishna tells us about Damah ben Netinah, a Gentile:
> Rabbi Abbahu said: Rabbi Eliezer the Great was asked by his disciples: "Can you give a [good] example of honoring parents?" He replied: "Go and see what [the idolatrous Gentile] Damah ben Netinah of Askelon did. His mother was mentally ill and used to slap him in front of his colleagues, and all he would say was, 'Mother, it is enough!'"
> Once the Sages came to him... to buy... a precious stone for... the vestments of the [High] Priest, and they agreed... on a price of 1,000 golden pieces. He entered the house and found his father asleep with his leg stretched out on the chest containing the stone. He would not trouble him and came out empty-handed... The Sages thought he wanted a higher price, and raised their offer to 10,000 golden

pieces. When his father awoke, Dama entered and brought out the stone. The Sages wished to give him 10,000 golden pieces, but he exclaimed: "Heaven forbid! I will not make a profit out of honoring my parents. I will only take the price we agreed, 1,000 golden pieces."

And what reward did the Holy One, blessed be He, give him? Our Rabbis report that in the very same year his cow gave birth to a red heifer, which he sold for more than 10,000 golden pieces. See how great the merit of honoring father and mother is? [Deuteronomy Rabbah 1:15; also Peah Y 5b-6a]

The Torah tells us that Esau, Jacob's evil twin brother, was very solicitous towads his father Isaac. The Midrash says:

Rabbi Shim'on ben Gamliel said: No son has ever honored his parents as I have done, and yet I find that Esau honored his father even more than I. How? [He] said: I usually waited on my father dressed in soiled clothes, but when I went out into the street I discarded these clothes and put on instead handsome clothes. Not so Esau. The clothes in which he was dressed when attending on his father were his best... Hence you learn that Esau was most scrupulous in honoring his parents.
[Deuteronomy Rabbah 1:15]

The Zohar concludes:

There was not a man in the world who showed as much honor to his father as Esau did, and this is what gave him dominion in this world. [The Romans were Esau's descendants.] [Zohar, Bereshit 1:146b]

Honor your father and your mother.

Shabbat shalom.

Mishpatim
Ex. 21:1-24:18

B"H

Do not Mix Milk and Meat

In this week's Torah portion, *Mishpatim*, we are given a commandment that is repeated three times in the Torah:

לֹא־תְבַשֵּׁל גְּדִי בַּחֲלֵב אִמּוֹ

Lo tevashel g'di bachalev immo [Ex. 23:19, Ex. 34:26. Deut. 14:21]
You will not cook a kid in its mother's milk.

This commandment was interpreted to mean that using milk products and meat products together (in Hebrew: בשר בחלב *bassar be-chalav*) is not allowed. Let's explore this Jewish law in some detail and try to fathom the reasons for it.

Let's begin with a joke that summarizes the detail of the laws and addresses the fact that the injunction is repeated three times:

God says to Moses: You will not cook a kid in its mother's milk.
Moses replies: You mean we may not eat meat and dairy products together?
God says: You will not cook a kid in its mother's milk.
Moses replies: You mean we should have two sets of dishes and utensils, one for meat and one for dairy?
God says, for the third time: You will not cook a kid in its mother's milk.
Moses replies: You mean we should wait six hours after eating meat before we can eat dairy?
Then God sighs and says: Have it your way.

Actually, the Talmud interprets this triplicate commandment as meaning three different things. [Kiddushin 56b and Hullin 113b] First, do not **cook** milk and meat together. Second, do not **eat** milk and meat together. And third, do not **benefit** from a mixture of milk and meat. For example, you can't feed milk and meat to your pet. This is in contrast to non-kosher animals, from which Jews are permitted to derive benefit.

The Baal ha-Turim, 14th-century Spanish rabbi [Yaakov ben Asher, 1269- 1343], notes that the gematria of "Do not cook a kid" (לֹא־תְבַשֵּׁל גְּדִי), is the same as the gematria of "it is the prohibition of eating, cooking and deriving benefit". (In Hebrew, היא איסור אכילה ובישול והנאה -- *He issur achilah u'bishul v'hana'ah*.)

Let's look at the details. A "kid" means not only a baby goat but also a calf, or a lamb, or any tender young animal. Why? The Talmud [Hullin 113b] says that it is because, when only a baby goat is intended, the Torah says גְּדִי־עִזִּים *g'di 'izzim*, not just *g'di*. [Gen. 38:17, Gen. 38:20, Gen. 27:9]

The Talmud also interprets meat to include fowl, even though fowl do not produce milk. [Hullin 103b] This is a rabbinic prohibition (*mi-derabbanan*) due to Rabbi Akiva. However, the Rema, 16th-century Polish Rabbi Moses Isserles, ruled that one *may* derive benefit from a mixture of chicken and milk.

Meat, however, does not include fish or locusts. [Hullin 103b] So, fish and milk may be eaten together, although many Sephardic Jews avoid that mixture.

May one cook milk and meat together if one of them is from a non-kosher species? The Talmud says yes. [Hullin 113a] However, there is a dispute on the appropriateness of doing so because of *mar'it ayin,* which is doing something that may appear to be prohibited and give witnesses the wrong idea. Among the sages, the Rashba [Teshuvot 3:257] and the Rema [Yoreh Deah 87:4] say not to do it, whereas the Shakh and the Taz say it's OK to do it.

May one cook milk and meat together if the meat is from a kosher species, but was improperly slaughtered? (In Hebrew, a נְבֵלָה *nevelah*.) The matter is in dispute. The Rambam says one may do it, but the Rashba prohibits it. A practical implication is: Can you feed such a mixture to your dog?

If some milk falls accidentally in a meat dish, in a proportion of less than one part in sixty, the mixture may be eaten. One sixtieth is considered to be the threshold for being able to "taste or smell" the milk. [In Hebrew, that principle is called *batel b'shishim* -- nullified in sixty.]

Rav Moshe Soloveitchik rules that one may cook, but not eat, milk and meat together for a scientific experiment, if it yields a material benefit. [See Rabbi Hershel Schachter's *Peninei Ha-Rav*, p. 152]

Now, what are the reasons behind the prohibition of mixing milk and meat? We don't know, of course. The traditional answer is "Because God said so". But in the Talmud, Rabbi Akiva said we are enjoined to speculate on the possible reasons behind the commandments [טעמי המצוות -- *taamei ha-mitzvot*]. [Eruvin 54b] Provided, of course, we observe the commandments no matter what conclusions are reached.

One possible reason is that it is a discipline measure. Its purpose might be to introduce discipline in our lives, particularly where food is concerned, so we remember that food comes from God.

Another reason is its association with idolatry. Some idolaters of old did just that as a fertility rite. Some even sprinkled mixtures of milk and meat on fields to ensure good crop. Abravanel, the 15th-century Spanish sage, reports this was still done in his time. [Rambam, Moreh Nevukhim 3:48; Sforno; Solomon Luntschitz; Abravanel on Ex. 23:19]

Another reason is the avoidance of cruelty. The Ramban, 12th-century Spanish sage, notes that "You shall not cook a kid in its mother's milk" [Deut. 14:21] is right next to "You shall be a holy nation unto the Lord your God" in the Torah. So, the mixture is not inherently bad, but must be avoided because it is unholy and cruel. Cooking a baby in the milk that was intended to nourish it certainly sounds cruel. Sforno, 15th-century Italian sage, adds that it is an inhumane practice, akin to taking eggs from a nest while the mother bird is watching, a practice explicitly prohibited by the Torah. (In Hebrew: שילוח הקן - - *Shiluach Haken*.) [Deuteronomy 22:6, Hullin 140b, Yoreh Deah 292]

Another reason is that it is the wrong mixture of symbols. Meat symbolizes death and milk symbolizes life. The Shelah HaKadosh, 17th-century sage from Prague says that meat stems from God's attribute of justice and milk from God's attribute of mercy, and these two opposites must not be mixed.

Samson Raphael Hirsch, 19th-century German rabbi, suggests that meat is taking, and milk is giving, two opposites that must not be mixed. Some commentators assert that the mixture of milk and meat is bad for one's health, but so far no science has backed up this claim. Others say the rule was intended to set the Jews apart and make it harder for them to socialize with Gentiles.

Then there are mystical reasons, alluded to in the Sefer ha-Chinukh, the "Book of Education" from 13th-century Spain, which discusses all 613 commandments from a legal and a moral perspective.

A final reason may be that all mixtures are generally frowned upon in Judaism. [Leviticus 19:19, Deuteronomy 22:9-11] For example, there is:
- The prohibition against mixing wool and linen in clothes, called שַׁעַטְנֵז *shaatnez;*
- The prohibition against planting mixtures of seeds, grafting and crossbreeding seeds;
- The prohibition against crossbreeding animals;
- The prohibition against plowing a field using animals of different species; and
- The prohibition against combining two different occasions to celebrate, such as a wedding and a Jewish holiday.

In fact, an entire tractate of the Mishna, *Kil'ayim*, is dedicated to forbidden mixtures. It has a Gemara commentary in the Jerusalem Talmud.

So there you have it. The Jewish Zionist thinker Ahad Ha'am once said, "More than Israel has kept Shabbat has Shabbat kept Israel". He could have said that about any of the ritual commandments, such as not mixing milk and meat. They keep us together.

Shabbat shalom.

140

Terumah
Ex. 25:1-27:19

B"H

Where is God?

This week's Torah portion, *Terumah*, deals with the Israelites building the *Mishkan*, the Tabernacle. It begins with:
> The Lord spoke to Moses, saying: "Speak to the children of Israel… [and tell them to] make Me a sanctuary and I will dwell in their midst." [Exodus 25:1-2, 8]

A few chapters later, still in the Book of Exodus, God says:
> וְשָׁכַנְתִּי בְּתוֹךְ בְּנֵי יִשְׂרָאֵל וְהָיִיתִי לָהֶם לֵאלֹהִים
> And I will dwell among the Children of Israel and I will be their God. [Exodus 29:45]

What does this mean? Does God really need a place to stay? Aren't we taught that God is ubiquitous, that He is everywhere? When King Solomon built the first Temple, the *Bet Hamikdash*, the successor of the *Mishkan*, he said:
> The heavens, and the heavens above them, cannot contain You, [O God], how much less this house that I have built. [1 Kings 8:27]

The Midrash says that Moses questioned how the Almighty could dwell in the small *Mishkan*, if His Glory fills heaven and earth. God replied: I do not think as humans think… I could even confine My Presence to one square cubit. [Exodus Rabbah 34:1]

In the Talmud, God is frequently referred to as *Ha-Makom*, which means "The Place", and is translated as "The Omnipresent", indicating that God is everywhere. The Midrash says:
> Rabbi Huna said, in Rabbi Ammi's name: Why do we give a changed name to the Holy One, blessed be He, and call him *Ha-Makom* ["The Place"]? Because He is the Place of the world. [Genesis Rabbah 48:9]

This means that God is bigger than the world: The world is contained in God, but God is not contained in the world.

But the Talmud also says that God is more in certain places than in others, in the guise of the Divine Presence, the *Shechinah*, literally "the dwelling". More on that later.

Furthermore, we are taught that God does not have a body, and so cannot be localized. The second commandment forbids us from making images of God. When we sing the *Yigdal*, which recounts the Rambam's 13 principles of faith, we see that the 3rd principle is:

אֵין לוֹ דְּמוּת הַגּוּף וְאֵינוֹ גוּף -- *En lo d'mut ha-guf v'eno guf*
He has no image or body.

Yet the Bible is full of anthropomorphisms:
- May the Lord make His *face* shine upon you. [Numbers 6:25]
- God said: I will stretch forth My *hand* upon Egypt, and bring out the people of Israel… [Exodus 7:5]
- Moses received two tablets of stone, written by the *finger* of God. [Exodus 31:18]
- God said: I will redeem you with a outstretched *arm*. [Exodus 6:6]
- The *eyes* of the Lord your God are always upon the land [of Israel]. [Deuteronomy 11:12]
- Thus says the Lord: The earth is my *foot*stool. [Isaiah 66:1]
- Moses talked to God *mouth* to mouth. [Numbers 12:8]
- God saw that the wickedness of man was great in the earth...and it grieved Him in His *heart*. [Genesis 6:5-6]
- God said: And I will take away My *hand*, and you shall see My *back*, but My *face* shall not be seen. [Exodus 33:23]
- Give *ear* to my prayer, O God. [Psalms 55:2]
- With the blast of [God's] *nostrils* the waters were piled up [Exodus 15:8]

Scripture also says that God experiences love, compassion, hatred, joy, sadness, regret, anger, or jealousy.

Many commentators do not hide their discomfort with these anthropomorphisms. For example, the Talmud says:
> Rabbi Yosei stated: The Shechinah never descended to earth, nor did Moses or Elijah ever ascend to Heaven, as it is written [in the Book of Psalms, also used in Hallel]:
> הַשָּׁמַיִם שָׁמַיִם לַיהוָה וְהָאָרֶץ נָתַן לִבְנֵי־אָדָם
> *Ha-shamayim shamayim l'Hashem, v'haaretz natan livnei Adam*

> The heavens are the heavens of the Lord, but the earth He has given to the sons of men. [Psalms 115:16]
> [Sukkah 5a]

Maimonides vociferously insisted that all anthropomorphisms are allegories, and that it is downright heretical to take them literally, as some did before him. He condemned books that took this allegory too far as idolatrous. He is credited with doing away with all vestiges of anthropomorphisms in Jewish thought.

So these anthropomorphisms are there just to make the message less abstract, more personal, more understandable to us. The Talmud says:
> דברה תורה כלשון בני אדם -- *Dibrah Torah k'lashon b'nei Adam*
> The Torah speaks in the language of men. [Yevamot 71a, Sifrei Numbers 112]

-In this vein, Rashi tells us that when God says: "Make Me a sanctuary and I will dwell in their midst", He means "make a sanctuary in My name", not *for* me.

-The Shelah ha-Kadosh, 17th-century mystic, says: The verse does not say, "I will dwell in the sanctuary," but "I will dwell in their midst", meaning, I will dwell within each and every one of them, not in a building.

-The Midrash says that God really meant for us to build a special house for the Torah:
> God said to Israel: "I have given you the Torah. I cannot part with her, and I also cannot tell you not to take her. But I request this of you: Wherever you go, make a house for Me in which I may dwell." [Exodus Rabbah 33:1]

To reinforce that point, the Talmud says:
> Rabbi Hiyya ben Ammi [said] in the name of Ulla: "Since the day that the Temple was destroyed, the Holy One, blessed be He, has nothing in His world [to dwell in] except the four cubits of Jewish law alone." [Berakhot 8a]

So God will return to the Land of Israel only when the Temple is rebuilt. That's why the 17th blessing of the Amidah says:
> וְתֶחֱזֶינָה עֵינֵינוּ בְּשׁוּבְךָ לְצִיּוֹן בְּרַחֲמִים: בָּרוּךְ אַתָּה יְהֹוָה הַמַּחֲזִיר שְׁכִינָתוֹ לְצִיּוֹן
> May our eyes behold your return to Zion in mercy!

Blessed are You, O God, who returns His Divine Presence to Zion.

So now God dwells in Jewish law. Where else does God dwell?

-God is present when people pray together. The Talmud says:
>Whenever ten are gathered for prayer, there the Shechinah rests. [Sanhedrin 39a]

-God is present when a court gives a righteous judgment. The Talmud says:
>When three sit as judges, the Shechinah is with them. [Berakhot 6a]

-God is present when people need healing. The Talmud says:
>The Shechinah dwells over the head of the sick man's bed. [Shabbat 12b]

-God is present with Israel in exile. The Talmud says:
>Wherever they were exiled, the Shechinah went with them. [Megillah 29a]

This echoes what Joshua told Israel before they entered the Holy Land:
>חֲזַק וֶאֱמָץ אַל־תַּעֲרֹץ וְאַל־תֵּחָת כִּי עִמְּךָ יְהוָה אֱלֹהֶיךָ בְּכֹל אֲשֶׁר תֵּלֵךְ
>*Hazzak ve-ematz* -- Be strong and of good courage. Do not be afraid, and do not be dismayed, for the Lord your God is with you wherever you go. [Joshua 1:9]

-God is with those who mourn the dead. The traditional formula for comforting mourners is:
>המקום ינחם אתכם בתוך שאר אבלי ציון וירושלים
>*HaMakom y'nachem etchem b'toch she-ar aveley Tzion v'Yerushalayim.*
>May God comfort you among the mourners of Zion and Jerusalem!

Note that here God is referred to as "The Place." People who have lost loved ones often feel that God has abandoned them. So we remind them that God is also standing where they are standing.

-God is in the smallest and most insignificant places. In the Book of Kings, the prophet Elijah, *Eliahu HaNavi,* is told to go to Mount Sinai, where the Torah was revealed:
>...and a great and strong wind tore the mountains, and broke the rocks in pieces...
>But the Lord was not in the wind.
>And after the wind an earthquake; but the Lord was not in the earthquake.
>And after the earthquake a fire; but the Lord was not in the fire.

And after the fire a still small voice... and [there was the Lord, and He] said, "What are you doing here, Elijah?" [1 Kings 19:11-12]

So where is God *not* to be found? The Talmud says:
> The Divine Presence does not rest upon people through gloom, nor through laziness, nor through silliness, nor through levity, nor through talk, nor through idle chatter, but only through a matter of joy in connection with a commandment, as it is said [in the Book of Kings]:
>> [And Elisha said:] ... Bring me a minstrel. And it came to pass, that when the minstrel played, the hand of the Lord came upon him." [2 Kings 3:15]
>
> [Shabbat 30b]

The Kotzker Rebbe, 19th-century Hassidic sage, said, "God is only where you let Him in." He was reportedly only five years old when he said this!

So we can conclude that, although God Himself said we can't really understand, God is "more likely", as it were, to be found wherever Jews follow commandments, or are in distress, or do things of which God approves. This brings to mind the modern theory of quantum mechanics, where presence anywhere is a matter of probability!

I usually don't like to end on a light note, but this one was too good to pass up:
> God is in Coke: He's the real thing.
> God is in Bayer Aspirin: He works miracles.
> God is in Hallmark Cards: He cares enough to send His very best.
> God is in General Electric: He brings good things to life.
> God is in Walmart: He has everything.
> God is in Delta Airlines: He's ready when you are.
> God is in Allstate Insurance: You're in good hands with Him.
> God is in Dial Soap: Aren't you glad you have Him?
> God is in a De Beers diamond: He is forever.
> God is in Maxwell House coffee: Good to the last drop.
> God is in the American Express card: Don't leave home without Him.
> God is in the Energizer Bunny: He keeps going and going and going.
> God is in the US Postal Service: Neither snow, nor rain, nor heat, nor gloom of night stays Him from the swift completion of His self-appointed rounds.

Shabbat shalom.

Tetzaveh
Ex. 27:20-30:10

B"H

Of Jews and Olives

This week's Torah portion, *Tetzaveh*, begins with instructions for the kindling of the menorah in the Tabernacle:

> וְאַתָּה תְּצַוֶּה | אֶת־בְּנֵי יִשְׂרָאֵל וְיִקְחוּ אֵלֶיךָ שֶׁמֶן זַיִת זָךְ כָּתִית לַמָּאוֹר לְהַעֲלֹת נֵר תָּמִיד:
> You shall further command the Israelites to bring to you pure oil from crushed olives for lighting, for kindling lamps continually. [Ex. 27:20]

Only olive oil must be used, not any other kind. Why?

The Jewish people are frequently compared to olives. The prophet Jeremiah compares Israel to an olive tree:
> The Lord has called you a leafy olive tree, beautiful, with choice fruit. [Jer. 11:16]

In the same vein, King David writes in the Book of Psalms:
> -But as for me, I am like a green olive tree in the house of God. I trust in the lovingkindness of God forever and ever. [Ps. 52:8]
> -When you eat the labor of your hands, you shall be happy, and it shall be well with you. Your wife shall be like a fruitful vine in the very heart of your house, your children like olive plants all around your table. [Ps. 128:1-4]

Why this analogy? The Talmud, Midrash and other sources find many reasons for it.

First, olives must be squeezed hard to yield their oil. Likewise, the Jews must be beaten, oppressed and persecuted before they repent and release their full potential of strength and wisdom for the benefit of the world. [Menaḥot 53b, Ex. R. 36:1]

Second, an olive is first bitter, then tasty. Likewise, the Jews suffer now, but will enjoy great good in the World to Come. [Midrash Pitron Torah to Num. 13:2]

Third, oil does not mix with other liquids. Likewise, the Jews are unique and separate from all other nations. [Ex. R. 36:1] In the Torah, the Gentile prophet Balaam says:
> [Israel] is a nation that will dwell alone, and will not be reckoned among the nations. [Num. 23:8-10]

Fourth, oil is always on top of other liquids. Likewise, the Jews are the chosen people and will always be morally guiding the world if they follow the Torah. [Ex. R. 36:1] Indeed, the Torah says:
> Now, if you obey the Lord your God and observe faithfully all of His commandments... [He] will set you high above all the nations of the earth. [Deut. 28:1]

Fifth, oil provides light. So do the Jews, giving the light of Torah to the world. [Ex. R. 36:1] The prophet Isaiah says:
> -And nations shall walk by your light. [Is. 60:3]
> -I [God] will give you as ... a light to the nations. [Is. 42:6]

Sixth, oil spreads on anything it is poured on. So do the Jews: They spread all over the world, usually out of necessity, and are always curious and eager to acquire new knowledge.

Seventh, the leaves of the olive tree do not fall off. Likewise, the Jews will never be cast off, neither in this world nor in the World to Come. [Menaḥot 53b] Also, Jews remain Jews when times are hard.

Eighth, the olive branch is a symbol of peace. Likewise, the Jews are not warlike. The Torah says that when you must wage war, you must first propose a peaceful settlement to the enemy. [Deut. 20:10]

Ninth, the olive tree is a survivor. Even in difficult terrain, it can last as much as 1,500 years. On average, it lasts 500 years. Likewise, the Jews have survived much and are here to stay.

Some questions come to mind. First, how can Jews spread the light if they do not mix with non-Jews? The Maharal of Prague, 16th-century scholar, said that non-Jews are like water, whereas Jews are like fire. [Netzach Yisrael, Ch. 25] Indeed, the psalmist says:
> Release me and rescue me from great waters, from the hand of strangers. [Ps. 144:7]

Also, the Torah says:
> God came from Sinai ... and presented the fiery Torah to them with his right hand. [Deut. 33:2]

When fire and water mix, the water extinguishes the fire -- unless there is a barrier between them. Only with that barrier can the fire heat up the water and bring it to a boil. The same is true with the Jews and the nations. Our mission is to heat up and ignite the world with a passion for God and His moral laws. We can only do this if we remain separate from our neighbors. If we remove the barrier, our fire will be extinguished by the waters of assimilation and we will fail in our mission to bring light to the nations.

Second, does antisemitism preserve Judaism? As we saw, the Midrash said that Jews must be oppressed before they yield their wisdom, just as olives must be squeezed hard to yield their oil. [Ex. R. 36:1] Is the pressure of persecution what motivates Jews to excel, to "show" the world? Note that Jews do not welcome suffering. The Talmud says:
> Rabbi Yoḥanan fell ill.
> Rabbi Ḥanina entered to visit him, and said to him: Is your suffering dear to you?
> [Rabbi Yoḥanan] replied: [I welcome] neither [suffering] nor its reward.
> [Berakhot 5b]

A convincing case can be made that antisemitism helps preserve Judaism. This is the subject of another presentation.

Shabbat shalom.

Ki Tisa
Ex. 30:11-34:35

B"H

The Quest for Knowledge in Judaism

In this week's portion, *Ki Tisa*, God decides to forgive Israel for the sin of the Golden Calf, after hearing a plea from Moses. God assures Moses that His presence will accompany Israel in their trek across the desert. But Moses is not satisfied. He wants more. The Torah says:
> And Moses said to God: "I beg you, if I have found favor in your sight, show me now your way, that I may know you... Show me your glory..."
> And God said: "I will make all my goodness pass before you, I will proclaim My name before you; and I will be gracious and show mercy to whom I please... But You may not see my face; for no man shall see me and live... You shall see my back; but my face shall not be seen." [Ex. 33:13-23]

Why not? What are we talking about here? First, does God have a face? That's not a Jewish concept. Even if so, is this face so terrifying that people die just from looking at it? Does it radiate so much light that people go blind and die when they see it? Surely not. There must be a figurative meaning here. Is the resulting "death" a punishment? Is it an automatic consequence? Is it a self-fulfilling prophecy?

I believe Moses is puzzled by this deity he cannot comprehend. He wants answers to ultimate questions. What is God's plan? What are God's motives? Why does evil exist? Moses wants knowledge. But God does not want to reveal this knowledge. God said he would drop hints -- his "presence", his "goodness", his "back" -- but will not give straight answers.

A similar theme is picked up in the Book of Job. Job criticizes God for all the undeserved catastrophes that descended on him, and asks the same questions. God answers these questions with other questions, in an extraordinary passage taking up 103 verses. God's questions merely expose Job's ignorance of God's plans, but provide no answers. Here is a sample:

> God answered Job out of the whirlwind and said: [Job 38:1]
> Where were you when I laid the foundations of the earth? [Job 38:4]
> Tell me, if you know, who determined its boundaries? [Job 38:5]
> What were those foundations attached to? [Job 38:6]
> Do you know what happens after death? [Job 38:17]
> Did you go inside the earth? Tell me, if you know it all. [Job 38:18]
> Come on, you are old enough to know. [Job 38:21]
> Where does the rain come from? [Job 38:28]
> And the ice? [Job 38:29]
> Can you shoot lightning bolts? [Job 38:35]
> Do you think you can just nullify my judgments, condemn me, and justify yourself? [Job 40:8]

This is what it says, verbatim! Yet Jews have always valued the pursuit of knowledge in all its forms. Education is always uppermost on the Jewish agenda. Einstein once said,
> The pursuit of knowledge for its own sake, an almost fanatical love of justice, and the desire for personal independence -- these are features of the Jewish tradition that make me [happy] I belong to it. [Albert Einstein, The World As I See It]

When I was growing up in Egypt, my father, a man of modest means, worked very hard to send his children to the best private schools. He used to say, "The Arabs can take everything from you -- your money, your house, your possessions, even the shirt on your back. But there is one thing they cannot take, and that's what's inside your head." Sure enough, they did take everything, and I survived with what my father arranged to have put inside my head.

The traditional morning prayer asks God:
> חָנֵּנוּ מֵאִתְּךָ דֵּעָה בִּינָה וְהַשְׂכֵּל -- *Channenu me'itcha de'ah, bina, v'haskel*
> Grant us knowledge, understanding, discernment.

We are always thirsty for more knowledge. So how can knowledge be bad?

Well, the Sources seem to say that, indeed, there are things we are not meant to know and should not inquire about.

Let's begin with the story of creation, in Genesis:

> -And God commanded the man saying, "Of every tree of the garden you may freely eat; but of the tree of knowledge of good and evil you shall not eat, for in the day you eat of it you will surely die." [Gen. 2:16-17]
>
> -[But] the snake said to the woman, "You will not surely die! God knows that when you eat of it, your eyes will be opened, and you will be as gods, knowing good and evil." [Gen. 3:4]
>
> -And God said, "Now that the man has become like one of us, knowing good and evil, what if he should stretch out his hand and take also from the tree of life and eat, and live forever!" Therefore God banished him from the Garden of Eden... and placed at the east of the Garden of Eden cherubim, and a flaming ever-turning sword, to guard the way to the tree of life. [Gen. 3:22-24]

So there is knowledge that God does not want us to have yet. God does not want us to be like Him.

Later, in Deuteronomy, the Torah says:
> הַנִּסְתָּרֹת--לַיהוָה, אֱלֹהֵינוּ; וְהַנִּגְלֹת לָנוּ וּלְבָנֵינוּ, עַד-עוֹלָם--לַעֲשׂוֹת, אֶת-כָּל-דִּבְרֵי הַתּוֹרָה הַזֹּאת
> Ha-nistarot l'Hashem elokenu, v'ha-niglot lanu ulvanenu 'ad 'olam la'asot et kol divrei hattorah hazzot
> The secret things belong to the Lord our God and the revealed things belong to us and to our children forever that we may follow all the words of this teaching.
> [Deuteronomy 29:28]

In an unusual flourish for emphasis, the words "For us and our children" include extra dots above each letter on the scroll.

The psalmist says:
> The heavens belong to the Lord, but the earth He gave over to man. [Ps. 115:16]

Ecclesiastes says:

> As you do not know the path of the wind, or how the body is formed in a mother's womb, so you cannot understand the work of God, the Maker of all things.
> [Ecclesiastes 11:5]

The Mishnah has similar admonitions:
> One should not discuss illegal unions unless there were three beside him,
> nor the creation unless there were two beside him,
> nor the divine chariot with [only] one individual, unless he was a wise man and had much knowledge of his own.
> Everyone who tries to know the following four things, it would have been better for him if he had never come into the world: What is above, what is below, what was before [creation], and what will be after [all is destroyed]. [Hagigah 2.1 -- 11b]

The Gemara quotes the apocryphal book of Ben Sira:
> Do not seek out the things that are too hard for you, and do not inquire in the things that are hidden from you. Instruct yourself in what is permitted. You have no business with the secret things. [Hagigah 13a; Ecclesiasticus 3:21-22]

The Talmud [Hagigah 14b] records the story of four rabbis who ventured into mysticism. Ben Azzai gazed and died. Ben Zoma became insane. Elisha ben Avuyah left Judaism and became an apostate. Only Akiva emerged unscathed, and went on to become one of the greatest rabbis in our history. On Ben Zoma becoming mad, the Talmud [Hagigah 14b] applies this quote from the Book of Proverbs to him:

> דְּבַשׁ מָצָאתָ אֱכֹל דַּיֶּךָּ פֶּן־תִּשְׂבָּעֶנּוּ וַהֲקֵאתוֹ:
> Have you found honey? Eat only as much as is enough for you, lest you consume too much of it and have to vomit it out. [Proverbs 25:16]

What do we make of all these passages?

One possibility is that God does not want us to suffer. God is withholding certain knowledge out of concern for our welfare. I can accept that, even though it's not clear to me what kind of knowledge could possibly cause me to suffer. (I am a physicist. How can anything be weirder than quantum mechanics or relativity?) Actually, it's not knowledge *itself* that God wants to shield us against, but *premature* knowledge of things we are not psychologically prepared to know. And the "premature" part applies to the individual, not to humanity as a whole. Note that the Talmud says, "It would have been better *for him* if he had not come into the world". The key part is *"for him"*.

In the same vein, when God is concerned that people might live forever, it may be because it would not be good *for people* to live forever. It is easy to figure out why: If we lived forever, we would have very little incentive to achieve anything, since there is always a tomorrow; and besides, young people would never get a chance to make progress by trying out new ideas, if their elders stay in charge forever.

But, if so, as we pursue knowledge, how do we know what's permitted and what's not? How do we know if we are ready or not? The tradition drops some hints. For example, the Talmud says:
> A five-year-old begins Scripture; a ten-year-old begins Mishnah; a 13-year-old becomes obliged to observe the commandments; a 15-year-old begins the study of Gemara; an 18-year-old goes to the marriage canopy; a 20-year-old begins pursuit [of a livelihood]; a 30-year-old attains full strength; a 40-year-old attains understanding; a 50-year-old can offer counsel... [Avot 5:25]

But still, that answer is incomplete.

A second possibility, as some commentators have suggested, is that we may physically not be able to understand certain things -- that we are just not smart enough. They say, "Can a monkey understand the theory of relativity?" I reject this view most emphatically, for three reasons:

-First, even if it's true, we cannot possibly know that it's true. We don't know the limits of our mind.

-Second, God did give us a mind. So God must want us to use it and *try* to understand. God also gave us the gift of curiosity. We *want to* know. It may take us 100 years or 10,000 years, but, as a scientist, I have faith that we will continue to understand more and more of the universe around us. Anything less is a defeatist attitude.

-Third, if that's the explanation, then God is just admonishing us against wasting our time, which doesn't seem to square with the urgency of the command to avoid certain lines of inquiry.

A third possibility is that God may fear that if we understood the Divine Plan, we could intentionally mess it up. Its success depends on us being ignorant of its details. That's the predominant feeling *I* get from reading these quotes, and this explanation may be right on the money.

What do we conclude from all this? Well, the world has always been leery of new knowledge, for the same reason change of any kind is not always welcome among people who feel reasonably satisfied. The new knowledge can be used for good or for evil. The new knowledge has given us the information explosion (through the Internet) as well as weapons of mass destruction. Judaism teaches that all knowledge is good, but only when you are ready for it. Unfortunately, it does not make it easy for us to determine *when* that is.

Shabbat shalom.

Vayakhel
Ex. 35:1-38:20

B"H

The Shabbat Goy

In this week's Torah portion, *Vayakhel*, we are reminded, again, to observe Shabbat:

שֵׁשֶׁת יָמִים תֵּעָשֶׂה מְלָאכָה וּבַיּוֹם הַשְּׁבִיעִי יִהְיֶה לָכֶם קֹדֶשׁ שַׁבַּת שַׁבָּתוֹן לַיהוָה
לֹא־תְבַעֲרוּ אֵשׁ בְּכֹל מֹשְׁבֹתֵיכֶם בְּיוֹם הַשַּׁבָּת

On six days work may be done, but on the seventh day you will observe a Shabbat of complete rest, holy to the Lord.
You shall kindle no fire throughout your habitations on Shabbat. [Ex. 35:2-3]

Earlier, it was made clear the prohibition extended to everybody, including animals:

לֹא־תַעֲשֶׂה כָל־מְלָאכָה אַתָּה ׀ וּבִנְךָ־וּבִתֶּךָ עַבְדְּךָ וַאֲמָתְךָ וּבְהֶמְתֶּךָ וְגֵרְךָ אֲשֶׁר בִּשְׁעָרֶיךָ

You shall not do any work [on Shabbat] -- you, your son, your daughter, your male slave, your female slave, your cattle, or the stranger who is within your settlements. [Ex. 20:10]

Yet, in spite of this, a tradition developed in Eastern Europe to hire a Gentile to do prohibited work on Shabbat. He is known as the שבת גוי "Shabbat goy" or "Gentile for Shabbat".

Famous examples are Russian writer Maxim Gorky, President Harry Truman, Secretary Colin Powell, Governor Mario Cuomo, film producer Martin Scorsese, and even famous singer Elvis Presley.

Does Jewish law allow this practice? Generally, no. The Code of Jewish Law specifically allows it for heating a house in extremely cold weather, because it may be a matter of life or death, in which case most commandments may be broken:

> It is permitted for a Gentile to make a fire [for Jews on Shabbat] ... when it is extremely cold, because everyone is at risk of catching a cold. [Shulḥan Arukh, Orach Chayim 276:5]

This was particularly important in Eastern Europe, where temperatures could dip very low in winter, whence the institution of the practice. It was allowed even when the cold was uncomfortable, but not a threat to life. The Shabbat goy would visit Jewish houses on Shabbat to add wood to the source of heat. Rabbi Moshe Feinstein [Igrot Moshe 3:42] also allows it when it is very hot, but not all agree with him.

Today, central heating, timers and thermostats have removed the need for the Shabbat goy.

But one may ask: If it is permitted for a Gentile, why is it not permitted for a Jew? It is, but only if a life is at stake, not just for comfort. [Shulḥan Arukh, Orach Chayim 328:17]

It is also allowed when great monetary loss might ensue, such as a fire in a house or place of business on Shabbat:

> If you are threatened with a loss -- for instance, if a barrel of wine has sprung a leak -- you may call in a non-Jew... provided you carefully avoid talking to him in a way that sounds like a request to repair it. You may say in his presence [but not *to* him]: "Whoever will save me from this loss, will not lose anything". [Kitzur Shulḥan Arukh 90:16]

The Ohr HaChaim, from 18th-century Morocco, in commenting on our verse, writes:

> The Torah may also wish to remind us that performance of work on Shabbat is prohibited whether performed by a Jew or by a Gentile on his behalf. The word לֹא־תֵעָשֶׂה *lo taaseh*, "[work] shall not be done", is in the passive form, which means that, whereas it is permissible for a Jew to have his work performed by Gentiles during the week, on Shabbat his work must not be performed at all by anybody.

In all other cases, it is generally prohibited to use a Shabbat goy, even if he works for free, even if he was hired before Shabbat. If he works on his own accord, or if someone else hires him, the Jew must protest and try to stop him.

If he fails, he may benefit from that work only after Shabbat is over. This is so even if the work is done far from the Jew's house.

A Jew may not have Gentile employees work at his place of business on Shabbat. However, if he has a Gentile *partner*, the latter may run the business as he sees fit on Shabbat.

However, a Gentile is allowed to do the work if paid by the job, without specifying when the job must be done. Example: cars or appliances sent out to be repaired. A Jew may not insist that the work not be done on Shabbat.

If a Gentile does prohibited work for his own purposes, a Jew may benefit from it. The Mishnah says:
> If a Gentile kindled a lamp [on Shabbat for his own benefit], a Jew may use its light ... [If a Gentile] drew water [from a well in the public domain] to give his animal to drink, a Jew may give [his own animal] to drink after him [from the same water]... If a Gentile made a ramp [on Shabbat] to disembark from a ship, a Jew may disembark after him...
> However, if the Gentile knows [the Jew], it is prohibited, [because he may have intended to benefit the Jew as well]. [Shabbat 122a]

The rule is simple: No work by or for Jews on Shabbat, except in rare cases.

Shabbat shalom.

Pekudei
Ex. 38:21-40:38

B"H

Should you Care What Others Think?

This week's Torah portion is *Pekudei* -- "Accountings". It is a detailed balance sheet. We learn exactly how Moses responsibly directed the use of every single item to build the Tabernacle:

> All the gold that was used for the work, in all the work of the sanctuary -- the elevation offering of gold -- came to 29 talents and 730 shekels by the sanctuary weight. The silver of those of the community who were recorded came to 100 talents and 1,775 shekels by the sanctuary weight: a half-shekel a head, half a shekel by the sanctuary weight, for each one who was entered in the records, from the age of twenty years up, 603,550 men. The 100 talents of silver were for casting the sockets of the sanctuary and the sockets for the curtain, 100 sockets to the 100 talents, a talent a socket. [Exodus 38:24-27]

Moses wanted everything to be transparent, above-board and in the open, so as to be beyond suspicion. He was applying the Jewish principle of מַרְאִית עַיִן -- *Marit Ayin*, literally: "Appearance to the eye".

Marit Ayin means that some permitted behavior is prohibited because it may appear to casual observers to be something prohibited. This would cause them to assume it is permitted, or, if they know it isn't, cause them to think ill of the one doing it.

One's behavior should not only be beyond reproach, but beyond suspicion as well. The Mishnah says:

> It is one's duty to *seem* to be free of blame before others as before God. As the Torah says:
>
> וִהְיִיתֶם נְקִיִּים מֵיְהוָה וּמִיִּשְׂרָאֵל
>
> And you shall be innocent before the Lord *and before Israel*. [Numbers 32:22]
>
> and the Book of Proverbs says:

וּמְצָא־חֵן וְשֵׂכֶל־טוֹב בְּעֵינֵי אֱלֹהִים וְאָדָם

And you will find favor and good understanding in the eyes of God *and of man*. [Proverbs 3:4]
[Shekalim 3:2]

Commentators have said it is far easier to fulfill the first half than the second. Obituaries in newspapers frequently say something like: "He found a cure for cancer but he was once convicted of jaywalking." Post one ambiguous picture on Facebook and your life may quickly change for the worse.

Here are some examples of actions that may carry the *appearance* of wrongdoing:

-Going into a non-kosher restaurant to buy something kosher, like a cup of coffee.
-Eating a cheeseburger in which either the cheese or the meat is fake.
-Eating fake treif, such as bacon bits or shrimp look-alikes, etc.
-Putting fake cream in coffee after meat meal.
-Going in a non-kosher butchery to buy bones for a dog.
-Eating Passover food that appears to be ḥametz. (For Ashkenazim, this includes kitniyot -- rice, corn, legumes, etc.)
-Doing these things while wearing a kippah (showing you are an observant Jew who knows the law).
-Some traditionalist rabbis even rule that a Jew should not enter a non-traditional synagogue when people there are praying, so as not to make it appear he agrees with their interpretations of Judaism.

The Talmud gives many examples:

-Do not recite the Ten Commandments during services, because heretics might claim they are the only commandments in force. [Berakhot 12a; Mishnah 5:1 in Tamid 32b]

-Do not hang up wet clothes on Shabbat, because people might think they were washed that day. [Shabbat 65a; Shulḥan Arukh, Orach Ḥayyim 301:45]

-If you are an official going into the Temple treasury, go barefoot and wear clothes with no pockets or folds, to make it clear you cannot hide any money. [Shekalim 3:2]

-If your house has two doors, light Hanukkah candles at both, so that if a passer-by sees one door but not the other, he should not think you did not fulfill the commandment. [Shabbat 23a]

-Especially if you are from a prominent family, punctiliously avoid behavior that might bring suspicion on your family:
> The Garmu family excelled in preparing the shewbread [for the Temple]... but they also never made fancy bread in their homes, so that people would not say that they sustained themselves from their art of preparing the shewbread [with ingredients that belonged to the Temple]...
> Similarly, the Avtinas family excelled in preparing incense [for the Temple]... but a perfumed bride never emerged from their homes, and when they married a woman from a different place, they stipulated with her that she will not perfume herself, so that cynics would not say that it is with the [Temple's] incense that they perfumed themselves.
> They [both] fulfilled that which is stated in the Torah:
>> And you shall be guiltless before the Lord and before Israel. [Numbers 32:22]
> [Yoma 38a]

-Do not serve fish blood in a serving bowl, because it might get confused with animal blood. The first is kosher, the second not. [Keritot 21b] Based on this, the Rashba prohibits cooking meat in human milk, even though human milk is pareve; and the Rama prohibits cooking meat in almond milk because it looks like cow's milk (unless you leave pieces of almond in the milk).

-Avoid even the appearance of idolatry. Maimonides writes:
> One who had a splinter stuck in his foot and he happens to be before an idol, should not bow down to take out because it will appear that he is bowing down to it.
> [Rambam, Mishneh Torah, Foreign Worship and Customs of the Nations 3:7]

One cannot help the feeling that the Sages always assumed that the average passer-by has the IQ of a cauliflower! ☺

Does *Marit Ayin* apply in private? Yes. The Talmud says:

אָמַר רַב יְהוּדָה אָמַר רַב: כָּל מָקוֹם שֶׁאָסְרוּ חֲכָמִים מִפְּנֵי מַרְאִית הָעַיִן — אֲפִילוּ בְּחַדְרֵי חֲדָרִים אָסוּר.

Rav Yehudah said that Rav said: Wherever the Sages prohibited an action due to the appearance of a prohibition; it is prohibited even in the innermost chambers, where no one will see it. [Shabbat 64b, Avodah Zarah 12a, Shabbat 146b; Shulḥan Arukh, Orach Ḥayyim 301:45]

Presumably this means that he might get so used to doing it that he would do it in public. Or, that he *thinks* he is not seen, but in reality somebody is watching. Some say it depends on conditions. The Talmud Yerushalmi presents it as a dispute [Kilayim 9:1].

Does *Marit Ayin* apply in front of ignorant Jews? No. For example, most locusts are kosher. But most Jews don't know that and assume they are insects, hence unkosher. The practice is not to refrain from eating them because of *Marit Ayin*. [Moshe Feinstein, Igrot Moshe Orach Ḥayyim 1:96; 4:82]

-Once applied, does *Marit Ayin* apply eternally? No. Prohibitions may get cancelled over time as people get used to new products or actions. [Shulḥan Arukh, Orach Ḥayyim 243:2] For example, non-dairy creamers are so common today that using them after a meat meal is no longer prohibited. Also, the Torah [Deut. 22:11] forbids wearing a mixture of wool and linen (שַׁעַטְנֵז -- shaatnez). The Mishnah [Kilayim 9:2-3] ruled that combining wool and silk was allowed, yet later rabbis forbade it due to *Marit Ayin*. Later still, it was allowed again [Shulḥan Arukh Yoreh Deah 298:1] because silk had become so common that it was easily recognizable.

The Mishnah says that Jews are supposed to practice דָן אֶת כָּל הָאָדָם לְכַף זְכוּת *dan l'khaf zekhut* [Avot 1:6] -- giving people the benefit of the doubt, judging them favorably [Leviticus 19:15], not thinking ill of them, but rather advising them as needed. [Shevuot 30a] Maimonides says that if you see someone you don't know do something that can be interpreted as good or bad, assume it's good. [Rambam on Avot 1:6] This softens one of the two reasons of *Marit Ayin*: Others might think ill of you.

In conclusion, you may not ignore what others will think of your actions, because their contempt might hurt you, or, most importantly, they may think your seemingly inappropriate behavior is something they should emulate. Because human nature makes one prone to suspect others, the principle of *Marit Ayin* is needed.

Shabbat shalom.

Vayikra
Lev. 1:1-5:26

B"H

Do Bad Thoughts Break Commandments?

In this week's Torah portion, *Vayikra*, we begin the Book of Leviticus. It gives details about the various animal sacrifices the Israelites had to bring to the Temple in biblical times. It opens with the *'olah,* or "burnt offering", the original holocaust. It is completely burned on the altar, and none of it can be eaten by anyone, unlike other sacrifices. *'Olah* comes from the root *ayin-lamed-heh,* which means "ascension". The word *aliyah* has the same root, and means moving "up" to Israel or going "up" to the bimah to read from the Torah. The *'olah* sacrifice represents a desire to commune with God and submit to His will.

The Talmud and the Midrash explain that the *olah* is brought to atone for sinful thoughts or *hirhur halev* [Shim'on Bar Yochai in Vayikra R. 7:3; Yoma Y 8:7, 45b]. So, apparently, sinful thoughts require divine forgiveness. Indeed, on Yom Kippur, we ask God's forgiveness for the 44 sins in the Ashkenazic list, the *Al chet,* one of which is sinful thoughts:

עַל חֵטְא שֶׁחָטָאנוּ לְפָנֶיךָ בְּהַרְהוֹר הַלֵּב
Al chet shechatanu lefanecha b'harhor ha-lev.
For the sin that we have committed before You by sinful thoughts.

The Midrash draws a distinction between "sin" and "sinful thought". A "sin" is a bad action and is prohibited, but a "sinful thought" is not a sin:
> Our Sages taught: The burnt offering is completely holy, because it was not brought for sins... but rather for thoughts of the heart. [Tanḥuma Tzav 13:13]

There are other references to avoiding bad thoughts in Jewish lore. The Shulḥan Arukh, or Code of Jewish Law, tells us that when you put on tefillin in the morning, you must be careful to avoid thinking about women. [Orach Ḥayyim, Siman 38] The Rema adds that if you can't help yourself, it's better not to put on tefillin at all. You are not allowed to think about the Torah in the bathroom. [Orach Hayyim, Siman 85] On Shabbat, you should not think about work matters. [Orach Hayyim, Siman 306] On Tisha b'Av, you should not think about studying Torah. [Orach Hayyim, Siman 554] The Talmud says that everybody commits these three transgressions every day: Sinful thoughts, expecting immediate results from prayer, and slander. [Bava Batra 164b]

All this may come as a surprise to many. After all, we are taught that Judaism is a religion of action, not a religion of thought or belief. It is a religion of deed, not of creed. We are judged by what we do, not by what we think. Our mind is our last refuge, and should be inviolable. Our thoughts are private and cause no harm. Some even say that fantasies should be encouraged, and are a sign of a healthy mind.

The Talmud says:
> הרהורי עבירה קשו מעבירה -- *Hirhurei 'averah kashu me'averah.* [Yoma 29a]

What does it mean? The word *kasheh* means "hard". So literally, it says:
> Sinful thoughts are harder than sin.

But "harder" in what sense? Some translate it as:
> Sinful thoughts are worse than sin.

This implies that merely thinking about transgressing commandments is a worse offense than actually transgressing them! Others translate it as:
> Sinful thoughts are more difficult than sin.

This implies only that it is more difficult to stop yourself from having bad thoughts than to stop yourself from acting on them.

Rashi adopts the second translation: Ridding yourself of bad thoughts is more difficult than stopping yourself from committing bad actions. And this extra difficulty brings a greater reward, because the Mishnah teaches:
> The reward for doing a good deed is in proportion to its difficulty. [Avot 5:26]

Maimonides, on the other hand, adopts the first translation: Sinful thoughts are a worse offense than the sin itself! In his *Guide for the Perplexed*, he writes:

> If a person sins, it is... due to his animal side. But thoughts are the treasure of a person. [They distinguish him from animals]... So if someone sins with his thoughts, then he sins with his greatest asset ... [because] the purpose of the mind is to cling to God, not to slip below [to the animal level]. [Rambam, Guide for the Perplexed 3:8]

How do we reconcile these two positions: (1) Bad thoughts are sinful and require atonement; and (2) You can't help your thoughts and must not be punished for them? In the standard Jewish fashion: By saying "You are right" and "You are right"!

Here is how the Talmud resolves it:
> [There is no punishment for mere intention to commit evil], for it is said [in the Book of Psalms]:
>> If I saw iniquity in my heart, The Lord would not hear. [Ps. 66:18]
>
> When intention [is followed by action] the Holy One, blessed be He, combines it with the action [and punishes both]. When intention [is not followed by action] the Holy One, blessed be He, does not combine it with the action [and there is therefore no punishment.] [Kiddushin 40a]

Here is what is particularly artful in this teaching. On the one hand, the rabbis could not very well say that bad thoughts are punished, because Judaism is clearly a religion of action, and not one of thought or belief. But on the other hand, they are reluctant to allow unbridled bad thoughts. If you go off in a corner and fantasize about doing terrible things to someone you don't like, it is very unhealthy. So the rabbis steer us away from it by warning us that, if bad thoughts are followed by bad actions, the punishment will be both for the thoughts and the action. In other words, you will get extra punishment just for the bad thoughts. But if *all* you have is the bad thoughts, there is no punishment. However, there is still a need to repent for having them, because they are unhealthy. This insightful teaching takes human nature into account, as the Talmud always does.

Also, there is no denying that our thoughts influence our attitude and our actions. Research into new drugs routinely shows that many patients get better when they think they are getting a revolutionary miracle drug, when in fact they are only getting a placebo with no medicine in it. A recent *Scientific American* article, entitled "Your Thoughts Can Release Abilities beyond Normal Limits", reports on the results of many studies along these lines. [Ozgun Atasoy, 13 August 2013]

So, to conclude: Evil thoughts *are* wrong, but not punished, and there is no commandment to refrain from having them. Such a commandment would, at any rate, be impossible to follow, and the Torah itself says that it does not command us to do anything we can't do. The Torah has four punishments for transgressions: Execution, flogging, fines, and shunning (note: no jail), and none apply here. Nevertheless, we must try hard, for our own sake, to avoid having evil thoughts, and it is proper that we should apologize on Yom Kippur for having them. The Sages say that the antidote to bad thoughts is the study of Torah. [Shim'on bar Yochai, Tanna d'Bei Eliyahu Zuta 16]

Shabbat shalom.

Tzav
Lev. 6:1-8:36

B"H

Thanksgiving

In this week's Torah portion, *Tzav*, we learn the details of the sacrifices. In particular, we learn about the *Korban Todah*, or Thanksgiving Offering, a form of the *Zevach Sh'lamim*, or Peace Offering:

> [He shall] offer, along with the thanksgiving offering, unleavened loaves mixed with oil, unleavened wafers anointed with oil, and cakes of choice flour with oil mixed in, well soaked... along with loaves of leavened bread... And the flesh of his... offering shall be eaten on the day it is offered up. He shall not leave any of it over until morning. [Lev. 7:12-15]

The Thanksgiving Offering is different from other sacrifices in three respects:

First, it's not just meat. It is a full meal that includes loaves, wafers, cakes, etc.

Second, you must eat everything, like a good boy, right after the offering. And there is a lot to eat. The Talmud says that ten loaves of each of the four types must be brought, for a total of *forty* loaves. [Menahot 77b]

Abravanel, the 15th-century Spanish commentator, concludes that since the entire offering had to be finished that same day, relatives, friends and neighbors had to be invited to eat and join in the celebration. This would ensure they would have the opportunity to hear the news of God's bounty that precipitated the offering, and thank God as well. So, in reality, you are throwing a party to celebrate your good fortune, by order of the Torah! One lesson here is that thanks must come quickly, right after the event for which one is thankful.

Third, the sacrifice was eaten by everybody, the people offering it and the kohanim – the priests. Note that other sacrifices were not necessarily eaten. For example, the Burnt Offering, or *olah* (the original "holocaust") was completely burned to ashes. Nobody ate it. Some were eaten only by the kohanim, such as the Meal Offering (or *minchah*), the Sin Offering (or *chatat*) and the Guilt Offering (or *asham*). The lesson here is: Share your good fortune.

The word for "thanks", *todah*, has the same root as the word for "Jew", *Yehudi* (vav, dalet, heh). When Jacob's son Judah was born, his mother Leah said:

הַפַּעַם֙ **אוֹדֶ֣ה** אֶת־יְהֹוָ֔ה -- This time I will thank God.

עַל־כֵּ֛ן קָרְאָ֥ה שְׁמ֖וֹ **יְהוּדָ֑ה** -- Therefore she named him Yehudah. [Genesis 29:35]

In a sense, then, a Jew is, by definition, one who offers thanks. That is what our very name means.

Now let's turn to the question: Who *must* make a thanksgiving offering? The Talmud answers:
> Four people are required to bring a thanksgiving offering:
> -One who crosses the sea,
> -One who crosses a desert,
> -One who was ill and recovered, and
> -One who was imprisoned and was released. [Berakhot 54b]

Psalm 107 describes these four situations. Presumably, a thanksgiving offering for other reasons is voluntary.

How often must Jews give thanks? Constantly. For example:

-The first prayer in the morning, upon awakening, while still in bed, is:
> מוֹדֶה אֲנִי לְפָנֶיךָ מֶלֶךְ חַי וְקַיָּים. שֶׁהֶחֱזַרְתָּ בִּי נִשְׁמָתִי, בְּחֶמְלָה. רַבָּה אֱמוּנָתֶךָ
> *Modeh ani lefanekha melekh ḥai v'kayam*
> *sheheḥezarta bi nishmahti b'ḥemlah, rabbah emunatekha.*
> I am thankful before you, living and eternal King, for You have returned within me my soul with compassion. Great is Your faithfulness!

with a slight pause between "compassion" and "great". [Kitzur Shulchan Aruch]

-In the Amidah, recited three times a day, we say:
מוֹדִים אֲנַחְנוּ לָךְ -- *Modim anachnu lach* -- We give thanks to You [O God].
This must be said by each person individually. In other blessings, one can listen to the cantor and answer "Amen". But not in this one!

-On Shabbat services, we sing:
טוֹב לְהֹדוֹת לַיהוָה -- *Tov lehodot l'Hashem*
It is good to give thanks to God. [Psalm 92:2]

In the Midrash, we read:
> In the Time to Come [the Messianic Age], all [obligations for] offerings will be cancelled, except for the thanksgiving offering, and all prayers will be cancelled, except the prayers of thanksgiving. [Lev. R. 9:7]

The only surviving offering and prayer will be for thanksgiving!

Jews are taught to always be grateful, in bad times as in good. There is a Jewish saying that goes: When you break a leg, be thankful to God you did not break both legs. If you break both legs, be thankful to God you did not break an arm. We must always be thankful to God for what we *do* have, and not dwell on what we *do not* have. The glass must always be seen as half full.

But is it too much to ask someone to thank or praise God when something bad happens to him? What if you are not truly grateful? Some of this is hinted at. For example, when someone dies, we tell the family:
ברוך דיין האמת -- *Baruch dayyan ha-emet* -- Blessed be the true judge.
Note the distinction: It is not thanks, but praise. It means "We trust that God knows best".

Consider also the Hallel, a set of six psalms (113-118) that thank and praise God. It is recited on Pessah, Shavuot, Sukkot, Hanukkah and Rosh Chodesh. But it is not recited on Purim, because the Purim miracle did not happen in the Land of Israel, and in the end the Jews were still subjects of a foreign ruler, unlike the case of Ḥanukkah. It is recited only partially on the last six days of Pessah. Indeed, the Talmud [Megillah 10b, Sanhedrin 39b] says that when the Egyptians drowned in the Sea of Reeds, God prevented the angels from singing songs of praise because "his handiwork was drowning in the sea". The Taz [Orach Chaim 490:3], Chavot Yair [225] and Or HaChaim [on Exodus 13:17] conclude from that that a full Hallel cannot be said on the last six days of Pessaḥ.

Is not reciting a full Hallel or not reciting Hallel at all equivalent to telling God: "You could have done better, so we are toning down thanks and praise."?

But a more fundamental question is: Does God need praise and thanks? No, but *we* need to express thanks. Consider the so-called Nun Study. In 1986, 678 American nuns, aged 75-106, participated in a study about aging. In 1930 they had written a short biography, including their reasons for becoming nuns. The study found that the more positive the emotions they expressed in these essays (contentment, gratitude, happiness, love, hope, etc.), the more likely they were to be alive and well sixty years later. Positive emotions increased their life expectancy by up to seven years. [Danner et al, Journal of Personality and Social Psychology, 2001, 80:5, 804-813]

Research shows that gratitude improves health and immunity against disease, makes people sleep better, enhances self-respect, reduces toxic emotions (such as resentment, frustration, regret, envy, desire for revenge), and makes depression less likely. Saying "thank you" also improves friendships and employee performance. There is an instinctive human need to give thanks, sometimes by giving something.

A question that is often asked is: Should American Jews celebrate the national holiday of Thanksgiving? Most American Jews, even if Orthodox, do celebrate it. A few, however, refrain, and cite laws forbidding Jews to follow non-Jewish customs. For example, the Torah says:
> You shall not copy the practices of the land of Egypt where you dwelt, or of the land of Canaan to which I am taking you; nor shall you follow their laws. [Leviticus 18:3]

Some interpret this to mean no gentile customs must be followed. However, Tosafot, in 12th-century France, says it means only that idolatry and "foolish customs" are forbidden. The Ran, from 14th-century Catalonia, and Maharik, from 15th-century Italy disagree and go further, saying that only idolatry is prohibited. Jewish law follows them. So, as long as no idolatrous rites are involved, Jews can follow local customs.

Here is what three contemporary rabbis say on the subject:
-Rabbi Moshe Feinstein says that Thanksgiving is not associated with any religion. It is a secular holiday and may be celebrated on a voluntary basis. It is prohibited, however, to turn it into an obligation or mitzvah.
-Rabbi Joseph B. Soloveitchik agrees, and notes that he once moved his lecture to an earlier time so he could catch a plane to Boston to have Thanksgiving dinner with his wife and sister.
-Rabbi Yitzchak Hutner, however, says that Thanksgiving is based on the Christian calendar and some people celebrate it with Christian religious rituals, and as such it is prohibited.

Jews warmed to the Thanksgiving holiday from the very beginning. When President Washington instituted it, Rabbi Seixas of Congregation Shearith Israel in New York arranged a special prayer service and called on Jews to "support [our] government, which is founded upon the strictest principles of equal liberty and justice."

At any rate, Jews don't *need* a Thanksgiving holiday -- they thank God multiple times a day every single day.

Shabbat shalom.

Shemini
Lev. 9:1-11:47

B"H

When Does Speculation Become Evil Gossip?

In this week's Torah portion, *Shemini,* we learn about the tragic and mysterious death of two of Aaron's sons, Nadav and Avihu. Here is the story, straight from the Book of Leviticus:

> And Nadav and Avihu, the sons of Aaron, took each of them his censer, and put fire in it, and put incense on it, and offered strange fire before the Lord, which He did not command them. And there went out fire from the Lord, and devoured them, and they died before the Lord. [Leviticus 10:1-2]

Why exactly did they die? What is this "strange fire" and why is it such a major infraction? We are not told. This left the field open for a lot of disturbing speculation that seems to "dump" on the brothers. We will first examine what the commentators said, and then ask whether this sort of negative speculation about what the brothers may have done wrong is permissible, when we don't really know what happened. When does this speculation become *lashon hara'*, or "evil gossip", and when does it serve a useful purpose?

The Midrash on Leviticus says:

> Bar Kappara said in the name of Rabbi Jeremiah ben Elazar: Aaron's sons died on account of four things: for drawing near, for offering, for the strange fire, and for not having taken counsel from each other.
> -"For drawing near" -- because they entered into the innermost precincts of the Sanctuary.
> -"For offering" -- because they offered a sacrifice which they had not been commanded to offer.
> -"For the strange fire" -- they brought in fire from the kitchen.

-"And for not having taken counsel from each other" -- as it says, "Each of them his censer," implying that each acted on his own initiative, without taking counsel from each other. [Lev. Rabbah 20:6]

Rabbi Mani of She'ab, Rabbi Yehoshua of Siknin, and Rabbi Yohanan in the name of Rabbi Levi said: The sons of Aaron died on account of four things...
-Because they had drunk wine, [whereas] it says [immediately following the incident], "Drink no wine or strong drink... so that you do not die" [Leviticus 10:9].
-Because they served in the Sanctuary without the prescribed number of priestly garments [Exodus 28:43].
-Because they entered the Sanctuary without washing their hands and feet [Exodus 30:21].
-Because they had no children... as it says, "And Nadav and Avihu died... and they had no children" [Numbers 3:4]. [Lev. Rabbah 20:9]

Abba Hanin says it was because they had no wives, for it is written [regarding the High Priest], "And [he shall] make atonement for himself, and for his house" [Leviticus 16:6]. "His house" refers to his wife. [Lev. Rabbah 20:9]

Rabbi Levi says that they were arrogant. Many women remained unmarried waiting for them. What did they say? Our father's brother is a king, our mother's brother is a prince [referring to Nachshon, the head of the tribe of Judah], our father is a High Priest, and we are both Deputy High Priests. What woman is worthy of us? ...

Moses and Aaron went first, Nadav and Avihu walked behind them, and all Israel followed, and Nadav and Avihu were saying: "When will these two old men die and we assume authority over the community?" Rabbi Yehudah in the name of Rabbi Aibu said that they uttered this to one another with their mouths, while Rabbi Pinchas said that they harbored the thought in their hearts. The Talmud adds:

> [Upon hearing this,] the Holy One, blessed be He, said to them: "We shall see who will bury whom." [Sanhedrin 52a]

Others say: They already deserved to die at Mount Sinai, when they callously feasted their eyes on the Divine [Exodus 24:9-11]. [Lev. Rabbah 20:10]

Rabbi Eliezer ben Yaakov stated: The sons of Aaron died only because they gave a legal decision in the presence of their master Moses.
What was the exposition they made? They interpreted the verse:

> And the sons of Aaron the priest shall put fire upon the altar. [Lev. 1:7]

This is to teach us, they said, that although fire [generally] came down from heaven, it is nevertheless a mitzvah to bring also ordinary fire. [This is indeed the law. Their sin was that they rendered a Halachic decision in the presence of their teacher.]
[Eruvin 63a, Lev. Rabbah 20:6]

Rashi says:
> Nadav and Avihu died because [their father] Aaron helped make the Golden Calf, as the Torah says:
>> [Moses said:] God raged to destroy Aaron; and I prayed for Aaron at that time. [Deuteronomy 9:20]
>
> "To destroy him" means the death of [his] children, as it is written [in the Book of Amos]:
>> And I destroyed his fruit from above. [Amos 2:9]
>
> Moses' prayer was halfway effective, so that two [of Aaron's children] died and two remained alive. [Rashi on Deut. 9:20]

However, to be fair, the commentators also offer speculation in defense of Nadav and Avihu, without impugning their character:

The Midrash Tanḥuma says:
> The death of the sons of Aaron is mentioned in four places, and each time their sin is mentioned with it, in order to teach you that this was their only sin. [Tanḥuma, Acharei Mot 6:6]

The 18th-century Moroccan commentator Ohr HaChayyim says:
> [The Torah says:]
> בְּקָרְבָתָם לִפְנֵי־יְהוָה וַיָּמֻתוּ -- They came close to God and died. [Leviticus 16:1]
> [This means] they approached the supernal light out of their great love of the Holy, and thereby died. Thus they died by "divine kiss" such as experienced by the perfectly righteous. It is only that the righteous die when the divine kiss approaches them, while they died by their approaching it... Although they sensed their own demise, this did not prevent them from drawing near to God in attachment, delight, delectability, fellowship, love, kiss and sweetness, to the point that their souls ceased from them.

The Zohar, the book of Jewish mysticism, says:

> After Pinchas acted zealously [by killing Zimri and Cosbi]... and the tribe of Shim'on came after him in anger, his soul left him, at which time the two souls of Nadav and Avihu [his uncles] entered him. [Zohar on Tzav 14b]

So Pinchas is a *tikkun*, an atonement, for the sin of Nadav and Avihu. But how did two people become one? The Zohar adds that Nadav and Avihu never married, so each is considered only half a person. [Zohar 3:57b; Arizal, Likutei Torah on Vayikra]. The Zohar even says that Pinchas was Eliyahu HaNavi, the Prophet Elijah! [Zohar on Pinchas]

While we are talking about Pinchas, let us also examine another case of speculative commentary. In the Torah portion *Pinchas*, a man named Tzelaf'chad dies, leaving five daughters. We are not told how or why he died. The Book of Numbers just says:

> The daughters of Tzelaf'chad ... [said] "Our father died in the desert, but he was not in the assembly that banded together against the Lord in Korach's assembly, but he died for his own sin, and he had no sons..." [Num. 27:1-3]

So we know he died presumably as punishment for some sin. But which sin?

The Talmud quotes Rabbi Akiva as saying: [Tzelaf'chad] was the man who gathered wood on Shabbat and was stoned to death as a result [Shabbat 96b]. That story is in the Book of Numbers [Numbers 15:32]. Rabbi Akiva was immediately chided by another rabbi:

> Rabbi Yehudah ben Betera said to him: "Akiva! In either case you will be called to task. If you are right, the Torah shielded him [by not naming him], while you reveal his identity [against the will of God]! And if you are wrong, you stigmatized a righteous man." [Shabbat 96b]

Here is another explanation. The Torah mentions that a number of Israelites set out to go to the Holy Land, before Moses and the other Israelites were ready. Moses chides them for that:

> And Moses said [to them], "Why do you now transgress the commandment of the Lord? ... Do not go up... the Lord will not be with you." But they [disobeyed and] went up to the hilltop [anyway]... [Numbers 14:41-44]

Rabbi Shim'on speculates in the Talmud that Tzelaf'chad was among those people, who ascended [the mountain] defiantly and died. [Rashi, Shabbat 97a]

In the Zohar, Rabbi Hiyya said: This is what is written [in the Torah about [Tzelaf'chad]: "But he died in his own sin [*ki b'chet'o met* -- with *chet'o* spelled *chet tet aleph vav*]" [Num. 27:3]; [which can be read as] "he died in the sin [*chet tet aleph*] of the *Vav*". Therefore, his sentence was left unsaid and not explained like other sentences, because this matter had to be in secrecy, veiled and not made known. Therefore, it was not mentioned openly. [Zohar on Shelach]

Or HaHayyim says that Tzelaf'chad was among those whose death in the desert God had decreed as a result of the debacle of the spies.

The Ramban says that Tzelaf'chad died a natural death in the wilderness in his bed. "In his sin" means that he was not worthy to enter the land.

The Tosafot say that the intention of the man gathering sticks on Shabbat was good, for the sake of Heaven, because the Israelites were saying that, since it had been decreed that they will not enter the Land because of the incident of the Spies, they are no longer obligated to keep the *mitzvot*. So he went and violated Shabbat [intentionally] so that he should be killed, and that others should see that the commandments still applied. [Tosafot on Bava Batra 119b]

The Maharsha concludes from this that he did not truly sin, since [by Torah law] "a work that is not needed for its product" does not violate Shabbat. In other words, his intention was not to make a fire with the sticks. Nevertheless, the court executed him, for a judge can only judge by what he sees, not by the intentions of the heart.

Now, back to our main question: Is such speculation really necessary when the Torah does not explain clearly the cause of someone's death?

To be sure, it is legitimate to try to understand what caused an unexplained, mysterious, or seemingly senseless death; at least so one can avoid making the same fatal mistake. Also, one can always attach a valid teaching to each speculative "explanation".

But when does this constitute dumping on the deceased by creatively trying to find fault with them? Is it rabbinically-sanctioned *lashon hara*, the evil tongue? What should be its limits?

In modern terms, it is as if a group of people reads an obituary in the newspaper about the untimely death of someone they know, and the cause of death is not given. Then one of them says, "I am pretty sure it was a suicide!" Another says, "No, I believe he was a homosexual and died of AIDS." A third says, "No, I think he had ties to organized crime and this was a settlement of accounts." Etc. Is this speculation kosher?

My conclusion from all this is that, when knowledge is lacking, it is always better to apply the advice found in the Talmud:

לַמֵּד לְשׁוֹנְךָ לוֹמַר "אֵינִי יוֹדֵעַ" -- *Lamed l'shoncha lomar 'eni yodea'*
Teach your tongue to say "I do not know". [Berakhot 4a]

Shabbat shalom.

Tazria
Lev. 12:1-13:59

B"H

Is Gossip Good?

The Torah portion for this week, *Tazria*, deals with skin diseases common in biblical times and their associated purification rites. Although we are mercifully no longer subject to these diseases today, *Baruch HaShem*, Talmudic and later commentators have taught that what is really referred to here is *spiritual* impurity, in the form of *lashon hara*, that is, gossip.

Everybody is prone to gossip. The Talmud goes so far as to say that it is one sin everybody engages in. [Bava Batra 165a] Is gossip good or bad? The Jewish tradition unequivocally characterizes it as bad. But psychological studies conducted in the past few years have asserted that gossip can sometimes be beneficial. You could read, for example, the article "The Virtues of Gossip", by Feinberg et al in the May 2012 issue of the *Personality and Social Psychology Bulletin*.

We will examine their findings. But before we do that, let us summarize the Jewish position on *lashon hara*:
- You may not speak ill of others, even if you are telling the truth, even if they are dead, even to the people closest to you.
- You may not speak ill of yourself.
- You may not *imply* ill, through body language, tone of voice, omissions, or ambiguous expressions.
- You may not speak *what will be interpreted* as ill, even if you say you don't *mean* ill.
- You may not relay damaging information even if you say you are not sure it is reliable.

-You may not relay information about someone who does not want it relayed.

Exceptions are few and far between. You may speak ill of others if you are:
-Saving a life;
-Or testifying in court;
-Or writing a letter of recommendation on request;
-Or warning someone against dealing with people who have been crooked in dealing with *you* (and only with you);
-Or referring to the misdeeds of people *currently* serving a legal sentence *for those misdeeds*;
-Or teaching about cruel and crooked historical figures to avoid history repeating itself;
-Or speaking to someone, in private, to advise him on how to correct the faults you perceive in him.

The Talmud says:
> Anyone who shames another in public is as if he had shed blood. [Bava Metzia 58b]

It also says:
> Slander destroys three persons: He who speaks evil, he who listens to it, and he who is spoken about. [Arachin 15b]

Now, what are these recent psychological studies saying? They established, based on a huge amount of eavesdropping in public places, that two-thirds of the time, when people talk, it is gossip that comes out. They tried to answer the question: Why is that? Why do people love to spread gossip? To quote Robin Dunbar, a psychology professor at the University of Liverpool:
> Language evolved for social purposes, not spreading technical information, like whether it will rain or how to get from New York City to Washington, D.C. Knowledge of the social world has a much deeper purpose. It's not just the fact that I saw Jimmy kiss Penelope, but how that incident relates to me and the group.
> [http://www.apa.org/monitor/apr06/bonding.aspx]

Here is what some psychologists speculate. First, they say that gossip fosters bonding. When two people exchange slander about others, they create an association: Two superior people versus the inferior masses. Also, when we gossip, we show others we trust them enough to share such information, which reinforces the bonding.

This bonding extends to entire groups. A study showed that spreading good news about the group's friends and damaging news about the group's enemies makes the group as a whole feel good, which helps to buttress group goals. Some also suggest that negative talk in a group, about a member of the group who deviates from group norms, can be used as punishment, and as a means to get the offending member to mend his ways.

Second, they say that talking about people who are less skilled or of lower status bolsters our own self-esteem.

Third, some psychologists view gossip as evolution of the species. Natural selection pressured us to learn as much as possible about the people around us, as a means of protection against them. As Frank McAndrew, an applied social psychology professor at Knox College said:
> If you weren't curious about others, you'd pay the consequences.

Fourth, Sarah Wert, a researcher at Trinity College and Yale University, suggests that gossip gives us something to talk about. She says:
> We don't tend to like people that don't have anything to talk about. Talking about other people gives us an infinite source of conversational material.

Fifth, gossiping about prominent people can be used to test the limits of acceptability. When people talked about President Clinton's affair with Monica Lewinsky in the late 1990s, they were also trying to see whether their social circle was ready to accept extramarital affairs as normal behavior in a changing world. (Hey, if this flies, maybe I can join the fun!)

Sixth, when you spread dirt, you become popular -- most of the time.

Charlotte De Backer, a psychologist at the University of Antwerp and a researcher on the use of gossip as a social agent, says:
> Gossip is like chocolate. Humans are drawn to fatty, sweet foods like chocolate because such high-calorie foods were once our lifeblood in lean times. As a result, people crave those foods -- even when they are not in dire need of calories. Likewise, the pleasure that people derive from gossip can create a tendency to "dish dirt" -- even when the subject matter doesn't affect our lives, such as with celebrity gossip, or when divulging information could be more risky, such as at work.

So there you have it. None of this is particularly new or unexpected. These psychologists are correct. *Of course* you will derive benefit from gossip. In fact, you believe you will derive benefit from everything you do, or you wouldn't be doing it, even if that benefit is just a feeling of satisfaction. That's not the point. The real point is, *does this benefit outweigh the harm done to others?* Our tradition answers this question with a resounding and unambiguous "No!" For example, when two Gentiles who are not particularly antisemitic share antisemitic jokes, they *do* bond; but they also unwittingly set the stage for the next Holocaust.

It is not surprising, then, that Jewish tradition likens the spreading of gossip to murder, idolatry and sexual immorality rolled into one:
> There are four things for which punishment is exacted from a person in this world, while the principal punishment remains intact for him in the World to Come: Idolatry, sexual immorality, and murder. And *Lashon Hara* [the evil tongue] is equal to them all. [Peah Y 8a]

Shabbat shalom.

Metzora
Lev. 14:1-15:33

B"H

In Praise of Praise

In this week's Torah portion, *Metzora*, we read about the rituals for cleansing people who are afflicted with a skin disease, or צרעת *tzaraat*, sometimes identified with leprosy. In the Torah, Miriam was punished with *tzaraat* for badmouthing her brother Moses. [Num. 12:1–15] Because of this, the Sages understood the disease to be caused by *lashon hara*, "the evil tongue" or malicious speech. The Talmud says:
> Rabbi Yosei ben Zimra says: Anyone who engages in malicious speech will be afflicted by leprous marks coming upon him, as it is stated [in Psalms]:
>> I will destroy he who slanders his friend in secret. [Ps. 101:5]
>
> [Arakhin 15b, 16a]

The Sages were always very emphatic in telling us to avoid speaking ill of others. The Talmud warns us:

> -There are four things for which punishment is exacted from a person in this world, while the principal punishment remains intact for him in the World to Come: Idolatry, sexual immorality, and murder [the three cardinal sins of Judaism]. And *lashon hara* [the evil tongue] is equal to them all. [Peah Y 8a]

> -Slander destroys three persons: He who speaks evil, he who listens to it, and he who is spoken about. [Arakhin 15b]

When God charged Moses with leading the Exodus, Moses said of the Israelites: "They will not believe me". [Ex. 4:1] The Torah then says:
> The Lord said to him further, "Put your hand into your bosom."
> He put his hand into his bosom; and when he took it out, his hand was encrusted with snowy scales!
> And [God] said, "Put your hand back into your bosom."

He put his hand back into his bosom; and when he took it out of his bosom, there it was again like the rest of his body. [Ex. 4:6-7]

Rashi understands this passage to mean that Moses was punished for speaking ill of the Israelites.

One might think that one way to avoid *lashon hara* is not to say anything. Indeed the Sages praised silence. The Mishnah tells us that Rabban Gamliel's son Shim'on used to say:
> All my days I grew up among the sages, and I have found nothing better for a person than silence... Whoever indulges in too many words brings about sin. [Avot 1:17]

It adds that Rabbi Akiva said:
> רַבִּי עֲקִיבָא אוֹמֵר, סְיָג לַחָכְמָה, שְׁתִיקָה- -- A fence to wisdom is silence. [Avot 3:13]

Bartenura, from 15th-century Italy, clarifies that this advice does not refer to words of Torah, which we are supposed to actively engage in, or about malicious speech, which the Torah has already forbidden, but only to optional speech, which he says must be minimized. Along those lines, Rabbi Abraham ben Shmuel ibn Hasdai Halevi, from 13th-century Catalonia, wrote:
> Man was given two ears and one tongue, so that he may listen more than speak. [Ben haMelekh ve-haNazir 26]

On a more down-to-earth level, Mark Twain said:
> It is better to keep your mouth shut and be thought a fool than to open your mouth and remove all doubt.

However, the problem with silence is that, while it may prevent us from sinning, it generally does not accomplish any good. This raises the question: Should you go out of your way to praise others?

The Sages laid down a principle: A negative commandment implies a positive commandment and vice-versa:

-[The Torah says:]
> כַּבֵּד אֶת־אָבִיךָ וְאֶת־אִמֶּךָ לְמַעַן יַאֲרִכוּן יָמֶיךָ -- Honor your father and your mother so that your days may be prolonged. [Ex. 20:12]

This means that if you honor them, your days be prolonged, and if not, they will be shortened, because the words of Torah are terse, the positive implies the negative and the negative implies the positive. [Mekhilta d'Rabbi Yishmael 20:12]

-[The Torah says:]
וְלִמַּדְתֶּם אֹתָם אֶת־בְּנֵיכֶם ... לְמַעַן יִרְבּוּ יְמֵיכֶם וִימֵי בְנֵיכֶם
And you shall teach [these words] to your children... so that your days and the days of your children may increase. [Deut. 11:19-21]
[This implies:] If not, your days will be shortened, because the words of Torah are expounded as follows: From the negative, you infer the positive; and from the positive you infer the negative. [Sifrei Devarim 46:1]

In other words, if you don't honor your parents or instruct your children, your life won't just not be extended, but it will actually be shortened. Rabbi Meir disagreed [Nedarim 11a, Sotah 17a], but he was in the minority.

This principle implies that if speaking ill of others is forbidden, then speaking well of them should be required. The opposite of *lashon hara* should be *lashon hatov* -- the "good tongue". Yet that expression is not found in our Sources.

Maimonides endorsed it heartily:
לְפִיכָךְ צָרִיךְ לְסַפֵּר בְּשִׁבְחוֹ
One is obliged to speak in praise of his neighbor. [Rambam, Hilkhot Deot 6:3]

Rabbi Joseph Telushkin's 2009 book *A Code of Jewish Ethics, Volume 2 -- Love Your Neighbor as Yourself* has a whole section on *lashon hatov*, arguing that it follows directly from "Love your neighbor as yourself". [Lev. 19:18]

What is the best way to praise people? Three general guidelines can be found.

First, focus your praise. The Mishnah mentions that Rabban Yohanan ben Zakkai used to praise his students as follows:
-Rabbi Eliezer ben Hyrcanus has an excellent memory. [This was important when the Oral Law was still oral and books were rare and expensive.]

-Shimon ben Netanel is pious and reverential.
-Elazar ben Arakh is creative in his interpretations of Torah.
[Avot 2:8]

The lesson is: Don't be too effusive and concentrate specifically on what is salient. For example, "He is always scrupulously honest" is better than "He is a great guy". Rabbi Jonathan Sacks calls it "focused praise" and strongly endorses it.

Second, lie to make people feel good, if necessary. The Talmud says you must tell the bride she is beautiful on her wedding day, even if you think she is ugly as sin. [Ketubot 16b-17a] Lying is also permitted to keep the peace. This is called *shalom bayit*. [Yevamot 65b, Bava Metzia 87a]

So, no matter what you really think, tell the bride she is beautiful, praise other people's purchases, tell them you missed them, tell them they haven't aged, tell them you like their gift, tell them some people you both know have good feelings towards them even if it stretches the truth a bit (as Aaron did [Avot D'Rabbi Nathan 12:3]), etc.

Third, praise efforts more than absolute attributes. Rabbi Jonathan Sacks argues that it is better to praise effort than praise fixed characteristics, to encourage growth. He notes that:
 -Rabbi ben Zakkai praised Rabbi Eliezer for his memory, but later Rabbi Eliezer was placed under cherem for refusing to accept the majority view. [Bava Metzia 59b]
 -Rabbi ben Zakkai praised Rabbi Elazar for his originality, but later Rabbi Elazar decided to live far from the center of scholarship and forgot his knowledge, to the point that he could not read correctly a Torah scroll. [Shabbat 147b]

The second brings to mind what Hillel said:
וּדְלֹא מוֹסִיף, יָסֵף -- He who does not increase his knowledge loses it. [Avot 1:13]

Rabbi Sacks concludes that absolute praise creates a mindset that avoids risk, for fear or not living up to the description; while praising effort encourages risk as the price for growth:

> It may be that praising his students for their innate abilities rather than their effort, Rabban Yoḥanan ben Zakkai inadvertently encouraged the two most talented of them to develop a fixed mindset rather than engage with colleagues and stay open to intellectual growth. [https://rabbisacks.org/metsorah-5774-praise/]

Rabbi ben Zakkai might have told Rabbi Eliezer: "I wish somebody could remember what's in these particular hard-to-find books" or told Rabbi Elazar: "These particularly hard-to-interpret passages need some fresh thinking applied to them."

Some argue that by praising people's qualities, even if they are not salient, may reinforce them, bring them to the fore, and cause people to work on improving them. Positive speech leads to positive actions.

However, there is pushback. Not all Sages agree others should be praised. The Talmud warns:
> Rav Dimi, brother of Rav Safra said: A person should never speak about the goodness of another, because speaking about his goodness will lead to disparaging him. [Arakhin 16a, Bava Batra 164b]

The fear is that he or his listeners may then try to temper the praise with criticism. Maimonides applies this only to one's enemies:
> One who tells of the good qualities of his fellow in the presence of his fellow's enemies is guilty of a form of evil speech אֲבַק לְשׁוֹן הָרַע, because he provokes them to disparage him. [Rambam, Hilkhot Deot 7:4]

This raises the question: How far should one go in seeking the good in evil people and advertising it? Should we even say that Hitler was very affectionate with his dogs?

Also, telling someone you expect miracles from him on a specific task, especially in front of others, puts tremendous pressure on him to deliver, knowing that if he doesn't people will think less of him.

Finally, praising everybody lavishly may lead to nobody believing you. Professors who write glowing letters of recommendation for all their students, without any balance, are usually roundly ignored, even if they are famous.

Conclusion: Praising others is… praiseworthy; but only up to a point.

Shabbat shalom.

Acharei Mot
Lev. 16:1-18:30

B"H

Imagine!

This week's Torah portion, *Acharei Mot,* contains 79 commandments, or 13% of the 613 commandments in the Torah, more than any other single portion. That's a lot of commandments. If you follow diligently all these commandments, then after you die you are guaranteed a place in *Olam Haba*, the World to Come, heaven. If not, you will spend up to a year in Gehennom, and if you do not repent, your soul and your name will be erased forever.

For those who don't like this scenario, let's use our imagination and think of alternatives.

Imagine: There's no heaven. No hell. Above us only sky.
And no religion too. It's easy if you try.
Imagine: There's no countries, no borders. One united world!
Imagine: No possessions! All the people sharing all the world.
Imagine: A brotherhood of man! All the people living life in peace!

You may say I'm a dreamer.
But I say I have nightmares.
And I'm not the only one.
I hope some day you'll join me,
And realize that these nightmares will not repair the world.

They will only make it worse.

Why? Let's examine these points one by one.

First, there is no need to "imagine" a world without religion. Most of us have experienced it firsthand. It's called the twentieth century. The secular ideologies of the twentieth century – fascism, Naziism, communism -- have killed far more people than all the wars of religion combined. Hitler's genocidal frenzy murdered 11 million in concentration camps and 3 million in prisoner-of-war camps. In the name of communism, Mao Tse Toung of China killed up to 100 million civilians, Stalin of the Soviet Union killed 20 million, Pol Pot of Cambodia killed 2 million, and other lovers of the hammer and sickle, in Cuba, Vietnam, Korea, Eastern Europe and elsewhere, killed millions more. King Leopold II of Belgium killed 10 million blacks in the Congo because they weren't working fast enough as slaves.

Let's consider a religious counterpart: The Inquisition of the Catholic Church. In its name, Christian clerics spied on Jews who had been forced to convert to Christianity. If they caught one of them practicing Judaism in secret, they arrested him, jailed him and tortured him savagely to extract a confession from him. Then, they tried him in a kangaroo court, and sentenced him to be burned alive. This murder, which they called an auto-da-fé, was carried out in a public place, in front of thousands of enthusiastic onlookers, happy to see justice being done and using the occasion for a family picnic.

Now, think of all the time, the energy, the money, the manpower required to kill just *one* person in the name of religion. Compare it to the Nazis happily murdering thousands of Jews every single day on an efficient, industrial scale, without bothering with spying, charges, confessions or trials. Who is worse in the end, the Inquisitors or the Nazis?

In the secular ideologies, human lives are expendable. All that counts is the cause. The end justifies the means. It is always easier to kill than to argue, to convince, to spy, to jail, to restrict, or to tolerate. By contrast, in all modern religions, life counts for something. In Judaism, the Mishnah says:
> Whoever destroys one life is considered as if he had destroyed an entire world; and whoever saves one life is considered as if he had saved an entire world. [Sanhedrin 4:1 (22a)]

You often hear the argument that many people who don't practice any religion are nevertheless "good". Certainly, but what is clear to me is that these people got their "goodness" from religious values passed down to them through the generations from parents, teachers and leaders. They were not born that way. Remember that the so-called "good" people of 5,000 years ago believed there was nothing wrong with slavery, with sacrificing children to angry gods, with pedophilia, with the notion that might makes right, with the survival of the fittest and the most cunning, and with many other things that, thanks to religion, are no longer taught as "good".

In fact, the Torah tells us:
יֵצֶר לֵב הָאָדָם רַע מִנְּעֻרָיו -- *Yetzer lev ha-adam ra' min'urav.*
The inclination of a man's heart is evil from his birth. [Genesis 8:21; 6:5; see also Talmud, Berakhot Y 3:5]

This means that our natural instincts are evil. Goodness has to be learned. This is why the Torah was given. Absent the Torah, it would be natural to ask: "If I see something I like, why can't I steal it, if I can get away with it? Why can't I kill anybody who stands in my way, if I am strong enough?" The Torah does not command us to do anything we would do naturally. The purpose of the ethical commandments is precisely to help us overcome our natural evil inclination.

Steven Weinberg, a Jewish physicist, who received a Nobel Prize in 1979, famously said:
> With or without religion, you would have good people doing good things and evil people doing evil things. But for good people to do evil things, that takes religion.
> [Address at Conference on Cosmic Design, American Association for the Advancement of Science, Washington, D.C., April 1999]

He is wrong. One could say, just as appropriately: "For evil people to do good things, that takes religion." One could also say: "Good people can be led to do evil things even without religion." We can certainly at least say: "For evil people to do less evil things, that takes religion." You saw that when we compared Inquisitors and Nazis.

Second, let us address the "One World" idea. It is not good. In a single, centrally-managed world, where would persecuted people go? When the Christians persecuted us Jews, we went to the Muslims; when the Muslims persecuted us, we went to the Christians. Where would we go if the whole world was under one government and that government hated the Jews? It would be the end of Judaism.

Also, a diversity of approaches to progress is important. If we had a single government, it would support only what *it* likes and many good ideas would be squelched. What fosters huge leaps forward is the competition between different states or entities. Without the Cold War, we would not have gone to the moon, we would not be exploring space, we would not have the GPS, we would not have the Internet and so many other fruits of modern technology.

Third, let's tackle the "No possessions" idea. Is it good? The communists thought so: Everything belongs to everybody, everybody shares everything and everybody works for the good of society. They failed miserably. They failed because they ignored human nature. People want to work for themselves and their families, not for society, not for a cause. Idealists are few and far between. A good system is one that allows people to work for themselves in a way that also benefits society as a whole. It is not a zero-sum game.

Finally, what about the utopian society, "no greed or hunger" under "the brotherhood of man"? Think about it for a minute. No more wars, no more diseases, no more natural disasters, no more accidents, no more famine, no more crime, no more hatred. All material needs are satisfied for free for everybody: Food, shelter, comfort, sex, entertainment, perfect health, perfect weather, etc. Robots and machines do all the physical work. Ask anything and it's yours at no cost and no effort.

You would feel worthless in such a world. You would feel bored to the point of despair because life would have no challenges, no unanswered questions, no mountains to climb, nothing to do that would make you feel proud of yourself or look forward to the future. We need a reason to live. We need challenges.

It is a paradox, to be sure, but a concern just the same. Indeed, the Midrash tells us that we *need* evil; we need our natural evil inclination to achieve anything worthwhile:
> Without the evil inclination, no man would build a house, take a wife, beget a family, and engage in work. [As King] Solomon [said in Ecclesiastes]: "I saw that all labor and all achievement was the result of man's envy and rivalry with his neighbor." [Eccl. 4:4] [Genesis Rabbah 9:7]

The line "I hope some day you'll join us, and the world will live as one" is particularly ironic. Isn't that what all religious fundamentalists say? "I hope some day you'll join us, and the world will live as one"? Note that we Jews never say "I hope some day you'll join us." There is nothing wrong with being a Gentile. Judaism is not an upgrade.

So, in the end, if John Lennon's little song moves you to tears, remember: Be careful what you wish for; you might get it.

Shabbat shalom.

Kedoshim
Lev. 19:1–20:27

B"H

Love Your Neighbor as Yourself

This week's Torah portion, *Kedoshim*, includes what is probably the most quoted line in the Bible:

וְאָהַבְתָּ לְרֵעֲךָ כָּמוֹךָ -- *V'ahavta l're'acha kamocha*
And you shall love your neighbor as yourself. [Leviticus 19:18]

It is a very inspirational and edifying line. But what does it really mean? First, who is my neighbor? Is a Jew in Uzbekistan my neighbor? Is a non-Jew in Uzbekistan my neighbor? It says "your neighbor" (*re'a*) and not "your fellow human beings" (*ha-briot*). Does that imply that some people are excluded? If so, who? Should I love my enemy? If I hate myself, should I hate my neighbor also? Note that the Torah does not command you to love yourself. It has only two commandments to love: To love God [Deuteronomy 6:5] and to love your neighbor [Leviticus 19:18].

Second, what is love? What about tough love? If you rough up somebody for what you think is his own good, does it count as "love"?

Third, how can you be commanded to "love"? How can you make yourself have certain feelings?

Fourth, is it even possible to truly love another as you love yourself? The Torah implies that it is, when it says לֹא בַשָּׁמַיִם הִוא *Lo bashamayim hi*, meaning "it [the Torah] is not in heaven" [Deut. 30:12]. What the Torah commands to do is always doable.

Fifth, there is a saying that goes "He who loves everybody loves nobody." Can we realistically ask a mother to love all children as much as she loves her own children?

Let us tackle these questions one by one, and see if we can find answers in our Jewish tradition.

First, who is my neighbor? Are the "neighbors" in question fellow Jews only or everybody? Here are the arguments for each possible answer.

On the one hand, why does "your neighbor" mean only "your fellow Jew"? Because the full verse is:
> You shall neither take revenge from nor bear a grudge against the sons of your own people. You shall love your neighbor as yourself. I am the Lord. [Lev. 19:18]

The first part clearly refers only to fellow Jews: The sons of your people, *bnei 'ammecha*. So the rest of the verse does also. This is Maimonides' conclusion. [Rambam, Yad, De'ot 6:3]

Also, a little later in the same chapter, we are told:
> When a stranger sojourns with you in your land, you shall not taunt him. The stranger who sojourns with you shall be as a native from among you, and you shall love him as yourself; for you were strangers in the land of Egypt. I am the Lord, your God. [Lev. 19:33-4]

Since love of the resident stranger (the *ger*) is enjoined later in the same chapter, it makes sense that the two injunctions should refer to two different categories of people, the first to Jews only, the second to Gentiles only. However, the Sages say that *ger* here means "convert to Judaism", so it not a different injunction. The second injunction merely reinforces the first by saying it does not apply only to *born* Jews.

Finally, the Talmud restricts interaction with "idolaters". This complicates applying the commandment of neighborly love to all, even though there is no injunction anywhere to hate idolaters.

Now for the other side: Why does "your neighbor" means "all of humankind"? Because *Re-a* (neighbor) is used elsewhere in the Bible to refer to Gentiles as well.

Also, in the Jerusalem Talmud, Rabbi Akiva says: "Love your neighbor as yourself" is a great principle of the Torah [*Kelal gadol ba-Torah*]." [Sifra 19:45; Nedarim Y 9:4]. His colleague Ben Azzai retorts: Even greater is "God created man... in His image." [Gen. 5:1] The Midrash concludes that two creatures in the likeness of God are bound to love each other, so the second statement implies the first, and applies to all creatures. [Sifra 19:18; also Genesis Rabbah 24:7] The Midrash Tanḥuma says that if you hate any man, you hate God who made man in His image. Note, however, that this does not tell us to love, only not to hate.

Note that the full quote is: "Love your neighbor as yourself. I am the Lord". Why the addition of "I am the Lord"? Ben Azzai implies: Do this because I am the Lord and *all humans* are in My image.

The Maggid of Trisk, 19th-century sage, noted that the gematria of "love" (*ahava*) is 13, and the gematria of "The Lord" (The Tetragrammaton) is 26. So he concludes: "Love of self" + "Love of neighbor" = "Reaching God".

Pinchas Peli, an Israeli rabbi, said that the phrase should be read: Love your neighbor [because he is] like yourself [in the image of God]. He noted that it does not say "as you love yourself" but "as yourself".

In Pirkei Avot, Hillel says:
 אוֹהֵב אֶת הַבְּרִיּוֹת -- *Ohev et ha-briot* (Love people). [Avot 1:12]
However, he adds: וּמְקָרְבָן לַתּוֹרָה -- *Um-karvan la-Torah* (And being them closer to the Torah). Does this imply Jews only, since the full Torah is for Jews only, or is proselytizing intended? Hillel also said:
 דַּעֲלָךְ סָנֵי לְחַבְרָךְ לָא תַּעֲבֵיד — זוֹ הִיא כָּל הַתּוֹרָה כּוּלָּהּ, וְאִידַּךְ פֵּירוּשָׁהּ הוּא, זִיל גְּמוֹר
 What is hateful to you, don't do to others. This is the whole Torah. All else is commentary. Go and study it. [Shabbat 31a]

"Others" means "the rest of humankind". This principle has been embraced by other faiths as the "Golden Rule".

Also in Pirkei Avot, Rabbi Meir said:
> [Whoever engages in Torah study] ... loves God and loves people [הַבְּרִיּוֹת אוֹהֵב אֶת - - ohev et ha-briot]. [Avot 6:6]

Another relevant teaching is that we must be concerned about the welfare of non-Jews at least in the interest of peace, *mi penei darkhei shalom*. The Maimonides said:
> We bury the dead among the Gentiles, comfort their mourners and visit their sick, because this is the way of peace. [Rambam, Yad, Avel 14:12]

The implication of expediency does not detract from the commandment: Either we do it or we don't, and we are supposed to do it.

The conclusion the rabbis reached is that the commandment refers to Jews only [*Ahavat Yisrael*], but the extension to all mankind is encouraged. There is nothing wrong with a commandment referring to loving Jews only. It does not imply you should hate everybody else. For example, "Honor your father and your mother" does not imply you should be disrespectful towards everybody else. It is natural to prioritize affections: First immediate family, then extended family, community, co-religionists, co-nationals, people with whom we have some affinity, etc.

Let us now turn to the question: Does loving your neighbor imply loving your enemy? There are four relevant Jewish teachings:
- First, you may not hate your enemy. The Torah says:
> Do not hate an Edomite, because he is your brother. Do not hate an Egyptian, for you were strangers in his land. [Deut. 23:8]
- Second, you must occasionally help your enemy. The Torah says:
> If you see the donkey of one who hates you lying down under its burden, do not just walk by: Stop and release him. [Ex. 23:5]

The Book of Psalms adds:
> If your enemy is hungry, give him bread to eat; and if he is thirsty, give him water to drink. [Prov. 25:21]

-Third, you should try to turn your enemy into a friend. The Talmud says:
> Who is a hero? מי שעושה שונא אוהבו -- One who turns an enemy into a friend.
> [Avot d'Rabbi Natan 23:1]

-Fourth, you may have to kill your enemy, if that is the only way to save yourself or others. The Talmud says:
> If someone comes to kill you, kill him first [if that is the only way to stop him].
> [Berakhot 58a; derived from Ex. 22:1]

What about tough love? In the Midrash, Rabbi Jose ben Rabbi Hanina said:
> Reproof leads to love, as it says [in the Book of Proverbs]:
>> Reprove a wise man, and he will love you. [Prov. 9:8]
>
> Love not accompanied by reproof is not love. [Genesis Rabbah 54:3]

The next question is: How can you be commanded to love? You can't, really. But you can be commanded to act in ways someone who loves would act, in hopes that it will lead to genuine love. The 19th-century opus הכתב והקבלה *HaK'tav v'HaKabbalah* [The Written and Oral Tradition] suggests nine ways:

> 1-Do not fake affection for others
> 2-Treat them with respect
> 3-Seek the best for them
> 4-Join them in their pain
> 5-Greet them with friendliness
> 6-Give them the benefit of the doubt
> 7-Assist them physically
> 8-Give them small loans and gifts
> 9-Do not consider yourself better than them
> [HaK'tav v'HaKabbalah, as reproduced in Stone Chumash, p 662]

The Rambam said about love of God: If we just looked into nature and contemplated God's wondrous creation, we would be filled with love of God. We ask ourselves: Can the same idea be applied to people?

The next question: Is it even possible to truly love another as you love yourself? Rabbi Samson Raphael Hirsch, from 19th-century Germany, notes that the Torah does not say: *V'ahavta et re'acha kamocha*, but *V'ahavta l're'acha kamocha*:

-The first, *V'ahavta et reacha kamocha* would mean: "Feel the same love for others as you feel for yourself," which is impossible.
-But the second, the actual quote from the Torah, *V'ahavta l're'acha kamocha*, means "Love that which pertains to your neighbor as if it pertained to you", meaning his well-being and happiness.

The Ramban wrote in the 13th century: We should wish our neighbors the same well-being we enjoy ourselves.

Deep, emotional love is not what our verse refers to. That kind of love is expressed with different words in the Tanach. For example, in the Book of Samuel we read:
> Jonathan loved [David] as his own soul (*ke-nafsho*). [1 Sam 18:1, 20:17]

Another possibility is that the commandment is meant to be just an *upper limit* on love: Do not love your neighbor *more* than yourself. You don't have to give him more than you have yourself. You don't have to die to save his life. In the Talmud, Rabbi Akiva himself ruled that "Your life takes precedence over another's life." [Bava Metzia 62a]

Some say that "your neighbor" means "those physically closest to you". They are harder to love because we interact with them, whence the need for a separate commandment to love them! It's easier to love someone far away, as a theoretical abstraction. As a rule, the Torah only tells us to do what we would *not* normally do.

Hassidic Rabbi Schneur Zalman of Liadi said:
> All souls are of a single essence, united in their source in God.

His master the Baal Shem Tov, founder of Hassidism, said:
> One must love the lowliest of men as much as the greatest Torah scholar. When a person gets up in the morning and looks at himself in the mirror he thinks, "I am basically a good person. I have my faults and foibles; I am not perfect. But I am more good than bad." This is how we must evaluate our neighbor: He is basically good; I will overlook his faults.

Shabbat shalom.

Emor
Lev. 21:1-24:23

B"H

Why is Blasphemy Such a Major Infraction?

In this week's Torah portion, *Emor*, we read the following story:

> Now, the son of an Israelite woman... [and] an Egyptian man... quarreled... with an Israelite man..., pronounced the [Divine] Name and cursed. So they brought him to Moses [and]... placed him in the guardhouse, [until] the word of the Lord specified his sentence.
>
> Then the Lord spoke to Moses, saying: "Take the blasphemer outside the camp, and all who heard [his blasphemy] shall lean their hands on his head. And the entire community shall stone him. And to the children of Israel, you shall speak, saying: Any man who blasphemes his God shall bear his sin. And he who blasphemes the name of the Lord, he shall surely be put to death, and the entire congregation shall certainly stone him; both the stranger and he who is born in the land, when he blasphemes the name of the Lord, shall be put to death." [Lev. 24: 10-16]

Indeed, the third of the Ten Commandments is:

לֹא תִשָּׂא אֶת־שֵׁם־יְהֹוָה אֱלֹהֶיךָ לַשָּׁוְא כִּי לֹא יְנַקֶּה יְהֹוָה אֵת אֲשֶׁר־יִשָּׂא אֶת־שְׁמוֹ לַשָּׁוְא׃

You shall not take the name of the Lord your God in vain; for the Lord will not hold him guiltless who takes his name in vain. [Ex. 20:7]

It is also one of the seven Noahide laws, which are binding on all humankind, not only on Jews. [Sanhedrin 56a-60a]

Why is "No blasphemy" so major a commandment?

Let us begin by defining blasphemy. Blasphemy is disrespectful or irreverent use of God's name, with or without intention to pray or speak of holy matters. The Hebrew word is *gidduf*, but frequently *Birkat HaShem* is used. Literally, it means "the blessing of God", where "blessing" is understood as a euphemism for "cursing".

As we saw above, the Torah says that the punishment for blasphemy is death by stoning, but later commentaries have considerably softened the penalty. First, the Mishna says that the death penalty applies only if one specific name of God is used, namely the Tetragrammaton (יְהוָה -- referred to as *HaShem*) and no other. Also, there must be at least two witnesses. The Mishnah says:
> The blasphemer is punished only if he utters the [divine] name [HaShem].
> Rabbi Yehoshua bar Karha said: The whole day [of the trial] the witnesses are examined by means of a substitute for HaShem, [for example] Yosei. [This was because Yosei also has four letters like HaShem, and its gematria is 81, the same as that for Elokim, another name of God.]
> When the trial is finished, the accused is not executed on this evidence, but all persons are removed [from the court], and the chief witness is told, "State literally what you heard". When he does so, [using HaShem], the judges then arise and rend their garments, which are not to be sewn back. The second witness states "I too have heard as he said" [but not uttering HaShem], and the third says: "I too heard as he said." [Sanhedrin 7:5]

As a matter of fact, the correct pronunciation of God's name HaShem has been lost for over two millennia, so no one can technically blaspheme today. There is no record of trials for blasphemy since that time.

Second, the Talmud states that for any other name of God, only corporal punishment is applied. [Sanhedrin 56a] Also, *teshuva*, or repentance, is possible for blasphemy. The Rambam adds that blasphemy includes the erasure of God's name (for example, on paper).

Third, today's penalty for blasphemy is *cherem* – shunning by the community. The *Shulḥan Arukh*, the Code of Jewish law, also states that whoever hears blasphemy, whether with HaShem or any other name [of God], in any language, from a Jew, must rend his garment. [Yoreh Deah 340:37]

Now, in the Talmud, Rabbi Akiva says that one is allowed, even enjoined, to speculate on the reasons behind the commandments *(taamei ha-mitzvot)* [Eruvin 54b]. Provided, of course, that one observes the commandments regardless of the conclusions reached. So let us speculate on the reasons why blasphemy is not allowed:

-First, it demeans the authority of God. Refraining from mocking the ultimate authority is one way to preserve respect for the Torah, even if one is lax in following its commandments.

-Second, even though blasphemy does not harm God Himself, it hurts believers, and their feelings must be taken into account.

-Third, their feelings may be so strong that offensive words may spur them to commit acts of violence, and that is very much to be avoided.

-Fourth, it burns our bridges to believers.

But, on the other hand, there is the issue of freedom of speech, so important to the Western, democratic way of life. Blasphemy, along with six others of the Ten Commandments, is not punishable by secular law in the United States. Banning blasphemy means we may not utter anything that others find sacrilegious, even if *we* do not consider it sacrilegious. Blasphemers may even think they are doing a service to society by speaking out and calling into question other people's beliefs, thereby stimulating healthy discussion. Truth, after all should be able to withstand even the most intense scrutiny. But the issue is: Does this questioning have to include insulting language?

The discussion continues.

Shabbat shalom.

Behar
Lev. 25:1-26:2

B"H

The Meaning of Freedom

In this week's Torah portion, *Behar*, God decrees the Jubilee Year, *Yovel*, with the famous words:

וּקְרָאתֶם דְּרוֹר בָּאָרֶץ לְכָל־יֹשְׁבֶיהָ -- *Ukratem dror ba-aretz, lechol yoshveha.*
And you shall proclaim liberty throughout the land, unto all the inhabitants thereof.
[Lev. 25:10]

This line is found on the Liberty Bell, that iconic symbol of American freedom and independence.

When we celebrate the holiday of Pessaḥ -- Passover -- at the seder table, and remember the Exodus from Egypt and the transition from slavery to freedom, we recite *Dayyenu*, a poem with 14 lines, each of which says, "If God had done this for us, but had not done that, it would have been enough." For example, "If God had brought us to Mount Sinai, but had not given us the Torah, *Dayyenu* -- it would have been enough."

There is only one statement in the list that is not so qualified: The first: "If God had brought us out of Egypt". We never say, for example, "If God had kept us alive, but not brought us out of Egypt, it would have been enough." This is the one non-negotiable item in the list. It's as if the Haggadah is echoing Patrick Henry's famous line, "Give me liberty or give me death." In fact, another name for the holiday of Pessah is *Zman Ḥerutenu* – The time of our freedom.

So "freedom" is obviously of central importance to us. But that does not mean the word is clearly defined. So what, exactly, is freedom?

When my youngest son was eight, he said he was going to come to the seder table without wearing shoes. He added that he was a "free man". I appreciated the appropriateness of his remark. In the end, I convinced him to put shoes on, but I thought: What does freedom really mean, when you can't even come to the dinner table barefoot? When you have to constantly follow laws, commandments, rules, regulations, conventions, customs, practices; and society's expectations?

The Maharal of Prague, that 16th-century luminary, went so far as to say that Pessaḥ does not celebrate true freedom, but rather the change of masters from Pharaoh to God. What did he mean? Is there really no difference between the two?

Actually, there are at least two aspects in which the two "slaveries" differ. First, slavery to Pharaoh was malevolent and for the benefit of the master only, but "slavery" to God is benevolent and for our own benefit. God told us that a life that follows the Torah is more satisfying and meaningful than one that does not. Further, if we refused to obey, retribution was immediate and harsh in the case of Pharaoh, but not so, if it ever came, in the case of God. God told us specifically we have the power to choose. God allowed for *teshuvah* – repentance. Pharaoh did not.

The Mishnah argues that the only true freedom is freedom of the mind. It says:

אֵין לְךָ בֶן חוֹרִין אֶלָּא מִי שֶׁעוֹסֵק בְּתַלְמוּד תּוֹרָה.
En lekha ben chorin ella mi she'osek b'talmud Torah.
No one is free except one who engages in the study of Torah. [Avot 6:2]

This is an odd statement. Studying the Torah may make life more meaningful, more useful, more endurable, more pleasurable, but why more *free*? The Maharal explains: Slavery refers only to the body, which is enslaved by the laws of the universe. The spiritual world is not enslaved by these laws, and it is attained only by study, whence the quote. There are no limits to how much you can let your imagination soar, to how far your thoughts can take you, to what's going on in your own head. You are completely free in that regard.

So in the end, a person is never really free. He has to worry about a multitude of material problems and is constrained by the world around him. True freedom can only be attained by involvement in matters of the mind, and these are never constrained.

Shabbat shalom.

Bechukkotai
Lev. 26:3-27:34

B"H

Why Did God Create Predators?

In this week's Torah portion, *Bechukkotai*, God promises that if we follow His commandments, many good things will happen to us, including:

וְהִשְׁבַּתִּי חַיָּה רָעָה מִן־הָאָרֶץ -- *V'hishbatti chayyah ra'ah min haaretz.*
I will remove evil beasts from the land. [Leviticus 26:6]

This brings up the question: Why did God create the evil beasts in the first place? They must kill just to survive. People have free will and can survive on a vegetarian diet, so they can *choose* whether to harm, kill, or inflict pain on man or beast. But predators, or carnivorous animals, don't have that choice. They *must* do these things to survive. Why did God create them, if His goal was a world at peace?

Let's review what the Torah says on the matter before attempting to answer the question.

First, the Torah reports that originally, every living thing was vegetarian. The Book of Genesis says:

> God said [to Adam]... "Behold, I have given you every herb bearing seed, which is upon the face of all the earth, and every tree, on which is the fruit of a tree yielding seed; to you it shall be for food. And to every beast of the earth, and to every bird of the air, and to every thing that creeps upon the earth, where there is life, I have given every green herb for food; and it was so." [Gen. 1:28-30]

So carnivores did not exist then, but they exist today, and seem designed to kill, with their large and sharp teeth, their claws, and their great strength. Why?

Second, the Torah does not say that Adam was afraid of some of the animals, or that they tried to harm him. Maybe they didn't. Adam was simply told to *name* all newly-created animals:
> And out of the ground the Lord God formed every beast of the field, and every bird of the air, and brought them to Adam, to see what he would call them. And whatever Adam called every living creature; that was its name. And Adam gave names to all cattle, and to the bird of the air, and to every beast of the field. [Gen. 2:19-20]

Now, names are critical in Judaism. If God asked Adam to name the animals, it was for Adam to determine the purpose of each animal through its name, to become a "co-creator", as it were. Similarly, the patriarch Jacob identified the mission of each of his sons on his deathbed. For example, he said:
> The staff shall not depart from Judah, nor the scepter from between his feet... and to him shall the obedience of the people be. [Gen. 49:10]

Indeed, the royal house of Israel is from Judah.

Did Adam decide that some animals should be predators? Why?

Third, on Noah's Ark, the predators lived in peace with the other animals, since they all survived the Flood. Noah could not have fed them meat.

Fourth, in our Torah portion we saw that God promises that if we are observant, wild beasts will no longer threaten us. Does that mean that the carnivores were created to be our punishment for lack of observance? The Sifra, a Midrash on Leviticus, says that this means that the animals will be transformed, so they no longer cause harm to other creatures. [Torat Kohanim on Lev. 26:6].

Fifth, God declared the world "very good":
> וַיַּרְא אֱלֹהִים אֶת־כָּל־אֲשֶׁר עָשָׂה וְהִנֵּה־טוֹב מְאֹד
> *Vayyar Elokim et kol asher 'asa, v'hinne, tov me'od.*
> And God saw every thing that He had made, and, behold, it was very good. [Gen. 1:31]

The psalmist adds:
> טוֹב־יְהוָה לַכֹּל וְרַחֲמָיו עַל־כָּל־מַעֲשָׂיו׃

Tov HaShem lakol, verachamav 'al kol maasav
The Lord is good to all, and His mercy is over all His works. [Ps. 145:9]

So, presumably, there is some good in predators. In fact, the Talmud teaches that everything God created has a purpose:

> Rav Yehudah said in Rav's name: Of all that the Holy One, blessed be He, created in His world, He did not create a single thing without purpose. [Shabbat 77b]

So let us speculate on possible reasons for the creation of carnivores.

One reason for carnivores could be population control, to make sure the herbivore population doesn't grow too fast. Biologists have identified "predator-prey cycles", where the predators feed on the prey until little prey is left. Then they start dying of starvation. This lull allows whatever prey is left to reproduce exponentially, thus providing new food for predators, who thus also start growing in numbers. The cycle then repeats indefinitely. But could God not simply make the herbivores less fertile? Can't the herbivores control their own population based on the supply of food available, without the need to die a painful death in the mouth of predators?

A second reason for predators might be that they were created to serve as bad examples to human beings. Evidence for that theory is that no predators are kosher. Jews may not eat them. The Ramban went so far as to say that we may not eat them *because* they are cruel and we do not want to absorb their bad traits. Note also that all sacrificed animals were prey, not predators. The Midrash says:

> The Holy One, Blessed be He said: An ox is pursued by a lion, a goat by a leopard, a sheep by a wolf. Do not offer before Me the pursuers, but rather the pursued...
> [Eccl. R. 3:19; Lev. R. 27:5; Tanḥuma Emor 9]

The Book of Ecclesiastes says:

> And God [takes the side of] the pursued. [Eccl. 3:15]

But if so, isn't it better for an animal's sake to be non-kosher? Shechitah may minimize the pain inflicted in slaughtering kosher animals for food, but it does not eliminate it.

Some say that if there were no non-kosher animals, we could not get rewards for not eating them, so their role is simply to tempt us!

A third possible reason for predators is that people can use them in ways other than a source of food or population control. For example, bears and minks are used for clothing; crocodiles are used to make leather goods, such as wallets, purses and belts; whale oil was used for lighting for a long time; dogs are used for protection; snake venom and carnivorous plants are used to make medical products; leeches are still used in surgery; rats are used in medical research; falcons in hunting; dolphins are used by the military to detect mines and lost swimmers, or to retrieve objects; zoological gardens are used for education; circus animals can be used for entertainment; cats are used for companionship.

We can also learn from the behavior of all animals. The Book of Job says:
> [God] teaches us from the animals of the land, and from the birds of the heavens He makes us wise. [Job 35:11]

The Book of Proverbs says:
> Go to the ant, you sluggard, observe her ways and become wise; for although there is neither officer nor guard, nor ruler over her, she prepares her food in the summer, and gathers her food in the harvest. [Prov. 6:6-8]

The Talmud says:
> Rabbi Yohanan observed: If the Torah had not been given, we could have learned modesty from the cat, honesty from the ant, chastity from the dove, and good manners from the rooster. [Eruvin 100b]

A commentator added: And devotion and loyalty from a dog.

But these various uses do not *require* the animals to be carnivores. They could be herbivores and still fulfill these roles. Note, in passing, that Jewish law allows us to benefit from predators. (However, it does not allow us to benefit from mixtures of milk and meat.)

A fourth reason for predators might be a concession to man's own predatory instincts, his "evil inclination", or *yetser hara*, which the Talmud tells us is necessary for a useful life. It is worth noting in this respect that people like to use expressions that glorify wild beasts (usually predators) and vilify domesticated and useful animals (usually herbivores). For example, being called a lion, a tiger, an eagle, a fox, or an owl, is a compliment. Lions and tigers convey strength, eagles convey majesty, foxes convey cleverness, and owls convey wisdom. But being called a pig, or a dog, or a cow, or a weasel, or a chicken, or a turkey, or an ass, or an elephant, or a goat, or a monkey, or a rat, or a shrimp, or a toad, or a worm, is a grave insult! Cruelty and violence has always attracted huge crowds: Fights to the death, lethal games, public executions, and the like.

Our own Talmud is not exempt from lapsing into such dubious glorification:
> Rabbi Yehudah ben Teima used to say: Be bold as the leopard, light as the eagle, swift as the deer, and strong as the lion, to do the will of your Father in Heaven. [Avot 5:20]

Even in the Torah itself, Jacob, on his deathbed, compares some of his sons to predators. Judah is identified with a lion [Gen. 49:9], Dan with a serpent [Gen. 49:17] and Benjamin with a wolf [Gen. 49:27].

A fifth reason for predators could be improvement of the species. When the lion devours the gazelle, *which* gazelle does he devour? The swift and clever one or the slow and dumb one? Answer: The slow and dumb one. By removing the weakest from the prey population, predators improve the species. The survivors are the ones able to escape, and they are the ones that reproduce and pass on their ability: Survival of the fittest.

One can even generalize and say that everybody needs challenges to improve themselves and the world. These challenges frequently come in the form of stress, violence, death and devastation. Much human progress is due to competition, and even war. It is military requirements that gave us nuclear energy, the computer, the Internet, the GPS, the sonar, the radar, the microwave oven, the drone, night vision, rocket technology, space travel, canned food, freeze-dried food, the jet engine, the digital camera, and plastic surgery, not to mention improvements over existing technologies.

A sixth possible reason for predators is to keep enough plants for humans. When there were droughts and plants got scarce, humans got first dibs on the

plants. Herbivores had to become carnivores to survive. After all, humans come first. As God said to Adam:
> Have dominion over the fish of the sea, and over the birds of the air, and over every living thing that moves upon the earth... [Gen. 1:28]

Also, carnivores may have been originally herbivores, but then saw prey as easy targets of opportunity. It is easier and faster to get calories through eating animals than through eating plants. Evolution then adapted their bodies to their new diets. But this evolution can be reversed. Some carnivores are already omnivores: They eat both flesh and plants. The panda bear has the same digestive system as the grizzly bear and the black bear, both carnivores, yet it is an herbivore: It eats bamboo. The coyote is a carnivore, but can also live on melons, berries and cactus fruit. The raccoon can switch between being a carnivore and an herbivore. During the two world wars, when meat was rationed, zoos fed plants to their carnivorous animals, and they survived. Early in this century, a lioness was raised and survived on a vegetarian diet of cheesy pasta, potatoes, and green vegetables. She was called Lea, the "Spaghetti Lioness". She particularly liked Neapolitan sauce.

So the division between carnivore and herbivore may indicate preference and digestive system design, but it is not absolute.

In conclusion, it appears the world took a wrong turn when some animals became carnivores. "Converting" them to eating plants is part of the Jewish mission of *tikkun olam*, "repairing the world". After all, the prophet Isaiah promised us that one day animals will no longer threaten us, or one another. He said:
> And the wolf shall live with the lamb, and the leopard shall lie down with the kid, and the calf and the young lion and the fatling together...
> And the cow and the bear shall feed; their young ones shall lie down together; and the lion shall eat straw like the ox.
> And the sucking child shall play on the hole of the asp, and the weaned child shall put his hand in the vipers' den. [Isaiah 11:6-8]

And that is our hope for the future.

Shabbat shalom.

Bamidbar
Num. 1:1-4:20

B"H

Counting Jews

The first portion in the Book of Numbers, *Bamidbar,* begins with a census of the Israelites (whence the name "Numbers"). It is the third in the space of a year!

> On the first day of the second month, in the second year following the exodus from the land of Egypt, the Lord spoke to Moses in the wilderness of Sinai, in the Tent of Meeting, saying:
> שְׂאוּ אֶת־רֹאשׁ כָּל־עֲדַת בְּנֵי־יִשְׂרָאֵל לְמִשְׁפְּחֹתָם לְבֵית אֲבֹתָם בְּמִסְפַּר שֵׁמוֹת כָּל־זָכָר לְגֻלְגְּלֹתָם
> Take a census of the whole Israelite community by the clans of its ancestral houses, listing the names, every male, head by head.
> You and Aaron shall record them by their groups, from the age of twenty years up, all those in Israel who are able to bear arms. [Numbers 1:1-3]

The Midrash adds that Israel was counted on ten occasions:
> -Once when they went down to Egypt [Genesis 46:27].
> -A second time when they came out [Exodus 12:37].
> -A third time after the incident of the Golden Calf [Exodus 30:12].
> -Twice in the Book of Numbers:
> > -once in connection with the formation of the camps [Numbers 1],
> > -and once in connection with the division of the land [Numbers 26].
>
> -Twice in the days of Saul [1 Samuel 11:8, 15:4].
> -The eighth time in the days of David [2 Samuel 24:9].
> -The ninth time in the days of Ezra [Ezra 2:64; Nehemiah 7:66].
> -The tenth time will be in the future era of the Messiah, when, [as Jeremiah said:]
> > The sheep shall pass again under the hands of one who counts them [said the Lord]. [Jeremiah 33:13]
>
> [Numbers Rabbah 2:11]

Why all these censuses? There are many possible reasons.

First, there are practical reasons. Leaders need to know how many must be fed, how many can fight, how many survived, etc.

Second, because God loves Israel. Rashi writes that God counted Israel often because of His great love for Israel. The Ramban notes that a Hebrew word for "count", *pakod*, also means "to remember", "to be concerned with".

However, when King David ordered a census, against the advice of his chief of staff, Joab, God became angry and 70,000 people died of a plague. The Torah indeed warns there is risk in a census:
> Then God said to Moses, "When you take a census of the Israelites to count them, each must give to God a ransom for his life at the time he is counted. Then no plague will come on them when you number them. Everyone who is entered in the records shall pay ... a half-shekel as an offering to the Lord." [Ex. 30:11-13]

Perhaps David's people did not do that and counted directly? David repented of his mistake:
> But afterwards David reproached himself for having numbered the people. And David said to the Lord, "I have sinned grievously in what I have done. Please, O Lord, remit the guilt of Your servant, for I have acted foolishly." [2 Sam. 24:10]

Third, a census implies that each individual is significant. The line in the Torah translated as "Take a census of the whole Israelite community" is, in fact, "Lift up the heads of the whole Israelite community" (שְׂאוּ אֶת־רֹאשׁ *Se'u et rosh*): Make each person count, and, in so doing, affirm the worth of the individual. As is well-known, the Mishnah says:
> Whoever destroys one life is considered as if he had destroyed an entire world; and whoever saves one life is considered as if he had saved an entire world. [Sanhedrin 4:1 (22a)]

Rav Nahman of Breslov strongly emphasized this point:
> הַיּוֹם בּוֹ נוֹלַדְתָּ הוּא הַיּוֹם בּוֹ הֶחְלִיט הקב"ה שֶׁהָעוֹלָם אֵינוֹ יָכוֹל לְהִתְקַיֵּים בַּלְעָדֶיךָ
> *Hayom yom noladta hu hayom bo hechlit Ha-Kadosh Baruch Hu she-haolam eno yakhol lehit-kayyem bal'adekha.*

> The day that you were born is the day God decided the world could not be preserved without you.

Minority opinions are recorded in the Talmud. They are not silenced. Two Jews produce three opinions. Jews are small in number yet achieved great things: It's the individual who counts.

Fourth, a census implies that each individual counts the same as another. It's an equalizer. All the people are created equal in the image of God. Rich or poor, the Torah says they must pay a half-shekel each.

Yet this still reduces an individual to a number. During the Holocaust, the Nazis tattooed a number on the arms of Jews in concentration camps. Perhaps as a reminder of that, the Jewish tradition *does not allow us to count Jews directly*. Why not? The Talmud explains:
> Rabbi Eleazar said: Whoever counts Israel transgresses a prohibition, as the prophet Hosea said:
>> The number of the Children of Israel shall be like that of the sands of the sea, which cannot be measured or counted. [Hosea 2:1]

Indeed, as mentioned above, the Torah says that, rather than count the people directly, they collected a half-shekel from each person then counted the coins. Also, King Saul counted his soldiers by requiring each to give one shard of pottery, and then the shards were counted [1 Samuel 11:8]. Later he used kid goats. [1 Samuel 15:4]

Why this prohibition? There are many opinions. Rashi believes that when Jews are counted directly and are not deemed worthy and may get punished; that counting them puts an "evil eye" spotlight on them. Others reinforce this: When Jews are in a group, they are connected to God by their collective merit, but when they are counted, they become individuals and come under individual scrutiny. [Rabbenu Bahya, Panim Yafot on Exodus]

Sforno argues that a census draws attention to who is dead and who is still alive, which raises the dangerous question: Why am I alive and others are dead? Rabbi Jonathan Sacks points out that we are very small in number:

only one-fifth of one percent of humanity. Milton Himmelfarb adds that the number of Jews is smaller than a statistical error in the Chinese census. Their concern is: If we emphasize this, it may lower our morale.

Our strength is not in our numbers. The Torah says: Ask Jews to give, then count their contributions. It's the contributions that "count". We gave the world a lot, far out of proportion to our low numbers.

Finally, there are reasons of security. We must not create lists or counts that antisemites could use against us.

However, this prohibition is not in the Code of Jewish Law, although it is a well-entrenched custom. The matter is discussed by many commentators.
[Magen Avrohom 156; Alter Rebbe on Shulḥan Arukh 156:15]

So, in practice, Jews may be counted only in an indirect manner. Maimonides writes:
> It is forbidden to count Israelites except by means of some other object. [Rambam, Mishneh Torah, Daily Offerings and Additional Offerings 4:4]

Further, there must be a valid purpose for the counting. The Ramban writes that counting Jews without a purpose is forbidden. This may have been another of King David's errors.

One is allowed to count by saying "Not one, not two, etc." For a minyan, one may use a Torah verse that contains ten words, [Kitzur Shulḥan Arukh 15:3] such as:

הוֹשִׁיעָה ׀ אֶת־עַמֶּךָ וּבָרֵךְ אֶת־נַחֲלָתֶךָ וּרְעֵם וְנַשְּׂאֵם עַד־הָעוֹלָם

Hoshiah et amecha u'varech et nachalatecha ur'em venas'em ad ha'olam.
Save Your people and bless Your inheritance, and tend them and elevate them forever. [Psalms 28:9]

One may count body parts, such as noses, but not body parts whose removal would be fatal, such as the head.

There is a dispute as to whether one can count Jews in one's head.

Once the count is completed, one may say the total out loud. The reason is that the total numbers of the various tribes are stated in the Torah.

One may not participate in a counting even if one is not doing the counting. This gave rise to another dispute: May one participate in a census in Israel? Some say it's OK because one counts written names, not people, and non-Jews are included. Many others disagree unless the number of people per family is not calculated.

Shabbat shalom.

Naso
Num. 4:21-7:89

B"H

Queen Berenice: Heroine or Traitor?

This week's Torah portion, *Naso*, teaches that God allowed people to take Nazirite vows, to set themselves apart "for the sake of the Lord", and thereby achieve a higher level of holiness. [Numbers 6:2]

This vow included forms of abstinence. The Nazirite, man or woman, was not allowed to drink wine or other grape products, get a haircut, or come in contact with the dead. The duration of the vow varied from 30 days to life.

There were many possible reasons for the vow: Achieving a higher level of holiness; subduing the desire for pleasure by abstaining from wine; being distressed; paying for the fulfillment of a wish, such as the birth of a child [Nazir 1:7, 9-10]; or having an opportunity to make a sin-offering. [Nedarim 10b]

The most famous Nazirite was Samson. His mother promised to dedicate him to God during his whole life, saying:
> [Lord,] if You will grant Your maidservant a male child, I will dedicate him to the Lord for all the days of his life, and no razor shall ever touch his head. [1 Samuel 1:11]

Prominent rabbis opposed asceticism. They called sinners and evil-doers those who fasted or became Nazirites or took any vow whatsoever, even if the vow was fulfilled. [Nedarim 9a-b, 20a, 77b; Nazir 4a; Taanit 11a]

The practice fell into disuse, and no one is known to have taken Nazirite vows since the Middle Ages.

Let us examine in particular the case of Queen Berenice. She was a first-century Jewish princess of Judea, sister of King Herod Agrippa II, with whom she shared power. She was a great-granddaughter of Herod the so-called Great, whose family ruled Judea for 131 years, from 39 BCE to 92 CE, as a vassal-state of Rome.

King Agrippa had her marry a foreign king (Polemon II, king of Cilicia) for political reasons, but she agreed only after he accepted to convert to Judaism and be circumcised. She later left him and he gave up Judaism.

She lived through the Jewish rebellion of 66-70, which resulted in the destruction of the Temple, one million Jewish dead and 100,000 Jews taken away as slaves.

In the year 66, Florus, the procurator of Judea, systematically antagonized the Jews. He plundered the Temple for "taxes", crucified rioters, and sparked rebellion. Incensed and desperate, Berenice took a Nazirite vow, came before Florus crying, barefoot, hair shorn and nails uncut, disheveled, debasing herself before the Romans, begging for mercy for her fellow Jews. But Florus refused. The Roman soldiers tortured and killed Jews before her eyes, and would have killed her also, but she found refuge in the palace, where she spent the night surrounded by her guards. [Josephus, *The Jewish War* 2.15.1]

King Agrippa implored the people to stop rioting, but they burned down his palace. In 67, Emperor Nero sent Vespasian and his son Titus to put down the rebellion. Berenice and Agrippa sided with Rome, gave them intelligence and even material help. [Tacitus, Histories 2.81.2] The historian Josephus, a Jewish general, did likewise, betrayed his people in the field and supported the Romans. Many Jews did not support the uprising and even fought one another, to the point that the Talmud said that the Temple was destroyed because of "senseless hatred" – *sin'at chinam*. [Yoma 9b]

Berenice fell in love with Titus in 68 and began a long affair with him. [Tacitus, Histories 2.2.1; Suetonius, Titus 7.1; Cassius Dio, Roman History 66.15.3–4] **He was so jealous that** he had one of his generals killed when he suspected him of having an affair with Berenice. [Aurelius Victor, Epitome 10:7]

The Talmud reports: What did Titus do [when he conquered the Temple]? He took a prostitute with his hand, and entered the Holy of Holies [with her]. He then spread out a Torah scroll and committed a sin [had sex with her] on it. [Gittin 56b] It is believed this "prostitute" was Berenice.

Josephus tells us that Titus commanded that the Temple be spared, but Berenice herself set fire to it, believing the Jews would not surrender as long as it was standing... When Titus heard that the Temple was burning, he ran to help put out the fire, but he came too late, for the flames had already enveloped the whole Temple. Some of what Josephus wrote is frequently called self-serving; as he goes out of his way to make the Romans look good.

In 75, after the war, Berenice went to live with Titus in Rome. He was now the son of the Emperor. Public pressure made him send her away. When Titus became emperor in 79, she tried to go back to him but failed.

From the 17th century on, many works of art about Berenice and her affair with Titus were created: Plays, novels, operas, etc. I, myself, studied in school the play *Bérénice* by French playwright Racine.

Can we call her a heroine? She was religious, cared about her people, placed her life at risk, was true to her convictions.

Can we call her a traitor? She sided with the enemy, provided him with advice, information and material help, and even had an affair with him.

One can look at it both ways. People are complicated.

Shabbat shalom.

Behaalotecha
Num. 8:1-12:16

B"H

Democracy and Judaism

In this week's Torah portion, *Behaalotecha*, Moses appoints 70 elders to help him judge and govern Israel. The Sanhedrin is born: A body of 71 Sages ruling on Torah matters:
> And the Lord said to Moses: "Gather... seventy men of the elders of Israel... and bring them into the tent of meeting... and they shall bear the burden of the people with you, so that you don't have to bear it by yourself alone." [Numbers 11:16-17]

Since the Sanhedrin made decisions by majority vote, it is an early example of democracy, and gives us a good opportunity to ask the question: To what extent is modern democracy consistent with Judaism? Let us explore the matter, with some examples.

First of all, what is democracy? Most people will agree that it should have five pillars:
-First, free and fair elections of leaders;
-Second, few and reasonable restrictions on who can be a candidate;
-Third, only one vote per person;
-Fourth, all are equal before the law; and
-Fifth, perhaps most importantly, basic rights and freedoms secured by a constitution.

Indeed, without such a constitution (such as the Torah for Jews), democracy is not good and not Jewish. For example, in Nazi Germany, in the modern Gaza strip, or in France right after their revolution, leaders were elected, but without a constitution guaranteeing anything. We saw the results: Warmongers, terrorists, genocidal maniacs and murderous despots. Also, the name "democracy" can easily be usurped, as in the People's Democratic Republic of North Korea, of Algeria, of Yemen, etc.

That "all are equal before the law" is a principle instituted by Judaism. Indeed, Judaism has always stressed the importance of the individual. The Talmud says:
> Whoever destroys one life is as if he had destroyed an entire world; and whoever saves one life is as if he had saved an entire world… All people descend from one man so that no one can say, "My ancestors were greater than your ancestors".
> [Sanhedrin 37a]

Let us take a look at how collective decisions were arrived at in the history of Judaism.

First, in the period of the Patriarchs, God gives broad guidelines. In the period of Moses and the Exodus, God gives very detailed instructions, and, as we saw, instructs Moses to appoint 70 elders to help him judge and govern Israel.

Then, in the period of the Judges, Israel is a loose confederation of tribes, each with its own leaders. Some "judges" are recognized by consensus, to lead in battle in times of crisis and reconcile disputes. That period lasts about 450 years and is characterized by lawlessness. The Book of Judges states:
> In those days there was no king in Israel. Every man did that which was right in his own eyes. [Judges 21:25]

There are prophets to advise and report what God told them, but they have no enforcement powers. The Sanhedrin makes religious decisions, but has limited temporal power.

Fed up with lawlessness, the people demand a king with absolute power. God and the prophet Samuel strongly advise Israel not to have a king. Let's hear that exchange in the Book of Samuel:
> And the Lord said to Samuel, "Listen to the voice of the people in all that they say to you; for they have not rejected you, but they have rejected Me, that I should not reign over them... But you should solemnly warn them, and relate to them the customary practice of the king who shall reign over them..."

> And [Samuel] said [to the people], "This will be the customary practice of the king who shall reign over you. He will take your sons, and appoint them for himself, for his chariots, and to be his horsemen; and some shall run before his chariots.
> And he will appoint for himself captains over thousands and captains over fifties; and will set them to plow his ground, and to reap his harvest, and to make his instruments of war, and instruments of his chariots.
> And he will take your daughters to be perfumers, and to be cooks, and to be bakers.
> And he will take your fields, and your vineyards, and your olive trees, the best of them, and give them to his servants.
> And he will take the tenth of your seed, and of your vineyards, and give it to his officers, and to his servants.
> And he will take your menservants, and your maidservants, and your best young men, and your asses, and put them to his work.
> He will take the tenth of your sheep; and you shall be his servants.
> And you shall cry out in that day because of your king, whom you shall have chosen; and the Lord will not hear you in that day."
>
> But the people refused to obey the voice of Samuel; and said, "No. We will have a king over us; so that we may be like all the [other] nations; and so that our king may judge us, and go out before us, and fight our battles."
> And Samuel heard all the words of the people, and he repeated them in the ears of the Lord. And the Lord said to Samuel, "Listen to their voice, and make them a king." [1 Samuel 8:7-22]

So Samuel relents and anoints a king, Saul, and after Saul comes David, then Solomon, then a long line of kings, some good, some bad -- mostly bad. That period lasts 434 years, from 1021 to 587 BCE. It is followed by foreign occupation, and then the monarchy is restored in the 103 years of the Hasmonean period, from 140 to 37 BCE.

The kings were not absolute rulers. There were three checks and balances to their power – a sort of constitutional monarchy:

-First, the prophets. They could loudly tell the people things the king did not want to hear. The king sometimes harassed them and even killed them for it.

-Second, the priests. Led by the High Priest, they had their own religious responsibilities, separate from kings, prophets or rabbis; and were influential.

-Third, the Sanhedrin. It decided legal matters and ran an independent judiciary. Here are some examples of the limits it placed on kings. The Talmud says:
> -The king may neither judge nor be judged, testify nor be testified against. [Sanhedrin 18a]
> -The king or the High Priest may not be members of the [Sanhedrin's] board for the intercalation of the year [that is, to decide when to add a leap year]: The king on account of the upkeep of the army, and the High Priest because of the cold. [Sanhedrin 18b]

Here is what this means. The king is presumed to be biased in favor of adding a month because he pays his soldiers by the year, so adding a month makes the year longer. So he is excluded from the board. The High Priest is presumed to be biased against adding a month, because he has to immerse himself five times in the mikvah on Yom Kippur, and if Yom Kippur falls a month later the water is colder. So he is also excluded from the board. [Yoma 31b] These are very human considerations!

Note, before we go on, that whether or not to add a month to the Jewish year no longer has to be decided each year. The Jewish calendar we use today tells us when to do it. It was issued in 358 CE by Hillel II, as the last gift of the last Sanhedrin, before it was banned by the Romans.

Later, the view on kings changed. Rabbi Nehemiah writes that it is *not* a religious duty for the people to have a king. [Sifrei to Deut. 17:14] Abravanel writes, in 15th-century Spain, that a republic is better than a monarchy because it is better that power be shared.

The Sanhedrin was closest to democracy. All decisions were made by majority vote and each rabbi had only one vote. That practice is based on the verse in Exodus:
> לֹא־תִהְיֶה אַחֲרֵי־רַבִּים לְרָעֹת -- *Lo tihyeh acharei rabbim lera'ot.*

You shall not follow the majority for evil. [Exodus 23:2]
The Talmud interpreted this to mean:
> If you must not follow the majority for evil, then surely you must follow the majority for good. [Sanhedrin 2a]

The Sanhedrin instituted three types of courts:
- The basic bet din, with three judges, for ordinary cases;
- The Small Sanhedrin, with 23 judges, for capital offenses and other life-and-death matters; and
- The Great Sanhedrin, the "Supreme Court" of Israel, with 71 judges, to decide Jewish law. The number of judges always had to be odd, to avoid a tie.

Rabbis who refused to accept and teach the majority decision were expelled from the Sanhedrin and placed under cherem. Examples are Rabbis Eliezer and 'Akavya ben Mahalal'el. This is not full democracy, in that not everyone gets a vote: Only designated judges appointed to decide specific matters posed before them get to vote. The Talmud states:
> God [said]: "The majority must be followed. When the majority declares a thing permitted, it is permitted, and when the majority declares a thing forbidden, it is forbidden... The Torah is capable of interpretation, with 49 points [arguing one way] and 49 points [arguing the other way]." [Sanhedrin Y 22a]

They followed the principle of אַחֲרֵי רַבִּים--לְהַטֹּת *Acharei rabbim l'hattot*: When there is a dispute between an individual and the many, the halacha follows the many. [Berakhot 9a] Even God cannot overrule a majority opinion, as demonstrated by the famous story in the Talmud in which God's opinion on a law is overruled by the majority of rabbis. [Bava Metzia 59a]

How about the common people? Do they have any voice? The rabbis have a tradition of listening to them. Three rules attest to that.

The first is פּוּק חֲזִי מַאי עַמָּא דְּבַר *Puk chazi mai 'ammah d'var* – "Go out and see what the people are doing". Here are two examples from the Talmud.

-Rava, son of Rabbi Ḥanan, said to Abaye, "What is the law?"
He replied: פּוֹק חֲזִי מַאי עַמָּא דְבָר -- "Go out and see what the people are doing."
[Berakhot 45a, Eruvin 14b]

-They said, "Does anyone know whether Pessah overrides Shabbat?"
Hillel... knows... So they summoned him... and said..., "Master, what if a man forgot and did not bring a knife on the eve of Shabbat?"
[Hillel] answered, "I have heard this law, but have forgotten it. But leave it to Israel: if they are not prophets, they are the children of prophets!" [Go and see what the people actually do.]
The next day, [they found that] those who had a lamb as a Pessah sacrifice stuck the knife in its wool; and those who had a goat as a Pessah sacrifice stuck it between its horns. [Pesachim 66a]

So the people figured out the law by using their heads. Note that we are talking about deferring to what *observant* Jews do. Unlike what some say, Judaism is not "what Jews do". Sadly, in any generation, the majority does not know and does not follow many rules.

The second is: The rabbis will not issue a ruling that the people can't follow. The principle is:

אין גוזרין גזרה על הצבור אא"כ רוב צבור יכולין לעמוד בה
En gozrin g'zerah 'al ha-tzibbur ela im ken rov tzibbur y'kholin la'amod bah
We do not enact a decree upon the community unless a majority of the community is able to live up to it. [Bava Batra 60b]

Three examples from the Talmud:
-The rabbis declined to prohibit meat and wine after the destruction of the Temple [Bava Batra 60b];
-The rabbis declined to prohibit non-Jewish oil [Avodah Zara 36a]; and
-The rabbis declined to prohibit raising large animals in Israel [Bava Kamma 79b]. Today, some ultra-Orthodox rabbis refrain from prohibiting TV or the Internet because of this principle.

The third is: In the Talmud, Rabbi Yitzhak said: We must not appoint a leader over a community without first consulting the people. [Berakhot 55a] However, he left the exact meaning of "consulting" up for interpretation.

Now let's ask: Today, how are Jewish leaders chosen and how are Jewish decisions arrived at?

-In the State of Israel, there is a Western-style democracy.

-For new religious decisions, each rabbi is essentially on his own. There is no Sanhedrin to make central decisions. Majority rule is a thing of the past. New halachic decisions are made by individual rabbis, who make them stick only by virtue of the respect they inspire. Their decisions are sometimes controversial even centuries after their death. Maimonides is an example. Generally, Jews shop for a community whose practices most closely reflect their views.

-In congregations and Jewish institutions, there is minimal, fig-leaf democracy to select secular leaders and reach decisions. A Board handpicks a nominating committee, who handpicks the next leaders as a package, then the entire congregation or membership votes yes or no on the whole package. There are no opposing candidates, no running for office, no campaigning, no resumes circulated, no debates, no interaction, no candidates advertising their qualifications, their experience, their plans, or their vision to the people.

What can we conclude? Jewish law does not preclude democracy as practiced in the West, but does not mandate it either. The operating principle is: We must listen to the people. Even God, while agreeing with the prophet Samuel that a king is a bad idea, nevertheless tells Samuel:

> Listen to the voice of the people in all that they say to you...
> Listen to their voice... [1 Samuel 8:7-22]

Shabbat shalom.

Shlach Lecha
Num. 13:1-15:41

B"H

Fear of Success

In this week's Torah portion, *Shlach Lecha*, Moses sends 12 spies to scout the land of Israel, at the request of the people. [Deut 1:22] The people want this because do not take God's word that the land is good and that they will be successful against its inhabitants.

Ten of the 12 spies bring back an alarming report and say that the enemies cannot be defeated:
> The inhabitants are mighty, and the cities are extremely huge and fortified...
> We are unable to go up against the people, for they are stronger than we...
> The land... consumes its inhabitants, and all the people we saw in it are men of stature... giants... descended from the giants. In our eyes, we seemed like grasshoppers, and so were we in their eyes. [Numbers 13:1-33]

God then gets angry and decrees that the people will wander for forty years in the desert. This will ensure that the offenders will die before reaching the land and that only their children will settle in it.

What did the spies do wrong? Didn't they do what spies are supposed to do? I covered this in another d'var Torah and found ten possible answers in the Sources:

1-They scared and demoralized the people.
2-They doubted God's power.
3-They wondered if God had changed His mind after Israel built the Golden Calf.
4-They did not report that the inhabitants may have feared Israel.
5-They were fearful of facing the inhabitants, being former slaves.
6-They wanted go on living in the desert, isolated and directly connected to God.
7-They reported by using alarmist language.

8-They reported to the whole people, not only to the leaders.
9-They spoke lashon hara against the land and against God.
10-They were affected by the Israelites' distrust of God.

Let us now ask the question: Who were the spies? The Torah tells us:
כֻּלָּם אֲנָשִׁים רָאשֵׁי בְנֵי־יִשְׂרָאֵל
All [these] men were leaders of the Children of Israel. [Num. 13:3]

So they were not simple people. They were leaders to begin with. So they must have understood, better than the common folk, that God was with them, that God will protect them and allow them to conquer the land. God had already proved his abilities. So why did they discourage the people?

Hassidic sources [Likkutei Torah on Shlach] conclude that the spies' fear was precisely that God *would* keep His promises. In the desert, God was taking care of them completely: Manna from heaven, water from Miriam's well, miracles to keep the pursuing Egyptians away from them, teachings… In the Promised Land, they feared, God would be more distant, even while still keeping watch over them. They would have to do things they did not have to do in the desert: Fight battles, cultivate the land, earn a living, and build an entire country. And *think*.

In other words, they would have to live in the real world. So they resisted. Like most leaders, they did not welcome change.

The fact that the spies intended to give an alarming report all along was already hinted at in the Talmud:
> [The Torah says: "And the spies] went and they came" [Numbers 13:26]. Rabbi Yoḥanan said in the name of Rabbi Shim'on bar Yoḥai: This verse likens their going to their coming. Just as their coming back was with wicked counsel, so too, their going to Eretz Yisrael was with wicked counsel. [Sotah 35a]

The Lubavitcher Rebbe further points out that it is easy to find God while living isolated and with no responsibilities. [Likutei Sichot Vol 4 p1041]

Another Hassidic luminary, Rav Naḥman of Breslov, advocated doing just that, every now and then. He preached that to be close to God you have to speak to God "as you would with a best friend" in a natural setting, such as a field or forest, among the natural works of God's creation, to avoid man-made distractions. And speak to God in your own words, in your mother tongue, for at least one hour every day. He called it *hitbodedut*, meaning self-seclusion. It is central to his thinking. He described it as follows:

> It is very good to pour out your thoughts before God like a child pleading before his father. God calls us His children, as it is written [in the Torah]:
>
> בָּנִים אַתֶּם לַיהוָה אֱלֹהֵיכֶם
>
> You are the children of the Lord your God. [Deuteronomy 14:1]
>
> Therefore, it is good to express your thoughts and troubles to God like a child complaining and pestering his father.

As one commentator described it:

> During a session of *hitbodedut*, the practitioner pours out his heart to God in his own language, describing all his thoughts, feelings, problems and frustrations. Nothing was viewed by Rebbe Naḥman as being too mundane for discussion, including business dealings, conflicting desires and everyday interactions. Even the inability to properly articulate what one wishes to say is viewed as a legitimate subject to discuss with God. One should also use the opportunity to examine his behavior and motivations, correcting the flaws and errors of the past while seeking the proper path for the future.

But God wants us to live in the real world. It is difficult to find God in everyday life, surrounded by busy people who are sometimes animated by unholy motives. That is the challenge.

So the spies were *not* afraid of failure. They were afraid of *success*. It is a common occurrence.

Let us take an example. You are happy with your life. One day, you are offered a new job: More pay, more perks, more impact. You know you can do it, so you are not afraid of failure. But it entails more responsibility, so it will require:

-more of your time (which means less time for family, friends and hobbies),
-more work (and you are lazy),
-more scrutiny and media exposure (meaning less privacy),
-more managing and firing and causing pain (and this hurts you),
-more interaction with people at new income level (they may not be your type),
-more interaction with people in general (assuming you don't like it),
-more envy and enmity generated by your success, and even
-more risks (more liability for mistakes, possible threats, etc.).

It will change your life. All change is painful. The fear of the unknown can be paralyzing. It will lower your quality of life. So you refuse. The world will have to miss your positive impact. The price is too high.

In 1971, psychologist Abraham Maslow called it "The Jonah complex". In the Bible, God told Jonah to go to Nineveh and tell the Assyrians to repent or He will destroy them. Jonah keeps refusing and escaping, but God steers him back to his mission every time. Finally he reluctantly accepts, warns Nineveh and they repent, and God spares them.

We may *want* to succeed, but *fear* what the new responsibilities entail. That may have been the spies' dominant thinking.

Shabbat shalom.

Korach
Num. 16:1-18:32

B"H

What did Korach do Wrong?

The Torah portion of this week, *Korach*, tells us about Korach: Korach, the rebel; Korach, the bad guy; Korach, who dared to challenge the authority of Moses. What can we say about Korach, in these free and democratic United States, in the 21st century?

First, the story. Moses appoints his own brother High Priest, and his own cousin Chief Levite. Korach, a Levite, wanted that last position. Angry at what appears to be a clear case of nepotism and because of what he sees as a one-man show, Korach assembles 250 distinguished leaders of Israel, and together they confront Moses and Aaron. They tell them:

רַב־לָכֶם כִּי כָל־הָעֵדָה כֻּלָּם קְדֹשִׁים וּבְתוֹכָם יְהוָה וּמַדּוּעַ תִּתְנַשְּׂאוּ עַל־קְהַל יְהוָה

You take too much upon yourselves. All of us here are holy, every one of us, and God is among us. Why then do you raise yourselves above everyone else? [Numbers 16:3]

In other words, as the Midrash expounds: Every one of us heard God's commandments at Sinai, so we are all equal in God's sight. If you alone had heard God, you could have claimed superiority, but since we all heard God, you cannot [Numbers R. 18:6]. Who elected you? Who appointed you? When did you ever consult us on anything? What gives you the right to lord it over us? Some of us have other ideas on what to do next. Do we not have a say in the matter? We are all in dire straits, here in the desert. Do we not have the right to decide our own future, by majority vote?

Moses attempts conciliation, but fails. The Torah then tells us that God has the earth swallow up Korach and his 250 immediate followers, and follows up with a plague that destroys 14,700 more followers at large.

Yet we, as modern-day Americans, certainly resonate to Korach's argument. We hold that all people are equal. We require our leaders to be elected by the people. We insist that power be shared among three independent branches of government. We celebrate these principles on a regular basis. More to the point, we as *Jews* have never taken kindly to authority from any source. We like to argue, to debate, to dispute, and that is the foundation of our success.

Abraham argued with God. Tevye, in the musical *Fiddler on the Roof*, argued with God. Every page of the Talmud is filled with disagreements among rabbis. Demolishing conventional wisdom is a Jewish pastime, and the source of many Jewish accomplishments. We take the second commandment seriously: You shall not make unto thee any graven image. You shall have no idols. This means no idols of wood and stone, but it also means no idols of the mind. We are an iconoclastic people. We like to break idols.

> A new rabbi comes to serve a congregation. During services, when it comes time to recite the Shema, half the congregation stands and the other half sits. The half that stands says, "We stand for the Shema. It's the creed of Judaism. Thousands of Jews have died with the Shema on their lips." The half that remains seated says, "No, the Shema is just another part of the service."
> This drives the new rabbi crazy. One day he learns that the last founding member of the congregation is a 98-year-old man who lives in a nearby nursing home. So the Board appoints a delegation of three to go visit him: One who stands for the Shema, one who sits, and the rabbi himself.
> The man who stands for the Shema rushes over to the old man and says: "Wasn't it the tradition in our synagogue to stand for the Shema?"
> The old man says, "No, that wasn't the tradition."
> The other man jumps in excitedly. "So the tradition was to sit for the Shema, right?"
> The old man says, "No, that wasn't the tradition."
> At this point, the rabbi can't contain himself, takes the old man aside, and tells him: "Look, I don't care *what* the tradition was! Just tell them one or the other. Do you know what goes on in services week after week? Those who stand for the Shema yell at those who sit, and those who sit yell at those who stand."
> And the old man says, "*That* was the tradition!"

And, of course, you heard the one about two Jews shipwrecked on a desert island who build three synagogues: One for each of them to pray in, and one for each of them to say that he would not be caught dead praying in. What I find particularly significant about this story is that we Jews have always recognized the importance of having a full spectrum of views openly debated. That's why we always *want* that third synagogue to be there, even if we don't go to it.

Getting back to Korach, what did he really do that was so bad? Two things.

First, he picked the *wrong* time to make his point. Even the most committed democracies can suspend liberties and even proclaim martial law when facing a severe crisis. When Rome was a Republic, every time the enemy was at the gate, the first thing they did was appoint a "dictator". That dictator made all major decisions until the danger was passed, and was not legally responsible for anything he did while in office. In critical times, follow the leader. Korach didn't.

Indeed, God never says that Korach's point is invalid for all time. To wit, Korach's name was not blotted out in Israel. In fact, contrary to the impression left in this week's Torah portion, we learn later in Parshat Pinchas that "the sons of Korach did not die" [Num. 26:11]. These three sons composed eleven psalms, all recorded in the Book of Psalms [Ps. 42, 44-49, 84-85, 87-88]. Finally, we learn in the first Book of Chronicles that Korach had a very distinguished descendant, who got *two* books of the Bible named after him [1 Chron. 6:16ff]. Even Moses cannot claim this much! If you don't know who that was, I'll tell you at the end.

Most importantly, Korach's point was ultimately upheld. The priests, the Levites, the Sadducees, the Jewish aristocracy eventually lost power when the Temple was destroyed, 1,500 years later. Today, spiritual power in Judaism is vested in the rabbis, who rise to their position thanks to their own actions, their own merit, their own knowledge, not by virtue of their birth. The kohanim and leviim have only ceremonial positions today.

The last Lubavitcher Rebbe wondered why we allowed an entire Torah portion to be named after Korach, if he was such a bad person. He answered: Korach's desire for high spiritual office was, in and of itself, a positive thing. While the story tells us that we should not act against the will of God, even for the loftiest goals, it also teaches us that we should desire and yearn for the highest ideals. The end is good even if the means are not.

The second thing Korach did wrong is this. The Mishnah says:
> Every controversy that is for the sake of heaven will endure in the end; but one that is not for the sake of heaven will not endure in the end. Which is a controversy that is for the sake of heaven? The controversy between Hillel and Shammai [two rabbis who frequently argued Jewish law]. And which is a controversy that is not for the sake of heaven? The controversy between Korach [and Moses]. [Avot 5:17]

So the *motive* of the controversy is another factor against Korach. He was not trying to strike a blow for democracy or trying to understand Torah better; he was just trying to obtain personal gain.

Let me now close the loops and not keep you in suspense. The Code of Jewish Law says that you can recite the Shema in almost any position. [Shulḥan Arukh, Orach Ḥayyim 63:1] If you are seated when you come to the Shema during the service, you may stay seated; if you are standing, you may stay standing.

And Korach's distinguished descendant was the prophet Samuel.

Shabbat shalom.

Chukat
Num. 19:1-22:1

B"H

What Did Moses Do Wrong?

In this week's Torah portion, *Chukat*, the people complain that they have no water to drink. So God gives them water in the following manner:
> The Lord spoke to Moses, saying, "You and your brother Aaron take the rod and assemble the community, and before their very eyes speak to the rock to yield its water. Thus you shall produce water for them from the rock and provide drink for the congregation and their beasts."
> Moses took the rod from before the Lord, as He had commanded him.
> Moses and Aaron assembled the congregation in front of the rock; and he said to them, "Listen, you rebels, shall we get water for you out of this rock?"
> And Moses raised his hand and struck the rock twice with his rod. Out came copious water, and the community and their beasts drank.
> But the Lord said to Moses and Aaron, "Because you did not trust Me enough to affirm My sanctity in the sight of Israel, you shall not lead this congregation into the land that I have given them." [Num. 20:7-12]

So, to summarize, Moses strikes the rock instead of talking to it, and his punishment is that he won't be allowed to go into the Promised Land! It seems a bit out of proportion, doesn't it?

The mystery deepens when we remember that forty years earlier, God had indeed told Moses to strike a rock to bring water!
> [God said:] I will be standing there before you on the rock at Horeb. Strike the rock and water will issue from it, and the people will drink." And Moses did so in the sight of the elders of Israel. [Ex. 17:6]

Even earlier, God gave Moses yet a different instruction to bring water:

[Israel] traveled three days in the wilderness and found no water. They came to Marah, but they could not drink the water of Marah because it was bitter. That is why it was named Marah. And the people grumbled against Moses, saying, "What shall we drink?" So he cried out to the Lord, and the Lord showed him a piece of wood. He threw it into the water and the water became sweet. [Ex. 15:22-25]

So what was Moses' sin? There is plenty of speculation from our commentators.

First, he failed to teach the importance of following commandments. Rashi says:
> [God was telling Moses:] If you had spoken to the rock and it had brought forth water, I would have been sanctified in the eyes of the community. They would have said: "Now if this rock, which can neither speak nor hear, and does not require sustenance, fulfills the word of the Omnipresent, how much more should we do so."

So Moses missed teaching the people that if even a *rock* obeys God, how much more should *they*. Indeed, note that God had told Moses to do this "before their very eyes", meaning that He *wanted* the people to witness the miracle. The miracle is much more apparent if the rock yields water after being spoken to, rather than after being struck.

The Ramban says, in Moses' defense, that God said to him: "Take the rod ... and speak to the rock." He wondered: "What is the rod for? I must have misunderstood. God meant 'strike the rock with the rod', like last time." [Ramban on Numbers 20:8]

Second, he failed to follow instructions to the letter, no matter how seemingly trivial. God didn't like improvisations at that time. For example, God killed Nadav and Avihu because they offered "strange fire" before the Lord, which He did not command them. [Leviticus 10:1-2] My personal view on such punishments is this. God is saying, in effect, "OK, this is the beginning of Judaism and I must set the tone *now*. You must perform commandments *exactly* as ordered, or else. No variation whatsoever is allowed. Because if I allow variations, before too long you will be sacrificing your children to me to show me your great devotion, torture animals to death to offer me their pain, and other such nonsense, and I don't want any of that."

Third, he got angry. He angrily told the people, "Listen to me, you rebels." He gave a bad example. The people might have concluded that anger is permissible, or that God was angry with them. (He was not.) Standards must be higher for more important people. [Rambam, Shemonah Perakim 4]

Fourth, he took credit. He said "Shall *we* bring forth water for you from this rock?" This implied that it was he and Aaron, not God, who were bringing water from the rock. [Ramban on Numbers 20:8]

Fifth, he insulted the congregation. He called them "rebels". He lumped them with the direct followers of Korach who had already been punished. The Ran, from 14th-century Catalonia, says:
> Our Sages of blessed memory [directed leaders to be in] awe of the congregation, to the point of their saying: "Let the fear of the congregation be always upon you." [Sotah 40a] And we find the chief prophet himself [Moses] to have been punished in this regard, having said: "Listen, now, you rebels," [Numbers 20:10] as if each one of them as an individual merited the rebuke. [Darashot HaRan 1:4]

Sixth, he did not appreciate that his audience had changed. A good leader must tailor his words and actions to his audience. Forty years earlier, when talking to former slaves, hitting the rock is what they understood must be done to get results. But for their children, born free, gentle persuasion (as in speaking) must be tried first. Moses just assumed he should do the same as before -- strike the rock. So God concluded from that that a new generation of leaders was needed at this point, as they were about to enter the Land.

Another explanation is that the punishment was for an earlier sin. God does not say it was the matter of the rock that caused the punishment. Abravanel says it was because of previous offenses: Aaron made the Golden Calf and Moses sent the spies. Or, possibly, it was indeed for the matter of the rock, but that was simply the last straw, and, by itself, would not have justified the punishment. Or, to protect their honor, God pretended that the rock was the reason for their punishment, not the heavier sins. Or God had already decided that Moses was not the right leader for the task ahead, and used the rock as an excuse. Possible justification: Why else would Aaron be punished also? He didn't strike the rock.

There are other views. Perhaps Moses was getting old and forgetful: He forgot God just told him to "speak", but remembered that 40 years ago God told him to "strike"? The old are better at remembering events of long ago than recent ones.

Rabbi Jonathan Sacks notes that Miriam, Moses' older sister, had just died [Num. 20:1] and he was very close to her. Also, the Talmud gives her credit for the water:
> The well was given to the Jewish people in the merit of Miriam... When Miriam died the well disappeared... "And there was no water for the congregation". [Numbers 20:2] [Taanit 9a]

Perhaps, in his bereavement, Moses could no longer cope with crises and had to yield leadership?

Perhaps it wasn't Moses' fault, but the people's fault. In Deuteronomy, Moses says:
> [I told God:] "Let me, I pray, cross over and see the good land on the other side of the Jordan, that good hill country, and the Lebanon." But the Lord was angry with me on your account and would not listen to me. The Lord said to me, "Enough! Never speak to Me of this matter again!" [Deuteronomy 3:25-26]

Likewise, Psalm 106 states:
> They caused [God's] anger by the waters of Merivah and Moses suffered because of them. [Psalm 106:32]

Perhaps God wanted a direct connection with the people as they were about to enter the land, without the intermediaries Moses, Aaron and Miriam. [Tikkunei haZohar]

The episode is certainly a bit of a mystery. We have all done things in our lives that we didn't think were particularly significant or wrong, but suffered very bad consequences on their account. Sometimes they are even things we may have done before without any adverse consequences or any consequences at all.

As the Talmud says on such matters: *Teku* -- Let it rest.

Shabbat shalom.

Balak
Num. 22:2-25:9

B"H

Was the Prophet Balaam Good or Bad?

In this week's Torah portion, *Balak*, we learn that Balak, the king of Moab, is afraid of the Israelites, who are numerous and physically close. So, three times Balak sends emissaries to enlist Balaam, a non-Jewish prophet, to curse Israel. Balaam refuses the first two times, saying that God has already blessed Israel. But the third time he accepts and follow them. King Balak then shows him Israel from three different "angles". Each time, Balaam blesses Israel against his will and predicts victory for them. This is what Balaam says, in the Torah:

> [Balaam said: Even] if [King] Balak gave me his house, full of silver and gold, I cannot transgress the word of the Lord, and do either good or evil on my own. Only what the Lord speaks can I speak. [Num. 24:13]

> How goodly are your tents, O Jacob, your dwelling places, O Israel! They extend like streams, like gardens by the river, like aloes which the Lord planted, like cedars by the water. Water will flow from his wells, and his seed shall have abundant water. His king shall be raised over Agag, and his kingship exalted. God, Who has brought them out of Egypt with the strength of His loftiness, shall consume the nations that are his adversaries…Those who bless you shall be blessed, and those who curse you shall be cursed. [Num. 24:5-9]

> How can I curse whom God has not cursed, and how can I invoke wrath if the Lord has not been angered? ... [Israel] is a nation that will dwell alone, and will not be reckoned among the nations. Who [can count] the dust of Jacob or the number of the seed of Israel? [Num. 23:8-10]

> There shall shoot forth a star out of Jacob and a scepter shall rise out of Israel, which will crush the princes of Moab and uproot all the sons of Seth. Edom shall be

possessed, and Seir shall become the possession of his enemies, and Israel shall triumph. [Num. 24:17-18]

The Talmudic interpretation of "How goodly are your tents, O Jacob!" is that Balaam saw that the entrances of the tents were not facing each other, to allow for privacy. [Bava Batra 60a]

The Midrashic interpretation of the line "[Israel] is a nation that will dwell alone" is:
> When Israel rejoices, no other nation rejoices with them...
> And when the [other] nations prosper, Israel will prosper with them...
> [Tanḥuma Balak 12, Num. Rabbah 20:19]

Maimonides interprets the line "There shall shoot forth a star out of Jacob" to refer to King David, and the line "And a scepter shall rise out of Israel" to the future Messiah, a descendant of King David. [Rambam, Mishneh Torah, Laws of Kings 11-12]

On his way to King Balak, Balaam's ass sees an angel with a sword blocking his way and gets off the road. Balaam never sees it, strikes the ass every time, and brings him back to the road. Finally the ass speaks and asks Balaam why he is hitting him. Kli Yakar, from 17th-century Prague, writes:
> This was to impress upon Balaam that he should not feel proud that he has been given the gift of prophecy. If it suits God's purposes, even an ass will see angels and make speeches.

God then comes to Balaam and asks him:
> Who are these men with you? [Num. 22:9]

The Midrash comments:
> That villain [Balaam] thought: [God] does not know them! There are times, then, when [God] does not know what is going on, and so I shall do with His children all that I please. [God is not omniscient, so I will find a time when I am able to curse, and God will not realize it.] [Tanḥuma Balak 5, Numbers R. 20:9]

Now, let's step back and ask the question: Who was Balaam? The Talmud tells us that Balaam was one of "the seven prophets who prophesied to the [non-Jews]". (The other six were: Balaam's father, Beor; Job; and Job's four friends.) [Bava Batra 15b] The Midrash adds:

God raised up Moses for Israel and Balaam for the peoples of the world. [Num. R. 20:1; Tanḥuma Balak 1]

It also tells us that Balaam was greater than Moses in many respects:
[The Torah says:] And there has not arisen since, in Israel, a prophet [like Moses] [Deut. 34:10]. In Israel there had not arisen one like him, but there had arisen one like him among the nations of the world. This was in order that the nations of the world might have no excuse for saying: "If we had possessed a prophet like Moses, we would have worshipped the Holy One, blessed be He." What prophet did they have who was like Moses? Balaam the son of Beor. There was a difference, however, between the prophecy of Moses and that of Balaam...

-Moses did not know who was speaking with him, while Balaam knew...
-Moses did not know when the Holy One, blessed be He, would speak with him, while Balaam knew...
-Moses did not know what the Holy One, blessed be He, would speak to him about, while Balaam knew...
-Moses could not speak with [God] whenever he pleased, but Balaam could...
[Numbers Rabbah 14:20]

Also that:
-Balaam knew the exact time of God's anger. [Avoda Zara 4a–b; Sanhedrin 105b] [Berakhot 7a]

This is what allowed his curses to be effective.

The Talmud makes clear that Balaam's prophecies are included in the Torah:
Moses wrote his own book [Deuteronomy] and the parts dealing with Balaam [Num. 23-24] and the Book of Job. [Bava Batra 14b]

There is an extra-biblical reference to Balaam. In 1967, a plaster was discovered in Tell Deir 'Alla, in Jordan, in a language similar to biblical Hebrew, dated about the 8th century BCE, with an inscription bearing the name of *bl'm br b'r:* "Balaam, son of Beor". He is referred to as "a divine seer" [*'zh < lhn*], who dreamt that the gods told him of an impending disaster that would devastate the land. He then tells the people about it, and is viewed as a heroic figure, who tried to save his people and the land.

Now we can turn to our central question: Should the prophet Balaam be considered good or bad? Here is some evidence that he was good:

-First, Balaam obeyed God, and made clear he would not depart from what God told him to say. In the Book of Micah, Balaam's role is interpreted as a sign of God's providence over his people. [Micah 6:5]

-Second, Balaam may have had bad thoughts, but one is judged by actions, not thoughts.

-Third, Balaam's is the only prayer in the Jewish liturgy written by a non-Jew:
מַה־טֹּבוּ אֹהָלֶיךָ יַעֲקֹב מִשְׁכְּנֹתֶיךָ יִשְׂרָאֵל
Mah tovu ohalecha Yaakov, mishkenotecha Yisrael!
How goodly are your tents, O Jacob, your dwelling places, O Israel! [Num. 24:5]

But here is evidence that Balaam was bad:

-First, the Talmud says so:
> Balaam was a *rasha*, a wicked one [Berakhot 7a; Taanit 20a; Num. R. 20:14].
> An evil eye, a haughty spirit, and a proud soul, are the marks of the disciples of "Balaam the Wicked". [Avot 5:19]

-Second, God protected Israel by not allowing Balaam to curse them, and implies that Balaam intended to do just that. The Book of Joshua says:
> [God said:] Balak... sent Balaam to curse you. But I would not listen to Balaam. Therefore, he blessed you. So I saved you from his hand. [Joshua 24:9-10]

-Third, the Midrash says what Balaam wished:
> [Balaam wished] to uproot an entire people for naught and for no reason. [Num. R. 20:1; Tanḥuma Balak 1]

He advised Balak on how to destroy them. The Talmud concludes that this caused the Holy Spirit to depart from the Gentiles, and since then prophecy existed only in Israel. [Bava Batra 15b]

-Fourth, the Talmud says that Balaam was one of Pharaoh's counselors, along with Jethro and Job. His advice was that the male Israelite children should be cast into the Nile. [Sanhedrin 106a]

Eventually Balaam was killed; Jethro argued against harming Israel and was rewarded; Job was silent and was punished.

-Fifth, Balaam led Israel to worship Baal Peor. That episode follows the account of Balaam's blessing in the Torah [Numbers 31:8, 16]:
> Balaam arose, went, and returned home, and Balak went on his way. Israel settled in Shittim, and the people began to commit harlotry with the daughters of the Moabites. They invited the people to the sacrifices of their gods, and the people ate and prostrated themselves to their gods. Israel became attached to Baal Peor, and the anger of the Lord flared against Israel. [Num. 24:25, 25:1-3]
> Behold, [the women] caused the people of Israel, *through the counsel of Balaam*, to commit trespass against the Lord in the matter of Peor. [Num. 31:16]

-Sixth, the Torah implies that because Balaam had been retained by King Balak of Moab to curse Israel, God prohibited the conversion to Judaism of Ammonite and Moabite men. The Torah says:
> An Ammonite or Moabite [masculine] shall not enter into the congregation of the Lord...forever, because they met you not with bread and with water in the way, when you came out of Egypt; and because they hired against you Balaam the son of Beor of Pethor of Mesopotamia, to curse you. Nevertheless the Lord your God would not listen to Balaam; but the Lord your God turned the curse into a blessing to you, because the Lord your God loved you. [Deuteronomy 23:4–6. See also Neh. 13:2]

-Seventh, Balaam was killed fighting the Israelites, together with the kings of Midian, during the war against the Midianites:
> They also slew with the sword Balaam ben Beor. [Num. 31:8]

-Eighth, Balaam was demoted. He is referred to as *ha-qôsem* ("the diviner") in the Book of Joshua. [Joshua 13:22] The Talmud comments:
> [It says in Joshua: The children of Israel also slew with the sword] Balaam ben Beor, the soothsayer. A soothsayer? But he was a prophet! Rabbi Yoḥanan said: At first he was a prophet, but later he [was demoted to] soothsayer [as punishment for wishing to curse Israel]. [Sanh. 106a]

-Ninth, he was cruel to that poor ass.

-And tenth, what he wanted to say was bad, even though God made him say the opposite:

> Rabbi Yohanan said: From the blessings of that wicked man [Balaam] you may learn his intentions. [Every blessing is the opposite of the curse he wanted to utter.] Thus he wished to curse them
> -That they [the Israelites] should not possess any synagogues or school-houses. [This is deduced from] "How goodly are your tents, O Jacob." [Num. 24:5];
> -That the Shechinah should not rest upon them: [Deduced from] "And your dwelling places, O Israel [*mishkenotecha*, or tabernacles]" [Num. 24:5];
> -That their kingdom should not endure. [Deduced from] "They extend like streams." [Num. 24:6];
> -That they might have no olive trees and vineyards. [Deduced from] "As gardens by the river's side." [Num. 24:6];
> -That their odor might not be fragrant. [Deduced from] "As the trees of aloes which the Lord has planted." [Num. 24:6];
> -That their kings might not be tall. [Deduced from] "And as cedar trees beside the waters." [Num. 24:6];
> -That they might not have a king the son of a king. [Deduced from] "He shall pour the water out of his buckets." [Num. 24:7];
> -That their kingdom might not rule over other nations. [Deduced from] "And his seed shall be in many waters." [Num. 24:7];
> -That their kingdom might not be strong. [Deduced from] "And his king shall be higher than Agag." [Num. 24:7];
> -That their kingdom might not be awe-inspiring. [Deduced from] "And his kingdom shall be exalted." [Num. 24:7]
>
> [Yet] Rabbi Abba bar Kahana [noted]: All [these blessings eventually] reverted to a curse, [Balaam's intention was fulfilled with the fall of the house of David, the destruction of the Temple, and the Exile] except the synagogues and schoolhouses, for it is written:
>> But the Lord your God turned the curse into a blessing for you, because the Lord your God loved you. [Deut. 23:6.]
>
> The curse, but not the curse**s**. [Only one curse was permanently turned into a blessing: the one concerning synagogues and schoolhouses, as these never disappeared from Israel.] [Sanhedrin 105b]

There is an implication here that the "feelings" of a prophet matter, even if his words belie them.

Ultimately, Balaam had the free will to do as he pleased, except in cursing whom God had blessed, because the words of a prophet are fulfilled. But one may ask: Why did God first tell Balaam that He disapproved of his trip, yet let him go and try to curse Israel, and finally prevent him from doing so? Why not just stop Balaam right away? The Talmud answers: Free will:

> One is allowed to follow the road he wishes to follow. [For example], it is written, "God said to Balaam, 'You shall not go with them,'" [Num. 22:12] [but Balaam clearly wanted to go with them, so] then it is written, "If the men came to call you, rise up and go with them." [Num. 22:20]
> [Makkot 10b]

Balaam had a complex personality, to be sure, but he was clearly more bad than good.

Shabbat shalom.

Pinchas
Num. 25:10-30:1

B"H

The Fate of Moses' Children

In this week's Torah portion, *Pinchas*, we hear the story of five unmarried sisters. Their father, Tzelaf'chad, died, and had no sons to inherit his land. They went to Moses and asked him to be allowed to inherit it. The daughters' tribe, Manasseh, was not opposed, but said they then *had* to marry within their tribe, so the land would not end up in the tribes of their husbands. Moses consulted with God, and God decided the daughters would *both* inherit the land *and* marry within their tribe. So they married their cousins.

Immediately afterwards we read about who will lead Israel after Moses:
> The Lord said to Moses: "Ascend these heights of Abarim and view the Land that I have given to the Israelite people. [Then you will die,] for you disobeyed My command to uphold My sanctity in their sight by [striking the rock instead of talking to it to bring] water." ...
> [Moses said to God:] Let the Lord, Source of the breath of all flesh, appoint someone over the community who shall go out before them and come in before them, and who shall take them out and bring them in, so that the Lord's community may not be like sheep that have no shepherd.
> And the Lord answered Moses, "Single out Joshua son of Nun, an inspired man, and lay your hand upon him." [Num. 27:12-18]

Why are these two stories next to each other? The Midrash answers:
> Why did [Moses] make this request [right] after ordering [that the women should inherit]? Simply this. When he saw that the daughters of Tzelaf'chad inherited the properties of their father, he thought, "This is the time for me to make my own request. If daughters inherit, it is [also] proper for my sons to inherit my glory." [But] the Holy One, blessed be He, said to him [quoting Proverbs]:
>> He who tends a fig tree will enjoy its fruit. [Proverbs 27:18]

> Your sons sat idly and were not involved with Torah [study]. It is [more] appropriate that Joshua, who served you, serve Israel and not lose his compensation. [Midrash Tanḥuma, Pinchas 11]

So Moses' sons were not sufficiently meritorious. The mantle of leadership passed to Joshua, a disciple of Moses, not to his sons.

But what happened to Moses' sons? Moses had two sons: Gershom and Eliezer. They were not part of the Exodus proper. While still in Egypt, Moses had sent them off with their mother Zipporah to their grandfather Jethro in Midian. After the Exodus, they joined their father in the desert. [Exodus 18:1-6] This is the last mention of them in the Torah.

Their descendants are mentioned much later in the Book of Chronicles:
> The sons of Moses [were] Gershom and Eliezer. The sons of Gershom [were] Shebuel the Chief. And the sons of Eliezer [were] Reḥavia the Chief (הָרֹאשׁ רְחַבְיָה). Eliezer had no other sons, but the sons of Reḥavia were very numerous. [1 Chronicles 23:14-17]

So Moses had a lot of descendants. We just don't know who they are. They disappear from history. The Talmud adds:
> From where do we [derive that all of God's promises are fulfilled?] From Moses our teacher. [God said to him...] "I will make from you a mighty nation." [Deut. 9:14] ... This promise was fulfilled, as it is written ... "the sons of Reḥavia [Moses' grandson] were very many" רָבוּ [1 Chronicles 23:15–17]...
> And Rav Yosef taught in a baraita: "Many" means more than 600,000. [Why? Because it says here] "[the sons of Reḥavia] were very many" [and it is written in Exodus with regard to the Israelites in Egypt]: "And the children of Israel became numerous and multiplied and were very many." [Exodus 1:7]
> [Berakhot 7a]

And the Torah says that the children of Israel were 600,000. [Ex. 12:37]
Note: 600,000 is about $2^{19.2}$. Assuming every descendant has two children, it takes less than 20 generations for one person to engender 600,000.

We also learn that King David appointed Moses' grandson as his treasurer:
> And Shebuel, the son of Gershom, the son of Moses, was ruler over the treasuries. [1 Chronicles 26:24]

Now, did Gershom's line descend into idolatry? The Book of Judges, which begins after Joshua's death, says:
> The Children of [the Tribe of] Dan erected graven images for themselves; and Jonathan son of Gershom son of Menashe [וִיהוֹנָתָן בֶּן־גֵּרְשֹׁם בֶּן־מְנַשֶּׁה], and his descendants, served as [idolatrous] priests to the tribe of Dan until the land went into exile. [Judges 18:30]

The Talmud enlightens us:
> Was Gershom the son of Menashe? No, he was the son of Moshe (Moses). But his actions were not like those of Moses his father, so they added a *nun* to connect him to Menashe instead. [Avot d'Rabbi Natan 34:4]

Why Menashe? The Talmud says:
> [Although he was the son of Moses] he acted like Menashe [the wicked king of Judah who was notorious for idol worship], so the verse linked him to Menashe. [Bava Batra 109b]

Rashi adds that the extra *nun* is raised above the line:
> In deference to Moses, the letter *nun* was included, thus altering the name. It is scripturally suspended to indicate that he was actually not "Menashe", but "Moshe".

Here is the raised *nun* in the Aleppo Codex, dating from the 10th-century:

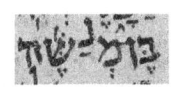

בֶּן־מְנַשֶּׁה

But one wonders. What does the raised *nun* accomplish? If anything, it brings attention to the fact that Moses' grandson descended into idolatry, which is what the *nun* attempts to hide in the first place. Perhaps it is there precisely for us to know the story, as a warning to take the education of our children seriously. Also, if the written word hides, why did the Sages reveal? Besides, like all humans, biblical characters have flaws which the Torah not only mentions but frequently highlights. So what is the lesson here?

The Jerusalem Talmud offers another explanation [Berakhot Yerushalmi 9:2]:

The hanging *nun* is meant to teach the power of *teshuva*: *If* Jonathan son of Gershom repents of his idolatry, *then* he will be considered like a son of Moses, but if not, he will be considered like a son of the idolatrous King Menashe. In this approach, Jonathan has no biological links to either Moses or Menashe.

Back to: "The sons of Gershom [were] Shebuel the Chief." Why the plural when only one is listed? Is the other son (Jonathan, the idolater) not listed to erase his memory? Unlikely, because the same is done for the child of Gershom's brother Eliezer, who was not recorded as idolatrous. The Talmud says that Shebuel and Jonathan were the same person, who repented:

> When King David saw that money was excessively precious [to Jonathan], he appointed him [as director] of the treasuries of the Temple, as it is stated: "And Shebuel, the son of Gershom, the son of Moses, was ruler over the treasuries". [1 Chronicles 26:24]
> And was his name really Shebuel? Wasn't his name Jonathan? Rabbi Yoḥanan says: [He is called Shebuel because he repented and] returned to God [*shav la'el*] with all his heart. [Bava Batra 110a]

The Midrash adds that Jonathan only took up idolatry as a job to survive!

> The rabbis expressed surprise: After [Jonathan] became a priest to idolatrous worship, how could he have lived so long? [There are some 200 years from the Judges to King David.] ... Because he tried to discourage idolatry ... by shaming [those who engaged in it].
> One cunning fellow … asked him: "Why then do you sit here and serve [idols]?"
> He replied: "I am paid for it, but I despise it."
> When [King] David heard of him he sent for him and said, "Do you, the grandson of so righteous a man practice idolatry?"
> He replied: "I have received this teaching from the house of my father's father [Moses]: Sell yourself to idolatry rather than be dependent on your fellow-creatures."
> [David] said to him: "God forbid! That is not so. What it means is: Sell yourself to a service which is foreign to you [i.e., which you consider to be below your dignity] rather than depend on your fellow-men." [Song of Songs Rabbah 2:18]

The Talmud indeed says:

> Rav said to [his student] Rav Kahana: Skin a carcass in the marketplace and take payment [if you need money], but do not say: I am a great man and this work is beneath me. [Bava Batra 110a]

The Midrash continues:
> So David saw [Jonathan's] love of money and put him in control of his treasury. They say that after David died [Jonathan] returned to his evil ways. [Song of Songs Rabbah 2:18]

Why the relapse? The Jerusalem Talmud says that that was because, when King David died, King Solomon replaced all the ministers, including Jonathan, so Jonathan was again out of work. It includes this amusing story:
> [A man came to Jonathan and asked him what offering he should prepare for the idol.] Jonathan said: "Go, prepare and bring to me one dish of fine flour and place upon it ten eggs, then put it before the idol, and he will eat from all that you bring and I will appease him on your behalf." As soon as the person would go on his way, Jonathan would eat the foods himself. [Berakhot Yerushalmi 9:2]

This brings up the question: Should one take legal but ethically questionable jobs out of necessity, like Jonathan? Should one take advantage of people's gullibility, arguing that, if these people feel good afterwards and everybody's happy, there is no harm?

To complicate the story, the Mekhilta tells us that Moses agreed to have idolatrous descendants!
> When Moses said to Jethro, "Give me your daughter Tzipporah as a wife", Jethro answered, "If you do what I ask of you, I will give her to you as a wife."
> Moses said: "What do you ask?"
> Jethro replied: "Your first son must serve idolatry. The following sons may serve God in heaven."
> Moses accepted.
> Jethro said: "Swear."
> And Moses swore. [Mekhilta d'Rabbi Yishmael 18:3]

Why would Jethro make such a request of Moses in the first place? Jethro said in the Torah:
> Now I know that the Lord is greater than all the gods. [Ex. 18:11]

Hearing that, God Himself told Moses to welcome Jethro into Judaism with great honor. [Midrash Tanḥuma, Yitro 6]

One answer is provided by Rabbi Shim'on Schwab, from 20th-century Europe and the US. The Midrash says that Jethro worshipped all existing idols and concluded only God was real:
> Jethro said: I have not neglected to worship any idol in this world, but I have found no god like the God of Israel. [Midrash Tanḥuma, Yitro 7]

So Jethro wanted a grandson to do as he did: Worship all existing idols and conclude only God was real. This would give him a better appreciation of monotheism. [Mayan Bet Hashoeva on Yitro 18, 4] To be sure, this is a dubious interpretation of the injunction to teach Torah to our children:
> וְשִׁנַּנְתָּם לְבָנֶיךָ -- Veshinantam levanecha -- and you will teach it to your children. [Deut. 6:7]

Perhaps, since Gershom lived with his grandfather Jethro in Midian for a long time, Jethro's bad influence indoctrinated him into idolatry. Later, when Jethro converted to Judaism, it was too late to turn Gershom around. Moses' other son, Eliezer, was younger and was not irrevocably influenced.

One may wonder: Is this why Moses at first did not circumcize Gershom, and God threatened to kill him, and his wife Zipporah had to do it in his stead?
> The Lord met [Moses], and sought to kill him. Then [Moses' wife] Tzipporah took a sharp stone, and cut off the foreskin of her [newborn] son... So [God] let [Moses] go... [Ex. 4:24-26]

Perhaps Moses intentionally did not want Gershom circumcised because of his promise to Jethro.

Early on, Judaism struck a balance between hereditary rights and meritocracy. Priesthood and kingship were hereditary; prophecy and scholarship were not. The Mishna says:
> Rabbi Shim'on said: There are three crowns: the crown of Torah, the crown of priesthood, and the crown of royalty. [Avot 4:13]

The Rambam adds:
> Aaron merited priesthood, David merited monarchy, but the crown of Torah remains for anyone who wants to be crowned with it. [Rambam on Avot 4:13]

Aaron got a hereditary dynasty to last forever -- the kohanim. But Torah scholarship is *not* hereditary. It belongs to all of us. The Torah states:

תּוֹרָה צִוָּה־לָנוּ מֹשֶׁה מוֹרָשָׁה קְהִלַּת יַעֲקֹב -- Moses commanded us the Torah as an inheritance of the congregation of Jacob. [Deut. 33:4]

Another question arises from this narrative. The Torah says:
> This is the line of Aaron and Moses at the time that the Lord spoke with Moses on Mount Sinai. These were the names of Aaron's sons: Nadav, the first-born, and Avihu, Eleazar and Ithamar. [Numbers 6:1-2]

But only Aaron's four sons are listed! Moses' sons are not. The Talmud says:
> Moses' nephews are considered as his children because he taught them Torah ... Anyone who teaches another person's son Torah, it is as if he fathered him. [Sanhedrin 19b]

The Midrash adds:
> Rabbi Natan says: Moses was saddened that one of his sons did not stand [in his place], whereupon the Lord said to him: Are the sons of your brother Aaron not like your sons? [Sifrei Devarim 305:2]

So Moses taught the sons of Aaron but not his own? Why? The Torah that he preached says:

וְשִׁנַּנְתָּם לְבָנֶיךָ -- And you will teach it to your children. [Deut. 6:7]

Does teaching other children replace teaching your own? Or perhaps it is better to let others educate your children, on the grounds that the teacher-student relationship is fundamentally different from the parent-child relationship?

Finally, a disturbing question to which there is no definitive answer: Are the children of important and charismatic people doomed to a life of mediocrity, wrongdoing and irrelevance? It is true that in many cases important people have little time for family and that their children suffer for it. There are examples and counterexamples. Sadly, Moses' children are an example.

Shabbat shalom.

Matot
Num. 30:2-32:42

B"H

Are Jews Responsible for One Another?

Today we discuss a Jew's responsibility towards other Jews. The Talmud says:
כל ישראל ערבים זה בזה -- All Jews are responsible for one another.
How far does this responsibility extend?

In this week's Torah portion, *Matot*, the Israelites are at the gates of the Promised Land. All they need to do is cross the Jordan River. But some don't want to:

> The descendants of Reuben and Gad had an abundance of livestock ... and they saw the land of Jazer and the land of Gilead, and behold, the place was a place for livestock...
>
> They [said to the leaders:] ... Let this land be given to [us and] do not take us across the Jordan...
>
> Moses said "Shall your brothers go to war while you stay here?" (לַמִּלְחָמָה הַאֲחֵיכֶם יָבֹאוּ וְאַתֶּם תֵּשְׁבוּ פֹה)
>
> Why do you discourage the children of Israel from crossing over to the land which the Lord has given them? This is what your fathers did [in the incident of the spies and God was angry and made us wander in the desert for 40 years]... And behold, you have now risen in place of your fathers as a society of sinful people... If you turn away from following [God], He will leave you in the desert again, and you will destroy this entire people."
>
> They approached [Moses] and said, "We will build here pens for our livestock and cities for our children. We will then arm ourselves quickly [and go] before the children of Israel until we have brought them to their place. Our children will reside in the fortified cities [... but] we shall not return to our homes until each of the children of Israel has taken possession of his inheritance. We will not inherit with them on the other side of the Jordan and beyond, because our inheritance has come to us on the east bank of the Jordan."

> Moses said to them, "If you do this... you shall be freed [of your obligation] from the Lord and from Israel and this land will become your heritage before the Lord."
> [Numbers 32:1-32:22]

That is what was done in the end. The tribes of Gad and Reuben were given the land they wanted, on the east side of the Jordan.

This episode raises many questions.

First, is it mandatory for Jews to live in Israel? Did God make entry in the Promised Land mandatory? Are all Jews today commanded to live in Israel? The point is in dispute. Since the Talmud does not list the 613 mitzvot, there is no definitive list. The Rambam's list [jewfaq.org/613.htm] is the most often quoted and used. It does not include a commandment to live in Eretz Yisrael. But the Ramban's list does. Both sages acted on their beliefs. When the Rambam was forced out of Spain, he lived only very briefly in Israel, then moved to Egypt, did all his work there and died there. When the Ramban was forced out of Catalonia, he went directly to Israel and worked and died there.

Second, did Gad and Reuben act properly in refusing to settle in Israel? Yes, because they have freedom of choice. Rabbi Simcha Zissel of Kelm, from 19th-century Lithuania, writes:
> Why do Jews [today] continue to live outside Israel -- on the other side of the Jordan or the other side of the Atlantic? Because they have found good grazing lands for their cattle, and it's a shame to give it up.

Indeed, Moses did not say that their action was illegal. He only said they had a moral duty to help in the war.

Third, did Gad and Reuben have a responsibility to fight for the Promised Land if they didn't want to settle in it? Yes. This is especially true because all Israelites helped them get the land they are in now. Otherwise, the other Israelites would think that they did not trust God, that they just wanted to avoid war (as in matter of the spies), and that only material goods are important to them.

Many ask today: Is it right that the State of Israel should fight "for us" while we live in comfort far away? Note that only 5% of *post*-Holocaust Jewry was in Israel when it became independent, on 14 May 1948: 600,000 out of 12 million.

This question brings us to our responsibility towards other Jews. The Talmud says flatly:
> כל ישראל ערבים זה בזה – *Kol Yisrael aravim zeh bazeh*
> All Jews are responsible for one another.
> [Shevuot 39a, Sanhedrin 27b; also Sifra Bechukotai 7:5; Mishneh Torah on Oaths 11:16; Or HaChaim on Deut. 29:9; Shaarei Teshuvah 3:72]

The literal translation is: All Jews are *guarantors* for one another. It is derived from the Torah:
> And each man will stumble over his brother. וְכָשְׁלוּ אִישׁ־בְּאָחִיו [Lev. 26:37]

The Talmud interprets this verse as:
> One Jew may suffer because of the sin of another Jew. [Sanhedrin 27b]

Traditionally, the line also means that a Jew may perform a mitzvah in the place of another Jew.

But what does being "one people" entail? First and foremost, it entails collective responsibility, and this also means collective punishment. This was demonstrated very early. During the battle of Jericho, one (and only one) Israelite engages in looting, which was forbidden:
> Achan ..., of the tribe of Judah, took of that which was proscribed, and the Lord was incensed with the Israelites. [Joshua 7:1]

God is angry at everybody for the actions of a single individual! As a result, the Israelites lose the next battle, at Ai (עַי) [Joshua 7:5]. Joshua investigates and discovers Achan's action. Achan confesses, is tried and stoned to death. Joshua tells Achan:
> What calamity you have brought upon us! [Joshua 7:25]

This idea is also vividly expressed in a Midrash: A man with two heads claimed a double portion of his father's estate. King Solomon covered one of the heads and poured hot water over the other head. The covered head cried from the pain, proving that it was really one person. [Tosafot on Menaḥot 37a]

The fall of Temples was due to collective sins, even though many did not commit them. The logic behind collective punishment is: When bad behavior is widespread and tolerated, it slowly becomes acceptable to all. The bad apple spoils the lot.

In spite of their forced dispersion, Jews feel united and interdependent. When a Jew suffers anywhere, fellow Jews throughout the world express concern and try to help. This is heartfelt and not simply obeying commandments. Also, it is not a choice. The Midrash says:
> The people of Israel are similar to a ship. If there is a hole in the lower hold, one does not say, "Only the lower hold has a hole in it." Rather they must immediately recognize that the ship is liable to sink and that they must repair the hole down below. [Tanna Debei Eliyahu Rabbah 11]

Should Jews be quiet and avoid the limelight? Especially for a persecuted minority, the actions of one reflect on the whole. In olden days, Jewish community leaders did not want Jews to become too prominent, because their mistakes would have repercussions on the whole community. Better to stay in the shadows. But being "prominent" is no sin. Should we accept this philosophy today?

The Torah tells us to rebuke sinners:
> הוֹכֵחַ תּוֹכִיחַ אֶת־עֲמִיתֶךָ וְלֹא־תִשָּׂא עָלָיו חֵטְא:
> Rebuke your fellow and incur no guilt because of him. [Lev. 19:17]

The clear implication is: If you don't rebuke him, you will be punished on his account. Don't hate him, don't avoid him, don't harm him, don't kill him, only rebuke him. The Talmud says:
> [Rava] said: [You must rebuke another] even 100 times… [Even] a student [must rebuke] a teacher [if necessary]. [Bava Metzia 31a]

Rashi adds that the rebuke must be done in private. [Rashi on Lev. 19:17]

How far does the notion of being punished when another person sins extend? To the whole world, if you don't *speak up* against the sins:

> Rav, Rabbi Ḥanina, Rabbi Yoḥanan, and Rav Ḥaviva taught: …
> Anyone who can protest [the sinful conduct] of the members of his household and does not protest, [he himself is] apprehended [… and punished].
> [If he can protest the sinful conduct of] the people of his town [and does not do so, he is] apprehended [and punished].
> [If he can protest the sinful conduct of] the whole world [and does not do so], he is apprehended for [the sins of] the whole world. (נִתְפָּס עַל כָּל הָעוֹלָם כּוּלוֹ) [Shabbat 54b]

Now, to be responsible for other Jews, we must first know where they are. But we don't always know who is Jewish and who isn't. It is likely that the vast majority of halachic Jews today have no idea they are Jewish. A single Jewish woman who was forced to convert out a thousand years ago could have thousands of matrilineal descendents today, all halachically Jewish, all ignorant of the fact. Do we have an obligation to conduct genealogical research to find out who is Jewish, inform them of the fact and instruct them? If not, why not? Isn't it a logical implication of the Talmudic phrase?

What should we do to keep peace in the house and truly become "one people"? Jews are argumentative: Two Jews, three opinions. Jews are religiously divided, especially Ashkenazim. Rabbi Jonathan Sacks suggests seven principles to enhance the feeling of "peoplehood":

> 1-Keep talking to one another.
> 2-Listen to one another. *Shema Yisrael.*
> 3-Work to understand those with whom you disagree. The law follows Hillel, not Shammai, because Hillel's students were kind and humble, and always quoted the other side's opinions before their own, as the Talmud says:
>> Rav Abba stated in the name of Samuel: For three years there was a dispute between Beth Shammai and Beth Hillel, the first saying, "the halachah agrees with us" and the second [also] saying, "the halachah agrees with us". Then a heavenly voice [bat kol] was heard saying:
>> "אלו ואלו דברי אלהים חיים" -- *Ellu v'ellu divrei Elokim Chayyim* – These and these are the words of the living God; but the halacha agrees with Beth Hillel."

> However, since both are the words of the living God, what was it that entitled Beth Hillel to have the halachah agree with them? It was because they were kind and modest, and studied both their own rulings and those of Beth Shammai and were even so [humble] as to mention the opinions of Beth Shammai before their own. [Eruvin 13b]

4-Do not seek victory. Think first of the overall good of Jews and Judaism.
5-Give respect to get respect.
6-Even if you do not agree with fellow Jews, show that you care about them.
7-Remember that God chose us *as a people*. God did not choose only you, but me as well.

Anti-Semites do not make distinctions between Jews. We are united by shared memory, shared identity, shared fate, shared faith, even as we differ on the details. As Benjamin Franklin said, "We must hang together or, most assuredly, we will hang separately."

Shabbat shalom.

Mass'ei
Num. 33:1-36:13

B"H

The Wandering Jews

This week's Torah portion is Mass'ei:
אֵלֶּה מַסְעֵי בְּנֵי־יִשְׂרָאֵל -- *Elleh mass'ei B'nai Yisrael*
These are the journeys of the children of Israel. [Numbers 33:1]

It begins by recounting all the places where the Israelites encamped in their forty-year saga from Egypt to Israel; all forty-two places, one by one. An average of about one move a year: Long enough to gain a modicum of stability in every place, but also long enough to feel the pain of uprooting from surroundings that had become familiar and akin to home. The length of each stay was never known in advance: A few days here, a few months there, a few years yonder. We hear about:

- Yam Suf, where God split the sea;
- Marah, where God provided water in spite of the people's grumblings;
- Refidim, where they fought the Amalekites;
- Sinai, where they received the Torah;
- Mount Hor, where Aaron died;
- and so on.

Rashi tells us that God demonstrated kindness to the people in one way or another at every stop.

The Sfat Emet, 19th-century Chassidic sage, tells us that in each of the 42 stops the Jewish people accomplished a specific *tikkun*, a "spiritual repair".

Maimonides tells us that the 42 stops are recalled by name in the Torah so that future generations could not say, "The forty-year wandering was a myth and never took place."

Other commentators tell us that each stop was an opportunity for new and necessary growth, that the best path between two points is not necessarily the straight line, and that the journey can be even more important than the destination.

The Israelites were looking forward to some stability in their destination, the Promised Land. Little did they know that what they had just experienced was merely a harbinger of things to come! Indeed, for most of our history, we were the "Wandering Jews", forced to roam the earth in the elusive search of a home. After 1,500 years of relative stability in the Land, punctuated, to be sure, by wars, invasions, deportations, and subjugation by foreign nations, we began a long, 2,000-year diaspora, where "wandering" was the name of the game. This dispersion is foretold in the Torah. The Book of Deuteronomy says:

וְהֵפִיץ יְהוָה אֶתְכֶם בָּעַמִּים וְנִשְׁאַרְתֶּם מְתֵי מִסְפָּר בַּגּוֹיִם אֲשֶׁר יְנַהֵג יְהוָה אֶתְכֶם שָׁמָּה
The Lord will scatter you among the nations, and you will be left few in number among the nations where the Lord will drive you. [Deut. 4:27]

Our history since the Romans expelled us from the Land of Israel was a depressing series of expulsions and resettlements, of perpetual uprooting, sometimes several times in a single lifetime. Antisemites, religious fanatics or mere plunderers would expel us from one place; then enlightened leaders, recognizing our value, and sometimes for a hefty fee, would invite us to some other place; then a new leader would come on the scene and expel us yet again. Jews have been banished or forced out from more places on earth than any other people. Most of the time it was a physical expulsion, and some of the time our tormentors made life so unbearable for us that we *had* to leave, abandoning all our possessions. Let us recount just a few of these expulsions:

-From Israel to Babylon in 597 BCE
-From Israel to the larger Roman Empire in 70 and 135 CE – the Diaspora
-From Alexandria, Egypt, in 415
-From Arabia in 635, as Islam appeared on the scene
-From many places in Germany: From Mainz in 1012, from Brandenburg in 1510, from Bavaria in 1593, from Frankfurt in 1614, from Vienna in 1670, among others
-From many places in Italy: From Bologna in 1172; from Trani in 1380, from a lot of communities in the 16th century
-From France in 1182, 1254, 1322, 1359, and 1394, where they played the game of expulsion and confiscation of all property, readmission for ransom many years later, and then expulsion and plunder yet again
-From England in 1290, where the ban was in force for 350 years
-From Spain in 1492, after my ancestors enjoyed a Golden Age there
-From Portugal in 1497
-From the Papal States in 1569
-From Recife, Brazil, in 1654
-From Norway in 1687, where the ban lasted 164 years
-From Europe in the 1940s, when most Holocaust survivors chose to live elsewhere
-From all Arab countries after the creation of the State of Israel in 1948
-From Russia at the time of the pogroms, or from its worthy successor the Soviet Union
-From Iran, when getting through the day became a challenge

The list is never-ending. Most of you are unusual Jews, in that you are still living in the land of your birth. I am not like you in that respect. I am an "ordinary" Jew. I was born and raised in Egypt, where my entire, large extended family lived, then I was forced out and now live in the United States. My extended family was literally scattered to the five continents:
-Looking *only* at my uncles and aunts, they went to France, Belgium, Brazil, Italy, and Venezuela.
-Some encountered even more antisemitism or had difficulty adapting, or wanted to rejoin family, and had to uproot themselves a second time. They went to Spain, Israel, and Belgium.
-Many of their children and grandchildren, my cousins, did not stay in the land of their birth. For various reasons, they emigrated to Israel, the US, Australia, Italy, Colombia, Mexico, Switzerland, France, and Costa Rica.

-Looking beyond my immediate family, I would not be surprised if I had relatives in every Western country.
-My father's native language was Ladino, or Judeo-Spanish. My mother's was Arabic. My native language is French. My children's native language is English. All of us have ties to many different cultures.

Is all this wandering good or bad? Certainly, while you are living it, it does not feel good. Constantly having to adapt to change, to new cultures, learning new languages and new ways of surviving, starting over from scratch again and again to provide for loved ones, all of this takes its toll.

But looking back on it, as I am doing now, does any good come out of it? Yes. First and foremost, we survived. Fortunately for us, the world is not a single country, and each country has its own policies towards the Jews. Second, we are the world's roving ambassadors. We are the repositories of the collective wisdom of the entire world. We keep moving and learning new things. We take the best from the many cultures we come in contact with, blend it with our own homegrown Judaism, and offer the world new points of view, new approaches, new angles, new solutions to problems. We offer creative and imaginative ideas that result from the combined wisdom of the world. We separate the wheat from the chaff and take only the best, what is consistent with Judaism.

The Midrash says:
אִם יֹאמַר לְךָ אָדָם יֵשׁ חָכְמָה בַּגּוֹיִם, תַּאֲמֵן ... יֵשׁ תּוֹרָה בַּגּוֹיִם, אַל תַּאֲמֵן
If a person tells you there is wisdom among the nations, believe him...
If a person tells you there is Torah among the nations, do not believe him.
[Lamentations Rabbah 2:13]

So we wander all over the globe, look for the wisdom, take it wherever we find it, blend it with our own Torah teaching, and produce something good and uniquely Jewish. This explains in part why we tend to excel wherever we go, and encourage others to excel as well. The Talmud says:
לֹא הִגְלָה הַקָּדוֹשׁ בָּרוּךְ הוּא אֶת יִשְׂרָאֵל לְבֵין הָאוּמּוֹת אֶלָּא כְּדֵי שֶׁיִּתּוֹסְפוּ עֲלֵיהֶם גֵּרִים

> The Holy One, blessed be He, exiled the Jews among the nations only so that converts might join them. [Pesaḥim 87b]

Well, for most of the past 2,000 years proselytizing would have cost us our lives, so the Talmud's observation must be interpreted figuratively, to mean that part of the Jewish mission is to spread the values of Judaism, the wisdom of Torah, and the seven Noahide laws, to the entire world, to fulfill the injunction we received through the prophet Isaiah to be "a light unto the nations" [Is. 42:6, 49:6], so that one day, in whatever sense one wishes to understand it, the prophecy of Zechariah will be fulfilled:

וְהָיָה יְהוָה לְמֶלֶךְ עַל־כָּל־הָאָרֶץ בַּיּוֹם הַהוּא יִהְיֶה יְהוָה אֶחָד וּשְׁמוֹ אֶחָד
And the Lord shall be king over all the earth. On that day the Lord shall be One, and his name One. [Zech. 14:9]

So we march through the world, much as a farmer marches through his field, throwing seeds left and right as he moves, confident that they will one day bring fruit.

Jewish mysticism has its own take on our wandering. It teaches that, at the time of Creation, a vessel holding divine holiness burst, and dispersed its contents throughout the world. Jews were then made to wander far and wide just so they could gather these "sparks of holiness" and make them available to all. [Arizal, quoted in Petech Anayim by Chida, Yoma 38]

To bolster the point, the Hebrew word for exile is גּוֹלָה *golah* and the Hebrew word for redemption is גאולה *geulah.* So you just add the letter aleph to get from exile to redemption. Aleph represents the number one, which in turn represents God, the One. Thus, Jews went into exile to bring God to the world, thus bringing about the redemption and the coming of the Messiah.

In fact, Rabbenu Beḥaye, 13th-century Spanish mystic, says that there were sparks of holiness in the 42 places where the Israelites encamped in the desert, listed in our Torah portion, and that God made the Israelites go there just so they could gather them.

Will our wandering ever stop? When the State of Israel was created, only 5% of the Jewish people lived there. That fraction has steadily risen. Today, it is 42%. Most of the increase was due to necessity, not ideology. Necessity is the practical reason why we have a state. Today, for the first time since Talmudic days, there are more Jews in Israel than in any other single country. (The US is a close second.) Their observance is even on the way up. As the poet wrote:

> We shall not cease from exploration
> And the end of all our exploring
> Will be to arrive where we started
> And know the place for the first time. [T S Eliot, Little Gidding]

So wandering makes you appreciate your origins in the end.

Will all Jews ever live in Israel? That depends more on the rest of the world than on us Jews. The better they treat us the fewer of us will make aliyah to Israel.

And *should* all Jews live in Israel? That depends on religious ideology. Tradition says that the Messiah will bring about the ingathering of the exiles into their homeland, in Hebrew קיבוץ גלויות *kibbutz galuyot*. So tradition is unmistakably clear: *All* Jews *should* live in Israel. But there are also practical considerations. With antisemitism on the rise, and showing no sign of disappearing, *should* all Jews live in one small place, in this age of weapons of mass destruction? Iranian leaders have said that Israel is a "one-nuclear-weapon" country. And, for the mystics, have all the sparks of holiness scattered throughout the world been gathered already?

Only one thing is certain: Jews make themselves useful wherever they live.

The term "wandering Jew", to be sure, is a term of derision, a label stuck on our backs by antisemites. To them, we are the grievous sinners, condemned by the Almighty to wander the earth with the mark of Cain on our forehead, reviled and despised wherever we go, a testament to the wages of sin. It is time for us to claim that term of derision for our own, and wear it as a badge of honor. For without the so-called "wandering Jew", humanity would be worse off.

A botanist with a sense of history gave the name "Wandering Jew" to a certain plant. Here is what his web site says about this plant:
> This plant is unique. When given minimal sustenance it will spread out and grow. Cutting out its roots and planting it in other soil will make it regenerate itself and start to grow. It adapts easily to various environments and conditions. The plant is very pretty, doesn't require a lot of care, and is really hard to kill.

As we conclude Bamidbar, the Book of Numbers, we say the phrase our Sages have taught us when we complete a book of the Torah:
> חזק חזק ונתחזק -- *Chazzak, chazzak, v'nit-chazzek*
> Be strong, be strong, and may we be strengthened.

May we continue to travel from strength to strength in our peregrinations throughout the world, and may we be continually strengthened by our enforced wandering, as God intended.

Shabbat shalom.

Devarim
Deut. 1:1-3:22

B"H

Esau, Edom, Rome and the Jews

In this week's Torah portion, *Devarim*, the Israelites are positioned to enter the Land of Israel. But to do so they must pass through the land of the Edomites, south of the Dead Sea. The Edomites are the descendants of Edom, who is also known as Esau, Jacob's "evil twin". The Edomites refuse passage, so God tells the Israelites to leave the Edomites alone and bypass them:

> And the Lord spoke to [Moses], saying…Command the people, saying: "You are to pass through the border of your brothers, the children of Esau, who live in Seir. They will be afraid of you. Be very careful. You shall not provoke them, for I will not give you of their land, no, not as much as the breadth of a single foot, because I have given Mount Seir to Esau as an inheritance." [Deuteronomy 2:2-5]

Why is God being so protective of the Edomites? Isn't Esau a "bad guy"? One answer is provided in the Torah:

> לֹא־תְתַעֵב אֲדֹמִי כִּי אָחִיךָ הוּא
> You will not hate an Edomite, for he is your brother. [Deut. 23:8]

OK. Brotherhood is worth something. But that cannot be the whole story, because our tradition paints Esau as the very epitome of wickedness. The Talmud says:

> Rabbi Yoḥanan said: That wicked man [Esau] committed five sins [in one] day. He dishonored a betrothed maiden, he committed a murder, he denied God, he denied the resurrection of the dead, and he spurned [his] birthright. [Bava Batra 16b]

Moreover, our tradition tells us that the Edomites are the ancestors of the Romans, and indeed of all Europeans and the entire Christian world. The Midrash says:

> Two orphans were left to [Esau], namely Remus and Romulus, and You [God] gave permission to a she-wolf to suckle them, and afterwards they arose and built... Rome. [Esther R. 3:5]

Now, the Romans, and their successors the Byzantines, dominated the land of Israel for seven centuries: From 63 BCE, when Pompey conquered Jerusalem, to 638 CE, when the Muslim Caliph Omar Ibn al-Khattab (عمر ابن الخطاب) conquered Jerusalem. The Romans oppressed the Jews, destroyed their Temple, and exiled them from their land. So why did God protect them and allow them to do this?

The Midrash and the Zohar offer another answer: Esau merited land and power because he honored his father. The Midrash tells us:
> Rabbi Shim'on ben Gamliel said: "All my life I attended to my father's needs, yet I did not do for him one hundredth of what Esau did for his father. I used to attend to my father in soiled garments and go out in the street in clean ones, but when Esau attended to his father, he attended upon him in royal robes, for, he said, 'Only royal robes befit my father's honor.'" [Genesis R. 65:16]

Commenting on our portion, Rabbi Yudan says in the Midrash:
> When Israel came to wage war with [the children of Esau], the Holy One blessed be He showed Moses the [Cave of Machpelah] where the Patriarchs are buried and said to him: "Moses, say to Israel, you may not engage [Esau] in battle, because he still deserves reward for the honor he gave to [some of] those who are buried in this mountain [i.e., his parents]." [Deuteronomy R. 1:15]

The Zohar adds:
> Rabbi Yesa said: It is written [in Malachi]:
> בֵּן יְכַבֵּד אָב וְעֶבֶד אֲדֹנָיו
> A son honors his father and a servant his master. [Mal. 1:6]
> Such a son was Esau, for no man in the world showed as much honor to his father as he did, and it is thanks to this that he obtained dominion in this world [through his descendants the Romans]. [Zohar, Bereshit 1:146b]

Five centuries later, in King David's day, the Edomites attacked Israel many times. Israel was, of course, allowed to defend itself, but God would not allow David to annihilate them or take their land. In the Midrash, God tells David:

> I know you can [defeat Edom], but I wish to subdue My world through them [i.e., through Rome]... I need [Rome] for future generations [until the final Redemption]... Moses, your teacher, already wished to engage [the Edomites] in battle, but I said no to him. [Deuteronomy R. 1:16]

The Midrash adds:
> Rabbi Yehoshua ben Levi said: "When the [Roman] enemies came to destroy Jerusalem, there were 600,000 destructive angels standing at the gate of the Temple ready to engage them in battle. However, when they saw the Divine Presence observing in silence ... they, too, made way [for the enemy to enter]." Rabbi Yehudah bar Sima said: "[God] saw [Esau] destroying His Temple and remained silent ... [because Esau] still deserves reward for honoring his parents [and must not yet be defeated] ... The Holy One, blessed be He, said: 'I am paying [Esau his] dues.' [Deuteronomy R. 1:17] ...Command the heads of [all future] generations to treat [Esau] with respect." [Deuteronomy R. 1:20]

This is certainly a big reward for honoring your father and your mother! On the one hand, one can almost understand Rome being given power and influence as a reward. But on the other hand, why should this reward include oppressing the Jews for seven centuries, destroying their Temple and stealing their land? These are two different things. Nowhere in Judaism does it say that part of your reward for anything will be to get away with murder. Nowhere does it say that in civil law either.

Sometimes, in hindsight, we can recognize that God's plan requires us to suffer. Slavery in Egypt was a case in point. We didn't do anything wrong to deserve it. God simply said to Abraham:
> Know for certain that your offspring will be strangers in a strange land, and will be enslaved and afflicted for four hundred years. [Genesis 15:13]

No reason was given. Evidently God thought slavery was necessary. But why? Many answers come to mind:
> -First, for our protection. Jacob's clan in Israel was an easy target for neighbors. In Egypt, a superpower protected us, albeit to exploit us.
> -Second, to build up our numbers in safety, to build up our identity and community spirit, to minimize contact with the idolatrous outside world,

and to eliminate the possibility of intermarriage. (Egyptians would not want to marry slaves.)
-Third, to allow God to show the whole world that He was in charge, by performing impressive miracles when He freed the Jews.
-Finally, the gratitude felt upon liberation, coupled with the acquired slave mentality, made it easier for us to accept the Torah.

Furthermore, our tradition says that all the bad things that evil perpetrators inflict on us are punishment for our lack of observance, but it also says that that God does not choose who those perpetrators are. They choose themselves, of their own free will, and as a result for their bad choices they *will* be punished for their evil deeds. That being so, how can the Midrash say that God allowed the Romans to almost destroy Judaism as a *reward* for their ancestor Esau's good behavior towards his father? There is a contradiction there.

It is all very difficult to understand. I don't. Do you?

Shabbat shalom.

Va'etchanan
Deut. 3:23-7:11

B"H

The Mission of Judaism

This week's Torah portion, *Va'etchanan*, features the Ten Commandments, which many consider to be the centerpiece of Judaism. They are a good starting point to reflect on the meaning and mission of Judaism in the world.

We will be discussing the mission of Judaism, not the mission of mankind in general or the purpose of Creation. At any rate, Judaism is not clear on the latter. The Talmud is even pessimistic, saying:

> Our Rabbis taught: For two and a half years the School of Shammai and the School of Hillel argued, the School of Shammai saying that it would have been better if man had not been created, and the School of Hillel saying that it is better that man has been created. They finally took a vote and decided that it would have been better if man had not been created, but now that he has been created, let him investigate his past deeds [and make amends if he finds them at fault], or, as others say, let him examine his future actions [before committing them]. [Eruvin 13b]

In other words, now that humanity is here, let's make the best of a bad situation.

The first question is obviously: Does Judaism have a mission? The answer is yes. The Torah says that Jews are the Chosen People, and chosenness implies mission. These are the words God used when He chose the Jews:

> -For you are a holy people to the Lord your God. The Lord your God has chosen you to be a special people to Himself, above all peoples that are upon the face of the earth. The Lord did not set his love upon you, nor choose you, because you were more in number than any people; for you were the fewest of all peoples. [Deut 7: 6-7; also Deut. 14:2]

> -Understand therefore, that the Lord your God does not give you this good land to possess because of your righteousness, for you are a stiff-necked people. [Deut 9:6]

So God "loves" us and "chose" us, not because we were numerous and not because we were righteous. The Torah therefore explicitly rejects the notion of the innate superiority of the Jews.

The Torah does not say why God chose us, nor for what mission. Its words include apparent criticism: We are "stiff-necked". This criticism is repeated no less than eight times in the Torah! [Ex. 32:9, 33:3, 33:5, 34:9; Deut. 9:6, 9:13, 10:16, 31:27] Perhaps we were chosen *because* we are stiff-necked? God may have been saying, in effect, "I need someone with the determination, the endurance, the staying power, to do what I have in mind." The implication is that the mission is to do what God has in mind in spite of the resistance and inevitable persecutions that will ensue. So the mission must *require* stubbornness, or "stiff-neckedness".

The Midrash compares Israel to an olive. Just as the olive yields its oil only after being squeezed hard, so Israel must endure great oppression and hardship in order to yield its wisdom. [Exodus R. 36:1]

The Torah drops hints about our mission:

> -We are called to high office:
> וְאַתֶּם תִּהְיוּ־לִי מַמְלֶכֶת כֹּהֲנִים וְגוֹי קָדוֹשׁ
> *Ve-atem tihyu li mamlekhet kohanim vegoy kadosh*
> And you shall be unto me a kingdom of priests and a holy nation. [Ex. 19:6]
>
> -We are chosen to imitate God, by being holy:
> קְדֹשִׁים תִּהְיוּ כִּי קָדוֹשׁ אֲנִי יְהוָה אֱלֹהֵיכֶם:
> *Kedoshim tihyu ki kadosh ani HaShem Elokechem*
> You shall be holy, for I, the Lord your God, am holy. [Lev. 19:2]
>
> "Holy" means "separated", "distinguished", "set apart". Indeed, the Torah says:
> הֶן־עָם לְבָדָד יִשְׁכֹּן וּבַגּוֹיִם לֹא יִתְחַשָּׁב:
> *Hen, 'am levadad yishkon uva-goyim lo yit-chashav*

> Behold, [Israel is] a nation that will dwell alone and not be reckoned among the nations. [Num. 23:9]

So we are alone, on our own, among all the peoples of the earth, to fulfill our mission.

So what is the mission of Judaism? It is not clearly spelled out in the Torah. The Torah just says: "Follow the commandments", implying "and let God worry about the rest". The rest of the Bible, and the Talmud, give at least three possibilities. They are not independent.

The first possible mission is to spread Jewish teaching. Is our mission to spread God's word and perhaps His commandments also? Through the prophet Isaiah, God said he wanted us to be to be "a light unto the nations":

> -I the Lord have called you in righteousness, and will hold your hand, and will keep you, and offer you for a covenant of the people, for a light to nations *[L'or goyim]* [Is. 42:6]

> -I will also give you for a light to the nations, so that my salvation may extend to the end of the earth. [Is. 49:6]

Clearly, then, part of the mission is to spread the values of Judaism. But spread how? By just living apart and unnoticed, and following our commandments? By making sure non-Jews see us, so we can give a good example? By interacting with non-Jews, or even proselytizing? The Talmud says:
> Rabbi Eleazar also said: The Holy One, blessed be He, exiled the Jews among the nations only so that converts might join them. [Pesachim 87b]

At the time of Rabbi Eleazar, Jews were actively proselytizing. Ten percent of the Roman Empire was Jewish -- 7.5 million people, according to the Roman census of the year 48. But for most of the past 2,000 years proselytizing would have cost us our lives, so we lost our appetite for it. We reinterpreted the Talmud to mean that we are to spread only the values of Judaism, the wisdom of the Torah, and at least the seven Noahide laws, to the entire world.

These laws are binding on all mankind, and are in the Talmud. They instruct every human being to refrain from idolatry, murder, blaspheming God's name, adultery, stealing, and eating live animals; and to establish courts of justice. [Sanhedrin 56a] The goal is the fulfillment of the prophecy of Zechariah, that we repeat at every service in the 'Alenu:

וְהָיָה יְהוָה לְמֶלֶךְ עַל־כָּל־הָאָרֶץ בַּיּוֹם הַהוּא יִהְיֶה יְהוָה אֶחָד וּשְׁמוֹ אֶחָד:
And the Lord shall be king over all the earth
On that day the Lord shall be One, and his name One. [Zech. 14:9]

Should Jews go back to full-scale proselytizing? All suggestions in that direction have been met with indifference.

The second possible mission is to excel for the benefit of mankind. Jews as a group excel at what they do. That is a fact. Judaism is a "package deal" that works. Which parts of the package can get credit for what achievement? This is a matter of dispute. Maybe the package is indivisible. Is our mission to excel for the benefit of all mankind, to be agents of change, of progress, of improvement? In the Torah, God tells Abraham:

וְאֶעֶשְׂךָ לְגוֹי גָּדוֹל -- I will make you a great nation. [Gen.12:2]

There are hosts of Jewish accomplishments. One is spreading the knowledge of God, with its attendant responsibilities. Hitler was quoted as saying that the Jews' greatest crime was to give the world a conscience. Another is material wealth, which creates jobs. A third is intellectual wealth, which increases knowledge and solutions to problems. Indeed, only one-fifth of 1% of humanity is Jewish, yet Jews get one-third of the Nobel Prizes --150 times more often than their small numbers suggest. There is also economic prowess; witness tiny Israel's meteoric rise in modern living and technology, and its accession to the rank of regional economic powerhouse even though it has almost no natural resources. There is military prowess, witness tiny Israel victorious against large and mighty combined Arab armies -- or Greek armies, as the case may be. There is disproportionate representation in the professions -- physicians, lawyers, captains of industry, bankers, leaders, teachers, researchers, etc. There is disproportionate representation among college graduates. There is disproportionate representation wherever revolutionary ideas are brewing. Jews can be found in every camp, every field, frequently in leadership positions; including camps in which *I* don't particularly care to find Jews.

It is precisely these achievements that are the sole source of antisemitism -- but that's another subject.

The third possible mission is to perform *Tikkun 'Olam*, the "repair of the world", that is, to make the world a better place. The origin of the term is in the Mishnah. The rabbis would render rulings *Mip'nei tikkun ha-'olam* – "for the sake of the repair of the world". These rulings are not required by the Torah, but are deemed necessary to keep order in the world. [Example: Gittin 32a]. This concept of going beyond strict commandments is used in the Talmud only for technical matters.

In the second half of the 'Alenu we hope for the day when we will be able "to perfect the world under God's kingship" -- לְתַקֵּן עוֹלָם בְּמַלְכוּת שַׁדַּי -- *l'takken 'olam b'malkhut Shaddai*.

In the 16th century, this concept was expanded in Isaac Luria's mysticism. He taught that at Creation, a vessel holding divine "sparks of holiness" burst, and the sparks spread throughout the world. Jews were then made to wander far and wide just so they could gather these "sparks of holiness" and make them available to all. That is the needed "repair". [Isaac Luria (the Arizal), quoted in Petech Anayim by Chida, Yoma 38]

Traditional Judaism holds that the way to *tikkun 'olam* is to perform commandments, both ritual and ethical. The more performance, the more the world will inch towards perfection in the Messianic age. The Talmud says:
> Rabbi Yochanan said in the name of Rabbi Shim'on bar Yoḥai: If all Jews kept two Shabbatot in a row according to all the laws of Shabbat, redemption will come immediately. [Shabbat 118b]

Non-Orthodox Jews have expanded the Mishnaic interpretation of *tikkun 'olam* and put it at the center of their philosophy, by emphasizing justice and social action. The big question is: Can non-Orthodox Jews and their descendants survive as Jews with only a strong emphasis on two secular enterprises, social action and the State of Israel, to the detriment of rest of Judaism? The jury is still out, but early observations are not reassuring. In a recent column, Joel Alperson, past national campaign chair for what is now the Jewish Federations of North America, said the following:

> Judaism is more than *tikkun 'olam*... Jews increasingly try to find their Judaic meaning in social/political causes, [such as] immigration reform, Supreme Court appointments, environmentalism, women's rights, etc. Putting aside the merit of the positions taken, let's be honest: These *tikkun 'olam* pursuits might feel good and even do some good, but they do little to build Jewish communities...
>
> If Jews continue to prioritize these social/political efforts over proven religious practices, we must have the courage to acknowledge that we have substituted all these secular causes for Judaism... They are increasingly taking the place of serious Jewish education and Jewish practice...
>
> It is the discipline of leading a traditional Jewish life that also reminds us how best to engage in repairing the world...Ironically, by overemphasizing *tikkun 'olam* we could ultimately, through lack of Jewish knowledge and experience, lose the very impetus that put us in the *tikkun 'olam* business in the first place.
>
> ...We'll be severely weakened if we don't acknowledge that we must repair ourselves far more urgently than we must repair the world.
>
> [http://www.jta.org/news/article/2011/07/27/3088736/op-ed-judaism-is-more-than-tikkun-olam]

So we need to find a proper balance. We can't have it all.

In conclusion, perhaps the Torah is intentionally vague about the mission of Judaism, and all of the above might apply, in some proper balance. Perhaps the most important thing is for Jews to continue to feel strongly that God chose them for *some* mission, so they can live their lives fully and passionately, and, with the help of Jewish observance and values, perform for the betterment of all mankind. The Talmud summarizes it beautifully:

לֹא עָלֶיךָ הַמְּלָאכָה לִגְמֹר, וְלֹא אַתָּה בֶן חוֹרִין לִבָּטֵל מִמֶּנָּה

Lo 'alecha hamlacha ligmor, v'lo atta ven chorrin libatel mimmena

You don't have to complete the task, but you may not desist from it entirely either.

[Avot 2:16]

Translation: You must have goals and purpose in life, consistent with Jewish observance and values. You don't have to fulfill them completely, but you must *have* them and work on them.

Shabbat shalom.

Ekev
Deut. 7:12-11:25

B"H

Why Did Moses Break the Tablets?

In this week's portion, *Ekev*, Moses recounts to the Israelites how he broke the first set of tablets of the Law once he saw that they had engaged in idolatry by building and worshiping a golden calf:

> And I saw, and behold, you had sinned against the Lord, your God. You had made yourselves a molten calf. You had deviated quickly from the way which the Lord had commanded you. So I gripped the two tablets, flung them away with both my hands, and smashed them before your eyes. [Deuteronomy 9:16-17]

This parallels the account in Exodus:

> As soon as Moses came near the camp and saw the calf and the dancing, he became enraged; and he hurled the tablets from his hands and shattered them at the foot of the mountain. [Exodus 32:19]

Why did he do that? What purpose did it accomplish? Wasn't it an affront to God, since the tablets were holy? Didn't it shatter the authority of the very commandments that told the Israelites not to worship idols? Was it just a spontaneous reaction, a public display of anger, a temper tantrum? Did Moses just forget himself? Why didn't he just return them to God, or at least get God's approval before smashing them? Yet he was not admonished!

Our Sources offer six answers.

First, Moses smashed the tablets because God told him to do it. The Talmud reports that four prominent rabbis said that God told Moses to break the tablets: Meir, Akiva, Eleazar ben Azariah, and Yehudah ben Bathyra. [Avot deRabbi Natan 3; also Tanḥuma on Ki Tisa 30]

Second, it was because the tablets were too heavy! The Talmud says that the tablets were two large sapphire stones, and weighed too much to be possibly carried by one person. The letters God engraved on them miraculously lightened them. This allowed Moses to carry the tablets. When the letters "saw" the Golden Calf which the Jewish people had made, they were revolted and "flew" out of the tablets, back to their divine source, leaving Moses with a burden he could not bear. So Moses dropped them. [Taanit Y 4:5; also Tanhuma on Ki Tisa 30] It's been calculated that the tablets weighed a thousand pounds.

Third, it was because idolaters have no stake in the Torah. The Talmud says:
> And he broke the tablets following the sin of the Golden Calf. What source did he interpret that led him to do so? Moses said: With regard to the Paschal lamb, which is only one of 613 mitzvot, the Torah stated:
>> And the Lord said to Moses and Aaron: This is the ordinance of the Paschal offering; no alien shall eat of it. [Exodus 12:43]
>
> This referred not only to Gentiles, but to apostate Jews as well...
> [The Israelites] at that moment were apostates, because they were worshipping the calf, so they were not worthy of receiving the Torah. [Shabbat 87a]

The Midrash clarifies:
> Why did he shatter them? Rabbi Yishmael said: ... Since the paschal sacrifice, which is only one commandment, was not permitted to idolaters... how much more so would it not be fitting to give the entire Torah to idolaters! That is why he broke them. [Tanhuma on Ki Tisa 30]

Fourth, it was to lessen the punishment of the Israelites. The Midrash says:
> What did Moses witness that compelled him to break the tablets? It may be compared to a king who travels abroad, while his wife remains at home with the servants. Because she was alone with them, rumors began to circulate concerning her behavior. The king heard them, and when he returned home, he wanted to kill her. His advisor learned this and tore up her marriage certificate. He said: "If the king should say, my wife has done such and such, we can reply, she is no longer your wife." The king inquired about her and found that she had done nothing wrong. Only the maidservants had acted shamefully. He became reconciled with her immediately. His advisor then said to him: "Master, write another marriage contract, since the first one was torn up." [Tanhuma on Ki Tisa 30; see also Exodus Rabbah 43:1]

Daat Zkenim, from 12th-century Europe, explains:
> [The advisor] tore up the marriage certificate because it was in that woman's interest: instead of becoming an unfaithful wife ... [she was considered] unmarried [and therefore] subject to a lesser penalty. The same happened with the relationship between God and Israel at that time. Israel had become betrothed to God at time of the revelation at Mount Sinai. The Tablets were meant to be the marriage document that He would give His people forty days later. When Moses saw how corrupt they had become in the interval, he decided that it was in their best interest to tear up the marriage document, i.e. the Tablets, so as to make their legal status less serious. [Daat Zkenim on Deuteronomy 9:16]

Fifth, it was to save the Israelites on the grounds that they did not know the law. The Midrash says:
> When Moses saw that [the Israelites] were doomed, he sought a pretext through which to save them. He said: It is written on the tablets that he who sacrifices to gods will be excommunicated, and so, I will break them and say to the Holy One, blessed be He: Until now they did not know the punishment for idolatry. If they had, they would not have done it. [Tanḥuma on Ki Tisa 30]

Chizkuni adds:
> Moses smashed the tablets in front of the people and said: I did this so as not to make you guilty of transgressing the laws written on these tablets. It was written on them that you are not to have other deities, and you had made a Golden Calf for yourselves!

Sixth, it was to commit a sin that would make him share the punishment of the Israelites. The Midrash says that Moses broke the tablets because he thought God would destroy the Jews for their sin and create a new chosen nation from Moses and his descendants. Indeed, back in Exodus, God tells Moses:
> Now, let Me be, that My anger may blaze forth against them and that I may destroy them, and make of you a great nation. [Exodus 32:10].

The Midrash concludes:
> Upon breaking the tablets, [Moses] told God, "Now I am a sinner just like them. If You decide to eradicate them, destroy me as well." [Exodus Rabbah 41:1]

What do the last three explanations have in common? It is the fact that Moses placed his people above the Torah. The Lubavitcher Rebbe views this as Moses' greatest achievement:
> Which was Moses' greatest achievement? Taking the Jews out of Egypt? Splitting the Red Sea? Receiving the Torah from God and transmitting it to humanity? If we are to judge by the Torah's final summation of his life, Moses' greatest deed was his breaking the Two Tablets of the Covenant, inscribed with the Ten Commandments by the very hand of God!

Indeed, the last phrase in Deuteronomy is:
> No other prophet has arisen in Israel like Moses, who knew the Lord knew face to face ... and possessed great might and awesome power that he displayed in the sight of all Israel. [Deut. 34:10-12]

The Jerusalem Talmud tells us that the phrase "great might" refers to the breaking of the tablets. [Taanit Y 4:5] Rashi comments that Moses' heart inspired him to shatter the Tablets before the eyes of all the people. So the Torah ends with an approving account of its own destruction! It was destroyed to preserve it. The Rebbe says:
> With its closing words the Torah establishes that it sees its own existence as secondary to the existence of the people of Israel.

It is seen as one of his greatest acts of leadership. A leader must make his followers feel they are his first concern, not pawns.

Did God approve the breaking of the tablets? Yes. The Talmud derives this from a play on words:
> And from where do we derive that the Holy One, Blessed be He, agreed with [Moses' reasoning]? Because in the Torah God refers to the tablets as follows:
>> The first tablets which you broke [אֲשֶׁר שִׁבַּרְתָּ -- *asher shibarta*] [Exodus 34:1]
>
> and Resh Lakish said: The word *asher* refers to the phrase יִישַׁר כֹּחֲךָ שֶׁשִּׁבַּרְתָּ -- *yishar koḥakha sheshibarta* -- May your strength be enriched by your breaking [of the tablets]. [Shabbat 87a; Yevamot 62a]

This is the origin of the phrase:
> יישר כחך *Yasher koach! (Shkoiyech!* in Ashkenazic. ☺)

It means: "Your action was worthy of my validation and may it strengthen you!" The correct version is the Talmud's, *yishar koḥakha,* but most people say *Yasher koach* anyway.

Yasher Koach was originally intended to compliment the Torah reader. In antiquity, the scroll was held upright. So Sephardim made Sifrei Torah in self-standing hard cases. Ashkenazim didn't, so their Torah reader had to be strong to keep the Torah scroll upright while he was reading from it. So he was told *Yasher Koach* - More power to you! We use the phrase today to wish strength to those holding the Torah, but the original meaning refers to the incident in which the Torah was smashed on the ground!

The Midrash even says that God rewarded Moses:
> God told [Moses]: Do not feel bad about the first tablets, for they only contained the Ten Commandments. However, the second set of tablets I am giving you will also have halakhot, Midrash and Aggadot [the Oral Law]. אֲנִי נוֹתֵן לְךָ שֶׁיְהֵא בָהֶם הֲלָכוֹת מִדְרָשׁ וְאַגָּדוֹת [Shemot Rabbah 46:1]

The Talmud adds that Moses became wealthy as a result:
> Rabbi Ḥama, son of Rabbi Ḥanina, said: Moses became wealthy only from the waste remaining from hewing the Tablets of the Covenant, as it is stated:
>> Hew for yourself two tablets of stone like the first. [Ex. 34:1]
>
> The command "Hew for yourself" means that their waste shall be yours. As the tablets were crafted from valuable gems, their remnants were also valuable... However, Moses treated the Torah with generosity and gave it to the Jewish people. [Nedarim 38a]

The Talmud says:
> This is one of the things that Moses decided on his own, and his decision was in accordance with the will of the Omnipresent. [Avot deRabbi Natan 2]

Was Moses really angry or pretending? Maimonides said in his Mishneh Torah:
> Anger is an extremely evil tendency. One should distance oneself from it by going to the other extreme. One should train oneself not to get angry, even when something appears to justify it. ... The ancient sages said,

-One who yields to anger is as if he had worshipped idols. [Nedarim 22b]
-Whoever yields to anger, wisdom leaves him if he is wise and prophecy leaves him if he is a prophet. [Pesaḥim 66b]
-The life of an irritable person is not a life. [Pesaḥim 113a]

Therefore, they have commanded us to keep far from anger, to train ourselves to stay calm even when provoked. This is the good way. The conduct of the just is to take insults but not give insults, hear themselves flouted but make no reply, do their duty as a work of love, and bear affliction cheerfully. [Rambam, Hilkhot Deot 2:3]

But he also says it's sometimes useful to act angry:
> If one desires to instill reverence in his children and his household, or in public if he is the head of a community, and he wishes to show them his anger so as to bring them back to the good way, he should only act angry in their presence so as to reprove them, but within himself he must remain calm. He should act the part of an angry man, when in reality he is not angry. [Rambam, Hilkhot Deot 2:3]

So maybe Moses' action was just an act. That's why parents sometimes put on a show of anger in front of their children, for shock value, the equivalent of shock treatment!

The Rambam notes that when the people complained of lack of water and Moses responded:
> Listen, you rebels, shall we get water for you out of this rock? [Num. 20:10]

Moses was *really* angry and it was not justifiable, because not all of them had been rebels in the Korach rebellion and all were suffering from thirst. So God did not forgive him. [Rambam, Shemoneh Perakim 4]

But God quickly approved when he broke the tablets seemingly in anger. Why? Possibly because God knew the anger was not real, only staged.

Ecclesiastes wrote:
> עֵת לְהַשְׁלִיךְ אֲבָנִים וְעֵת כְּנוֹס אֲבָנִים
> There is a time for throwing stones and a time for gathering stones. [Eccl. 3:5]

Daat Zkenim points out a direct parallel: There is a time for throwing the tablets (the first set) and a time for gathering the tablets (the second set).

But the first tablets are still important. The Talmud says:
> Had the first tablets not been shattered, the Torah would not have been forgotten by the Jews. [Eruvin 54a]

Rav Naḥman of Breslov explains. He notes that Malachi says: *Zikhru Torat Moshe* (Remember the Torah of Moses) [Malachi 3:22]. The first letters spell TaMmuZ without a *vav*. When the first tablets were broken, during the month of Tammuz, the *vav* departed. Now, the size of the tablets was *vav* by *vav* – that is 6x6 handbreadths. [Bava Batra 54a] So when the first tablets were broken, forgetfulness came into existence. [Likutei Moharan 217:1:1]

The Talmud also says:
> Rav Aḥa bar Yaakov said: Had the first tablets not been shattered, no nation or tongue would ever have ruled over Israel. [Eruvin 54a]

He derives this from the verse in Exodus:
> And the tablets were the work of God, and the writing was the writing of God, engraved upon the tablets. [Ex. 32:16]

He also derives it from a play on words:
> Do not read engraved [חָרוּת -- *ḥarut*] but rather freedom [*ḥerut*]. [Eruvin 54a]

The Midrash says that the death of the righteous is as tragic to God as the day on which the tablets were broken.
> Rabbi Yudan asked: Why was the death of Aaron recorded in close proximity to the breaking of the tablets? Simply this: To teach that Aaron's death was as grievous to the Holy One, blessed be He, as the breaking of the tablets. [Lev. R. 20:12]

What happened to the broken tablets? The Talmud says that they were still holy and its pieces were preserved:
> From where does [Rabbi Meir] derive that the broken pieces of the first set of tablets were placed in the Ark? ... [From the fact that God told Moses: "Hew for yourself two tablets of stone like the first...and I will write on the tablets the words that were on the first tablets,] which you broke, and you shall put them in the Ark" [Deut. 10:1-2]. This teaches that both the second set of tablets and the broken pieces of the first set of tablets were placed in the Ark. [Bava Batra 14b]

A major teaching emerged from this episode:

Be careful [to continue to respect] an elder who has forgotten his Torah knowledge due to circumstances beyond his control. As we say: Both the tablets of the Covenant and the broken tablets are placed in the Ark. [Berakhot 8b] ... One may not behave toward him in a degrading manner. [An elder who forgot his knowledge is like the broken tablets.] [Menaḥot 99a]

Shabbat shalom.

Re'eh
Deut. 11:26-16:17

B"H

Why Eat Only Kosher Foods?

This week's portion, *Re'eh*, summarizes the Jewish dietary laws. Foods that Jews may eat are called *kasher*, meaning "fit", in the sense of "fit to eat". Let us review what these foods are and speculate on possible reasons why we are not allowed to eat the other foods.

The Torah says:
- לֹא תֹאכַל כָּל־תּוֹעֵבָה -- You shall not eat any abomination. [Deut 14:3]
- These are the animals that you may eat: ox, lamb, and kid; gazelle, deer, and antelope, ibex, chamois, bison, and giraffe. And every animal that has a split hoof and has a hoof cloven into two hoof sections, [and] chews the cud, is among the animals that you may eat. [Deut 14:4-6]
- These you may eat of all that are in the waters: all that have fins and scales, you may eat. But whatever does not have fins and scales, you shall not eat; it is unclean for you. [Deut 14:9-10]
- You may eat every clean bird. But these are those from which you shall not eat: [follows a list of 21 birds] [Deut 14:11-12]
- Every flying insect is unclean for you. [Deut 14:19]
- You shall not eat any thing that dies of itself [that is, an animal not properly slaughtered]. You may give it to the stranger, who is in your cities, that he may eat it, or you may sell it to a foreigner; for you are a holy people to the Lord your God. [Deut 14:21]
- You shall not cook a kid in its mother's milk. [Deut 14:21]

From these verses and similar ones, the rabbis extracted the following rules.

Animals that do not both chew the cud and have split hooves may not be eaten. Both conditions must be there. For example, the camel, the hyrax, and the hare, which chew the cud but do not have split hooves, are forbidden. The pig, which has split hooves but does not chew the cud, is also forbidden.

Also, the products of forbidden animals, such as milk or eggs, are also forbidden.

The Torah only lists birds that are *not* kosher. Does this mean all other birds are kosher? No. Rabbis are reluctant to allow birds with no tradition of being eaten, because they might be related to the forbidden ones. Fish that do not have both scales and fins, such as shellfish, may not be eaten. Neither can reptiles or amphibians.

Not all kosher animals are eaten. For example, the giraffe is kosher, but is not eaten because of the high cost, the difficulty in restraining it, and the fact that it is an endangered species. Also, although there is no biblical basis for it, some foods are deemed more unkosher than others. Pork is an example. As someone once put it: "Shrimp is naughty, but pork is antisemitic!"

Also, animals must be properly slaughtered to be fit to eat. Proper slaughtering is called *shechitah*. The Talmud elaborates:
>-Land animals, which were created from the soil, are rendered fit to eat by severing both vital passages, that is, the windpipe and the gullet.
>-Fish, which were created from the water, do not require any special slaughtering.
>-Birds, which were created from a mixture of soil and water, are rendered fit to eat with the severing of either one of the two vital passages. [Hullin 27b]

Thus, carrion (*nevelah*) is forbidden.

Animals with significant defects or injuries may not be eaten. Seventy categories of abnormalities disqualify them. Insects may not be eaten, except for some locusts. This is why all vegetables must be checked for infestation before they can be eaten. Blood may not be eaten, and is removed through salting [Lev. 3:7, 17:11]. Some fats, called *chelev*, may not be eaten [Lev. 7:23-25]. The sciatic nerve of a permitted animal may not be eaten, because Jacob's sciatic nerve was damaged when he fought with the angel [Genesis 32:33].

One may not eat the limb torn off of a living animal. [Genesis 9:4] This is even one of the 7 Noahide laws, which apply to all mankind, not only to Jews.

Other categories of prohibited foods are untithed food (*tevel*) [Leviticus 22:15]; fruit grown during the first three years of the life of a tree (*orlah*) [Leviticus 19:23]; fresh grain until a certain time [Leviticus 23:14]; wine that may have been used for idolatrous purposes (*yayin nesech*); and finally, leavened items, called *ḥametz*, during the week of Passover.

There are also two kinds of mixtures prohibited by the Torah. The first is mixtures of milk and meat. [Ex. 23:19, 34:26; Deut. 14:21] This requires Jews to use two sets of dishes and utensils, one for dairy and one for meat, and to wait up to 6 hours after eating meat before eating dairy. Some also wait up to 3 hours after eating dairy before eating meat, but most don't. Fish are considered neither milk nor meat, a category called *pareve*. However, Sephardic Jews avoid eating fish with milk. Jews are not even allowed to derive any benefit from mixtures of milk and meat, although they are allowed to derive benefit from other non-kosher food.

The second prohibited mixture is plants or animals that are crossbred, or *kil'ayim*, because the Torah says:
> You shall not sow your field with a mixture of seeds. [Lev. 19:19]

Because of this phrasing, some authorities allow eating that mixture, but not planting it.

In addition to all the foods prohibited by the Torah, the rabbis added new ones on foods produced by non-Jews, although observance varies. For example, wine produced by non-Jews is not allowed because of the old fear that it may have been produced for idolatrous purposes. Today, such possibilities are low in the Western world, but it is easier to ban all such wine rather than pick and choose who is trustworthy enough, at the risk of offending the rest. Milk produced by non-Jews may include milk from non-kosher animals, and cheese produced by non-Jews may contain non-kosher rennet, so they are not allowed. The Shulḥan Arukh, the Code of Jewish Law, even prohibits all bread and food produced by non-Jews [Shulḥan Arukh, Yoreh Deah 112:1, 113:1ff], although "produced by" is subject to interpretation. It even prohibits food the Talmud considers unhealthy, such as mixtures of fish and meat [Pesaḥim 76b;

Shulḥan Arukh, Yoreh Deah 116:2], saying they may be eaten in the same meal, but not mixed together. Again, observance of these rabbinic prohibitions varies widely even among Orthodox Jews.

In the 1960s and 1970s, the kosher-food company *Hebrew National* ran a massive campaign, aimed at the general public, claiming that their food is good and healthy because, as their slogan says, "We answer to a higher authority". Since then, many non-Jews have regularly bought kosher food. In fact, today, non-Jews account for 80% of the kosher market in the US. That market includes Muslims, Hindus, vegetarians, vegans, people allergic to dairy products, people who believe kosher is healthier and kinder to animals, philosemites, and others.

Now we come to our central question: Why are these injunctions in the Torah? What are possible reasons for kashrut?

The first reason is: Because God said so. Kashrut is an example of a *chok*, that is, a commandment whose rationale is not obvious. Our tradition allows us to speculate on possible reasons for commandments, as long as we continue to observe them no matter what conclusions we reach. [Rambam, Mishneh Torah, Korbanot, Temurah 4:13]

A second reason is that kashrut severely limits the killing of animals for food. It directs us to slaughter animals in a humane fashion, to minimize pain. Some say the laws of kashrut encourage us to be vegetarian, by making the consumption of meat difficult. And separating milk from meat reminds us that milk represents life and meat represents death.

A third reason may be health-related. We know now that incompletely cooked pork can cause trichinosis, and that shellfish easily accumulates bacteria and toxins. This is an unlikely reason because the Torah says: "You may give [unkosher meat] to the stranger who is in your cities, that he may eat it, or you may sell it to a foreigner." Surely, if that food was harmful, the Torah would not be telling us to give it to non-Jews to eat, and kashrut would be among the seven Noahide laws, binding on all mankind.

A fourth reason is that kashrut teaches self-discipline. Actually, any constraint achieves that goal.

A fifth reason is that kashrut encourages cohesion of the Jewish people. But it also discourages socialization with non-Jews.

A sixth reason is: You are what you eat. The Ramban, Nahmanides, from 13th-century Spain, writes:
> The birds and many of the mammals forbidden by the Torah are predators, while the permitted animals are not. We are commanded not to eat those animals that have a cruel nature, so that we should not absorb these qualities into ourselves. [Nahmanides, bi'ur on Leviticus]

The Talmud notes that all fish that have scales also have fins, so the Torah could have written only "scales", without mentioning "fins". Then it explains, cryptically:
> Rabbi Abbahu said, as was taught in the house of study of Rabbi Yishmael: This is so that, [as stated in Isaiah:]
>> The Torah may be magnified and made glorious. [Isaiah 42:21]
>
> [Niddah 51b]

This is understood to mean that even a word that appears unnecessary adds to the greatness and glory of the Torah. A contemporary rabbi explains that our soul is influenced by what we eat. Kosher birds are not aggressive. Kosher animals must have split hooves, which are used for fleeing, as opposed to claws, which are used for attacking. Kosher animals must chew the cud, so they can flee when attacked and still retain enough food to survive. Kosher fish have fins to help them flee and scales to protect them. Therefore, fins and scales make them the hunted and not the hunters.

Finally, there are mystical reasons. Isaac Luria, the great Kabbalist, taught that everything possesses a "divine spark". When something is used for a worthy cause, this divine spark achieves the purpose for which it was created.

Thus, eating kosher meat, and using its energy to perform a mitzvah, elevates the divine spark in it. But when eating non-kosher meat, no such "elevation" takes place, even if the energy is used for a worthy cause, because God disapproves.

Shabbat shalom, bon appétit, and *lechayyim!*

Shoftim
Deut. 16:18-21:9

B"H

Violence and Judaism

In this week's Torah portion, *Shoftim*, we hear, repeated for the third time, the so-called law of retaliation:

עַיִן בְּעַיִן שֵׁן בְּשֵׁן -- An eye for an eye, a tooth for a tooth. [Deut. 19:21]

In reality, the rabbis have always interpreted this law to mean monetary compensation, not physical violence. We'll get back to this point in a minute. Today, we are going to review the Jewish attitude towards using violence.

In short, Jews are traditionally against using violence to settle disputes. I remember a live comedy show in New York where the entertainer was describing how various ethnic groups react to being mugged in a dark alley. When he came to the Jews, he said, "A Jew would say: 'You mess with me and I'll sue your tail!'" (No violence!)

Judaism may disdain violence, but it is not pacifist. Violence is permitted in self-defense. The Talmud says:

אִם בָּא לְהָרְגְךָ — הַשְׁכֵּם לְהָרְגוֹ

If someone comes to kill you, kill him first [if that is the only way to stop him]. [Berakhot 58a]

Judaism has sharply reduced its endorsement of violence throughout its history. Here are some examples.

First, the law of retaliation, "An eye for an eye, a tooth for a tooth" has always interpreted as monetary compensation, as mentioned above. [Bava Kamma 83b-84a] There is a long list of clever reasons for this in the Talmud, among them the following:

> Rabbi Dostai ben Yehudah says: It does not mean actual retaliation, because if the eye of one was big and the eye of the other small, one weak and one strong, they would not be equivalent, and the Torah says in Leviticus:

> You shall have only one standard of law, for you, for your countrymen, and for the stranger. [Lev. 24:22]

The argument here is that justice must be evenly applied. Therefore, monetary compensation is implied. Money is the great equalizer.

> -Rabbi Shim'on bar Yoḥai says: "Eye for eye" means monetary compensation. If it really meant retaliation, what would you do if a blind man put out the eye of another man, or if a person missing both hands cut off the hand of another, or if a person missing both legs broke the leg of another? You could not physically retaliate in kind. Yet the Torah says, "You shall have only one standard of law", which implies that the law should be applied the same way to all. So it means monetary compensation.

> -Abaye said [in the name of the School of Hezekiah]: It says in Exodus: "life for life, eye for eye". It does not say "life *and eye* for eye". If one retaliated in kind, it could happen that the offender would die while he is being blinded. This would be unfair, and cannot be predicted or prevented, so monetary compensation is meant.

Second, the death penalty. It has not been applied in Judaism since the year 30 CE. The Talmud lists many strict legal requirements before it can be applied: There must be two Jewishly observant independent male eyewitnesses to the event; they must be unrelated to the accused or to each other; the accused must have been instructed ahead of time that his would be a capital crime, etc. All this made conviction close to impossible. The Mishnah says:

> A court that sentences one person to death in seven years is a bloody court.
> -Rabbi Eleazar ben 'Azariah said: "No, it's once in seventy years."
> -Rabbis Tarfon and Akiva said, "If we had been on the court, no one would ever have been put to death."
> -Rabbi Shim'on ben Gamliel pushed back, saying, "Great, and then murderers would have a field day in Israel." [Makkot 7a]

There is also the issue of reasonable doubt. Maimonides said:

> It is better… to acquit a thousand guilty persons than to put a single innocent person to death. [Rambam, Sefer Hamitzvot, negative commandment 290]

Third, corporal punishment. Flogging was the last legal violent punishment. It is discussed in Tractate Makkot in the Talmud. It slowly fell into disuse and has not been applied since the Middle Ages. It was replaced by monetary fines. [Luria, 16th century, Yam shel Shlomoh, BK 8:48]

The **fourth** and most important aspect of violence is war. Unfortunately, war is rarely a matter of choice, and Jews have been forced to engage in it. There are three types of war. [Rambam, Laws of Kings 5:1]

The first is *milchemet chovah*, a holy or obligatory war, directed directly by God in the Tanach. For example, the war against Amalek [Deut.25:17] and the war against the seven nations of Canaan [Deut. 20:16] in Deuteronomy. It is not applicable today because we can no longer identify these people. The Talmud says:
> But Sennacherib, King of Assyria, had come up already and confused all the lands as it is said in Isaiah, "I have removed the bounds of the peoples", [Isaiah 10:13] So the rabbis decreed that the seven nations of Canaan no longer exist because the Assyrians [and not the Israelites] wiped them out. [Yoma 54a]

19th-century Turkish rabbi Hayyim Palacci said that we lost the tradition of how to distinguish Amalekites from others, so we should not presume to be able to fulfill the commandment to wipe them out. [Eynei Kol Hai, 73, on Sanhedrin 96b]

The second is *milchemet mitzvah*. It is a commanded war, in self-defense, waged after being attacked.

The third is *milchemet reshut*. It is a discretionary war, such as a war of conquest, exemplified by King David's expansions; or a pre-emptive war, such as the Six-Day War, to prevent Israel from being annihilated by the Arabs; or a war to help an oppressed people overthrow a tyrant, such as the US in Iraq. This type of war requires permission of the Sanhedrin. The king alone cannot initiate it. Today, unfortunately, there is no Sanhedrin.

Many commandments are intended to mitigate the effects of war. For example, the Torah says:
> -Always seek a just peace before waging war. [Deut. 20:10]

-Do not destroy fruit trees [Deut. 20:19-20], or break vessels, or tear clothing, or wreck that which is built up, or stop fountains, or destroy food, or kill animals needlessly.

-To besiege a city, surround it on only three sides to allow people to escape. [Rambam, Laws of Kings 6:11]

In addition, Jews must minimize injury to noncombatants or property, and be lenient towards the enemy after victory. One reason to be lenient towards the enemy is that the wicked do not always stay wicked. They or their descendants may eventually see the light. The Talmud says:

The greatest hero is one who turns his enemy into a friend. [Avot d'Rabbi Natan 23:1]

Examples of such occurrences are the sons of Korach, who wrote eleven of the 150 psalms. The Talmud records many others [Sanhedrin 96b]:

-Naaman, a Syrian commander in the days of the Kingdom of Israel, [2 Kings 5:1] became a resident alien, a *ger toshav*, one who gives up idolatry in exchange for citizenship.

-Nebuzaradan, the Babylonian commander who destroyed Jerusalem and the First Temple and deported the Jews of Judah, [2Kings 25:8] became a righteous convert to Judaism.

-Sisera, the Canaanite general who oppressed the Israelites for twenty years [Judges 4:2], had descendants who studied Torah and taught children in Jerusalem [Gittin 57b]. The great Rabbi Akiva was his descendant. He was killed by Yael, and, when he died, the Midrash says that his mother cried 101 cries, and that's why we blow the shofar 100 blasts on Rosh Hashanah: 100 of her cries were anger at the Jews, and the shofar drowns these out; one cry for love for her son, and we do not counter that one.

-Sennacherib, the Assyrian king who waged war against the kingdom of Judah [2 Kings 18:13], had descendants who taught Torah to the multitudes.

Some of them were Shema'iah and Avtalion, the lead rabbis who preceded Hillel and Shammai.

-Haman, the wicked Persian minister who tried to destroy the Jews in the story of Purim [Esther 3:1], had descendants who studied Torah in Bnai Brak.

Note that the only descendants identified by name were those who themselves revealed their non-Jewish origin.

Isolated acts of violence are regularly condemned by the Jewish establishment, especially vigilantism -- latter-day Pinchases. Judaism is a religion of laws and commandments, and no individual can take the law in his own hands.

Jews do not glorify violence. There is no "dancing in the streets" after enemies are of necessity killed in war. The Book of Proverbs says:
> Do not rejoice when your enemy falls, and do not let your heart be glad when he stumbles, lest the Lord see it and it displease him, and he turn away his wrath from [your enemy]. [Proverbs 24:17-18]

Concessions are always allowed for sake of peace, if they will save lives. When trouble arises, Jews always call for "dialogue", to avoid bloodshed.

Yet, can all necessary tasks be accomplished without violence? No. Change is sometimes necessary and sometimes only violence can bring it about, even if it goes against official teaching. Consider the following five events in Jewish history:

-1- In 164 BCE, the Jews were wondering whether to rise against the Greeks. That's the story of Hanukkah.
-2- In 70 CE, the Jews were wondering whether to rise against the Romans. That's the story of the fall of the Second Temple.

-3- In 135 CE, the Jews were wondering whether to rise against the Romans again. That's the beginning of the Diaspora.
-4- In the early 1930s, the Jews of Europe were wondering whether to try to leave when Naziism was slowly on the rise. That's the beginning of the Holocaust.
-5- In the 1980s, the Lubavitch Hassidim were wondering whether to leave New York in light of problems with the Black community.

What do all these events have in common? Simply this: In all cases, the leaders counseled against change. They always do. They are old, set in their ways; they want to keep power, they are confident in their ability to deal peacefully with the devil they know, etc. They are sometimes right, as in events 2, 3, and 5; and sometimes wrong, as in events 1 and 4:

-The rabbis counseled against fighting Greek oppression, and they were wrong. We won.
-The rabbis counseled against fighting Roman oppression, and they were right. We lost big.
-The rabbis counseled against leaving Europe, saying that Hitler was just a temporary phenomenon and would blow away, and that Jews should especially avoid going to America where they would assimilate, or going to the Holy Land and be ensnared by godless secular Zionists. They were wrong, big time. They all perished in the Holocaust, as night descended on the Jews of Europe.
-The Lubavitcher Rebbe told his people that they should stay where they were, predicting that calm will return and all problems with the Black community would be worked out. He was right.

All this suggests that if the people really feel fundamental change is needed, they must go against teachings and Establishment and flee or engage in violence. In the end they may be right or wrong, but real change will never come from the Establishment.

Finally, Jews have always been recognized as fundamentally non-violent by the Gentiles around them who are not antisemitic. This is summarized by French philosopher Jean-Paul Sartre, who wrote:
> The Jews are the mildest of men, passionately hostile to violence. That obstinate sweetness which they conserve in the midst of the most atrocious persecution, that sense of justice and of reason which they put up as their sole defense against a hostile, brutal, and unjust society, is perhaps the best part of the message they bring to us and the true mark of their greatness. [Réflexions sur la Question Juive, 1946]

Shabbat shalom.

Ki Tetze
Deut. 21:10-25:19

B"H

The Rebellious Son

In this week's Torah portion, *Ki Tetse*, we find an astounding passage:
> If a man has a stubborn and rebellious son [בֵּן סוֹרֵר וּמוֹרֶה -- *ben sorer u-moreh*], who will not hearken to the voice of his father, or to the voice of his mother, and who, even though they discipline him, will not hearken to them; then his father and his mother shall seize him, and bring him out to the elders of his city, and to the gate of his place. And they shall say to the elders of his city, "This, our son, is stubborn and rebellious. He will not hearken to our voice. He is a glutton and a drunkard." And all the men of his city shall pelt him with stones, and he shall die. So shall you remove evil from your midst, and all Israel shall hear and fear. [Deut. 21:18-21]

So: Father and mother will have their son executed for not listening to them? And for being "a glutton and a drunkard"? These are not capital sins! In fact, they are not sins at all: There are no commandments against them. The Talmud says that he must have stolen to buy all this food and drink. [Sanhedrin 71a] But even stealing is not a capital offense! Should he not even be given the opportunity to repent, to undergo *teshuva*? Note that if he is an adult, his parents do not have authority over him. So he must be a minor. But a minor is not responsible for the commandments! Should we execute him anyway? Something is not right here.

Indeed, the Sages of the Talmud state flatly:
בן סורר ומורה לא היה ולא עתיד -- This never happened and never will. [Sanh. 71a] They also made sure of it by putting so many requirements before a death sentence can be carried out, that it is extremely unlikely it ever will be. Let us review these clever requirements.

First, the Torah says "a son". So, if the culprit is a daughter, none of this applies. Half the people are automatically exempt! [Sanhedrin 68b]

Second, only his parents can request his execution, and both must agree on it, using the same words, or the case cannot proceed. The Mishnah says:
> [If the boy's] father wishes to have him declared stubborn and rebellious and his mother does not so wish, or vice-versa, he is not liable. [Sanhedrin 71a]

Third, if either of his parents is handicapped in a relevant way, the case cannot proceed. The Mishna says:
> If [his father or his mother] was missing a hand; or was lame, mute, blind or deaf, he does not become a "stubborn and rebellious son", because it is written [in the Torah]:
> -"Then his father and his mother shall seize him". This excludes those missing a hand. [You need hands to seize.]
> -"And bring him out". This excludes lame parents. [You need to be able to walk to "bring him out".]
> -"And they shall say." This excludes the mute.
> -"This, our son." This excludes the blind [because the phrase "this, our son" implies that they see him].
> -"He will not hearken to our voice." This excludes the deaf [because they cannot hear his response when they admonish him]. [Sanhedrin 71a]

Fourth, if the boy is deaf, he is exempt, because it says: "He will not hearken to our voice". [This is not in the Sources, but it's logical.]

Fifth, if his parents don't have similar voices, the case cannot proceed:
> The Torah states: "He will not hearken to *our* voice". [This teaches that the boy's parents must have similar voices]. [Sanhedrin 71a]

Rabbi Yehudah even adds that the parents must also have the same appearance and height, as an implication of having similar voices!

Sixth, if he is below bar mitzvah age, the case cannot proceed:
> A minor is exempt, since he has not yet entered the realm of the commandments. [Sanhedrin 68b]

Seventh, if he is older than bar mitzvah age, he is under parental control only for about 3 months, so all this can happen only in these 3 months. The Mishnah says:
> When does a stubborn and rebellious son become liable to the [death] penalty? From the time that he produces two [pubic] hairs [after the age of 13] until he has full pubic hair. [Sanhedrin 68b]

Eighth, if he is not properly warned and punished first, the case cannot proceed. The Mishna says:
> [His parents] must warn him before three [judges] and the court [must] flog him. If he repeats his misdeeds afterwards, he is judged by a court of 23, [which must include] the original three judges, for it is stated [in the Torah] "*This*, our son", [meaning that they can point to the original judges and say:] "This is [the son] who was flogged in your presence." [Sanhedrin 71a]

Ninth, if he flees and is caught too late, the case cannot proceed. The Mishnah says:
> If [the boy] flees before his [guilty] verdict is reached, and [when he is caught] he has already grown full pubic hair, he is exempt. [Sanhedrin 71b]

Tenth, if the boy was fathered by a minor, the case cannot proceed:
> [The Torah says:] "If a *man* has a stubborn and rebellious son." [If his father is not a man, he is exempt.] [Sanhedrin 68b]

Eleventh, if he eats and drinks less than a specified (and large) amount of food and drink, all at one time, the case cannot proceed. The Mishnah says:
> When does he become liable? When he eats a tartemar of meat and drinks half a log of Italian wine. Rabbi Yosei said: A mina of meat and a log of wine. [Sanhedrin 70a]

These are large quantities!

Twelfth, if his overeating and overdrinking occurred while he was involved in a religious act, such as a holiday, or a celebration, such as a wedding, in the company of others (even crooks), the case cannot proceed. The Mishnah says:
> [If the boy over-]ate [and drank] at a gathering that involved a mitzvah... he is not liable. [Sanhedrin 70a]

Thirteenth, if his overeating and overdrinking is not of meat and wine, the case cannot proceed. The Mishnah says:
> If he ate any food but meat, or drank any drink but wine, he does not become a "stubborn and rebellious son". [He must] eat meat and drink wine. [Why?] Because it is written,
>> He is a glutton [*zolel*] and a drunkard [*ve-sove*].
>
> And ... it is [also] written [in Proverbs],
>> Do not be not among wine bibbers [*ve-sov'ei*]; among gluttonous eaters of flesh [*ve-zol'lei*]. [Prov. 23:20]
>
> [The use of the same words implies wine and meat.]
> [Sanhedrin 70a]

One can wonder: Did the Torah use words that hint at all these exclusions on purpose, so this execution would never happen?

Now, one is entitled to ask: Why is this passage in the Torah at all? Commentators have speculated as follows:

First, it's there only to teach us things. The Talmud says:
> Rabbi Shim'on said: There never has been a stubborn and rebellious son [who was executed] and there never will be one in the future. Why then was the law written? [God said:] Study the passage and you will receive reward for doing so.
> [Sanhedrin 71a]

But what does it mean to say "It is there only to study and receive reward"? Perhaps it means to appreciate the seriousness of the problem, and take action. Also, the case is so "far out" that it makes for captivating reading, and makes Torah study more interesting. We "learn" by asking why such a law is there and admire the rabbis' ingenuity in placing restrictions on its application!

Kli Yakar, from 16th-century Prague, offers a proof that it will never happen:
> When the Torah commands an execution, an announcement is made to warn the people, concluding with "so that this will never happen again". Examples are:
>> -And all Israel shall hear and fear, and shall no longer engage in such wickedness. [Deut. 13:12]

> -And all the people shall hear and fear, and do no more presumptuously. [Deut. 17:13]

But in the case of the rebellious son, there is no such statement. Only:
> And all Israel shall hear and fear. [Deut. 21:21]

So this cannot happen. There is no need to say "it will never happen again" because it could never have happened in the first place.

But the Talmud notes a dissenter:
> Rabbi Yonatan said: I saw [such a son] and I sat on his grave. [Sanhedrin 71a]

However, commentators note that Rabbi Yonatan was a kohen, and so was prohibited to touch a grave, much less sit on one. [Enayim Lamishpat on Sanhedrin 71a] Also, it is questionable whether it is proper to sit on a grave. [Pischei Teshuvah to Yoreh Deah 364:2] Maybe Rabbi Yonatan just meant to point out that it *could* happen?

The Talmud speculates on another reason: To show that the "rebellious son" is likely to do terrible things in future, so it's best if he dies now:
> It has been taught: Rabbi Yosei the Galilean said: Did the Torah decree that the rebellious son be brought before the court and stoned merely because he ate a tartemar of meat and drank a log of Italian wine? [No.] The Torah foresaw his ultimate destiny. After dissipating his father's wealth, he will [still] seek to maintain his [bad] habits, and being unable to do so, he will go to the crossroads and rob people. Therefore the Torah said: Let him die while he is still innocent, and let him not die guilty [of capital crimes]. [Sanhedrin 72a]

Gluttony and drunkenness indicate a lack of self-restraint. They point to a future lack of self-restraint on more important matters. But, nevertheless, Judaism does not punish preemptively. For example, when Abraham chased away Ishmael and his mother Hagar, they were dying of thirst in the desert, but God opened up a well for them. The Torah says:
> God has heard the voice of the lad where he is. [Gen. 21:17]

The Talmud interprets "where he is" as follows:
> Rabbi Yitzhaq further said: Man is judged only according to his actions up to the time of judgment. [Rosh Hashanah 16b]

The Midrash adds:
> Rabbi Simon said: The ministering angels... exclaimed: "Lord of the universe, will you bring up a well for [Ishmael], who will one day slay your children with thirst?"

> God asked them: "At this moment, what is he?" "Righteous," they replied. [God answered:] "I judge man only as he is at the moment." [Gen. R. 53:14]

Besides, everyone can repent (do teshuva) and thereby be redeemed. The psalmist writes:
> Though my father and my mother have rejected me, the Lord will receive me. [Ps. 27:10]

Finally, we have free will. We do not know for sure what he will do in the future. In the Torah, God says:
> I have set before you life and death, blessing and curse. Choose life, so that both you and your seed may live. [Deut. 30:19]

Another reason for this passage may be to teach the seriousness of lacking respect for parents; or to teach the importance of good child rearing, because bad habits only get worse unless nipped in the bud; or to teach the importance for parents to agree on child rearing; or to deter juvenile misbehavior. The Torah says: "All Israel shall hear and fear". Kli Yakar wonders: Perhaps this passage should be taught to errant children?

Abravanel writes that the passage expresses concern that the son's bad example will cause others to sin.

This passage also has the salutary effect of pointing to limits of the father's power. Indeed, he needs the approval of the mother and of the court before ordering his son's execution. In other cultures, such as the ones ruled by the Hammurabi Code, a father had life-and-death power over his son. [Hammurabi Code 168-169]

The Talmud also sees this passage as a warning against marrying a "captive woman" (*Eshet Yefat To'ar*). She is defined in the Torah as follows:
> When... the Lord your God has delivered [your enemies] into your hands... and you see among them a beautiful woman, and desire her ... [you shall do these things and after...] a full month... you shall go into her, and be her husband, and she shall be your wife.

The Torah immediately continues:

> If a man has two wives, one beloved, and another hated... and if the firstborn son belongs to the one who was hated... he shall acknowledge the son of the hated as the firstborn, and give him a double portion of all that he has, [which is his due]...

And the Torah follows this up with our paragraph:

> If a man has a stubborn and rebellious son, [etc.] [Deut. 21:10-22]

The Talmud interprets this succession to imply that if you marry a captive woman, you will end up hating her, and the son you have from her will be a "stubborn and rebellious" son:

> Rav Yehudah said in Rav's name... Interpret the proximity of verses... For in proximity [to marrying the captive woman] it is written, "If a man has a stubborn and rebellious son." [This teaches that] whoever marries a beautiful woman [taken in battle will end up hating her and] will have a stubborn and rebellious son [from her].
> [Sanhedrin 107a]

King David married such a woman, Maacah, and had Avshalom, who tried to kill his father and usurp his throne; slept with his wives and caused war. [2 Sam. 3-20]

Rabbenu Bahya, 14th-century Spanish scholar, believes that this passage teaches us that our love of God must supersede even our love of our children, by making sure we and our children follow commandments. After all, Abraham accepted God's command to sacrifice his son Isaac.

My personal conclusion is that God phrased this Torah passage so as to allow many loopholes, thereby ensuring this would never happen. It is even possible to see this as evidence that God wrote the Torah, because no other known culture ever had this commandment.

Shabbat shalom.

Ki Tavo
Deut. 26:1-29:8

B"H

Is Life a Zero-Sum Game?

In this week's Torah portion, *Ki Tavo*, we read about offering God the first fruit of the harvest -- the commandment of *bikkurim*:
> You shall take some of every first fruit of the soil ... [and] put it in a basket...
> The priest shall take the basket... and set it down in front of the altar...
> [You shall say:] "I now bring the first fruits of the soil which You, O Lord have given me."
> You shall then leave it... and bow low before the Lord your God...
> And you shall enjoy, together with the Levite and the stranger in your midst, all the bounty that the Lord your God has bestowed upon you and your household.
> [Deuteronomy 26:2~11]

The priests later divided the fruit among themselves, to be eaten later, and gave back the ornate, expensive baskets to their owners.

So we give God the first fruit in exchange for His favor.

People have a deep feeling that, if they want to get something, they must give something in return, of equal or higher value. There is no free lunch. The Romans called it *do ut des,* which means "I give so that you will give". It's an entrenched belief.

In ancient times, people sacrificed human beings to their gods, in order to pacify them and obtain their favor. The gods were always angry. Children were the people's most valuable "possession". Teenage virgin daughters were next in line. In the Torah, Abraham did not protest when God told him to sacrifice his son. He protested only when God threatened to destroy both the righteous and the wicked in Sodom and Gomorrah.

Human sacrifice is found in just about every culture up to biblical times. We find it among the Japanese, the Mongols, the Scythians, the Tibetans, the Indians, the West Africans, the ancient Egyptians, the ancient Chinese, the Cretans, the Celts, the Etruscans, the Germans, the Phoenicians, the Hawaiian, the Carthaginians, the Incas, and others... In the year 1487, the Aztecs sacrificed 80,000 people in four days when they re-consecrated the Great Pyramid of Tenochtitlan. Parents and teachers raised children to consider it a high honor to be chosen for sacrifice.

God weaned Jews from human sacrifice. The Torah says:
> And you shall not let any of your seed pass through the fire to [the idol] Molech... [Lev. 18:21] [If you do,] you will surely be put to death [by stoning]. [Lev. 20:2; Mishna, Sanhedrin 53a]

However, to get people to accept the Torah, God could not completely remove the notion that He had to ask something tangible from them before granting His favor, so He asked for things such as animal sacrifices, first fruits, and what was needed to build the Tabernacle: Gold, fine linens, animal skins and precious stones.

As an aside, let us mention here that since the Middle Ages, Jews have often been maliciously accused of sacrificing Christian children to make Passover matzah. This is known as the "blood libel". Yet the Torah strictly forbids both human sacrifice and drinking blood! The bigger the lie, the more it is believed.

In his *Guide for the Perplexed*, Maimonides downplays sacrifices. He says they were a necessary transitional step between the human sacrifices of the pagans and the kind of worship God really wanted, which is prayer. If God had asked only for prayer back then, the people would not have followed. They were not ready to confine their worship to something so abstract:
> The custom in those days among all men...consisted in sacrificing animals. God did not command us to give [this] up, for this would have been contrary to the nature of man, who generally cleaves to that to which he is used.
> Sacrifices [however] are not the primary object [of the commandments about sacrifice]; prayers are. [To wit,] we were not commanded to sacrifice in every place,

> and in every time, or to build a Temple in every place, or to allow anybody to become a priest and sacrifice. Only one Temple was appointed, and only [as the Torah says] "in the place which the Lord shall choose". [Deut. 12:26] In no other place are we allowed to sacrifice. [The Torah says,] "Be careful not to give your burnt-offerings in every place that you see" [Deut. 12:13]. And only the members of a particular family were allowed to officiate as priests.
> All these restrictions served to limit this kind of worship. But prayer and supplication can be offered everywhere and by every person. Because of this, the Prophets rebuke people for being over-zealous in bringing sacrifices. [Rambam, Moreh Nevuchim (Guide for the Perplexed) 3:32]

The Midrash says that in the Messianic Age, all sacrifices will be discontinued, except for the thanksgiving offering. [Lev. Rabbah 9:7]

But Maimonides still emphasized that the best must be reserved for God:
> Everything that is for the sake of God should be of the best and most beautiful. When you build a house of prayer, it should be more beautiful than your own dwelling. When you feed the hungry, you should feed him of the best and sweetest of your table. When you clothe the naked, you should clothe him with the finest of your clothes. Whenever you designate something for a holy purpose, you should sanctify the finest of your possessions. As it is written [in the Torah]: [Leviticus 3:16] "The choicest is for God." [Rambam, Mishneh Torah, Things Forbidden on the Altar 7:11]

The Lubavitcher Rebbe added that if a school day includes both religious and secular studies, the religious should be taught in the morning when the mind is freshest and most receptive; and that if one has two jobs, one to make a living and one to benefit humanity, the latter must take priority.

Now, here is my central question: Why do most people have a strong feeling that life is a zero-sum game? Some of our life experiences suggest that it is not. For example, our knowledge increases as we get older. We create new things in our productive years. If you are nice to others, they may be nice to you: Both gain, no one loses. If you are surly to others, they may be surly to you: Both lose, no one gains. Zero-sum implies quantification, but some things cannot always be quantified, such as love, happiness, success, etc.

But other life experiences suggest life is indeed a zero-sum game, especially when resources are few and limited. For example, the Talmud says:
> [Suppose] two people are travelling [far from civilization]. One of them has a pitcher of water [sufficient for only one person; the other has no water]. If both drink, they will [both] die; but if only one drinks, he can reach civilization [and survive]... Rabbi Akiva... taught: [If the pitcher is yours, you may drink alone.] Your life takes precedence over his life. [Bava Metzia 62a]

There are three reasons why many people believe life is a zero-sum game.

First, people are convinced there must be a higher power that makes things happen. Given that, how do you make that higher power do what you want? Answer: Give it what you would wish to receive yourself: Children, fine food, luxury items, etc. If what you wish does happen, you conclude that your strategy worked. If it doesn't, you conclude the higher power is angry and that you must give him more.

Second, people find it reassuring to believe that there *is* a power they can bargain with, that life is not all luck and randomness.

Third, some people don't believe it naturally, but are taught to believe it by religious authorities who use this belief to control and exploit them.

Is this zero-sum-game belief changing? Yes, because it is rooted in expectations. In olden days, people did not expect anything. They felt deeply they had to work for everything, and provide some kind of payment for what they got. But this belief is changing in the West. Prosperity, democracy, basic rights made people feel entitled to a lot of things without having to give anything in return. Also, secularism is partly at fault. If you are secular and the authority is an elected government, you feel entitled and don't feel you need to give back. If you are religious and the authority is God, you feel the need to earn what you get!

Is "feeling entitled" a good attitude? Yes and no. It is good to feel entitled to intangibles, to rights; such as democracy, free speech, free exercise of religion, free enterprise, equality before the law, etc. But it is not good to feel entitled to tangible things, such as basic income, food, shelter, medical care, etc., especially if one is able to earn them, but doesn't. It is also not good to feel entitled to get more than others, tangible or intangible.

All in all, the feeling that we must earn what we get can only lead to good – as long as the "earning" does not involve doing evil.

Shabbat shalom.

Nitzavim
Deut. 29:9-30:20

B"H

The Jewish View of the Afterlife

In this week's Torah portion, *Nitzavim*, God tells the Israelites:
הַחַיִּים וְהַמָּוֶת נָתַתִּי לְפָנֶיךָ הַבְּרָכָה וְהַקְּלָלָה וּבָחַרְתָּ בַּחַיִּים
I have set before you life and death. Choose life! [Deut. 30:19]

Because of that exhortation, the Jewish emphasis has always been on the "here and now". There is never any encouragement to die because what comes after death is better than this life. Death is never depicted as something to look forward to. It is just another part of the divine plan. Death gives us the discipline to make the most use of our years on earth, because we know there will not always be a tomorrow. Let us now explore what the Jewish tradition has to say about life, death, and the afterlife.

In the Tanach – the Bible – three concepts are put forth:
-First, the body, or flesh, *bassar* in Hebrew.
-Then, the soul -- *nefesh* or *neshamah*.
-Finally, life, which is spirit -- *nishmat*, or breath -- *ruach chayyim*.
Life is the glue that keeps body and soul together.

In the Torah, life is identified with blood. In Genesis, we read:
> But flesh with its life, which is its blood, you shall not eat. [Gen. 9:4]

Life comes from God's breath. In Genesis, we also read:
> And the Lord God formed man of the dust of the ground, and breathed into his nostrils the breath of life; and man became a living soul. [Gen. 2:7]

At some point, life stops. The body and soul separate, life is taken away or returns to God. The psalmist writes:
> His breath goes out, he returns to his earth; in that very day his thoughts perish.
> [Psalms 146:4]

And Ecclesiastes adds:
> And the dust returns to the earth as it was; and the spirit returns to God who gave it.
> [Eccl. 12:7]

As soon that happens, the soul goes down to a place called "Sheol", where it leads a mysterious and shadowy existence. Here are some related biblical quotes:

From Numbers:
> [Korach's people] went down alive into Sheol... The earth closed over them and they vanished from the midst of the congregation. [Numbers 16:33]

From the Psalms:
> -For in death there is no remembrance of You. In Sheol, who shall give you thanks? [Psalms 6:6]
>
> -The dead do not praise the Lord, nor can any who go down into silence.
> [Psalms 115:17]

From Isaiah:
> For Sheol cannot praise You, death cannot celebrate You. Those who go down into the pit cannot hope for Your truth... The living, only the living, will praise You. [Isaiah 38:18-19]

From Ecclesiastes:
> For the living know that they shall die; but the dead know nothing, nor do they have a reward any more; for the memory of them is forgotten.
> Also their love, and their hatred, and their envy, are now perished; nor do they have any more a portion forever in anything that is done under the sun... So whatever your hand finds to do, do it with all your strength; for there is no work, no scheme, no knowledge, no wisdom, in Sheol, where you are going.
> [Eccl. 9:5-10]

Yet the psalmist says that God will also be in Sheol and will get us out of there:

-For You will not abandon my soul to Sheol; nor will You suffer your pious one to see the pit. [Psalms 16:10]

-But God will redeem my soul from the power of Sheol; for he shall receive me. [Psalms 49:16]

-If I ascend up to heaven, you are there! If I make my bed in Sheol, behold, you are there! [Psalms 139:8]

The Torah says that eternal life is not for man, but only for God and celestial beings. In Genesis we read:
And the Lord God said, Behold, the man has become like one of us, knowing good and evil. And now, what if he puts forth his hand, and takes also from the tree of life, and eats, and lives forever. [Gen. 3:22]

But the psalmist has faith in some kind of immortality:

-As for me, I will behold Your face in righteousness. I shall be satisfied, when I awake, with beholding Your likeness. [Psalms 17:15]

-You shall guide me with Your counsel, and afterwards receive me to glory. [Psalms 73:24]

-Return to your rest, O my soul; for the Lord has dealt bountifully with you. For you have saved my soul from death, my eyes from tears, and my feet from falling. I will walk before the Lord in the land of the living. [Psalms 116: 7-9]

On the other hand, Job expresses only a desire for an afterlife, but he does not seem to have faith that an afterlife exists:
But man dies, and is laid low; indeed, man perishes, and where is he? ...
So man lies down, and does not rise; till the heavens are no more, he shall not awake, nor shall he be raised from his sleep.
O that you would hide me in Sheol, that you would conceal me, until your wrath is past, that you would appoint me a set time, and remember me! If a man dies, shall he live again? I will wait all the days of my service, until my reward comes. [Job 14:10-14]

We read about the prophet Elijah, who ascends to "heaven" in a chariot of fire:

A fiery chariot with fiery horses suddenly appeared... and Elijah went up to heaven [*shamayim*] in a whirlwind. [2 Kings 2:11]

We read about the witch of Endor, who raises the spirit of the prophet Samuel from the dead to speak to King Saul. [1 Sam. 28:8ff]

We read about the prophecy of Daniel:
> Many of those that sleep in the dust of the earth will awake, some to eternal life, others to reproaches, to everlasting abhorrence. [Daniel 12:2]

So, in the end, the Tanach is not clear about the afterlife. It leaves room for a wide variety of theories.

In Ecclesiasticus, which is part of the Apocrypha, and therefore not accepted as Jewish teaching, Ben Sira believes Sheol is the final destination. He says:
> -Remember that death will not be long in coming, and that the covenant of the grave is not shown to you. [Sir 14:12]
> -For all things cannot be in men, because the son of man is not immortal. [Sir 17:30]
> -All men are but earth and ashes. [Sir 17:32]
> -At the end [of sinners] there is the pit of hell. [Sir 21:10]

Now let's move on to the Talmud. In the Talmud, the opinions on the afterlife are not always consistent or coherent, but agree on the existence of a "World to Come" – in Hebrew, *Olam Haba*. They also agree on the immortality of the soul and the resurrection of the dead, when the Messiah arrives -- *tehiyyat hammetim* in Hebrew.

Indeed, the second of the nineteen blessings in the Amidah is simply:
> בָּרוּךְ אַתָּה יְהוָה, מְחַיֵּה הַמֵּתִים
> Blessed are You, O Lord, who revives the dead.

And the morning prayer, extracted from the Talmud [Berakhot 60b], reads:
> אֱלֹהַי נְשָׁמָה שֶׁנָּתַתָּ בִּי טְהוֹרָה הִיא אַתָּה בְרָאתָהּ אַתָּה יְצַרְתָּהּ אַתָּה נְפַחְתָּהּ בִּי וְאַתָּה מְשַׁמְּרָהּ בְּקִרְבִּי וְאַתָּה עָתִיד לִטְּלָהּ מִמֶּנִּי וּלְהַחֲזִירָהּ בִּי לֶעָתִיד לָבוֹא
> My God, the soul that You gave me is pure. You created it, You fashioned it, You breathed it into me. You preserve it within me, and You will take it from me, but will restore it to me hereafter.

These beliefs were codified in Maimonides' "thirteen principles of faith", and summarized in the *Yigdal* song. The 12th says that the Messiah will come:
> יִשְׁלַח לְקֵץ הַיָּמִין מְשִׁיחֵנוּ, לִפְדּוֹת מְחַכֵּי קֵץ יְשׁוּעָתוֹ
> At the End of Days He will send our Messiah, to redeem those longing for His final salvation.

The 13th says that God grants eternal life:
> מֵתִים יְחַיֶּה אֵל בְּרֹב חַסְדּוֹ
> God will revive the dead in His abundant kindness.

The Talmud [Berakhot 17a] gives more details, summarized by Maimonides:
> There are no bodies and no bodily forms in the World to Come ... There is no eating or drinking there, nor is there anything which the human body needs in this world. Nor does there occur there any of the events which occur to the human body in this world, such as sitting, standing, sleep, death, distress, laughter, and so forth. The ancient sages say: "In the World to Come, there is no eating or drinking or procreation, but the righteous sit with their crowns on their heads and bask in the radiance of the Divine Presence... There is no way for us in this world to know or comprehend the great goodness which the soul experiences in the world to come, for in this world we know only of material pleasures, and it is these we desire.
> [Rambam, Yad, Teshuvah 8]

Many Jewish writers likewise emphasize the spiritual nature of the afterlife.

The wicked are punished by being denied this spiritual afterlife. Some say they go to Gehennom (*Gei ven Hinnom*), a valley outside Jerusalem, and are punished there. It is the Jewish version of "purgatory". It is also not eternal. The Talmud says:
> -There will be no Gehennon in future times. [Rosh Hashana 17a, Bava Metzia 58b, Nedarim 8b, Avodah Zara 3b]
> -The souls in Gehinnom are punished for up to twelve months, then continue on to Gan Eden [that is, to heaven]. [Eduyyot 2:10]
> -Those who [do not repent and] remain wicked, are annihilated. [Rosh Hashanah 17a]

This gave rise to the practice of mourning the deceased for only eleven months, so as not to imply that they need the full twelve months.

In Talmudic times, the Sadducees rejected the concept of an afterlife. They lost. The Talmud says:
> Those who deny the resurrection of the dead get no share in the World to Come. [Sanh. 10:1, 90b-91a]

This means, curiously, that if you don't believe in it, you won't get it. Does your belief *cause* its existence? Let's save that for another time.

Some Hassidim believe in reincarnation. Jewish mystics speak of eternity not as an endless length of time, but outside of time altogether. They say that "heaven" is a state, not a place, and that the soul is divided into several parts. It gets complicated. One thing is certain: Heaven is not for Jews alone. Our Sages said:
> The righteous of all nations have a share in the world to come. [Rambam, Mishneh Torah, Repentance 3:5, based on Sanhedrin 105a]

The bottom line is that, while there is agreement in rabbinic Judaism on the existence and main outline of an afterlife, there is no uniform Jewish view of the details. The emphasis is always on life here on earth. A basic paradox that puts emphasis on both this world -- *Olam Hazzeh* – and the World to Come -- *Olam Haba* -- was expressed by Rabbi Yaakov in the Mishnah:
> Better is one hour of repentance and good deeds in this world than the whole life in the World to Come. Yet better is one hour of blissfulness of spirit in the World to Come than the whole life in this world. [Avot 4:22]

Shabbat shalom.

Vayelech
Deut. 31:1-31:30

B"H

When it's Time to Die

This week's Torah portion, *Vayelech*, is the end of the road for Moses, physically and spiritually. It is the physical end of the road because it is the endpoint of the journey to the Promised Land; and God did not allow him to go into it. Also, he is going to die on that very day. It is the spiritual end of the road because he must pass the mantle of leadership to Joshua, as instructed by God.

The portion begins with:

וַיֵּלֶךְ מֹשֶׁה וַיְדַבֵּר אֶת־הַדְּבָרִים הָאֵלֶּה אֶל־כָּל־יִשְׂרָאֵל
And Moses went, and he spoke these words to all of Israel. [Deut 31:1]

Vayelech Moshe: And Moses went. *Where did he go?* Are we talking about physically going to another place or only about the emotional and psychological departure of a lame duck leader?

Where did Moses go?

Ohr HaChaim, from 18th-century Morocco, is also puzzled: We need to know where Moses went... The wording of the Torah is vague and does not provide a clue as to where Moses actually went...

The Ramban, from 13th-century Catalonia, notes that Moses left the encampment of the Levites, where the previous assembly had taken place, and went to the Israelites, to show them respect and to take his final leave of them, because on that very day he was to die on Mount Nebo. It is good manners to ask one's host for permission to absent oneself. (But "Israel", in our verse, refers to all Jews, not just Israelites.)

Ibn Ezra, from 12th-century Spain and Chizkuni, from 13th-century France, said that Moses went to each tribe to inform them that he was going to die, so that they would not be frightened, and that they should take heart and support their new leader Joshua.

Sforno, from 16th-century Italy, notes that another meaning of the word Vayelech (וַיֵּלֶךְ) is that the persons described acted on their own initiative.

The Zohar notes that forty days before a man dies his soul (נשמה) leaves him... "Moses went" means that his soul had gone from him just like in any other righteous person (צדיק) whose end is at hand. [Zohar 1:217]

Kli Yakar, the 16th-century Chief Rabbi of Prague, writes that "And Moses went" means that he went from tent to tent to everyone among the Israelites, and he "spoke these words" to their hearts -- that is, words of repentance -- to help them in their own journey towards repentance.

He also speculates that perhaps "Moses went" to seek peace. The Sages [Leviticus Rabbah 9:9] interpreted the verse "Seek peace and pursue it" [Psalms 34:15] to mean that peacemaking is not like other commandments. One is obligated to perform all other commandments [only] when one encounters them, but one is not obligated to chase after them. Yet with regard to peacemaking, one must "pursue" it. We are not allowed simply to wait and hope that peace will occur. We are obligated to "pursue" it.

"And Moses went and spoke these words". Spoke which words? The words spoken are words of *teshuvah* directed both toward God and toward one's fellow. For both of these are referred to by Hosea when he said:
> Take with you words and return to God. Say to Him: "Forgive all guilt and accept what is good". [Hosea 14:3]

The Hassidic masters said that "Moses went" into the minds and hearts of the people -- the highest places and the deepest places. As proof, they cite the Torah before and after our verse. Before our verse, it says:

That very day the Lord spoke to Moses: Ascend these heights of Abarim to Mount Nebo... You shall die on the mountain that you are about to ascend. [Deut. 21:48-50]

After our verse, it says:
> So Moses ... died ... in the land of Moab, and [God] buried him in the valley in the land of Moab, near Beth-Peor; and no one knows his burial place to this day. [Deut. 34:5-6]

So Moses "went" to both mountain and valley, metaphorically speaking.

Was Moses incapable of continuing? After our verse, the Torah notes:

וַיֹּאמֶר אֲלֵהֶם בֶּן־מֵאָה וְעֶשְׂרִים שָׁנָה אָנֹכִי הַיּוֹם לֹא־אוּכַל עוֹד לָצֵאת וְלָבוֹא

[Moses] said to them: Today I am 120 years old, I can no longer go out and come in. [Deut. 31:2]

"I can no longer go out and come in." *Go out where and come in where?*

Rabbenu Baḥya, from 14th-century Spain, explains:
> It means "I am no longer able to go out to war and to come back." Moses refers to the times he had led the Jewish armies against Sichon and Og.

The Talmud, however, excludes any physical explanation:
> What is the meaning of "I can no longer go out and come in"? It is not a [physical problem] because it is written later:
>> And Moses was 120 years old when he died. His eye was not dim, and his natural force was not abated. [Deut. 34:7]
>
> And it is written further:
>> And Moses went up from the plains of Moab to Mount Nebo. [Deut. 34:1]
>
> [So he was quite vigorous, because] it is taught in a baraita: There were twelve steps there [to ascend the mountain], and Moses stepped over all of them in a single step. [Sotah 13b]

The Midrash says "I can no longer go out" means "I am not permitted [to do things on my own initiative]" because leadership is being taken from me and given to Joshua. [Sifrei Devarim 72:1]

The Talmud goes even further: Moses' mind was feeling its limitations:
> Rabbi Shmuel bar Naḥmani says that Rabbi Yonatan says: [It means he could no longer] go out and come in with words of Torah. This teaches that the gates of

wisdom were closed off to him… Authority was taken from him and given to [Joshua]. [Sotah 13b]

A poignant elaboration is given in Midrash Tanḥuma:

> The Holy One, blessed be He, said to Moses, "Why all this anguish that you are experiencing?"
> [Moses] said, "Master of the world, I am afraid of the pangs of the angel of death."
> [God] said to him, "I am not delivering you into his hands."
> He said in front of [God], "Master of the universe, my mother Yocheved … will be distressed by my death."
> [God] said to him, "So has it come up in [My] mind. But it is it the way of the world. Every generation has its expositors, every generation has its administrators, every generation has its leaders. Up to now it has been your lot to serve in front of Me, but now your lot is over and the time of your disciple Joshua for him to serve [Me] has arrived."
> [Moses] said to him, "My Master, if I am dying because of Joshua, let me go and become *his* disciple!"
> [God] said to him, "If you want to do that, go ahead and do it."
>
> Moses arose and went early to Joshua's door. Now Joshua was seated expounding [Torah] … and did not see [Moses]… and Moses was standing… [The Israelites] said to Joshua, "What has come over you that Moses our master stands, while you sit?"
> When [Joshua] raised his eyes and saw [Moses], he immediately rent his clothes. Then sobbing and weeping, he said, "O my master, my master! My father, my father and lord!"
> The Israelites said to Moses, "Moses our master, teach us Torah."
> He said to them, "I am not allowed."
> They said to him, "We are not leaving you."
> A heavenly voice (*bat kol*) came forth and said to them: "Learn from Joshua."
> [So] they… sat and learned from Joshua. Joshua sat at the head with Moses to his right and [Aaron's sons] Elazar and Ithamar to his left.
> So [Joshua] sat and expounded in the presence of Moses…
> But Moses did not understand what Joshua was expounding.
> After the Israelites arose [from the session], they said to Moses, "[Explain] to us the Torah [we have just heard from Joshua]."
> He said to them, "I do not know what to answer you."
> So Moses our master was stumbling and falling.

> It was at that time that he said, "Master of the Universe, up to now I requested life, but now here is my soul given over to You."
> He had resigned himself to death... [Midrash Tanḥuma, Va'etchanan 6:1]

The Talmud records another story about how Moses could not understand even laws expounded in his name:

> Rav Yehudah says that Rav says: When Moses ascended on High, he found the Holy One, Blessed be He, sitting and tying crowns on the letters [of the Torah]. ... [God] said to him: There is a man who is destined to be born after several generations, and Akiva ben Yosef is his name. He is destined to derive from each and every thorn [of these crowns] piles and piles of laws. It is for his sake that the crowns must be added to the letters of the Torah.
>
> Moses said before God: Master of the Universe, show him to me. God said to him: Return behind you. Moses went and sat at the end of the eighth row in Rabbi Akiva's study hall and did not understand what they were saying. Moses' strength waned ... [Rabbi Akiva's] students said: My teacher, from where do you derive this? Rabbi Akiva said to them: It is a law transmitted to Moses from Sinai. When Moses heard this, his mind was put at ease. [Menaḥot 29b]

Why was Moses uncomfortable at first, then "his mind was put at ease" when he heard that? Possibly, because he realized he must have known it all along, but had forgotten it? If so, what is the point of the story? That we all get old? This is suggested in our verse. Or, because he was happy to see that what *he* started would continue and evolve, even beyond his own ability to understand? Perhaps Moses thought at first that Akiva was making things up, which made him uneasy, then realized Akiva was deriving it from what Moses himself taught, at which point he relaxed?

Traditionally, all halacha was given to Moses on Mount Sinai as the "Oral Law". Can we say: Perhaps not all, but some of it could be *inferred* from what was given, with logic that may have been too complicated for Moses to understand? If Euclid or Pythagoras could attend a lecture on modern mathematics, they, too, would be completely lost, yet modern mathematics is based on their work.

Now let us tackle our central question: When is it time to die?

Moses asked God to die when he felt he could no longer be useful. Was it an overreaction? He knew he was going to die very soon anyway. The Torah says:
> God said to Moses: The time is drawing near for you to die… You are soon to lie with your fathers. [Deut. 31:14-16]

Moses asked for more time, then changed his mind. But still, Judaism does not encourage this attitude.

The Bible says:
> כִּי־עָפָר אַתָּה וְאֶל־עָפָר תָּשׁוּב:
> For dust you are and to dust you will return. [Genesis 3:19]

and:
> לַכֹּל זְמָן וְעֵת לְכָל־חֵפֶץ תַּחַת הַשָּׁמָיִם: עֵת לָלֶדֶת וְעֵת לָמוּת עֵת לָטַעַת וְעֵת לַעֲקוֹר נָטוּעַ
> For everything there is a season and a time for every experience under heaven: A time to be born and a time to die; a time to plant and a time to uproot what has been planted. [Eccl. 3:1-2]

When is a "good" time to die? When you believe you can no longer contribute? When your betters come on the scene? When you reach mandatory retirement, sometimes referred to sarcastically as statutory senility? It is unclear, because we don't control our time. The Mishnah says:
> וְשׁוּב יוֹם אֶחָד לִפְנֵי מִיתָתְךָ -- Repent one day before your death. [Avot 2:10]

This may imply you know when that it, but it really means "Repent now *because* you don't know when death will come."

No suicide or euthanasia is allowed in Judaism. But is one allowed to pray for death? The Talmud says that one can pray for the death of someone who is incurably sick, in pain and dying. This is based on how Rabbenu Nissim, from 14th-century Spain, understood the Talmud [Nedarim 40a; Ketuvot 104a]. It was ratified by the Arukh HaShulḥan [Yoreh Deah 335:3] and by Rabbi Moshe Feinstein [Igrot Moshe CM 2:74]. This may imply, a fortiori, that one is allowed to pray for his own death.

In fact, permission to pray for death is implied in the Torah account we just studied. It is also implied in the rest of the Bible, as in the case of the prophet Jonah:
> Please, God, take my life, for I would rather die than live. [Jonah 4:2]

It is also implied in the Talmud, as in the story of Ḥoni the Circle-Drawer, a first-century Mishnaic scholar:
> Ḥoni became very upset, prayed for mercy, and died. [Taanit 23a]

It is also implied in a story in the Midrash:
> [There was] an old woman who became very advanced in years. She came before Rabbi Yossi ben Halafta and said to him, "Rabbi, I have [lived long and] I have become too old. At this point, [my] life has deteriorated. I have no taste for food or drink. I wish to be free from the world."
> He said to her, "To what do you attribute your longevity?"
> She said to him, "My custom is that, even if I have some vital matter to attend to, I set it aside, rise up early and go to the synagogue each day."
> He said to her, "Restrain yourself and do not attend the synagogue for three consecutive days."
> She went and she did so, and on the third day she took ill and died. [Yalkut Shimoni to Proverbs 8:34-35]

In all these cases there was no physical or mental impairment. The person was simply too upset or too tired to go on living.

What can we conclude? Nothing. There are too many issues involved in end-of-life matters, and there are no one-size-fits-all answers. Judaism always stresses the sanctity of life and never allows it to be shortened intentionally.

Shabbat shalom.

Haazinu
Deut. 32:1-32:52

B"H

The Resurrection of the Dead

In this week's Torah portion, *Haazinu*, Moses delivers a song exhorting Israel to remember the Exodus and follow the Torah or incur punishment, and a promise of future redemption. He quotes God as saying:

> רְאוּ ׀ עַתָּה כִּי אֲנִי אֲנִי הוּא וְאֵין אֱלֹהִים עִמָּדִי אֲנִי אָמִית וַאֲחַיֶּה מָחַצְתִּי וַאֲנִי אֶרְפָּא וְאֵין מִיָּדִי מַצִּיל:
> See, now, that I, even I, am He. There is no god beside Me. I kill and I give life. I have wounded and I will heal. And there is none who can deliver out of My hand.
> [Deut. 32:39]

The Talmud concludes that this verse implies a physical revival after death. God first says "I kill," then "I give life", which is not the sequence of events we witness; especially given that the words "wound" and "heal" are in the proper sequence:

> The Sages taught: [God said] "I kill and I give life." One might have thought that this refers to death for one person and life [meaning birth], for another person, in the typical manner the world operates. [However,] the verse adds: "I have wounded and I will heal." Just as the wounding and the healing [clearly] refer to the same person, so too death and life refer to the same person. This verse refutes those who say that there is no Torah source for the resurrection of the dead. [Pesachim 68a; also Sanhedrin 91b]

What happens after life is not revealed in the Torah itself. The dead go to "Sheol", a mysterious, ill-defined place. This leaves room for a wide variety of theories.

In the rest of the Tanach, there are more explicit hints at resurrection. Hannah, Samuel's mother, in her prayer of thanksgiving, uses the same language as our portion:

יְהוָה מֵמִית וּמְחַיֶּה מוֹרִיד שְׁאוֹל וַיָּעַל:
The Lord gives death and gives life; casts down into Sheol and raises up.
[1 Samuel 2:6]

Isaiah tells God:
Oh, let Your dead revive! Let corpses arise!
Awake and shout for joy, you who dwell in the dust! [Isaiah 26:19]

In addition, there are three specific examples of resurrection in Tanach:

First, the prophet Elijah prays for God to resurrect a young boy, and God does so:
After a while, the son of the mistress of the house fell sick, and his illness grew worse, until he had no breath left in him. She said to Elijah, "What harm have I done to you, O man of God, that you should come here to recall my sin and cause the death of my son?"
"Give me the boy," he said to her; and taking him from her arms, he carried him to the upper chamber where he was staying, and laid him down on his own bed. He cried out to the Lord and said, "O Lord my God, will You bring calamity upon this widow whose guest I am, and let her son die?" Then he stretched out over the child three times, and cried out to the Lord, saying, "O Lord my God, let this child's life return to his body!"
The Lord heard Elijah's plea. The child's life returned to his body, and he revived. Elijah picked up the child and brought him down from the upper room into the main room, and gave him to his mother. "See," said Elijah, "your son is alive." And the woman answered Elijah, "Now I know that you are a man of God and that the word of the Lord is truly in your mouth." [1 Kings 17:17–24]

Second, the prophet Elisha revives the son of the Shunammite woman, a child whose birth he had foretold: [2 Kings 4:8–16]
Elisha came into the house, and there was the boy, laid out dead on his couch. He went in, shut the door behind the two of them, and prayed to the Lord. Then he mounted [the bed] and placed himself over the child. He put his mouth on its mouth,

his eyes on its eyes, and his hands on its hands, as he bent over it. And the body of the child became warm. He stepped down, walked once up and down the room, then mounted and bent over him. Thereupon, the boy sneezed seven times, and opened his eyes.
[Elisha] called Gehazi and said, "Call the Shunammite woman," and he called her. When she came to him, he said, "Pick up your son." She came and fell at his feet and bowed low to the ground. Then she picked up her son and left. [2 Kings 4:32–37]

Third, a dead man is thrown into Elisha's grave, and he is revived when his body touches Elisha's bones:
> Once a man was being buried, when the people caught sight of a band [of Moabite thugs], so they threw the corpse into Elisha's grave and made off. When the [dead] man came in contact with Elisha's bones, he came to life and stood up. [2 Kings 13:21]

One can argue that these prophets knew how to revive someone who had just died, something modern surgeons frequently do. There is even a hint of cardiopulmonary and mouth-to-mouth resuscitation.

The Talmud sees more proof in the tense of verbs: [Sanhedrin 91b]

-In Psalms, the first line of *Ashrei* says:
אַשְׁרֵי יוֹשְׁבֵי בֵיתֶךָ עוֹד יְהַלְלוּךָ סֶּלָה
Ashrei yoshvei vetecha; 'Od yehallelucha selah [Ps. 84:5]
Happy are those who dwell in Your house! They shall praise You yet again.
The Sages asked: Why "They shall praise you yet again" instead of just "they praise you"? Because it alludes to the *future*, after resurrection, when they will praise God *again*! It means, "Just as they praised You in this world, so they shall praise You in the World to Come."

-In Exodus, it says:
> "Then Moses and the children of Israel will sing this song to the Lord." [Exodus 15:1] It is not stated "sang" but "will sing" [implying Moses will be revived and sing the song in the future.]

-In Joshua, it says:

> "Then Joshua will build an altar to the Lord God of Israel on Mount Ebal." [Joshua 8:30] It is not stated "built" but "will build" [implying that Joshua will be revived.

In Talmudic times, Sadducees and Samaritans rejected the notion of the resurrection of the dead. The Pharisees defended it passionately, arguing it was part of the Oral Law. They won out, and now it is mainline Jewish teaching. All rabbis agreed on the existence of a "World to Come", *Olam Haba* in Hebrew, on the immortality of the soul and the resurrection of the dead when the Messiah arrives (*tehiyyat hammetim*). These concepts are ubiquitous in Jewish thought and liturgy:

-The Mishnah says:
> These are those who have no portion in the World to Come: He who maintains that resurrection is not a biblical doctrine, that the Torah was not divinely revealed, and an Epicurean [who encourages people to seek out only the pleasures of this world.] [Sanhedrin 10:1]

This means, curiously, that if you don't believe in it, you won't get it. Does your belief cause its existence? Let's save that thought for another time.

-The second of the nineteen blessings in the Amidah is simply:
> בָּרוּךְ אַתָּה יְהוָה, מְחַיֵּה הַמֵּתִים -- *Baruch atta HaShem, mechayye ha-metim.*
> Blessed are You, O Lord, who revives the dead.

-The morning prayer, extracted from the Talmud [Berakhot 60b], reads:
> אֱלֹהַי. נְשָׁמָה שֶׁנָּתַתָּ בִּי טְהוֹרָה הִיא. אַתָּה בְרָאתָהּ. אַתָּה יְצַרְתָּהּ. אַתָּה נְפַחְתָּהּ בִּי. וְאַתָּה מְשַׁמְּרָהּ בְּקִרְבִּי. וְאַתָּה עָתִיד לִטְּלָהּ מִמֶּנִּי. וּלְהַחֲזִירָהּ בִּי לֶעָתִיד לָבוֹא.

> My God, the soul that You gave me is pure. You created it, You fashioned it, You breathed it into me. You preserve it within me, and You will take it from me, but You will restore it to me hereafter.

-These beliefs are codified in Maimonides' "thirteen principles of faith". The 12th says that the Messiah will come and the 13th says that God grants eternal life:

(12) I believe with perfect faith in the coming of the Messiah, and even though he may delay, nevertheless I anticipate every day that he will come.

(13) I believe with perfect faith that there will be a resurrection of the dead at a time that will please the Creator, blessed and exalted be his Name forever and ever.

What is the process of resurrection according to our Sages?

First, the body will be rebuilt from the *luz* bone, a tiny but very tough bone in the spine. (Read: DNA.)

> [The Roman Emperor] Hadrian... asked Rabbi Yehoshua ben Hanania: "From what part [of the body] will the Holy One, blessed be He, cause man to blossom forth in the future?"
> He replied: "From the nut of the spinal column."
> He asked: "How do you know that?"
> He replied: "Bring me one and I will prove it to you."
> He threw it into the fire, yet it was not burnt.
> He put it in water, but it did not dissolve.
> He ground it between millstones, but it was not crushed.
> He placed it on an anvil and smote it with a hammer. The anvil was cleft and the hammer split, yet it remained intact. [Genesis R. 28:3]

Second, you will come back as you went:

> As a man departs [this life] so will he be when he is resurrected. If he departs blind, he will return blind; if he departs deaf, he will return deaf; if he departs mute, he will return mute; if he departs lame, he will return lame; if he departs clothed, he will return clothed... God said, "Let them arise as they went, and afterwards I will heal them." [Genesis R. 95:1; also Sanhedrin 91b]

Third, the order of events is as follows. The Messiah comes, rebuilds the Temple in Jerusalem, and gathers all living Jews in the Land of Israel. Then, forty years later, the dead are resurrected, by descending order of righteousness: First the scholars who mostly studied Torah, then those who mostly followed mitzvot; first the dead of Israel, then the dead in the Diaspora. The latter will burrow through the earth until they reach Israel. That's why many Jews want to be buried in Israel.

Fourth, following the bodily resurrection is a spiritual life in the World to Come. The Talmud [Berakhot 17a] gives more details, summarized by Maimonides:
> There are no bodies and no bodily forms in the World to Come... There is no eating or drinking there, nor is there anything which the human body needs in this world. Nor does there occur there any of the events which occur to the human body in this world, such as sitting, standing, sleep, death, distress, laughter, and so forth. The ancient sages say: "In the World to Come, there is no eating or drinking or procreation, but the righteous sit with their crowns on their heads and bask in the radiance of the Divine Presence... There is no way for us in this world to know or comprehend the great goodness which the soul experiences in the world to come, for in this world we know only of material pleasures, and it is these we desire.
> [Rambam, Yad, Teshuvah 8]

Many Jewish writers likewise emphasize the spiritual nature of the afterlife.

Let us conclude. While the belief in resurrection and an afterlife is deeply rooted in Judaism, the Jewish emphasis has always been on the "here and now". In the Torah, God tells us:

הַחַיִּים וְהַמָּוֶת נָתַתִּי לְפָנֶיךָ הַבְּרָכָה וְהַקְּלָלָה וּבָחַרְתָּ בַּחַיִּים

I have set before you life and death. Choose life! [Deut. 30:19]

Death is never depicted as something to look forward to, only a part of the divine plan. Death gives us the discipline to make the best use of our time on earth, because we know there will not always be a tomorrow.

Shabbat shalom.

V'Zot HaBracha
Deut. 33:1-34:12

B"H

The (Reluctant) Death of Moses

In the last Torah portion of the year, *V'zot Ha-berachah*, traditionally read on Simchat Torah, we hear about the death of Moses:
> So Moses, the servant of the Lord, died there in the land of Moab... And [God] buried him in a valley...; but no man knows his grave till this day.
> And Moses was 120 years old when he died. His eye was not dim, nor had his natural force abated... And there has not arisen since in Israel a prophet like Moses, whom the Lord knew face to face. [Deut. 34:5-7, 10]

The Midrash on Deuteronomy gives a detailed account of the death of Moses. It reads like a thriller, which is unusual for ancient commentary. It tells about how Moses absolutely, positively does not want to die, and uses every argument he can think of to get a reprieve. He fights off the Angel of Death, even beats him up. He recites all his merits one by one. He asks to at least be allowed in the Promised Land, saying: Just as I witnessed Israel's troubles, I want to witness their good fortune. He tells God, "I served you faithfully all these years, and this is how You repay me?" He accuses God of not following His own Torah by not paying the laborer's wages on time. He asks God to turn him into a bird instead of dying. The angels refuse to take away Moses' soul. So God orders Moses' soul to leave his body, but the soul refuses! So God gives Moses the kiss of death, then cries...

This account is so poignant that it deserves to be read in full. Here are some excerpts. [Deuteronomy Rabbah 11:5-10]

[The Torah says:
> And this is the blessing that Moses, the man of God, bestowed upon the children of Israel before his death. [Deut. 33:1]]

What is meant by "before his death"? The Rabbis say: What did Moses do? He seized the Angel of Death and cast him down in front of him and [then] blessed the tribes, each according to its [appropriate] blessing.
Rabbi Meir said: The Angel of Death came to Moses and said to him: "God has sent me to you, for you are to depart this life today."
Moses replied to him, "Go away, for I wish to praise the Holy One, Blessed be He."...
The Angel of Death said to Moses: "Moses, why are you so arrogant? There are others in creation who can praise God. Heaven and earth praise [God] all the time."...
Moses replied to him, "I shall silence [heaven and earth] and praise [God]."
The Angel of Death then came to [Moses] a second time. What did Moses do? He pronounced over him the Ineffable Name [of God] and [the Angel of Death] fled.
When he came to him a third time, Moses said, "Since [this decree] is from God, I must accept the righteousness of His judgment."

Rabbi Yitzhaq said: The soul of Moses struggled to leave. Moses was conversing with his soul, saying: "My soul, perhaps you think that the Angel of Death is seeking to gain dominion over you?"
[His soul] replied: "God will [surely] not permit it."
[Moses then said to his soul]: "Perhaps you have seen Israel weeping and you wept with them?"
Whereupon she replied:
>[You have delivered] my eyes from tears. [Ps. 116:8]

Moses said to her: "Do you think then that they have sought to thrust you into Gehennom?"
Whereupon she replied:
>[You have delivered] my feet from stumbling. [Ps. 116:8]

Moses said to her: "And where are you destined to go?"
She replied:
>I shall walk before the Lord in the lands of the living. [Ps. 116:9]

When Moses heard this he gave her permission [to leave], saying to her:
>Return, O my soul, to your rest, [for God has been kind to you]. [Ps. 116:7]

When Moses was about to depart this world, the Holy One, blessed be He, said to him:
>Behold, your days are drawing near [to die.] [Deut. 31:14]

[Moses] replied before [God]: "Master of the Universe, after all my toil [for You and for Israel], You say to me, "Behold, your days are drawing near [to die.]"!
>I shall not die, but live, and declare the works of the Lord. [Ps. 118:17]"

Thereupon God said: "You cannot prevail [in this matter], for this is [the destiny of] all men." [Eccl. 12:13].

Moses then said: "Master of the Universe, I ask of You one favor before I die, that I may enter [the Land of Israel] and that all the gates of heaven and in the depths be opened so people will see that there is none beside You."
Whereupon God replied: "You said [regarding Me]:

אֵין עוֹד -- There is none else. [Deut. 4:39]

I, too, say,

And there has not arisen a prophet like Moses in Israel..." [Deut. 34:10]

[God said to Moses:]

Behold, your days are drawing near [to die.] [Deut. 31:14]

Rabbi Evu said: Moses said: "Master of the Universe, with the word [behold! (*hinne!*)] that I have used to praise You among the 600,000 Israelites who hallowed Your name, you decreed the death penalty upon me! [Deut. 10:14] [Don't you reward] measure for measure? [Why then do you repay me] a bad measure for a good measure, a short measure for a full measure, a grudging measure for an ample measure?"

The Holy One, blessed be He, answered: "Moses, My use of the expression "behold" is also a good measure, as it is said [in Exodus, Proverbs and Malachi]:

Behold, I send an angel before you. [Ex. 23:20]

Behold, the righteous shall be requited in the earth. [Prov. 11:31]

Behold, I will send you Elijah the prophet. [Mal. 3:23]

And just as you have exalted Me before 600,000, so will I elevate you in the Time to Come among 550,000 altogether righteous men."...

[Moses thought: "When I prayed for God to have mercy on Israel, God granted my request.] Since I have not sinned from my youth, does it not stand to reason that when I pray on my own behalf God should answer my prayer?" And when God saw that Moses made light of the matter and that he was not engaging in prayer, He seized the opportunity to swear by His great Name that Moses should not enter the Land of Israel...

When Moses saw that the decree against him had been sealed, he resolved to fast, drew a small circle, and stood inside it. He said, "I will not move from here until You nullify that decree." What else did Moses do then? He... wrapped himself with sackcloth, rolled himself in the dust and stood in prayer and supplications before the Holy One, blessed be He, until the heavens and the order of nature were shaken. They said: "Perhaps it is the desire of the Holy One, blessed be He, to renew His world." Whereupon a heavenly voice was heard proclaiming: "It is not yet the desire of the Holy One, blessed be He, to renew His world..."

What did the Holy One, blessed be He, do at that time? He proclaimed in every gate of each of the [seven] heavens, and in every Court, that they should not receive Moses' prayer, nor bring it before Him, because the decree against him had been sealed. God hastily summoned the Angel in charge of Proclamations, whose name was Achreziel, and commanded the ministering angels: "Descend quickly, bolt all the gates of every heaven, because the voice of [Moses'] prayer threatens to force its way to heaven."

And the angels sought to ascend to heaven because of the sound of Moses' prayer, for his prayer was like a sword which tears and cuts its way through everything, and spares nothing, seeing that his prayer was of the nature of the Ineffable Name which he had learned from Zagzag-el the Master Scribe of the children of heaven...

It is to that hour that [the prophet Ezekiel] alludes when he says:
> And I heard behind me the voice of a great rushing: Blessed be the glory of the Lord from His place. [Ezek. 3:12]

And "rushing" surely means trembling and "great" surely refers to Moses... What is the meaning of, "Blessed be the glory of the Lord from His place"? When the wheels of the [Divine] Chariot and the fiery Seraphim saw that God commanded that Moses' prayer should not be accepted and that He did not favor [Moses], did not grant him more life, did not bring him into the Land of Israel, they exclaimed: "Blessed be the glory of the Lord from His place," for [from His position and station] there is no favoritism for persons great or small...

Moses said to God: "Master of the Universe, the hard work and the effort I have devoted to making Israel believe in Your name are manifest and known to You, as is the trouble I have taken to teach them Torah and commandments. I thought that, just as I witnessed their troubles, so too will I witness their good fortune. But now that the time of good fortune for Israel has arrived, You say to me:
> You will not cross this Jordan. [Deut. 31:2]

You thus make Your Torah into a fraud, because in it You wrote [in regard to a paid worker:]
> You will pay him on the same day [that he worked]. The sun shall not set upon him [without his being paid], for he is poor, and his life depends on it. [Deut. 24:15]

Is this the reward I get for forty years of work, during which I toiled so that [Israel] should become a holy and faithful nation?"

Samael, the wicked angel, the chief of all the accusing angels, was awaiting the death of Moses every hour, saying, "When will the time arrive for Moses to die, so that I may descend and take away his soul from him?" ...There is no one among the accusing angels as wicked as Samael and there is none so righteous among the prophets as Moses... So Samael the wicked was waiting for Moses' soul saying, "When will [the angel] Michael [Protector of Israel] be weeping and I be filling my mouth with laughter?"...

Meanwhile, only one hour [of life] remained for Moses.
Moses said to the Holy One, blessed be He: "Master of the Universe, if You will not allow me to enter the Land of Israel, leave me in this world [outside the Land] so that I may live [there] and not die."
The Holy One, blessed be He, then said to Moses: "If I do not put you to death in this world, how can I bring you back to life in the World to Come? And what is more, you [would] make of My Torah a fraud, for in My Torah, written by your hand, it says:
> And no one can rescue from My hand." [Deut. 32:39]

Moses said to God: "Master of the Universe, if You will not bring me into the Land of Israel, let me become like the beasts of the field that eat grass and drink water, and live and enjoy the world. Likewise let my soul be like one of them."
Whereupon God replied:
> אַל־יֹ רַב־לָךְ אַל־תּוֹסֶף דַּבֵּר אֵלַי עוֹד בַּדָּבָר הַזֶּה׃
> Enough! [Never speak to Me of this matter again!] [Deut. 3:26]

Moses then prayed: "Master of the Universe, let me at least become in this world like a bird that flies about in every direction, and gathers its food daily, and returns to its nest towards evening. Let my soul likewise become like one of them." Whereupon God answered: "Enough!" What is the meaning of "Enough!"? God said to him: "You have spoken sufficiently."

When Moses saw that no creature could save him from the path of death, he exclaimed:
> The Rock, His work is perfect; for all His ways are justice; a God of faithfulness and without iniquity, just and righteous is He. [Deut. 32:4]

What did Moses do? He took a scroll and wrote down upon it the Ineffable Name. The Book of the Song [of Haazinu] had not been completely written down when the moment of Moses' death arrived.

At that hour the Holy One, blessed be He, said to Gabriel: "Gabriel, go out and bring Moses' soul."
He, however, replied: "Master of the Universe, how can I witness the death of one who is equal to 600,000, and how can I behave harshly to one who possesses such qualities?"
Then [God] said to Michael: "Go out and bring Moses' soul."
He, however, replied: "Master of the Universe, I was his teacher, and he was my student. I cannot therefore witness his death."

[God] then said to Samael the wicked: "Go out and bring Moses' soul."
Immediately [Samael] clothed himself with anger, girded on his sword, wrapped himself with cruelty, and went out to meet Moses. When Samael saw Moses sitting and writing down the Ineffable Name, and how the radiance of his appearance was like the sun and he was like an angel of the Lord of hosts, he became afraid of Moses and declared: "It is certain that angels cannot take away Moses' soul."

Now before Samael showed himself to Moses, Moses knew of his coming, and when Samael caught sight of Moses, trembling and fear took hold of him, as of a woman in travail, and he did not have the effrontery to speak to Moses, until Moses said to him:
אֵין שָׁלוֹם אָמַר אֱלֹהַי לָרְשָׁעִים:
There is no peace for the wicked, said God. [Isa. 57:21]
What are you doing here?
He replied: "I have come to take away your soul."
Moses asked him: "Who sent you?"
He replied: "He who created all the creatures."
Moses then said to him: "You shall not take away my soul."
Whereupon he replied: "The souls of all who come into this world are delivered into my hands."
Whereupon Moses said: "I have more power than all who come into this world."
[Samael] then asked: "And what [demonstrates] your power?" Moses replied:
"I, the son of Amram, emerged from my mother's womb circumcised. I did not need to be circumcised.
On the very day I was born, I found myself able to speak, walk and converse with my father and mother, and I had not yet even sucked [my mother's] milk.
When I was three months old I prophesied and declared that I was destined to receive the Law from the midst of flames of fire.
Once when I was walking in the street I entered the palace of the king and removed the crown from his head.
When I was eighty years old I wrought signs and wonders in Egypt and took out 600,000 before the eyes of all Egypt.
I divided the sea into twelve parts, I made the bitter waters sweet; I ascended heaven [to receive the Torah]; I engaged in battle with the angels; I received the Torah of Fire; and I dwelt under [God's] Throne of Fire.
I took shelter under the pillar of fire; and spoke with God face to face.
I prevailed over the Heavenly Assembly; and revealed [the angels'] secrets to the sons of man.
I received the Law from the right hand of God, and taught it to Israel.

I made war on Sihon and Og, the two giants of the heathens to whose ankles the waters of the flood did not reach because of their [great] stature. I caused sun and moon to stand still on high, and I smote [the two giants] with the staff in my hand and killed them. Is there any other man who can do the same? Go away from here, wicked one, and [do not dare compare me with other men]. Go, flee from before me. I will not surrender my soul to you."

Immediately Samael went back and reported to the Almighty.
Whereupon the Holy One, blessed be He, commanded Samael, "Go out [again] and bring Moses' soul."
Immediately [Samael] drew his sword from its sheath and stood over Moses.
Immediately Moses raged against [Samael], took the staff on which the Ineffable Name was engraved, and struck Samael with all his might until [Samael] fled from before him. [Moses] ran after him with the Ineffable Name, took a ray of majesty from between his eyes and blinded him.

At this point Moses' final moment arrived. A heavenly voice was heard, declaring: "The time of your death has come."
Moses said to the Holy One, blessed be He: "Master of the Universe, remember the day when You revealed Yourself to me in the bush and said to me:
> Come now, I will send you to Pharaoh, that you may take My people, the children of Israel, out of Egypt. [Ex. 3:10]?

Remember the time when I stood on Mount Sinai for forty days and forty nights? I implore You, do not deliver me to the hand of the Angel of Death."
Thereupon a heavenly voice was heard saying to him: "Fear not, I Myself will attend to you and to your burial."

At that hour, Moses arose and sanctified himself like the Seraphim, and God came down from the highest heavens to take away the soul of Moses. With Him were three ministering angels, Michael, Gabriel, and Zagzag-el. Michael laid out Moses' bed, Gabriel spread out a fine linen cloth at Moses' head, and Zagzag-el one at his feet. Michael stood at one side and Gabriel at the other side.

God said: "Moses, fold your eyelids over your eyes." And he did so.
He then said: "Place your hands on your chest." And he did so.
He then said: "Put your feet next to each other." And he did so.
Then the Holy One, blessed be He, summoned [Moses'] soul from the midst of [Moses'] body, saying to her: "My daughter, I have fixed the period of your stay in the body of Moses at 120 years. Now your end has come. Depart without delay."

Whereupon she replied: "Master of the Universe, I know that You are the God of all spirits and all souls, the souls of the dead and the living are in Your keeping, and You have created and formed me and placed me within the body of Moses for 120 years. And now, is there a body in the world purer than the body of Moses in which there has never been an offensive smell, or worm or maggot, or any kind of vermin? Therefore I love him and I do not desire to leave him."

Whereupon God exclaimed: "Soul, go out, do not delay, and I will raise you to the highest heavens and will place you under the Throne of Glory next to the Cherubim, the Seraphim, and other troops of angels."
The soul replied: "Master of the Universe, two angels, Uzah and Azael, came down from near Your Divine Presence, coveted the daughters of the earth, and corrupted their way upon the earth until You suspended them between earth and heaven. But...from the day You revealed Yourself to [Moses] at the [burning] bush, he has had no marital relations with his wife [and is therefore greater than the angels]...
I beg You: Let me remain in the body of Moses."

Thereupon God kissed Moses and took away his soul with a kiss of the mouth.
And subsequently, the Holy One, blessed be He, wept, as it were...

And the Holy Spirit said:
    And there has not arisen since, in Israel, a prophet like Moses. [Deut. 34:10]
The heavens wept and said:
    אָבַד חָסִיד מִן־הָאָרֶץ -- The devout one has disappeared from the earth. [Micah 7:2]
The earth wept and said:
    וְיָשָׁר בָּאָדָם אָיִן -- And the upright among men is no more. [Micah 7:2]
And when Joshua was looking for his master and did not find him, he also wept and said:
    Help, O Lord; for the devout one is no more, for truthful people have vanished from mankind. [Ps. 12:2]
And the ministering angels said:
    צִדְקַת יְהוָה עָשָׂה -- He executed the righteousness of the Lord. [Deut. 33:21]
And Israel said:
    וּמִשְׁפָּטָיו עִם־יִשְׂרָאֵל -- And His ordinances with Israel. [Deut. 33:21]
All were saying:
    יָבוֹא שָׁלוֹם יָנוּחוּ עַל־מִשְׁכְּבוֹתָם הֹלֵךְ נְכֹחוֹ -- He will come to peace. He who walks in his uprightness will rest in his bed. [Isa. 62:2]
    זֵכֶר צַדִּיק לִבְרָכָה -- The memory of the righteous shall be for a blessing. [Prov. 10:7]
    וְנִשְׁמָתוֹ לְחַיֵּי עוֹלָם הַבָּא -- And his soul [is destined] for life in the World to Come.

בָּרוּךְ ה' לְעוֹלָם אָמֵן וְאָמֵן, אָמֵן כֵּן יְהִי רָצוֹן
Blessed be the Lord forever, amen and amen, [Ps. 89:53]. Amen! May it be His will!
[Deuteronomy Rabbah 11:5-10]

Chag sameach!

Yamim Noraim

B"H

When Can Repentance Be Considered Complete?

The Jewish month of Elul is a month of repentance, in preparation for the High Holy Days. This is because, on the first of Elul, Moses went up Mount Sinai to receive the second set of tablets and stayed until Yom Kippur, which is the tenth of Tishri. He also obtained God's forgiveness for the Israelites following the incident of the Golden Calf.

In Aramaic, *Elul* means "search". We must search our hearts in preparation for Rosh Hashanah, which is the Day of Judgment, and Yom Kippur, which is the Day of Atonement, by engaging in *tefillah, teshuva*, and *tzedakah*; that is: prayer, repentance and charity. Elul is the month when we grant forgiveness to individuals who have wronged us, on a one-on-one basis, and ask the forgiveness of those *we* have wronged.

Repentance is of paramount importance in Judaism. All sources say that the one who repents is always forgiven. First, the Talmud says:
> He who sins and regrets his act is at once forgiven. [Hagigah 5a; Berakhot 12b]

It even adds that God Himself has to work to forgive:
> God prays to Himself that His mercy should prevail over His anger and that He should forgive, even when strict justice demands punishment. [Berakhot 7a]

The Midrash says:
> The Holy One says: Even if [your sins] reach to Heaven, if you repent I will forgive. [Pesikta Rabbati 44:185a; see also Yalkut Shimoni 835]

The Tosafot say:
> God's quality of forgiveness is 500-fold that of His wrath. [Tosafot on Sotah 4:1, based on Exodus 34:6–7]

The Rambam says:

> Even if a man has sinned his whole life and repents on the day of his death, all his sins are forgiven him. [Yad, Teshuvah 2:1]

Rav Naḥman of Breslov, the famous Hasidic leader, says:
> There is no sin that will not be forgiven by sincere repentance. Every saying to the contrary in the Talmud and the Zohar is not to be understood literally. [Likkutei Ezot ha-Shalem 119 (1913)]

I would now like to ask the question: At what point can repentance be considered complete? There are four possible stages:

-First, realize what you did was wrong, feel bad about it, and resolve not to do it again.
-Second, the above plus make restitution whenever possible.
-Third, all of the above, plus ask and receive forgiveness.
-Fourth, all of the above plus make the matter public.

Here are two examples:

Example 1 - You steal, then feel bad about it and return the money anonymously. Must you also confess and ask the victim for forgiveness? Must you also make the matter public?

Example 2 - You cheat on your spouse, then feel bad and break off your extramarital affair. Must you also confess to your spouse and ask for forgiveness? Must you also make the matter public?

The Rambam, from 12th-century Egypt, writes that there are three stages to repentance: First, confession to God; second, regret and restitution; and third, commitment not to repeat the sin when facing the same situation. [Mishneh Torah, Hilkhot Teshuva (Repentance)] The confession need not be public, but making it public is "highly praiseworthy". [Teshuva 2:5]

But the definitive treatise on repentance was written by Rabbenu Yonah, from 13th-century Catalonia: שערי תשובה – *Shaarei Teshuvah* -- The Gates of Repentance. In it, he details the following twenty steps for a full repentance:

1-Acknowledge the sin and regret it.

2-Resolve never to repeat the sin; quoting the prophets Ezekiel and Isaiah:

>-[Ezekiel:] As I live -- declares the Lord God -- it is not My desire that the wicked die, but that the wicked turn from their [evil] ways and live. Turn back, turn back from your evil ways, that you may not die, O House of Israel! [Ezekiel 33:11]

>-[Isaiah:] Let the wicked give up his ways, the sinful man his plans. Let him turn back to the Lord, and He will pardon him. Our God freely forgives. [Isaiah 55:7]

3-Feel grief.

4-Feel pain; quoting the prophet Joel:
>Yet even now - says the Lord - turn back to Me with all your hearts, and with fasting, weeping, and lamenting. [Joel 2:12]

5-Worry about the consequences of the sin; quoting Psalms:
>I acknowledge my iniquity. I am fearful over my sin. [Psalms 38:19]

6-Feel shame; quoting the prophet Jeremiah:
>Now that I have turned back, I am filled with remorse... I am ashamed and humiliated, for I bear the disgrace of my youth. [Jeremiah 31:19]

7-Speak humbly and feel low and submissive.

8-Act humbly; quoting the prophet Isaiah:
>And you shall speak from lower than the ground. Your speech shall be humbler than the sod. Your speech shall sound like a ghost's from the ground. Your voice shall chirp from the sod. [Isaiah 29:4]

9-Keep away from the sources of sin.

10-Act in a manner contrary to the sin; quoting the Midrash:
    If you have done piles of sins, do piles and piles of commandments that correspond to them. [Leviticus Rabbah 21:5]

11-Examine your ways; quoting Lamentations:
    Let us search and examine our ways, and turn back to the Lord.
    [Lamentations 3:40]

12-Recognize the punishments for the sin.

13-Consider the lighter sins as if they are severe.

14-Confess the sin; quoting the Torah:
    And he shall confess that he has sinned. [Leviticus 5:5]

15-Pray for atonement; quoting the prophet Hosea:
    Return to the Lord and say to Him: "Forgive all guilt and accept the good." [Hosea 14:3]

16-Correct the sin whenever possible.
    -If the sin is robbery and extortion, no atonement is possible until you return what was robbed.
    -If the sin is causing pain to another, harassing him or embarrassing him; or speaking ill of him, no atonement is possible until forgiveness is requested.
    -If the victim is unwilling to forgive, the perpetrator has done all he could and the *victim* is deemed to have sinned. [Tanḥuma Ḥukkat 19]

17-Engage in acts of kindness and truth; quoting Proverbs:
    Iniquity is atoned by kindness and truth. [Proverbs 16:6]

18-Remember the sin for the rest of your life; quoting Psalms:

> For I recognize my transgressions, and am always conscious of my sin. [Psalms 51:5]

19-Refrain from sinning again if the opportunity presents itself; quoting the Talmud:
> [If one has the opportunity to sin] with the same woman [he sinned with previously], at the same time and the same place, [but this time he overcomes his inclination, it proves his repentance is complete, and he is forgiven.] [Yoma 86b]

This is viewed as the ultimate test of true repentance.

20-Teach others to repent from their sins; quoting the prophet Ezekiel:
> Repent and make repent. [Ezekiel 18:30]

These twenty steps can be essentially summed up in our first two steps: Feel contrite, resolve not to do it again, and make restitution. They are always necessary.

Our third step, informing the injured parties and seek their forgiveness, applies only if someone was actually hurt and knows it. In the two examples shown, there is no need to inform the victim if the money was returned before the victim noticed it was gone, and no need to inform the spouse of the betrayal.

The fourth step, making the matter public, is also not required. An example is given in the Torah. When Joseph was about to reveal his identity to his brothers, the Torah says:
> Now Joseph could not bear all those standing beside him, and he called out, "Take everyone away from me!" So no one stood with him when Joseph made himself known to his brothers. [Gen. 45:1]

This is interpreted to mean that Joseph did not want his brothers' sins toward him to become public knowledge. It is not mandatory to let a sin go public, especially if it might embarrass others.

However, if one wishes to inform the unwitting victims and seek their forgiveness, or make the matter public with the consent of everyone involved, it is permitted.

לְשָׁנָה טוֹבָה -- *L'shana tovah* – and תִּזְכּוּ לְשָׁנִים רַבּוֹת -- *Tizku leshanim rabbot* -- Happy New Year and May you merit many years.

Sukkot

B"H

You Shall Rejoice!

Chag Sukkot sameach! On this holiday of Sukkot, the Torah tells us:

> וְשָׂמַחְתָּ בְּחַגֶּךָ -- *Vesamachta be-chagecha*. And you shall rejoice in your feast, you, and your son, and your daughter, and your manservant, and your maidservant, and the Levite, the stranger, and the orphan, and the widow, who are inside your gates.
> [Deut. 16:13-14]

Samachta. You shall rejoice. How can you be commanded to rejoice? How can you command an emotion? We can be commanded to follow the rites and go through the motions, but what if we can't feel the inner joy we are commanded to feel?

Let's turn to the Talmud for enlightenment. In tractate Pesachim, it says:

> Our Rabbis taught: A man has the duty to make his children and his household rejoice on a festival, for it is said, "And you shall rejoice in your feast" [Deut. 16:14] With what does he make them rejoice? ...
> Rabbi Yehudah said: Men with what is suitable for them and women with what is suitable for them.
> Men with what is suitable for them: With wine.
> And women with what? Rabbi Yosef said: In Babylonia, with colored clothes; in Eretz Yisrael, with ironed lined clothes. [Pesachim 109a]

So you rejoice with what makes *you* rejoice. It's different for every person. If you like wine, you should drink wine. If you like to wear fancy clothes, you should wear fancy clothes. This latitude is designed to make it easier for you to rejoice. Of course, there will be times when circumstances prevent you from rejoicing. But you must try. The Talmud realizes the difficulty by asking the question: "With what does he make them rejoice?" It is not obvious.

Note that the Talmud goes beyond the Torah. The Torah merely says that you must rejoice. But the Talmud says that, in addition to that, you must make others around you rejoice as well. It says: "A man has the duty to make his children and his household rejoice." That extra duty may actually make it easier for *you* to rejoice. Sometimes the road to your own happiness passes through other people's happiness.

Finally, the Torah clearly implies that you do not rejoice alone. You rejoice with "your son, and your daughter and your manservant, and your maidservant, and the Levite, the stranger, and the orphan, and the widow, who are inside your gates". You rejoice with your entire community. Companionship is a key element of rejoicing.
[I note that the list does not mention your spouse, but let it pass. ☺]

In spite of the flexibility of letting you rejoice with what is best for you, our Sages had a saying:
    אֵין שִׂמְחָה אֶלָּא בְּבָשָׂר וְיַיִן -- *En simḥah ella be-bassar ve-yayin*
    There is no rejoicing except with meat and wine. [Rambam, Hilchot Yom Tov 6:18]
This custom is deeply entrenched in our tradition, but fortunately it is only a custom. I am personally not a fan of meat or wine. I will have them on special days as custom requires, but I happen to "rejoice" mostly with fancy cheese and sparkling fruit juice, preferably apricot, but it has to be dark, concentrated, tart, and with very little sugar, or I won't like it. So don't force yourself to eat meat or drink wine if you don't really enjoy them. And if they hurt you, there is no question that you should not have them. That's where *pikuach nefesh* comes in: Most commandments fall by the wayside to preserve life.

Another key element of rejoicing is that it must be something that you not only like but don't do very often. The Talmud says, in Tractate Shabbat:
> The sons of Rav Papa ben Abba asked Rav Papa: We have meat and wine every day, so how shall we mark a change?
> He answered: If you are accustomed to [dine] early, postpone the meal, if you are accustomed to [dine] late, have the meal earlier. [Shabbat 119a]

So do something different for Shabbat and the holidays.

There is another Talmudic principle when it comes to rejoicing:

אין מערבין שמחה בשמחה -- *En me'arvin simchah besimchah*
Do not mix rejoicing and rejoicing. [Moed Katan 8b]

That is, you should not enjoy two different things at the same time. The Talmud in Tractate Ḥagigah is more explicit:

Rabbi Daniel ben Kattina said in the name of Rav: How [do we derive] that weddings may not take place during Ḥol Hamoed [the Intermediate Days of a festival]?
Because it is said [in the Torah]: "And you shall rejoice in your feast", [in your feast] but not in your wife. [Ḥagigah 8a-b]

Tractate Moed Katan elaborates:

-Rav Yehudah said, quoting Samuel; and Rabbi Eleazar said, quoting Rabbi Oshaia; and some say, Rabbi Eleazar, quoting Rabbi Ḥanina: [It's very important to attribute proper credit in our tradition!]: …
אין מערבין שמחה בשמחה -- One rejoicing may not be mixed with another rejoicing.
-Rabbah son of Rabbi Huna said: [One may not marry on Ḥol Hamoed because the groom would] abandon the rejoicing of the festival and busy himself with the rejoicing of his wife…
[Why is that a problem, as long as he rejoices?]
-Ulla said: Because the exertion [required to rejoice with his wife prevents the groom from enjoying the festival].
-Rabbi Isaac ben Nappaha said: Because it may [also] cause a decline in marriage and parenthood. [If people postponed marriage until a festival, they may not marry at all.] [Moed Katan 8b]

Therefore, Jewish law does not allow weddings to take place on Pessaḥ or Sukkot or Shabbat or other special times, because one is obligated to rejoice specifically because of the festival and not because of a new wife. The rabbis relented, however, when it came to Hanukkah, Rosh Chodesh and Purim and allowed weddings at those times, as they are more minor holidays. [Shulḥan Arukh, Orach Ḥayyim 696:8]

While we are on the subject, Judaism seems to be definitely against certain forms of mixing. We can't mix two different kinds of celebration, we can't mix milk and meat in our food, we can't mix wool and linen in our clothing, we can't sow a field with two different kinds of seeds, we can't plough with two animals of different species, we can't mix the holy and the secular in our activities (and when we switch from holy to secular we mark the switch with a *Havdalah* ceremony). Each activity must be experienced exclusively, and not shared with another activity. It's probably a bad idea to eat a good meal while watching a movie on TV. Another reason is that if something goes wrong with one activity, it does not spoil another activity.

In my experience, and in the same vein, it's also best to avoid two-track relationships. Your doctor should not be your friend, your lawyer should not be a relative, your significant other should not be your business partner, your boss should not be your spiritual advisor, your neighbor should not be your creditor. That's because when a problem develops with one track, you end up losing both tracks. If you fire your doctor because you don't think his advice is helpful, don't expect to keep him as a friend. And if you really like him as a doctor, but your friendship suffers because he ran off with your girlfriend, don't expect to keep him as a doctor either. But that's a subject for another discussion.

So let's summarize. How can you rejoice on a holiday when you don't feel like rejoicing? Our Sages give us six ways:

-First, go through the motions required by the holiday.
-Second, think of something special you can get for yourself.
-Third, do something different.
-Fourth, surround yourself with family, friends and community.
-Fifth, consider it your duty to make sure *they* rejoice.
-Sixth, try to focus on only *one* source for rejoicing at a time.

Chag sameach. Let us rejoice!

Hanukkah

B"H

Hanukkah and Purim: Similar yet Different

The next two holidays on the Jewish calendar are Hanukkah and Purim. Let us explore the differences and similarities between them.

Let's begin with the similarities.

Neither holiday is in the Torah. Both were mandated by the rabbis. The Torah only has Rosh Hashanah, Yom Kippur, and the three pilgrimage festivals – Pessah, Shavuot and Sukkot.

Both holidays are colorful, and because of that they stay in the minds of children and make for wonderful childhood memories and help create an emotional attachment to Judaism.

Both celebrate Jewish victory over persecution. Both are miraculous, and for both we recite a special prayer, *Al HaNissim,* as an addition to the Amidah and to the Birkat Hamazon, the Grace After Meals:

עַל הַנִּסִּים וְעַל הַפֻּרְקָן וְעַל הַגְּבוּרוֹת וְעַל הַתְּשׁוּעוֹת וְעַל הַנִּפְלָאוֹת וְעַל הַנֶּחָמוֹת שֶׁעָשִׂיתָ לַאֲבוֹתֵינוּ בַּיָּמִים הָהֵם בַּזְּמַן הַזֶּה

Al hanissim, v'al hapurkan, v'al hag'vurot v'al hat'tshuot v'al hamilchamot she-asita la-avoteinu bayyamim hahem bazman hazzeh.

We thank You for the miracles, for the redemption, for the mighty deeds and saving acts, wrought by You, as well as for the wars which You waged for our fathers in days of old, at this season.

Note that the State of Israel is no less a miracle than those celebrated by Hanukkah and Purim, and for that many congregations recite the above prayer on Israel's Independence Day, Yom Haatzmaut, as well.

Both are considered so important that the rabbis turned their observance into actual commandments. Two of the seven rabbinic commandments are to light the Hanukkah lights (*le-hadlik ner shel Hanukkah*) and to read the Megillah, or Scroll of Esther, on Purim (*al mikra megillah*).

The similarities end there.

The story of Purim has a book in the Bible (the Book of Esther), a tractate in the Talmud (Tractate Megillah) and a volume in the Midrash (Esther Rabbah). Hanukkah has none of these. Hanukkah rates only a few mentions in the Talmud in Tractate Shabbat [Shabbat 21a-24a], as an appendage to a discussion of what wicks and oils one may use for Shabbat lights.

The Book of Esther does not mention God, yet it is in the Bible. The Books of Maccabees, which relate the story of Hanukkah, do mention God, but are not in the Bible.

The story of Purim is not known outside the Bible, yet it is in the Bible. The events of Hanukkah *are* known outside the Bible, yet are not in the Bible.

The Hallel, a set of six psalms that praise God, is recited on Hanukkah, but not on Purim. The Talmud tells us that there are two reasons for this: The miracle of Purim did not happen in the Land of Israel, and after the miracle the Jews were still the subjects of a foreign king. The miracle of Hanukkah, however, happened in the Land of Israel, and after the miracle the Jews were free and independent. [Megillah 14a]

Hanukkah began with the physical (an armed rebellion) and ended with the spiritual (the rededication of the Temple). Purim began with the spiritual (with prayer and fasting) and ended with the physical (the Jews' armed resistance to the killers).

On Purim, the persecutors wanted to kill *all* the Jews. On Hanukkah, the persecutors wanted to kill only observant Jews, to stamp out Judaism in favor of Hellenism.

Hanukkah will not be observed forever, but Purim will be. The Bible says:
> These days should be remembered and kept throughout every generation, every family, every province, and every city. These days of Purim should not fail to be observed among the Jews, nor should the memory of them perish from their descendants. [Esther 9:28]

The Jerusalem Talmud adds:
> In the Time to Come all Prophets and Writings will lose their worth, except for the Torah of Moses and the Book of Esther. [Megillah Y 1:5]

and:
> Our rabbis taught: 48 prophets and 7 prophetesses prophesied to Israel, and they neither took away from nor added to what is written in the Torah, except for the reading of the Megillah. [Megillah 14a]

The Midrash states categorically:
> In the future, all festivals will be abolished except for Purim and Yom Kippur. [Yalkut Shim'oni on Proverbs 9:2]

There are eight books called "Maccabees", and they were all rejected by the Sages for inclusion in the Bible. The first two are preserved in the Apocrypha in Greek translation, as additions to the Christian scriptures. These books are not even mentioned in the Talmud. Tractate Yoma says:
> Why was Esther compared to the dawn? To tell you that just as the dawn represents the end of the whole night, so the story of Esther represents the end of all the miracles. [An objection was raised:] But there is Hanukkah [which happened after the time of Esther and also resulted in a miracle]? [The answer was:] We only refer to the miracles included in our Scriptures. [Yoma 29a]

Why were the Hanukkah books banned? We can only speculate. First, only a Greek translation was available, and holy books must be written in Hebrew.

One can counter that the Book of Daniel is in Aramaic, yet it was kept. Second, they are too recent. The age of prophecy ended long before the Maccabees came, and anything after that *cannot* be "divinely inspired". Third, the Maccabees were a priestly family, and the rivalry between the Sadducees, who were priests, and the Pharisees, who were rabbis, dissuaded the rabbis from their inclusion. Also, the rabbis did not approve that the Hasmonean dynasty, issued from the Maccabean revolt, assumed the kingship of Israel, instead of giving it back to David's family. The Torah says the kingship belongs *only* to David's family:

> The staff shall not depart from Judah [David's tribe], nor the scepter from between his feet, until Shiloh arrives, and to him shall the obedience of the people be. [Gen. 49:10]

The Ramban comments:

> In my opinion, the kings who reigned over Israel who came from tribes other than Judah, after David, were violating the expressed wishes of their forefather Jacob and were usurping Judah's rightful inheritance… And this was the punishment of the Hasmoneans who ruled as kings during the Second Temple [period]. [Now,] they were [certainly] righteous people, and if not for them, Torah and mitzvot would have been forgotten by the Jewish People. Even so, they were punished with great retribution: … All their descendants were killed off because of this sin. [Ramban on Gen. 49:10]

Finally, the rabbis did not want to encourage yet another revolt or provoke the Romans.

Why is Hanukkah celebrated less festively than Purim? A 17th-century Italian rabbi, Azariah Figo, answers a follows. First, the more people a miracle benefits, the greater its commemoration. King Ahashverosh reigned over all the Jews, but only some of the Jews lived under Antiochus Epiphanes. Second, the events of Hanukkah occurred in Israel when the Temple stood. The merit of the Land and the Temple make the miracle less surprising. Third, Antiochus was only against God's commandments, not against the Jews per se. It was expected that God would "defend Himself", as it were. Haman was against the Jews themselves, so God's action against him was a greater miracle. Fourth, the Purim miracle was greater in that it caused the king, who was also an antisemite, to act against his own free will by allowing the Jews to defend themselves. [Binah La'ittim: Drush Sheni L'Hanukkah]

On Purim we make noise with groggers and on Hanukkah we spin dreydels. Why these particular objects? One explanation is that the grogger is held from below, which indicates that the Jews were saved on Purim through their own efforts: Esther pleaded with the king and Mordechai concocted plans behind the scenes. The Book of Esther does not even mention God. The dreydel, on the other hand, is held from above, indicating that the Maccabees' upset victory over the Greeks was a miracle.

Let us end on a light note. A great American Jewish tradition is a Latkes–Hamantaschen Debate. It is a funny mock "debate" about the merits of each of these two delicacies. It originated at the University of Chicago in 1946 and spread from there. Latkes usually "win". Here are some notable arguments in the "debates".

First, latkes are nine times more popular than hamantaschen. A Google search gives 3,300,000 returns for "latkes", but only 385,000 for "hamantaschen".

Second, hamantaschen symbolize Haman's hat, so they represent eating the enemy, a violation of the Geneva Conventions.

Third, the US Supreme Court recognized latkes, but not hamantaschen. In the case County of Allegheny v. ACLU, the majority opinion, written by Justice Blackmun, says:
> It is also a custom to serve potato pancakes or other fried foods on Hanukkah because the oil in which they are fried is, by tradition, a reminder of the miracle of Hanukkah.

No Supreme Court decision ever mentioned hamantaschen.

Fourth, from a standpoint of energy efficiency, the latke is eight times more fuel efficient than the hamantasch.

Fifth, Kepler discovered that the orbits of the planets around the sun are ellipses by contemplating a well-cooked latke.

On the other hand, latkes increase our dependence on foreign oil.

And it was recently discovered that the Large Hadron Collider in Geneva, the world's largest particle accelerator, is secretly a Latke-Hamantasch Collider, as its acronym, LHC, demonstrates.

Finally, if someone tells you: "Hamantaschen are Republican: They're doughy", you can reply, "Oh, yeah? Well, latkes are Democratic: They are greasy and slimy."

Chag Hanukkah sameach.

Purim

B"H

Does Antisemitism Preserve Judaism?

In discussing the story of Purim, the Talmud makes a remarkable point:
> Rabbi Abba bar Kahana said: [When King] Ahashverosh [approved Haman's proposal to kill all the Jews, he] was more effective than the 48 prophets and 7 prophetesses who prophesied on behalf of the Jewish people. Indeed, they were all unable to return the Jewish people to the right way, but [the king's agreement to genocide] returned them to the right way. [Megillah 14a]

So Haman did more for the Jews spiritually than all the prophets in the Bible! The prophets told the Jews to repent and reform, and most Jews didn't listen. But Ahashverosh ordered all Jews killed, and all of a sudden the Jews went back to their traditions!

The message is clear: Antisemitism can preserve Judaism. It can do so in one of two ways:
  -The religious might say: "Antisemites are harming me because I sinned, so I will sin no more and become more observant."
  -The secular might say: "So these guys don't like Jews, eh? I'll *show* them by being even more Jewishly committed!"

Tractate *Makkot*, in the Talmud, makes the point even more strongly:
> Rav says: I am afraid of this verse [in the Torah, in which God says]:
>> [If you do not follow My commandments,] you shall perish among the nations … and the land of your enemies shall consume you … [Lev. 26:38]
>
> Mar Zutra [comments]: Perhaps [it means] like the consumption of cucumbers and gourds [which are not entirely consumed; and what is left can grow into new plants]. [Makkot 24a]

The Maharsha, from 16th-century Poland, explains: When a cucumber falls on the ground, it rots. Yet the *very ground* which causes it to rot is what allows it to take root and grow and be reborn. So it is with Israel in exile: Although many Jews will die, the hostile environment of persecution will itself cause them to experience a spiritual rebirth. [Maharsha, as quoted by Artscroll]

Even in the Torah, God makes the following prediction to Abraham:
> Know for certain that your offspring will be strangers in a strange land, and will be enslaved and afflicted for four hundred years. But know with equal certainty that I will judge the nation that enslaved them, and that afterwards they will leave with great substance. [Genesis 15:13-14]

This is not punishment for anything. Evidently God thought slavery was necessary – possibly to build up our identity and community spirit, under the (malevolent) protection of a superpower. We were all in the same boat, followed the same customs, and huddled together to face our oppressors.

Here is more historical evidence. After the Exodus, a lot of Jews lapsed into idolatry, and clung to it tenaciously and enthusiastically for 1,000 years. The Talmud says that Rav Ashi dreamed of King Menashe, the most wicked Jewish king who championed idolatry, found out that he was well-versed in Torah matters, and asked him: If you are so wise, why did you worship idols? King Menashe replied:
> If you had lived in my time, you would have done the same. You would have lifted the hems of your robes to run behind me to worship idols also. [Sanhedrin 102b]

Then, after the exile in Babylon, idolatry disappeared from Judaism, suddenly and completely, and has remained absent for the next 2,500 years, to this day. What happened?

Here is my own explanation. During the thousand years of idolatry, the Jews were essentially free and masters of their own house. They felt they could indulge in whatever appealed to them, as free people do. Many found idolatrous rites colorful and attractive and felt free to engage in them. But for the next 2,500 years, the Jews were subjugated and persecuted – by the

Persians, the Greeks, the Romans, the Christians, the Muslims, etc. They felt they *had* to keep their own traditions and not adopt the practices of their overlords, as an act of rebellion. They were even willing to die rather than be forced to indulge in idolatry or reject their traditions. The story of Hanukkah is a perfect example.

Here we have the historical evidence that antisemitism preserved Judaism.

If you could remove anti-Judaism, would you be removing Judaism as well? Is it true that "What doesn't kill you makes you stronger?"

This point has been made repeatedly in modern times also. Here are some examples.

-**Spinoza**, in 17th-century Holland, said: Only thanks to antisemitism do the Jews continue to exist as a separate people. [Theological-Political Treatise]

-**Rabbi Hirsch**, in 19th-century Germany, said that antisemitism is the tool through which the God of Israel preserves his people. In the Torah, we read about the first instance of antisemitism: How Isaac lived peacefully among his neighbors, then, through hard and honest work, became fabulously wealthy and powerful. So his neighbors envied him, hated him, then harmed him by depriving him of water – the very source of life – and finally expelled him. Here is the account in the Torah:

> Then Isaac sowed in that land, and reaped in the same year a hundredfold; and the Lord blessed him. And the man became rich, and gained more and more, until he became very wealthy. He had possessions of flocks, and possessions of herds, and large numbers of servants.
>
> And the Philistines envied him. And the Philistines stopped up all [his] wells ... and filled them with earth. And Abimelech [king of the Philistines] said to Isaac, "Go away from us; because you are much mightier than we are." And Isaac departed from there, and encamped in the valley of Gerar, and dwelt there.
> [Genesis 26:12-17]

Rabbi Hirsh adds: Had it not been for that jealousy, Isaac would have slid into a life of leisure and forgotten all about his divine mission. Jealousy is "one of the great vehicles of salvation... It warns [the Jews] again and again [against assimilation]".

-**Bet HaLevi**, in 19th-century Russia, notes that when Jacob was about to meet with his brother Esau, after decades of estrangement and enmity, he prayed:

> הַצִּילֵנִי נָא מִיַּד אָחִי מִיַּד עֵשָׂו -- *Hatzileni na miyad achi, miyad Esav*
> Save me, I beseech you, from the hand of my brother, from the hand of Esau. [Gen. 32:12]

Bet Halevi asked himself: Why the repetition: "from the hand of my brother, from the hand of Esau"? We know Jacob's brother is Esau. And he answered:

> We are threatened by two kinds of dangers from the nations of the world: The physical threat of hatred, expressed as crusade, pogrom and holocaust; and the spiritual threat of the welcoming arms of acceptance, which turns into the asphyxiating embrace of assimilation.
> These two dangers are expressed in Jacob's prayer here: "Save me from my brother..." refers to when he behaves with friendship and brotherhood…, and "from Esau", refers to when he reveals he is a Jew-hater seeking a final solution.
>
> Of the two threats, history has shown that the spiritual danger of assimilation is more formidable than the physical peril of annihilation, and for this reason, Jacob first prays to overcome the threat of his "brother", then prays to overcome the threat of "Esau".

-**Herzl**, in 1896, was totally secular and assimilated, but the Dreyfus trial in France convinced him that antisemitism will not disappear with assimilation. He concluded we need a Jewish state and founded Zionism, leading to the State of Israel. That state was founded by secular Jews. They would have totally assimilated and not bothered to even think of a Jewish state if they had been allowed to forget they were Jews.

-**Freud** said in 1926: "My language is German. My culture, my attainments are German. I considered myself German intellectually, until I noticed the growth of antisemitic prejudice in Germany and German Austria. Since that time, I prefer to call myself a Jew." [Quoted in: Peter Gay, Freud: A Life for Our Time, 1998, p 448]

-**Sartre** noted in 1948 that assimilated Jews are not preserved by their faith or their common past, but "by the Christian who suddenly halts the [Jew's] process of assimilation and creates a special role for him." [Anti-Semite and Jew]

-**Einstein** wrote in 1952: "My relationship to the Jewish people has become my strongest human bond, ever since I became fully aware of our precarious situation among the nations of the world." [Letter to Ben Gurion]

-**Nachum Goldmann**, Zionist leader and former head of World Jewish Congress, said: "Antisemitism is good for Judaism, but bad for the Jews. Lack of antisemitism is good for the Jews, but bad for Judaism."

-**Jonathan Tobin** wrote an article in 2013 called *Loving Us to Death: How America's embrace is imperiling American Jewry,* [Commentary Magazine, 25 Oct 2013] in which he said:

> [The recent Pew study shows that] there has been a startling increase over the past quarter century of Jews who say they ... have "no religion." Intermarriage rates in that group are now at 70%, and ... only 47% [give their children] a Jewish education.
>
> Jews are not being driven from Judaism due to social difficulties. Fewer than 20% claimed to have experienced even a snub in a social setting, let alone an antisemitic epithet, in the last year. Such numbers are not only without precedent in American history; they are without precedent in the millennia-long history of the Jewish people... It is now inarguable that American Jewry... is rapidly shrinking, and the demographic trend lines are stark... American Jewry is on the brink of a demographic catastrophe.
>
> And yet here is the paradox: This catastrophe is also a triumph—a triumph both for American Jews and for the American experiment.

-**Alan Dershowitz**, Harvard Professor, in his 2017 book *The Vanishing Jew* says that the absence of antisemitism in the US spells doom for American Jews… "The good times [we experience] may mark the beginning of the end of Jewish life in America as we know it." Now that most Jews are free, not constrained in their spiritual choices, and not decisively held back by antisemitism, especially in the West, many are abandoning Judaism.

We must balance this by the observation that it doesn't always work, and sometimes works in reverse. Many Jews have said: If such vicious persecution is the price for staying Jewish, it's too high for me. Here are three examples:

-When the Jews were expelled from Spain in 1492, only one third refused to convert to Christianity and left, among them my own ancestors. Another third converted, and the last third had already converted. Romantic stories abound about the Marranos, who practiced Judaism in secret while pretending to be Christians, but the reality is that that was at best a one-generation affair. The next generations were simply Christians, and the overwhelming majority had no intention of changing. It has been said that half of Spain today has some Jewish blood.

-In the 19th century, a tidal wave of conversion and assimilation swept European Jewry. Conversion was the ticket to acceptance, to opportunities, to universities, to guilds, to jobs, to high society, to coveted positions. Large numbers of Jews eagerly and willingly paid that price.

-Finally, many Holocaust survivors have covered their Jewish tracks and raised non-Jewish families that are ignorant of their Jewish roots, because they could not bear the possible consequences of being Jewish.

Is the small minority that survives slaughter, persecution and assimilation sufficient to sustain Judaism? So far, so good, but we cannot take it for granted that this miracle will repeat itself in every generation.

There are collateral questions that also need to be examined to shed light on the issue. Is the reason other civilizations disappeared from history that no one tried to suppress them? Were other peoples also strengthened by hostility towards them? (The Armenians come to mind.) Is the State of Israel kept Jewish by the hostility of its neighbors?

In conclusion, a convincing case can be made that antisemitism helps preserve Judaism. So, in the end, what should we wish for? Perhaps a carefully calibrated balance is the answer. When Jewish identity is looking up, wish for less antisemitism. When Jewish identity is looking down, wish for, ahem… more antisemitism – but of the non-lethal variety!

Chag Purim sameach.

Pessah

B"H

Why an Egg on the Seder Plate?

In a few days we will again celebrate the festival of Passover, commemorating our miraculous deliverance from slavery in Egypt to freedom in the Promised Land. The seder plate on the table will contain all the foods that remind us of the holiday:

-The *matzah*, to remind us that the Israelites had to leave in haste and their bread did not have time to rise,

-The shankbone, or *zeroa*, to remind us of the Passover lamb eaten on the eve of the Exodus from Egypt,

-The bitter herbs, *maror* and *ḥazeret*, to remind us of the bitterness of slavery,

-The *ḥaroset* paste, made of wine and dates or apples, to remind us of the mortar and bricks the Jewish slaves made to build Pharaoh's palaces,

-The vegetable, *karpas*, usually parsley, dipped in salt water to remind us of the tears shed by the slaves.

Did I forget anything? Oh yes, a roasted egg – *betzah*.

Why do we place an egg on the seder plate? That egg is never mentioned in the Haggadah, and is never eaten!

The answer is very simple: No one knows!

The first reference to it is by Rabbi Yitzhak ben Abba Mari in late 12th-century Marseilles, France. [*Sefer Ha'ittur* 2:133c] Let us speculate on its significance. But note carefully that none of these explanations appear in ancient Jewish sources!

First, the egg symbolizes the beginning of life, and the events of Pessaḥ mark the true beginning of Judaism.

It also symbolizes the renewal that occurs in springtime, the season of Pessaḥ.

Next, when the Temple stood, a festival animal offering, or *ḥagigah*, was brought on the afternoon before Pessaḥ, in addition to the Pessaḥ offering itself. It was also roasted and eaten at the Seder Meal. The Chafetz Ḥayyim, in his Mishnah Berurah, published in 1904, believes the egg is a substitute for the *ḥagigah*. [Mishna Berurah 11]

Next, eating an egg is a sign of mourning. It is traditionally the first food after a funeral. So, although we are celebrating our freedom, we still mourn the loss of our Temple, and the fact that, because if it, we can't offer the Paschal sacrifice anymore. That's why many people eat a hard-boiled egg dipped in salt water at the beginning of the seder meal. Also, the egg is smooth and has no opening, like the mourner who grieves silently and appears composed on the surface.

The Rema (Rabbi Moshe Isserles), notes that the eve of Pessaḥ is always on the same night of the week as Tisha B'Av – the day of the destruction of our Temple, another reason for mourning at the seder table. Also, Abraham died on the eve of Pessaḥ.

Note, however, that Rabbi Moshe Feinstein, who died in 1985, rejected any sign of mourning at the Seder, and therefore rejected eating eggs at that time (but did not reject putting an egg on the seder plate). [Igrot Moshe, Orach Ḥayyim 1:156]

Next, the egg is a symbol of fertility. A Sephardic custom I remember well from my youth in Egypt is that unmarried women would eat a hard-boiled egg behind a door, to express their hope that marriage and children were in the not-too-distant future.

Some say the roundness of the egg represents the cycle of life. Some also say that the egg reminds us that God has no beginning and no end. Some note that when the Jews left Egypt, they were like an unhatched egg. Only at Mount Sinai were they truly born, when God gave them the Torah. Political freedom without spiritual freedom is like an unhatched egg.

Rabbi Aharon Hacohen of Lunel, in 13th-century Provence, notes that, in Aramaic, the language of the people in everyday life, an "egg" is *beyah*, which also means "wanted". So the egg means: "Please, God, we want to be freed from slavery!"

Rabbi Yehudah Dov Singer writes in 1977 that the egg is a symbol of freedom because the Romans ate it at their feasts. [Ziv Haminhagim, 3rd ed., 1977, p 51]

Rabbi Shemtob Gaguine notes in 1934 that we use a shankbone and an egg because the Egyptians did not eat meat or eggs, and we want to distance ourselves from them.

Another opinion is that peeling an egg frees it from its shell. It is not easy to do. Likewise, it is not easy to free yourself from the slave mentality. This is quite true, and that is why God made the Israelites wander in the desert for forty years -- to make sure the generation of the Exodus died out, and that only their children, born in freedom, would get to start the new country.

Yet another opinion is that an egg cannot stand without help. Likewise, our ancestors needed God's help to free them from slavery.

And finally, my personal favorite, due to the Chatam Sofer, 19th-century German sage: The egg represents the Jewish people. Most foods become softer as they are cooked. But the egg becomes harder. So it is with the Jewish people: The more they are oppressed, the stronger they become.

Take your pick.

חַג כָּשֵׁר וְשָׂמֵחַ -- Chag kasher ve-sameach!

Yom HaAtsma'ut

B"H

The Secrets of Jewish Survival

A few days from now we will observe Yom HaAtzma'ut, the State of Israel's Independence Day. It celebrates the greatest miracle of modern times: The resurgence of the Jewish nation, phoenix-like, from the ashes of the Holocaust.

We Jews have suffered so many tragedies that we should have disappeared by now. But we are still here. Why? What made us survive as a people, as the same continuous community, when so many other ancient (or even modern!) groups and civilizations have been consigned to the dustbin of history? As Mark Twain put it in 1898:

> The Jews constitute [less than] one percent of the human race. It suggests a nebulous dim puff of star-dust lost in the blaze of the Milky Way... [Yet the Jew's] contributions to... literature, science, art, music, finance, medicine and abstruse learning are... way out of proportion to the weakness of his numbers. He has made a marvelous fight in this world in all ages; and has done it with his hands tied behind him. He could be vain of himself and be excused for it.
>
> The Egyptian, the Babylonian and the Persian rose, filled the planet with sound and splendor, then faded to dream-stuff and passed away. The Greek and the Roman followed and made a vast noise, and they are gone. Other peoples have sprung up and held their torch high for a time but it burned out, and they sit in twilight now, or have vanished.
>
> The Jew saw them all, beat them all, and is now what he always was, exhibiting no decadence, no infirmities of age, no weakening of his parts, no slowing of his energies, no dulling of his alert and aggressive mind. All things are mortal but the Jew. All other forces pass, but he remains.
> What is the secret of his immortality?
>
> [Mark Twain, Concerning the Jews, Harper's Magazine, March 1898]

Our obituary was written many times, obviously prematurely. The first recorded notice of our death is the Stele of Merneptah, a large slab of black granite by the Egyptian pharaoh Merneptah, dating from the 13th century BCE, two centuries after the Exodus. It reads:
> Israel is laid waste. Her seed is no more.

It is displayed in the Egyptian Museum in Cairo, the city where I was born and grew up. It is also the oldest reference to Israel outside the Bible.

I would like to propose seven possible answers to the question, "Why did the Jews survive?"

The first is: Faith made us survive. The Book of Lamentations recalls the sufferings of the Jews. Its Midrash gives examples, concluding each example with:
> עַל־אֵלֶּה ׀ אֲנִי בוֹכִיָּה עֵינִי -- *Al elleh ani vokiya.*
> For these things I weep. [Lam. 1:16]

Let's examine one such example, cited in both the Talmud and the Midrash [Lam. R. 1:50, Gittin 57b]. It ends with the question:
> All the peoples of the world cried out and said, "What does the God of these [people] do for them, that they are [willing to be] killed for His sake at all times?" [Lam. R. 1:50]

The "Emperor" in the story was Hadrian [Tanna DeVei Eliyahu Rabbah, a Midrash]. He ruled from 117 to 138 CE. He quashed the second Jewish revolt, banned all teaching and practice of Judaism, and killed many rabbis, many of whom are commemorated on Yom Kippur.

> It is related of Miriam, the daughter of the baker, that she was captured [by the Romans] with her seven sons... He had the eldest son brought and said to him, "Prostrate yourself before [this] idol." He answered, "*Chas v'shalom* -- Heaven forbid! I will not bow before an idol."... [The Emperor] immediately had him taken out and killed. [Likewise], he had the second son brought... [And the third, and the fourth, and the fifth, and the sixth,] and [they all refused to bow before the idol, and he had them killed.] He had the seventh son brought, who was the youngest of them all...

The Emperor begins by trying to bribe him:
> The Emperor said to him, "[My son,] your brothers, [who were older than you,] had their fill of years and of life and had experienced the pleasure of this world. But you are still young; you have not had your fill of years and life and have not yet experienced the pleasure of this world. Prostrate yourself before the idol and I will bestow favors upon you."
> The child replied, "It is written in our Torah:
>> The Lord shall reign forever and ever. [Ex. 15:18]
>
> [… How much are your offers worth, when] you and your kingdom shall cease to exist? You are only flesh and blood, alive today and dead tomorrow, wealthy today and destitute tomorrow. But the Holy One, blessed be He, lives and endures for all eternity."

The Emperor is now afraid of losing face before his people, so he offers a compromise: Just pretend to bow down:
> The Emperor said to him, "See, your brothers are dead before you! Look, I will throw my ring to the ground in front of the idol. Pick it up, so everybody will think you have obeyed my command."
> He answered, "A curse on you, O Emperor! If you are afraid of human beings who are the same as yourself, shall I not fear the supreme King of Kings, the Holy One, blessed be He, the God of the universe!"

The Emperor now tries to argue theology with him:
> [The Emperor] asked him, "But is there truly a God in the world?"
> He replied, "Woe unto you, O Emperor! Do you see that the world is abandoned?" [Clearly, there is a Power behind it.]…
> The Emperor said, "If your God has all these attributes, why does He not rescue you from my hands…?
> He answered, "…You [are able to kill us only because] we have been condemned to death by Heaven. [In fact,] if you do not kill us, God has many other executioners [who can do so]… But ultimately the Holy One, blessed be He, will exact payment from you for our blood."
> The king immediately ordered him put to death.
> The child's mother said to him, "…O Emperor, give me my son that I may embrace and kiss him [before you kill him]… Kill *me* first and then kill him."

The emperor now has the gall to quote Torah to *her*!

> He answered her, "I will not, because it is written in your Torah:
>> You shall not slaughter an ox, a sheep, or a goat, and his offspring, on the same day." [Lev. 22:28]

The woman answers him appropriately:
> You great fool! Have you already fulfilled all [of God's] commandments, and this is the only one you have left to fulfill?
> He [again] ordered [that the child be] put to death immediately. The mother threw herself upon her child, embraced him and kissed him.

She then instructs her son to tell the patriarch Abraham that his travails were nothing compared to what she had to endure!
> She said to him, "My son, go before your father Abraham and tell him: My mother says, [Abraham,] do not feel too proud [about your righteousness] by saying 'I built an altar and offered up my son, Isaac.' [My] mother built seven altars and offered up seven sons in a single day. [And] yours was only a test, but mine was actually done."

> While she was embracing and kissing him, the king gave an order and they killed him in her arms... A few days later, she went mad, fell from a roof and died... and the Holy Spirit cried out:
>> עַל־אֵלֶּה ׀ אֲנִי בוֹכִיָּה עֵינִי -- *Al elleh ani vokiya.*
>> For these things I weep. [Lam. 1:16]

And the passage concludes with our quote:
> At that time, all the peoples of the world cried out and said, "What does the God of these [people] do for them, that they are [willing to be] killed for His sake at all times?"

We survived because of the faith of people like this woman and her seven sons.

Similar stories abound and are documented. There is a similar story in the Apocrypha: The story of Hannah during the Greek persecution by Antiochus Epiphanes, leading to the events of Hanukkah, with "eat pork" instead of "serve idol". [2 Maccabees 7] Many Jews in history accepted death rather than be forced to stop practicing Judaism; or deny Judaism; or be forcibly converted to idol worship, or to Christianity, or to Islam, or to the new "ism" of the day. They died *l'kiddush HaShem* קידוש השם -- for the Sanctification of the Name.

The second reason is that God made us survive. In the days of the prophet Amos, about 750 BCE, the Jews were very prosperous and observance was lax, especially among the ten tribes in the North. God tells them through the prophet:
> Behold, the eyes of the Lord God are on the sinful kingdom [in the North], and I will destroy it from upon the face of the earth. But I will not utterly destroy the house of Jacob [in the South], says the Lord. For, behold, I will command, and I will scatter the house of Israel among all nations... [Amos 9:8-9]

Does that mean that only the righteous and observant are destined to survive as Jews? There is the Jewish tradition of the *Lamed Vav*, the 36 righteous people for whose sake God preserves the world.

The Passover Haggadah underscores this reason in the *Vehi-sheamda*:

אֶלָּא שֶׁבְּכָל דּוֹר וָדוֹר עוֹמְדִים עָלֵינוּ לְכַלּוֹתֵנוּ וְהַקָּדוֹשׁ בָּרוּךְ הוּא מַצִּילֵנוּ מִיָּדָם

In every generation they rise against us to destroy us.
And the Holy One, Blessed be He, saves us from their hands.

The third reason is that our stubbornness made us survive. God calls us "a stiff-necked people" eight times in Torah! [Ex. 32:9, 33:3, 33:5, 34:9; Deut. 9:6, 9:13, 10:16, 31:27]. Usually this is seen as criticism. But is it? The Torah says:
> -The Lord did not set his love upon you, nor choose you, because you were more numerous than any people; for you were the fewest of all peoples... [Deut 7: 6-7; 14:2]
> -The Lord your God does not give you this good land to possess because of your righteousness, for you are a stiff-necked people. [Deut 9:6]

So God "loves" us and "chose" us, but not because we were numerous or righteous. God does not say why He chose us, but He immediately adds: "for you are a stiff-necked people". Could it be that we were chosen *because* we are stiff-necked? That God wanted someone with the stubbornness, the determination, the endurance, the staying power, to follow His commandments and spread His word in spite of the inevitable persecutions that will ensue? Most people don't have that. Evidently, the Jews did.

The Midrash compares Israel to an olive. Just as the olive yields its oil only after being squeezed hard, so Israel must endure great oppression and hardship in order to yield its wisdom. [Exodus R. 36:1]

The fourth reason is that the teachings of Torah, Talmud and Tradition made us survive. They kept all Jews following the same laws, in tight communities, distinct from non-Jews. After the Romans destroyed the Second Temple, the rabbis made Judaism portable, not tied to a place, and emphasized study.

The fifth reason is that שֵׂכֶל *sechel* made us survive. *Sechel* is intelligence, wisdom, ingenuity, creativity, mental agility, street smarts, finding clever solutions rather than use brute force. In brief, it is a ייִדיש קאָפּ *yiddishe kop*, a "Jewish head".

The sixth reason is that antisemitism made us survive. Born of envy and jealousy at the achievements of the Jews, it forced the Jews to be smarter and more resourceful to survive. It also strengthened our resolve to refuse to give in. Even to God Himself, as shown in the story of the Jew who fled the Spanish Inquisition by sea, with his wife and child, on a rickety boat. A bolt of lightning killed his wife. A storm rose and threw his son into the sea. He reached a small, rocky island, shook his fist at God and said:
> God of Israel, I have fled to be able to follow Your commandments and sanctify Your name. You, however, are doing everything You can to make me stop believing in You. But it will not avail You. You may insult me, strike me, take away all that I hold dear, torture me to death, and I will always believe in You, I will always love You, even in spite of You!"

The seventh and last reason is that the Exile made us survive. The fact that we were scattered among the nations made it difficult for antisemites to destroy *all* of us. A network of scattered communities makes for resilience and survivability.

My conclusion is that it is faith, more than anything else, which has sustained us as Jews. Most Jews, then or now, are not like that woman and her seven sons. Yet Judaism has survived *only* because of people like them. Most Jews today, and probably in any age, are not fully observant. Survival rests upon the shoulders of the minority who are. We are the descendants of that minority. In 200 years, will all Jews descend from the few who are Orthodox today?

A Pew study from 2013 showed that, today, in the United States, 10% of the Jews are Orthodox, 18% Conservative, 35% Reform, and 36% unaffiliated, and switching is mostly in the direction of less observance:
    -Among the Orthodox, only 48% stay Orthodox.
    -Among the Conservative, only 40% stay Conservative or become Orthodox.
    -Among the Reform, only 7% become Conservative or Orthodox.

An earlier study, conducted in 2005, showed that, if present trends continue, then, in the 4th generation:
    -100 secular Jews will have produced only 7 Jews.
    -100 Reform Jews will have produced only 10 Jews.
    -100 Conservative Jews will have produced only 29 Jews.
    -100 mainline Orthodox Jews will have produced 434 Jews.
    -100 ultra-Orthodox Jews will have produced 3,401 Jews.
    [http://www.simpletoremember.com/vitals/will-your-grandchild-be-jewish-chart-graph.htm]

But still: On the one hand, sadly, we must frequently say:

    עַל־אֵלֶּה ׀ אֲנִי בוֹכִיָּה עֵינִי -- *Al elleh ani vokiya.*
    For these things I weep. [Lam. 1:16]

But on the other hand, we can also say:

    עם ישראל חי -- *Am Yisrael chai!* The Jewish people lives.

Yom HaAtzma'ut sameach!

Shavuot

B"H

The Law of the Land is the Law

On the first Shavuot, 3,500 years ago, the Jews received the Torah on Mount Sinai. Then, they lived for 1,000 years in the Land of Israel, masters of their own destiny, under the laws of the Torah. Then, they were defeated and exiled to Babylon. Once there, they did not know how to observe their religion. The psalmist wrote:

אֵיךְ נָשִׁיר אֶת־שִׁיר־יְהוָה עַל אַדְמַת נֵכָר

How shall we sing the Lord's song in a foreign land? [Ps. 137:4]

The prophet Jeremiah gave them this advice in a letter:

> And seek the peace of the city where I have caused you to be carried away captives, and pray to the Lord for it, for in its peace shall you have peace. [Jeremiah 29:7]

The Jews came back 70 years later and rebuilt the Temple, and for some 500 years they continued to live in the Holy Land, but under foreign domination. Nevertheless, the Mishna told them:

> Pray for the welfare of the government, because without the fear of the government, each man would swallow up his neighbor alive. [Avot 3:2]

Indeed, law and order are needed even if they come from malevolent and oppressive rulers.

Prayers for the government are the norm in Jewish services. In Egypt, where I grew up, we prayed for Nasser, even though he was our sworn enemy. And when the rabbi concluded with "HaNasi Gamal Abdel Nasser", everyone lustily responded "Amen!" I should also mention the inhibiting presence of the official spy sent by the government.

The Roman occupiers allowed us to rule ourselves according to Jewish law. But after the Bar Kochba revolt in 135 CE, they expelled most Jews from the land and the Diaspora began. The Jews were now living in foreign countries. New rules were needed. In the Talmud, 2nd-century Rabbi Shmuel of Nehardea in Babylonia laid down this guiding principle:

> דינא דמלכותא דינא -- *Dina de-Malkhuta Dina*
> The Law of the Land is the Law.

This dictum provided the basis for Jewish living in foreign lands. Let us explore what it means and how it was applied.

First, what else does the Talmud say about it? It mentions four, and only four, specific examples. Let us begin by reviewing them.

The first is taxation. The Mishna says:
> One may tell murderers, robbers or tax collectors that the produce they want to take is *terumah* [a food offering to be eaten only by the kohanim] even though it is not *terumah*; or that it belongs to the house of the king, even though it does not belong to the house of the king. [Nedarim 27b]

So you may lie to evil-doers to avoid a loss. The Gemara comments:
> But didn't Shmuel say: "The law of the kingdom is the law"? Since one must pay the tax determined by the kingdom, how did the Sages permit one to lie in order to avoid paying? ... A Sage of the school of Rabbi Yannai said: The Mishnah is referring to a self-appointed tax collector [a fraudulent one], not one appointed by the kingdom. [Nedarim 28a]

So we must pay all taxes set by the lawful authorities. The Tashbatz, from 15th-century Spain, ruled that evading the payment of taxes is considered robbery. [Tashbatz, 3:46] Contemporary Rabbi Joseph Soloveichik said: Do not shop at a store if the owner is known not to pay taxes, because you are then being a *lifnei iver* – one who puts a stumbling block "before the blind", by assisting him to sin.

The second is the status of gentile legal documents. They are accepted. The Mishnah says:
> All documents produced in gentile courts are valid [in Jewish courts], even though they are signed by gentiles, except for bills of divorce and bills of slave release. [Gittin 10b]

It was deemed important that husband or master have full control.

The third concerns eminent domain laws – the power of the state to take private property for public use. The Talmud rules:
> Shmuel says: "The law of the kingdom is the law."
> Rava said: Know [that this principle is true from the fact] that [the municipal authorities] cut down palm trees [without the consent of their owners] and build bridges [from them], and [yet we allow ourselves to] cross over them [even though Jewish law does not allow us to benefit from stolen property]. [Bava Kamma 113b]

So, even though Jewish law considers the bridge to be stolen property, Jews may still use it because the state has declared it otherwise. In his Mishneh Torah, Maimonides summarizes the matter:
> -The general principle is: Any law that a king decrees to be universally applicable, and not merely applying to one person, is not considered theft. But whenever he takes from one person... arbitrarily, it is considered theft. [Mishneh Torah, Robbery and Lost Property 5:14; Shulḥan Arukh, Ḥoshen Mishpat 369:8]
> -[In the case of] a king who cut down trees belonging to individual property owners and made a bridge out of them, it is permissible to cross the bridge. So too if he destroyed homes to make a path or a wall; [a Jew] is allowed to benefit from it. And so it is for all similar circumstances, for the king's law is the law. [Mishneh Torah, Robbery and Lost Property 5:17]

The Shulḥan Arukh, Code of Jewish Law, adds:
> It is forbidden to benefit from something that was stolen, even after the owner gave up the ownership. This applies when one knew that this specific thing was stolen. How?
>> -If he knew that this animal was stolen, it is forbidden to ride it or thresh with it.
>> -If he stole a house or field, it is forbidden to go through it or enter it on a sunny day for protection from the sun or on a rainy day for protection from the rain.
>> -If one inhabits it one owes rent to its owners if it was made for renting.
>> -If he stole palm trees and made a bridge with them, it is forbidden to cross it, and so on.

> But if it was a king who cut trees belonging to house owners and made a bridge with them, it is permitted to cross it. It is permitted even if the king had ordered his servants to cut trees from every person, and it is known that they cut all trees from just *one* person. And the same applies if he destroyed houses and made a way or a wall, it is permitted to benefit from it, and so forth, since the judgment of the king is [the final] judgment. And this applies as long as [the king's] coin is used in all those areas, since the dwellers of those areas all agreed, and it is clear to them, that he is their lord and they are his servants. If this is not the case, behold, he is like a robber and user of force. [Shulḥan Arukh, Ḥoshen Mishpat 369:2]

The fourth concerns the time when ownership is acquired. The Talmud says:

> Rav Yehudah quotes Shmuel saying: [If a] gentile sells property [to a Jew for money], it is [nevertheless ownerless] like a desert [until the Jew performs an act of acquisition]. Anyone who takes possession of it [in the interim] has acquired it. Why? The gentile relinquishes ownership of it when the *money* reaches his hand, [while the] Jew does not acquire it until the *deed* reaches his hand. Therefore, [in the period of time between the giving of the money and the receiving of the deed, the property] is like a desert, and anyone who takes possession of it has acquired it. Abaye said to Rav Yosef: Did Shmuel actually say this? But doesn't Shmuel say that the law of the kingdom is the law, and the king said that land may not be acquired without a document? [Therefore, taking possession should not be effective for acquisition.]
>
> [Rav Yosef] said to him: I do not know [how to resolve this contradiction], but there was an incident in Dura… in which a Jew purchased land from a gentile by giving money, and in the interim another Jew came and plowed it a bit. The two Jews came before Rav Yehudah for a ruling, and he decided the property belonged to the second individual.
>
> This agrees with Shmuel's ruling that the property is ownerless until a Jew performs an act of acquisition. [Bava Batra 54b]

Next question: Where does the principle "The law of the land is the law" come from? Here are some opinions.

The Meiri, from 13th-century Provence, and later the Vilna Gaon, from 18th-century Lithuania, say that it is a biblical law (*d'Oraita*) not a rabbinic law (*d'Rabbanan*). A biblical law takes precedence and is more strictly enforced. The opinion that it is a biblical law is based on what the prophet Samuel told the Jews, *in God's name*, when they requested a king:

And Samuel told all the words of the Lord to the people who asked him for a king: This will be the customary practice of the king who shall reign over you; He will take your sons, and appoint them for himself, for his chariots, and to be his horsemen; and some shall run before his chariots. And he will appoint for himself captains over thousands and captains over fifties; and will set them to plow his ground, and to reap his harvest, and to make his instruments of war, and instruments of his chariots.
And he will take your daughters to be perfumers, and to be cooks, and to be bakers. And he will take your fields, and your vineyards, and your olive trees, the best of them, and give them to his servants. And he will take the tenth of your seed, and of your vineyards, and give to his officers, and to his servants. And he will take your menservants, and your maidservants, and your best young men, and your asses, and put them to his work. He will take the tenth of your sheep; and you shall be his servants...
And the people refused to obey the voice of Samuel; and they said: No; but we will have a king over us, that we also may be like all the nations, and that our king may judge us, and go out before us, and fight our battles.
And Samuel heard all the words of the people, and he repeated them in the ears of the Lord.
And the Lord said to Samuel: Listen to their voice, and make them a king. [1 Sam. 8:10-22]
[Meiri on Nedarim 28a; Vilna Gaon Choshen Mishpat 369:34]

Thus, the Meiri held that the prophet was discussing the legitimate rights of a king, not just building a scare scenario to discourage the people from wanting a king.

-Rashi, from 11th-century France, said that the law stems from the Noahide code. Gentiles are required to observe seven commandments, one of them being "to establish courts of law" [*dinim*]. Therefore, Jews living in their society are bound by those laws. [Rashi on Gittin 9b]

-The Rashbam, from 11th-century France, says that it's a contractual obligation. It derives from the fact that all citizens accept to live in the king's land of their own free will, and so must follow the king's laws. [Rashbam on Bava Batra 54b]

-The Rambam, from 12th-century Egypt, added that these courts are only to enforce the other six Noahide laws.

-The Ramban, from 13th-century Catalonia, said that these courts are a general command to legislate laws for an orderly society.

Now, let us ask the most important question: To what extent does the principle apply? What are its limits? A commentator insightfully called it the "pragmatic recognition of brute force". Vigorous debates took place through the centuries on how far it extends.

-Some say that civil law is binding only when it does not conflict with Torah law. [Shulḥan Arukh, Ḥoshen Mishpat 49; Ḥatam Sofer, Resp. ḤM 44] The meaning is unclear, since Torah law is supposed to cover everything.

-The Tashbatz, from 15th-century Spain and Algeria, says that it does not apply to religious or ritual observances. This is considered so obvious that it is hardly ever mentioned. [Tashbatz 1:158] For example, Jews don't have to obey laws that say they must convert to another religion, that they can't teach Judaism, that they can't circumcize their sons, that they can't celebrate Shabbat, that they can't perform Jewish services, that they must eat non-kosher food, etc. However, if ritual slaughter is banned, they must obey and import their meat, or eat only vegetarian food.

-The Rambam, from 12th-century Egypt, said that the laws that Jews must comply with must be laws that apply equally to all citizens. [Rambam, Robbery and Lost Property 5:14; Shulḥan Arukh, Ḥoshen Mishpat 369:8] He also said that in times of unrest, if you don't know who the ruler is, you must follow the laws of the government whose currency you use. [Laws of Theft and Loss 5]

-The Rema, from 16th-century Poland, said that the law applies to anything designed to promote the well-being of general society. Examples, provided by Rabbi Eliyahu Fink, are criminal law, minimum wage laws, environmental laws, child labor laws, traffic laws, and the like.

-Commentators have noted that the ruler does not have to be a "king". Any leader backed by the authority of the people (to whom the land belongs) triggers *dina d'malchuta dina*. An obvious example is democratically elected leaders. [Knesset ha-Gedolah, Tur, HM 369; Kissei Mishpat 45, citing Responsa Chatam Sofer, Choshen Mishpat 44]

-Does the principle apply to the Land of Israel? The Ran, from 14th-century Catalonia, said no, since the Land belongs to God, not to the temporal ruler there. [Ran on Nedarim 28a] He quotes God in the Torah:
> The land is mine, for you are strangers and sojourners with me. [Lev. 25:23]

He was later overruled by Tashbatz and others, [Tashbatz, 4-1:14; Shulhan Arukh, Hoshen Mishpat 369:6; also Rambam, Hilkhot Gezelah 5:11 and Tur] as long as the source of authority is the agreement of the people, as is the case in modern Israel. [Rambam, Hilkhot Gezelah v'Aveda 5:18; Rashbam on Bava Batra 54b]

-The Rashba, from 14th-century Catalonia, says three things:
  -First, while *laws* must be recognized, the same is not true for popular *customs*, or "non-Jewish ways":
  > The law of the king is binding for us, but the laws of his people are not binding for us. [Rashba 6:149; Bet ha-Behirah, Bava Kamma 113b]
  -Second, it says *dina d'malchuta* – the law of the kingdom -- and not *dina d'melech* – the law of the king. So the principle applies only to laws normally enacted for everybody's benefit, not to laws enacted only for the king's personal benefit.
  -Third, it does not apply to the rules of inheritance. He writes:
  > The secular laws that apply when someone dies without a will generally contradict halacha, so those who agree to benefit from them are guilty of theft. Also, the deceased violated halacha if he died without a will that follows halacha. [Rashba 6:254]

-On the matter of the kippah, it is often the case that head covering is not allowed in certain settings, such as in the military. Since wearing a kippah is only a custom, not required by Jewish law, Jews must not wear it when it is not allowed.

-Jews must serve in the military of their country when asked to do so, even though it may entail eating non-kosher food, desecrating Shabbat, killing people in time of war, etc. All are acceptable under *pikuach nefesh*, the saving of a life.

-Rav Moshe Feinstein, from 20th-century Belarus and the US, ruled that the law must be followed only as practiced, not as written. For example, if the law says the speed limit is 60 mph, but the police only enforce 65 mph; Jews may drive close to 65. However, if you get a ticket for going 65, you have to pay it!

Many laws are on the books that are never enforced and never repealed. For example, in Massachusetts, it is a crime to spit in the street; in California, it is illegal to have caller ID; in Denver, it is illegal to mistreat rats; in Hawaii, it is illegal to place coins in one's ears; in Chicago, it is illegal to go fishing in pajamas; in Los Angeles, it is illegal to bathe two babies together in the same tub, etc. Naturally, this ruling raises the issue: How do you know what's enforced and what isn't? Rabbi Aharon Soloveichik, from 20th-century Russia and the US, says that you must stop at a stop sign, even at 2 am.

-Some commentators rule that a violator must not be reported if the punishment is greater than the Torah punishment, or if the violation is not a Torah violation. For example, this may entail not reporting theft in Muslim countries, where the punishment is to cut off the hand of the thief.

-The Chazon Ish, from 20th-century Belarus, says that when a case is between two Jews (*ben adam l'chavero*), we must judge it with Jewish law only. [Chazon Ish C.M. Likkutim 16:1] In fact, appeals to secular law are frowned upon in Orthodox circles. The Talmud says:
> Rabbi Tarfon used to say: In any place where you find non-Jewish law courts, even though their law is the same as Jewish law, you must not resort to them. [Gittin 88b]

-Finally, allowed doesn't mean forced. Just because the law of the land allows us to do something, doesn't mean we Jews should do it. This includes smoking, drinking alcohol to excess, disrespecting parents, blaspheming, not observing Shabbat, worshiping idols, etc.

In conclusion, we Jews are taught to be good citizens and always follow the law of the land where we live. But this law must allow us to teach and worship and conduct religious rituals in our own way.

Chag sameach!

Tish'a b'Av

B"H

What is the Proper Response to Being Wronged?

Tish'a b'Av is almost upon us – the saddest day on the Jewish calendar. History is full of catastrophic events that befell us Jews on Tish'a B'Av, the ninth of Av. The timing is sometimes accidental and sometimes intentional. The Mishnah [Taanit 4:6] says that, on that day, the spies Moses sent to scout the Promised Land brought back a largely negative report, which demoralized the Israelites; that both Temples were destroyed; that the Bar Kochba revolt against Rome failed when he was killed and the city of Betar was destroyed; and that Jerusalem was razed a year later, when the Exile began.

Since then many other catastrophes occurred on Tish'a b'Av:
-In 1095, the Pope began the Crusades. On the way to the Land of Israel, the Crusaders slaughtered 30 to 50% of the Jews of Europe.
-In 1242, 24 cartloads of handwritten Talmuds were burned in Paris.
-In 1290, the Jews were expelled from England.
-In 1306, the Jews were expelled from France.
-In 1492, the Jews were expelled from Spain, including my own ancestors.
-In 1626, the false messiah Shabtai Tzvi was born. His apostasy dashed the hopes of millions of Jews, one-third of the total, and severely disrupted their lives.
-In 1914, World War I began. It led to World War II and the death of 6 million Jews in the Holocaust. It facilitated the Communist Revolution in Russia, spelling 70 years of darkness for Soviet Jews.
-And in 1941, the Nazis ordered the Final Solution: The slaughter of all the Jews under their boot.

What should our attitude be towards the perpetrators of all these atrocities, and more generally towards anyone who has wronged us?

There are five possible responses:
-First, retaliate in kind: Do the same unto them – "An eye for an eye".
-Second, hate them, but take no action yet. Bide your time and secretly prepare for revenge.
-Third, forgive them.
-Fourth, love them.
-Fifth, ignore them.

Let's examine them one by one.

First, retaliation. Three times in the Torah it appears we are told to retaliate in kind: עַיִן תַּחַת עַיִן שֵׁן תַּחַת שֵׁן -- *Ayin tachat ayin, shen tachat shen* -- Eye for eye, tooth for tooth.
In Exodus:
> ...You shall give life for life, eye for eye, tooth for tooth, hand for hand, foot for foot, burning for burning, wound for wound, stripe for stripe. [Ex. 21:23-5]

In Leviticus:
> A fracture for a fracture, an eye for an eye, a tooth for a tooth. Just as he inflicted an injury upon a person, so shall it be given to him. [Lev. 24:20]

And in Deuteronomy:
> And you [shall have no] pity: life for life, eye for eye, tooth for tooth, hand for hand, foot for foot. [Deut. 19:21]

Antisemites talk about our cruelty, our lack of compassion, our lust for revenge allegedly embodied in that law. There is only one problem with this criticism: There is no record of Judaism ever sanctioning doing this.

The Oral Law says that this injunction refers only to financial compensation. Its purpose is to set a limit to it: Do not ask for more than the value of an eye for the loss of an eye. The penalty must be proportional to the offense, not higher than the offense. The Mishnah says:

One who injures another becomes liable for five things: damages, pain, medical expenses, incapacitation, and mental anguish.

-Damages: If he put out his eye, cut off his arm or broke his leg, the injured person is considered as if he were a slave being sold in the market place, and one must calculate how much he was worth before the injury and how much he is worth after the injury. [The difference is the amount to be paid.]

-Pain: One must calculate how much a man of equal standing would require to be paid to undergo such pain.

-Medical expenses: If he has struck another, he is under obligation to pay medical expenses... If the wound was healed but reopened, healed again but reopened, he would still be under obligation to heal him. If, however, the wound had completely healed [even though it may have reopened much later] he would no longer be under obligation to heal him.

-Incapacitation: The wages lost during the period of illness must be reimbursed.

-Mental anguish: Must be calculated in accordance with the status of the offender and the offended. [Baba Kamma 83b]

The Gemara that follows the Mishnah explains, with arguments that are quite clever:

-It says in Leviticus:
> He who kills a beast shall make it good: beast for beast. [Lev. 24:18]

All agree that "beast for beast" means monetary compensation; so it is for "eye for eye".

-It says in Numbers:
> You shall not take monetary compensation from a murderer. He must be put to death. [Num. 35:31]

This implies that it is only from a murderer that you may not take compensation, whereas you may take compensation for other offenses, such as loss of body parts.

-It says in Leviticus:
> You shall have only one standard of law, for you, for your countrymen, and for the stranger... [Lev. 24:22]

Therefore, "an eye for an eye" cannot mean actual retaliation, because if the eye of one was big and the eye of the other small, one weak and one strong, they would not be equivalent, and two standards of law would apply. Therefore, monetary compensation is implied. Money is the great equalizer.

-Rabbi Shim'on bar Yoḥai says: If "eye for eye" meant retaliation, what would you do if a blind man put out the eye of another man, or if a person missing both hands cut off the hand of another, or if a person missing both legs broke the leg of another? You could not physically retaliate in kind. Yet the law must be applied the same way to all. So it means monetary compensation.

-The School of Rabbi Ishmael taught: The Torah says in Leviticus:
> Just as he inflicted an injury upon a person, so shall it be given to him. [Lev. 24:20]

The word "given" can apply only to monetary compensation.

-The School of Rabbi Ḥiyya taught: The Torah says in Deuteronomy, "Hand for hand", meaning something that is given from hand to hand, that is, money.

-Abaye said [in the name of the School of Hezekiah]: It says in Exodus: "life for life, eye for eye". It does not say *life and eye* for eye". If one retaliated in kind, the offender may die while being blinded. This would be unfair, and cannot be predicted or prevented, so monetary compensation is meant.

-Rabbi Zebid said in the name of Raba: It says in Exodus, "Wound for wound". If retaliation were meant, a person who is delicate would suffer more pain than a person who is not delicate. This would be unfair, so monetary compensation is meant.

-Rav Papa said in the name of Raba: It says in Exodus:
> If men quarrel and one strikes the other... and forces him to stay in bed... then the offender ... shall pay for the loss of his victim's time, and shall [pay for] him to be thoroughly healed. [Ex. 21:18-19]

This refers explicitly to monetary compensation. Besides, flesh heals fast for some people but not for others, so retaliation would be unfair, and monetary compensation is meant.

-Rav Ashi said: It says in Exodus:
> ...If one man's ox [kills] another man's ox... he shall surely pay ox for ox... [Ex. 21:35-6]

> The word "for" in "he shall pay ox for ox" is the same as in "eye for eye" (namely, *Tachat*). So just as in the first monetary compensation is implied ("he shall pay"), so it is in the second.

As a final note, it must be stressed that the primary aim of Jewish justice is not so much punishment of the guilty, but restoration of the victim. Putting out the eye of the offender does not help the victim one bit, but financial compensation does. In the case of murder, however, no restoration of the victim is possible, so a different resolution is necessary.

The second possible response is hatred. Hatred and bearing grudges are not Jewish. Jews could not have contributed to the betterment of humankind as they did if they wasted time hating all those who have wronged them. As is well known, hatred eventually destroys the haters. The Torah tells us clearly not to hate:

> לֹא־תִשְׂנָא אֶת־אָחִיךָ בִּלְבָבֶךָ -- *Lo tisna et achicha bil'vavecha.*
> Do not hate your brother in your heart. [Leviticus 19:17]

The Talmud says:
> Why was the First Temple destroyed? Because [the people engaged in the three main sins:] idolatry, sexual immorality, and murder... But why was the Second Temple destroyed, given that in its time the people *were* occupying themselves with Torah, observance of mitzvot, and deeds of kindness? Because senseless hatred [שנאת חינם *sin'at chinam*] prevailed. That teaches you that senseless hatred is considered as serious as the three sins of idolatry, sexual immorality, and murder combined. [Yoma 9b]

So, even though the majority was punctiliously observant, the many groups harbored intense hatred towards one another. This infighting led to Rome's victory and the razing of the Temple. So, clearly, it's not enough to be technically observant, the hatred towards those who think differently must go also. One is reminded of a prayer uttered by a little girl: Dear God, please make the bad people good and the good people nice.

In Talmudic days, the school of Hillel was always pitted against the school of Shammai. In the end, the Sanhedrin decided to rule according to Hillel. Why? Because, it says, Hillel's disciples were kind and humble, and always quoted the other side's opinions before their own.

Now, if some hatred is "senseless", it implies that other hatred must make sense. When? The Talmud answers: You may bear ill will when you witness someone breaking the Torah. [Pesachim 113b] You must then intervene quickly *before* helping those you love [so that the ill will does not turn to hatred.] [Bava Metzia 32b] How do you know that you have reached the point of hatred? A hater [*soné*] is someone who does not speak to his fellow for three days because of enmity between them. [Sanhedrin 27b]

Hatred is bad and destroys the haters. The Talmud even proposes a prayer to be delivered from hatred:
> May it be Your will, O Lord our God and God of our fathers, that no hatred against any person come into our hearts, and no hatred against us come into the hearts of any other person, and may none be jealous of us, and may we not be jealous of anybody; and may Your Torah be our labor all the days of our lives, and may our words be as supplications before You. [Berakhot Y 8:6]

The third possible response is forgiveness. In Jewish law, the perpetrator must seek forgiveness from the victim, and the victim must forgive. A story in the Talmud illustrates this:
> Once, Rabbi Eleazar son of Rabbi Shim'on was coming from Migdal Gedor, from the house of his teacher, and he was riding leisurely on his ass by the riverside and was feeling happy and elated because he had studied much Torah.
> He came upon an extremely ugly man who greeted him, saying: "Peace be upon you, Sir."
> [The rabbi,] however, did not return his greeting but instead said to him: "You worthless person, how ugly you are! Are all the people in your city as ugly as you are?"
> The man replied: "I do not know, but go and tell the Craftsman who made me: 'How ugly is the vessel that You have made'."

> Rabbi Eleazar then realized that he had done wrong, so he came down from the ass and prostrated himself before the man and said to him: "I have sinned against you, forgive me."
> The man replied: "I will not forgive you until you go to the Craftsman who made me and say to him: 'How ugly is the vessel that you have made'."
>
> [Rabbi Eleazar] walked behind him [to appease him] until he reached his native city. The people of his city came out to greet him, saying to him: "Peace be upon you O Teacher, O Master!"
> The man [who had been insulted] then asked them: "Whom are you calling 'My Teacher, My Master'?"
> They replied: "The man who is walking behind you."
> He said: "If this man is a teacher, may there not be any more like him in Israel!"
> They asked him: "Why?"
> He replied: "He did such and such to me."
> They said to him: "Even so, [forgive him], because he is a great Torah scholar."
> The man replied: "For your sakes I will forgive him, but only on condition that he does not act this way in the future!"
> [Taanit 20a-b]

The Talmud concludes:
> Our Rabbis have taught: A man should always be gentle as the reed and never unyielding as the cedar [in granting forgiveness]. [Taanit 20a]

It also adds that, after payments have been made for harm, the perpetrator must seek the victim's forgiveness for the suffering he caused. [Bava Kamma 92a; Yad, Hovel u-Mazzik 5:9; Shulḥan Arukh, Ḥoshen Mishpat 422]

Why forgive? There are many reasons. The first is self-interest. Forgiveness to one's fellow earns forgiveness from Heaven. The Talmud says:
> He who is merciful [forgiving] to others, mercy is shown to him by Heaven, while he who is not merciful [forgiving] to others, mercy is not shown to him by Heaven.
> [Shabbat 151b; also Rosh Hashanah 17a, Megillah 28a]

So, to earn God's forgiveness, you must become more forgiving yourself.

The second is imitating God. The Talmud says: God is merciful, so imitate Him by forgiving those who have wronged you. [Shabbat 133b; see Lev. 19:2] Rabbi Naḥman of Breslov echoed these sentiments:

Imitate God by being compassionate and forgiving. He will in turn have compassion on you, and pardon your offenses.

The third reason to forgive is more subtle. If I believe God willed everything that happens to me, and everything God wills is for the good, then this, too, is for my own good, and I should forgive, and maybe even thank, the perpetrator!

Some commentators went further. One said:
> If the victim refuses to forgive when the perpetrator has asked for forgiveness three times, in the presence of others, then the victim is deemed to have sinned. [Tanhuma Hukkat 19]

Another said:
> The victim should pray that God forgive the perpetrator, even before the perpetrator asks for forgiveness. [Tosefta Bava Kamma 9:29; Sefer Hasidim 267:360]

This is based on the story in Genesis in which Abraham prays to God to forgive Abimelech. [Gen. 20:17] So the Talmud says:
> Whoever is merciful [forgiving] to his fellow man is certainly of the seed of our father Abraham, and whoever is not merciful to his fellow man is certainly not of the seed of our father Abraham. [Betzah 32b]

Contemporary rabbi Jonathan Sacks adds: When we forgive and are worthy of being forgiven, we are no longer prisoners of our past.

But, most importantly, all this assumes the perpetrator admits wrongdoing, repents, and *asks* for forgiveness. If he doesn't, the victim is not required to forgive. In our history, generally speaking, Christians have asked for forgiveness for the wrong they committed against us, but Muslims have not.

The fourth possible reaction to being wronged is to love the perpetrator. Loving one who has wronged you is not a Jewish requirement. Scientists even classify it as a disease. They call it the "Stockholm syndrome". Sociologists define it as a case in which "the victims develop positive feelings toward their captors and sympathy for their causes and goals, and negative feelings toward the police or authorities".

The origin of the term is a 1973 event in which hostages in a Stockholm bank robbery defended their captors after being released and refused to testify against them. The FBI estimates that 8% of victims suffer from it.

Here are some examples. In 1974, Patty Hearst was held hostage by an urban guerilla group. She publicly denounced her family and the police, proclaimed her sympathy for her captors and their goals, and worked with them to rob banks. In 2001, Yvonne Ridley was captured by the Taliban, and when released she became a fervent Muslim and denounced the values and lifestyles of the West. The syndrome even appears in fairy tales. In "Beauty and the Beast", "Beauty" ends up falling in love with the "Beast" who captured her and kept her imprisoned. The Stockholm syndrome afflicts victims of domestic abuse, child abuse, human trafficking, incest, prisoners of war, political terrorism, cult members, concentration camp prisoners, slaves, prostitutes, etc. Women are more prone to it than men. Studies show it even exists among animals.

Psychoanalysts believe it is just a survival mechanism. Victims are afraid the perpetrators will perceive their love as fake, so they end up deceiving themselves, believing their positive feelings are genuine.

Sadly, the Stockholm syndrome even causes Jewish self-hatred. Marginal or ignorant Jews accept the antisemitic feelings of the majority and join them in attacking Jews, Judaism, and the State of Israel.

The fifth and last possible reaction to being wronged is to ignore the perpetrators and move on. This is the Israeli response. They let their government and military deal with terrorism, but as individuals they ignore terrorists and go on with their lives. They waste no time hating them or plotting retaliation. They waste no time wondering whether to forgive them. They leave that to the far left.

This is by far the best Jewish response.

Let us conclude with the traditional words: May this be the last Tish'a b'Av we spend in mourning.

Personal

B"H

The (Jewish) Lessons of (My) Life

When you reach the venerable age of seventy, as I have, you look back critically on your life. What have I learned? What have I contributed? Did I do what I was supposed to do? What did I do right and what did I do wrong? Your mind drifts towards ultimate questions: What is the meaning of life? What is the purpose of the universe? I would like to try to answer some of these questions for myself.

Judaism teaches that the purpose of life on earth is to prepare ourselves for the afterlife – the World to Come. We do that first by studying the Torah (which includes, of course, the Talmud, the Midrash, the classical commentaries, etc.) and second, by following its ethical and ritual commandments.

There are 613 commandments in the Torah. At first I thought: Should I try to stack up my life against each of 613 commandments in 13 hours? Then I concluded I would quickly lose my audience, so I decided to summarize. ☺

The Talmud [Makkot 24a] recounts how kings and prophets tried to extract the essence of the Torah in a few words:

> -[King] David… reduced the [613 commandments] to eleven [principles]…
> Lord, who shall … dwell in your holy mountain? He who walks uprightly, does what is right, speaks the truth in his heart; does not slander nor harm his neighbor nor takes up a reproach against his neighbor; who despises the vile but honors those who fear the Lord; who keeps his oath, who does not lend at interest, nor takes a bribe against the innocent. He who does these things shall never be shaken… [Ps. 15]

-[The prophet] Isaiah... reduced them to six... He who walks righteously, and speaks uprightly; who does not profit from fraudulent dealings, who does not take bribes, who closes his ears when slander is spoken, and shuts his eyes from contemplating evil: He shall dwell on high... [Isa. 33:15-16]

-[The prophet] Micah... reduced them to three... It has been told you, O man, what is good, and what the Lord requires of you: Only to do justice, and to love mercy, and to walk humbly with your God... [Micah 6:8]

-Again ... Isaiah reduced them to two...: Keep justice and perform righteousness... [Isa. 56:1]

-[The prophet] Amos ... reduced them to one... Seek [God], and you shall live... [Amos 5:4]

-[The prophet] Habakkuk [also] ... based them all on one [principle]... The righteous shall live by his faith. צַדִּיק בֶּאֱמוּנָתוֹ יִחְיֶה [Hab. 2:4]

The last one means that faith in God leads to following His commandments.

Many centuries later, in the Talmud, Hillel issued his famous golden rule:
דַּעֲלָךְ סְנֵי לְחַבְרָךְ לָא תַּעֲבֵיד — זוֹ הִיא כָּל הַתּוֹרָה כּוּלָהּ, וְאִידָּךְ פֵּירוּשָׁהּ הוּא, זִיל גְּמוֹר
What is hateful to you, do not do to another person. That is the whole Torah. The rest is commentary. Now go and study it. [Shabbat 31a]

In the Bible, Kohelet (that is, Ecclesiastes) is a rich man looking for satisfaction. He tries drinking, women, music, philosophy, but nothing works. All is meaningless, all is vanity, all is wind, and there is nothing new under the sun. In the end, he says that only the Torah is worth pursuing:
סוֹף דָּבָר הַכֹּל נִשְׁמָע אֶת־הָאֱלֹהִים יְרָא וְאֶת־מִצְוֹתָיו שְׁמוֹר כִּי־זֶה כָּל־הָאָדָם:
The sum of the matter, when all is said and done, is: Revere God and observe His commandments! This is the whole [purpose] of man. [Eccl. 12:13]
He concludes that purpose and fulfillment are found in practicing Judaism.

Beyond the commandments, God tells us in the Torah:

קְדֹשִׁים תִּהְיוּ כִּי קָדוֹשׁ אֲנִי יְהוָה אֱלֹהֵיכֶם: -- *Kedoshim tihyu ki kadosh ani, HaShem elokechem* -- You shall be holy for I, the Lord your God, am holy. [Lev. 19:2]

[You shall be] מַמְלֶכֶת כֹּהֲנִים וְגוֹי קָדוֹשׁ -- *Mamlechet kohanim vegoy kadosh* -- A kingdom of priests and a holy nation. [Ex. 19:6]

What does that mean? What is holiness? A Google search for the word "holiness" yields 30 million returns. They include a sidebar that says, "Looking for holiness? Find it at ebay.com." (Good luck.) With so many returns, you would think the meaning of the word is well-known. But there is no firm definition. Nachmanides, writing in 13th-century Catalonia, offers an interesting approach:

> [The Torah] permits intercourse between husband and wife, and the eating of kosher meat and wine. This might allow a person to act in a lewd manner with his wife [perhaps even in public], gorge himself with meat, inebriate himself with wine, and use vulgar language as much as he desires. The Torah does not forbid any of these things, and he would be allowed to be a vile, disgusting person with the permission of the Torah. [So] "You shall be holy" means ["Restrain yourself even with what is permitted."] [Ramban on Lev. 19:2]

So, for Nachmanides holiness means doing everything that is permitted in moderation. I resonate to this definition.

More generally, Judaism has two types of commandments: Ritual commandments and ethical commandments. **The ritual commandments preserve Judaism. The ethical commandments make Judaism worth preserving.** You need both. If you think you can do away with one set or the other, Judaism will not survive.

Now let me compare all this to my own life.

In the Mishnah, the great Hillel said: To fulfill the commandment to be fruitful and multiply, you must get married and have a boy and a girl. [Yevamot 6:6] Check, I did that. I even threw in an extra boy for good measure!

I always stayed far away from the big three "sins" of Judaism: Idolatry, adultery and murder. As for the "lower" sins, I might have buzzed around a

couple on occasion, but they were no more than peccadilloes. What I *was* mostly guilty of, is sins of omission, not sins of commission. There are things I should have done, or done more of, but didn't. They did not suit my personality. To quote Ecclesiastes again:
> No one in the world is completely righteous, only doing good and never sinning.
> [Eccl. 7:20]

But my favorite quote on the subject comes from the Baal Shem Tov, the founder of Hassidism, a pious man if ever there was one. He is quoted as saying:
> When a person gets up in the morning and looks at himself in the mirror, he thinks, "I am basically a good person. I have my faults. I have my foibles. I am not perfect. But I am more good than bad."

"I am more good than bad." I like that. In fact, it is Maimonides' definition of a righteous person: One who is more good than bad:

> כָּל אֶחָד וְאֶחָד מִבְּנֵי הָאָדָם יֵשׁ לוֹ זְכִיּוֹת וַעֲוֹנוֹת. מִי שֶׁזְּכִיּוֹתָיו יְתֵרוֹת עַל? עֲוֹנוֹתָיו צַדִּיק. וּמִי שֶׁעֲוֹנוֹתָיו יְתֵרוֹת עַל זְכִיּוֹתָיו רָשָׁע
>
> Each and every person has virtues and vices. He whose virtues exceed his vices is a righteous man (צַדִּיק) and he whose vices exceed his virtues is an evildoer (רָשָׁע).
> [Rambam, Mishneh Torah, Sefer Madda, Laws of Repentance 3:1]

What did I learn in my seven decades? My life is like a check mark. It went slowly downhill while I was growing up in Egypt up to the Six-Day-War in 1967, then it went slowly uphill after I left Egypt at age 18 and it kept going up. I learned from both segments. Here are the top twelve lessons I learned and their connection to Judaism.

Lesson Number 1 - People are not rational.

Emotions run history. In my personal life, I frequently felt my position was airtight, ironclad, that I had all bases covered and all possible arguments answered – and I lost my case. In my professional life, whenever clear, concise, logical analysis was pitted against politics, politics won.

Historians always like to present leaders as cool, calculating and rational, making moves only after a careful cost-benefit analysis. They don't. But historians feel they *have* to make sense of history.

Consider antisemitism, an age-old disease. It is not rational. Jews are very useful people and have contributed enormously to the welfare of the world. Jews are only one-fifth of 1% of humanity, yet they get one-third of the Nobel prizes. So they get Nobel prizes at a rate more than 150 times larger than their small numbers would suggest. Their inventions would fill books: From vaccines against polio, hepatitis, cholera and bubonic plague; to the laser, the ballpoint pen, Google and Facebook. And they are always at the forefront in matters of justice and civil rights. You would think people would be happy to have them around, that they would protect them and encourage them to continue their work! But, sadly, the opposite is frequently the case. Jews are often persecuted, dispossessed, expelled and slaughtered.

Actually, their success is the very thing that fuels antisemitism. Envy is a most irrational reaction. Consider the story in the Torah of Isaac, the first person born Jewish:

> Then Isaac sowed in that land, and reaped … a hundredfold… And [he] became very wealthy … He had flocks, … herds, and large numbers of servants. And the Philistines envied him. [They] stopped up all [his] wells … and filled them with earth. And [the king of the Philistines] said to Isaac, "Go away from us, because you are much stronger than we are." And Isaac departed from there… [Genesis 26:12-17]

Now, Isaac gave the Philistines jobs and reflected wealth. But they were too envious of him and acted against their best self-interests. Antisemitism will continue as long as the Jews are successful.

Another example is the fact that many, perhaps most, people want to be big fish in small ponds, because it strokes their egos. They should want to be small fish in big ponds, so they can learn and grow to be bigger and better fish, rather than remain stunted in small ponds.

I am rational, perhaps too much so. One of my heroes is the Jewish philosopher and rabbi Maimonides, who lived some 850 years ago:

-He was Sephardic (that is, of Spanish origin) and so am I.
-He lived and worked in Egypt, and that's where I was born and grew up.
-His Hebrew name was Moshe (Moses) and so is mine.
-He was a rationalist, and so am I.
-He was a scientist of sorts, and so am I.
-He had very strong opinions, and so do I.
-And, oh yes: He was Jewish, and so am I.

Now, contrary to what many people believe, "rational" does *not* mean "one who does not accept anything without proof". All logical processes must begin with premises that are accepted without proof. Without these unquestioned premises, there is no reason or logic. Reason and logic are only the tools by which one goes from premises to conclusions. These premises are unquestioned. In mathematics they are called axioms. Change them and you get a different mathematics, which is just as valid. It has been done. In Judaism, these axioms are the Torah.

Lesson Number 2 - People do things for selfish reasons.

This is not really as bad as it sounds, because that reason may be just to feel good inside, to feel wanted, appreciated, and remembered. But, technically, this is still a selfish reason. In the Jewish tradition, every person has a good inclination and an evil inclination. But, unlike other traditions, Judaism teaches that the evil inclination can be a good thing! The Midrash says:
> Can the Evil Inclination be "very good"? That would be extraordinary! Yes, [because] without the Evil Inclination, no man would build a house, take a wife, beget a family, and engage in work.
> So said [Ecclesiastes]: "And I saw that all labor and all achievement in work was the result of man's envy and rivalry with his neighbor." [Eccl. 4:4]
> [Genesis Rabbah 9:7]

This suggests that we achieve things to show off and gain the admiration of others; to have more money or possessions; to "get the girl" (or the boy); to do better than our neighbors; to be ahead of the competition; to win prizes; to exercise power; to show those who said we would never amount to anything; or to leave worthy deeds behind, so we are remembered after we die.

None of this is altruistic. But without these incentives, we would not achieve anything. There would be no progress. If that is the way we are wired, so be it. We must accept it and make the best of it.

Lesson Number 3 - People are afraid of change.

People prefer the devil-they-know to the devil-they-don't-know. Fear of change makes us continue to work in jobs we hate, stay in bad relationships, or even continue to use outdated and inferior equipment.

During the biblical Exodus, many Israelites, faced with the uncertainty of the desert and of a new way of life, regretted life in Egypt and wanted to go back, in spite of their enslavement and in spite of all the miracles they witnessed. In my lifetime, I witnessed and experienced the pain of uprooting from modern-day Egypt. I was only 18 when I was forced out, but my elders continued, to their dying day, to wax nostalgic about their life in Egypt.

Leaders are always older and most resistant to change. Sometimes they are right and sometimes they are wrong, but they can always be counted on to resist change. Here are some examples from our history:

-The rabbis counseled against fighting Greek oppression. They were wrong. We won. This is the story of Hanukkah.
-The rabbis counseled against fighting Roman oppression. They were right. We lost the Temple, the land, and much of our independence.
-The rabbis counseled against leaving Europe when Naziism was on the rise. They were wrong. As a result, most European Jews were murdered in the Holocaust.
-The Lubavitcher Rebbe counseled his people not to move out of New York when relations with the Black community turned sour. He was right, tensions went down, and Chabad is still based in New York.
-My father did not want to leave Egypt. He believed things would get better. He was wrong. Things got worse.

Lesson Number 4 - Do only one thing at a time.

There are two reasons for that: Improving the chances of success and increasing enjoyment.

The first reason: Success. Rabbi Akiva advised that if you try to accomplish too much, you end up accomplishing nothing. [Based on Rabbi Akiva in Sifra Metzora Parshat Zavim 5 -- תָּפַסְתָּ מְרֻבֶּה, לֹא תָּפַסְתָּ]

The Talmud says:
> There is a general principle that one does not perform commandments in bundles. [Sotah 8a]

And also:
> One who is engaged in a commandment is exempt from performing another commandment. [Sukkah 25a]

As they say, "Jack of all trades, master of none."

The second reason: Enjoyment. Each activity must be experienced exclusively and given maximum attention. That way, if something goes wrong with one activity, it does not spoil another activity. For example, don't eat a good meal while watching TV. (But one can make allowances for snacks. ☺) Another is: Avoid two-track relationships: Your doctor should not be your friend, your significant other should not be your business partner, your lawyer should not be your relative, your boss should not be your spiritual advisor, your teacher should not be your creditor, etc. The reason is that when a problem develops with one track, you lose both tracks.

Judaism is against many forms of mixing. Our Sages said:
> אין מערבין שמחה בשמחה -- *En me'arvin simchah besimchah*
> Do not mix rejoicing and rejoicing. [Moed Katan 8b]

This means: Do not try to enjoy two different things at the same time. This is why no weddings are allowed on Shabbat. Shabbat must be enjoyed in its own right and a wedding must be enjoyed in its own right, so make them two separate occasions.

Also, we can't mix milk and meat in our food, we can't mix wool and linen in our clothing; we can't sow a field with two different kinds of seeds; we can't plough with two animals of different species; we can't mix the holy and the secular in our activities, etc.

Ecclesiastes summed it up well, as usual:
> לַכֹּל זְמָן וְעֵת לְכָל־חֵפֶץ תַּחַת הַשָּׁמָיִם
> To everything there is a season, and a time to every purpose under heaven. [Eccl. 3:1]

Lesson Number 5 - Avail yourself of all permitted pleasures.

Judaism may frown on extravagance, but it does not approve of asceticism. [Nedarim 10a, 22a; Taanit 11a] The Talmud warns us:
> A man will have to account [to God] for the allowed pleasures he failed to enjoy. [Kiddushin Y 4:12]

So, in the next life, God will ask us: Why didn't you have as much fun as you could have?

The Talmud also asks, rhetorically:
> Hasn't the Torah forbidden enough already that you want to forbid other things to yourself?! [Nedarim Y 9:1]

I was never an ascetic, but I was too anxious, and I feared the future too much. As a result, I enjoyed the present less than I could have.

Lesson Number 6 - Know your limits.

If you don't, then the Peter Principle will apply: You will rise to your level of incompetence and remain there for the rest of your life, doing bad or mediocre work. This Jewish story is frequently told:
> Before his death, Rabbi Zusya said, "In the World to Come, I will not be asked: 'Why were you not Moses?' I will be asked: 'Why were you not Zusya?'" [In Martin Buber's *Tales of the Hasidim*]

Be the best that you can, but don't try to be more. As President Abraham Lincoln said, "Whatever you are, be a good one."

I applied this principle by avoiding all management duties in my life and career. Most people want to keep getting promoted until they become director, president, chief, overseer, head honcho, big boss. I didn't, for two reasons. First, I didn't want the job. What I really enjoyed was doing the real work, not telling people what to do and evaluating them afterwards. Second, I knew I would not have been good at it. I would have been impatient with subordinates and would have ended up doing the work myself.

So: "Know your limits". Some people preach the opposite: "Always aim higher", but I disagree. When you are promoted up to your level of incompetence, you do mediocre work and stop being useful.

Lesson Number 7 - Don't expect anything from anybody.

The reality is that nobody owes you anything. I myself never expected anything. That way, I was never disappointed. Sometimes I got things (and it was a genuine and very pleasant surprise), and sometimes I didn't (and never even thought about it). I know it's hard to make yourself feel that way, but I was blessed with this natural inclination.

Lesson Number 8 - The greatest feeling is getting things long desired.

I had to abandon everything when I was forced out of Egypt. All my life, I looked for many things I was exposed to as a child or young adult. It could be little things: A song, a book, a show, a food item, a magazine, etc. When I found them, decades later, it was a small joy every time. The pace of re-acquaintance picked up when the Internet came of age. Now I am sad because my list is very close to being entirely fulfilled. I pity the rich who never have that joy. I am happy I was not born rich. I like to say: "Hell is having everything you want, all the time."

Lesson Number 9 - Whatever you can accomplish, do it with all your strength while you are able.

This is a direct quote from Ecclesiastes (again!):
כֹּל אֲשֶׁר תִּמְצָא יָדְךָ לַעֲשׂוֹת בְּכֹחֲךָ עֲשֵׂה [Ecclesiastes 9:10]

In my case, I should have, but didn't. Since a very young age I was in love with mathematics and physics. I always wanted to work on basic research problems in theoretical physics. However, when the time came, I gave priority to job security and became a government defense analyst. Because of my background as a refugee, an immigrant and a Jew, I craved stability and security.

At first I convinced myself that I could do both. I would come home from work, have dinner with Joan, then neglect Joan and go in the back room to work on physics. I was able to do it for five years and I published a dozen papers. Then, I didn't have time to do it anymore. Two more children came and the workload became heavier.

I don't know if I would have become what they call "a good physicist", but I did become a good defense analyst, at least judging by the high awards I received that my colleagues did not get. I am sure some will say, "If *he* is the best there is in government, heaven help us!"

Lesson Number 10 - Family is very important.

I always felt close to my large, extended family. Back in Egypt, we all lived within a square mile of one another. Then we were forced out, went to many different countries in different continents, and slowly lost touch. Twenty years ago, I searched for my relatives on the Internet and was determined to have them come to my house for the Passover seders. One year Spain came. One year Italy came. One year Venezuela came. One year Australia came. I am still connected with them and the computer shortens the distances.

Lesson Number 11 - Studying Torah is very important.

I did. The Talmud emphasizes its maximum importance:
> These are the [most important] things ... Honoring father and mother, practicing loving deeds, and making peace between people. But the study of Torah is equal to all of them put together [וְתַלְמוּד תּוֹרָה כְּנֶגֶד כּוּלָם] -- *V'talmud Torah k'neged kullam*].
> [Peah 1:1, Shabbat 127a, Kiddushin 40a, Tanhuma Yitro 14]

The underlying teaching is that study leads to practice.

Lesson Number 12 - Studying secular subjects is also important.

I did that too. As I mentioned, math and physics were my favorite subjects. The Midrash tells us there is wisdom to be sought among all those who study the world around us:
> If someone tells you there is wisdom among the nations, believe it... But if he tells you there is Torah among the nations, do not believe it. [Lamentations Rabbah 2:13]

I always experienced quite a thrill when I saw that the most complicated things in the world derive from simple equations, simple principles. Understanding the laws of physics and solving intricate problems always had me in awe and made me appreciate how "smart" God is. This is what Einstein called "cosmic religious feeling". It has to be experienced to be understood. As poet John Gillespie Magee put it:

> Oh! I have slipped the surly bonds of Earth...
> Put out my hand, and touched the face of God.

Thank you for your attention.

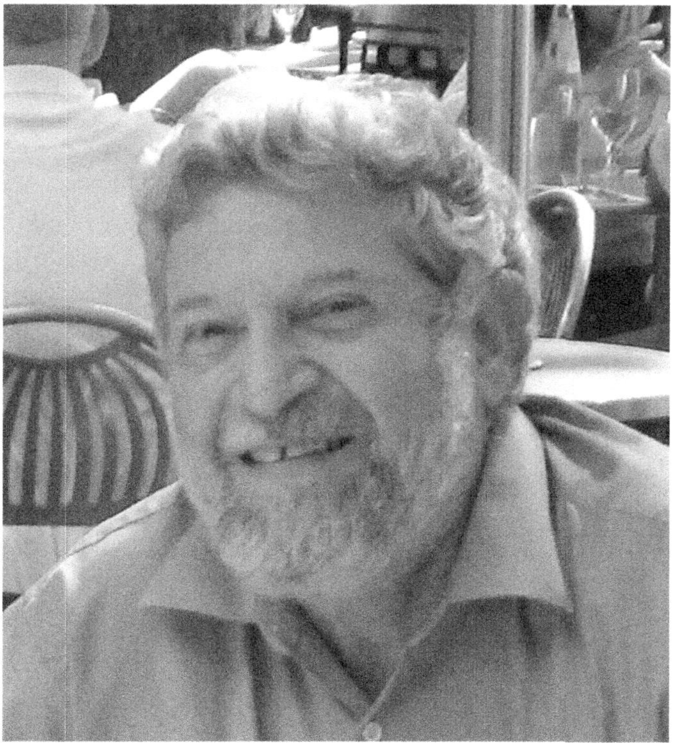

Made in the USA
Monee, IL
12 July 2021